CHARITIES

An Industry Accounting and Auditing Guide

CHARITIES

An Industry Accounting and Auditing Guide

Richard A Derwent

Contributing author
Jane Richardson MA, ACA, ATII
Peters Elworthy & Moore

Accountancy Books
Gloucester House
399 Silbury Boulevard
Central Milton Keynes
MK9 2HL
Tel: 01908 248000

No responsibility for loss occasioned to any person acting or refraining from action as a result of any material in this publication can be accepted by the author or publisher.

ISBN 1 85355 408 1

British Library Cataloguing-in-Publication Data.
A catalogue record for this book is available from the British Library.

Throughout this book the male pronoun has been used to cover references to both the male and female.

Typeset by J&L Composition Ltd, Filey, North Yorkshire
Printed in Great Britain by Bell & Bain

Preface and Acknowledgements

Charities are big business. The 1993 Annual Report of the Charity Commissioners reported that an estimate of the gross annual income of all charities on the register in that year amounted to some £11.444 billion. This compares with that of £17 billion, which is commonly quoted for the whole of the charitable sector. Walk down any high street and it is not building societies and estate agents opening new offices; it is charities opening new shops. With media coverage as well, charities enjoy a high profile in the UK today.

It is only proper, therefore, that charities should be more accountable to members of the public, without the generosity of whom they would not survive. Accordingly, charities are experiencing a period of dramatic change. The Charities Act 1992 was the most substantial piece of legislation to affect them for more than 30 years. The Charities Act 1993 has consolidated almost all of Parts I and IV of that Act, the Charitable Trustees Incorporation Act 1872 and, except for certain spent or transitional provisions, the Charities Act 1960. Sections 41 to 49 of the Charities Act 1993, the Regulations made thereunder and the revised charity SORP will create a new accounting framework for charities.

The objective of the revised charity SORP is 'to help improve the quality of financial reporting by charities'. The Charity Commissioners are committed to the need for high standards of accounting by charities. Without financial integrity and accountability, charities, particularly the larger, professionally run ones, cannot expect to maintain public confidence. High standards of accounting and good financial controls are equally important for the smaller charity. The 1993 Annual Report pointed out that much of the work of the Commissioners is directed at resolving inadequate financial controls in such charities, which often have no, or only a few, professional staff. The Commissioners are compiling a companion guide to the revised SORP for the smaller charity.

But the objective of the revised charity SORP is, also, 'to assist those who are responsible for the preparation of the charity's annual report and accounts'. The Charity Commissioners have a long record of working with charities. They have been taking steps to ensure that trustees are informed well in advance of the changes and place great emphasis on providing explanatory information about the implications of the new legislation. They are able to give a ruling on problems which trustees may have.

This book records and explains the new accounting framework. Emphasis has, also, been devoted to extracts from published accounts, demonstrating developments in current accounting practice and disclosure, the contrasting attitudes of trustees and auditors and the changes which will be necessary. Some of these changes have been, or are being, made, on an almost day-to-day basis, as trustees and their auditors come to terms with the new framework.

I am indebted to a number of people for their assistance with the publication of this book, notably Jane Richardson MA, ACA, ATII, Senior Tax Manager, Peters Elworthy & Moore, Cambridge for writing chapters 18 to 20.

Extracts from 'On trust: Increasing the effectiveness of charity trustees and management committees' and 'The Charities Acts 1992 and 1993: A guide for charities and other voluntary organisations' are reproduced with kind permission of the National Council for Voluntary Organisations. The former publication is a report, first published in 1992, of an NCVO/ Charity Commission Working Party on Trustee Training; and, the latter publication is the third edition, having been first published in 1992, and compiled by Lindsay Driscoll, Legal Adviser and Bridget Phelps.

Extracts from 'The Revision of SORP 2 (Accounting by charities): A commentary on the exposure draft' (1993), Certified Research Report 34, are reproduced with kind permission of The Chartered Association of Certified Accountants (CACA). This research report was funded and published by CACA and is available from CACA, P.O. Box 66, Glasgow G41 1BS.

Extracts from the revised charity SORP (dated 1 February 1995) and Annexes II and III of chapter 3 (which reproduce the *draft* Charity Commission guidance on the selection of independent examiners and *draft* general directions of the Charity Commissioners on the carrying out of an independent examination respectively) are reproduced with kind permission of the Charity Commissioners.

June 1995 Richard A Derwent

Abbreviations

Unless stated otherwise, the following abbreviations are used in this book:

Professional and regulatory bodies:

AAPA	Association of Authorised Public Accountants
APC	Auditing Practices Committee
ASB	Accounting Standards Board
ASC	Accounting Standards Committee
CACA	Chartered Association of Certified Accountants
CCAB	Consultative Committee of Accountancy Bodies
CIPFA	Chartered Institute of Public Finance and Accountancy
Commissioners	Charity Commissioners
DTI	Department of Trade and Industry
FASB	Financial Accounting Standards Board
IASC	International Accounting Standards Committee
ICAEW	Institute of Chartered Accountants in England and Wales
ICAI	Institute of Chartered Accountants in Ireland
ICAS	Institute of Chartered Accountants of Scotland
NCVO	National Council for Voluntary Organisations
Registrar	Registrar of Companies
UITF	Urgent Issues Task Force

Accounting and statutory terms:

1960 Act	Charities Act 1960
1981 Act	Companies Act 1981
1985 Act	Companies Act 1985
1989 Act	Companies Act 1989
1992 Act	Charities Act 1992
1993 Act	Charities Act 1993
AG	Auditing Guideline
ED	Exposure Draft
FA	Finance Act
FRAG	Financial Reporting and Auditing Group
FRED	Financial Reporting Exposure Draft
FRS	Financial Reporting Standard
HL Deb	House of Lords Debates

IAS	International Accounting Standard
ICTA	Income and Corporation Taxes Act
IHTA	Inheritance Tax Act
Para	Paragraph
Pt	Part
Reg	Regulation
s	section
SAS	Statement of Auditing Standards
Sch	Schedule
SFAS	Statement of Financial Accounting Standards
SI	Statutory Instrument
SOFA	Statement of Financial Activities
SORP 2	Statement of Recommended Practice 2 'Accounting by charities'
The revised charity SORP/the revised SORP	Statement of Recommended Practice 'Accounting by charities'
SSAP	Statement of Standard Accounting Practice
SSRA	Statement of Standards for Reporting Accountants
TCGA	Taxation of Chargeable Gains Act
The Regulations	The Charities (Accounts and Reports) Regulations 1995
TR	Technical Release

Contents

Chapter 1 – Definitions, registration, status and names

1.1 Introduction

The 1960 Act introduced a requirement for a register of charities to be established and maintained by the Commissioners and for all charities, generally unless exempt or excepted, to be registered.

The register provides both potential donors and other interested members of the public with access to basic information on the existence of registered charities, their purposes and administrative structure. It is, also, an important resource to the Commissioners in their monitoring and supervision.

To be effective, the register must be both accurate and up-to-date. In accordance with the recommendations of the Woodfield Report (*Efficiency scrutiny of the supervision of charities*), published in 1987, the register has now been computerised. The completion and submission of an annual return to the Commissioners (see chapter **3**, page 60) should ensure systematic updating.

Some changes have been made as regards the arrangements for exemptions and exceptions from registration. Larger registered charities are now required to state the fact that they are registered on certain business documents and provisions, similar to those in the 1985 Act, have been introduced regarding the acceptability of charity names.

1.2 Definition of a charity

Section 96(1) of the 1993 Act states that, unless the context otherwise requires, 'charity' means:

> '. . . Any institution, corporate or not, which is established for charitable purposes and is subject to the control of the High Court in the exercise of the court's jurisdiction with respect to charities'.

The definition provided by para 4 of Appendix 1 to the revised charity SORP is wider:

> 'A "charity" is any institution established for purposes which are exclusively charitable. Where the institution is involved in more than one activity, operates more than one fund, or is not centralised into one unit of operation, the term is used in this Statement to include all those activities, units and funds which fall within the scope of a single governing instrument (or instruments supplemental to the main instrument) or for which the trustees are otherwise legally liable to account (e.g., branches . . .).'

The aim has been to embrace all activities which fall within the charity trustees' responsibility. This should, *inter alia*, help trustees identify which activities should be accounted for within the accounts of the main charity.

1.2.1 'Any institution, corporate or not'

A charity is not a type of legal entity as such, but may be created in a number of different ways. For example, by declaration of trust, whereby a person declares that he holds certain property on trust or for a specific permitted object or purpose, or by conveyance to a trustee, whereby a person transfers property to another person in order for him to hold it on trust.

Another form of legal structure is the unincorporated association (although not partnerships, as trading with a view to making a profit would not be consonant with the charitable purpose). Many smaller local charities, such as parent/teacher associations, are set up in this way and produce a rule book to act as their governing instrument.

Charities incorporated under the Companies Acts are usually formed as companies limited by guarantee. They are subject, generally without dispensation, to the same accounting and disclosure provisions as companies limited by shares. Many of the larger charities, such as Barnardo's, are constituted as such.

Some charities are incorporated under the Industrial and Provident Societies Act 1965. This category includes the majority of housing associations which are subject to the complex accounting and disclosure requirements of the Housing Corporation, under the Housing Acts and statutory accounting requirements.

Several charities, for example Nightingale House (The Home for Aged Jews), whose original trusts have become out of date, may be governed by a 'scheme' made by the Commissioners under, what are now, s16 and s17 of the 1993 Act.

Some are incorporated by Royal Charter, including the Royal National Lifeboat Institution, the Royal Society for the Protection of Birds and the British Red Cross. Others are formed under their own special Act of

Parliament, such as The National Trust and the Royal Society for the Prevention of Cruelty to Animals. In these circumstances, their constitutions are governed by their own charter, or Act.

Paragraph 21(a) of SORP 2 recommended that 'an indication of the nature of the governing instrument or legal status of the charity' be disclosed, without specifically stating where. A review of accounts suggests that this information, where it is given, is found in a variety of positions within the annual report.

Some charities provide this information in the trustees' report, including Example 1.1 Action Research.

Example 1.1 Action Research
Report of the directors (part) (31 October 1993):

> FINANCIAL (part)
>
> The Charity was incorporated under the Companies Act 1948 as a Company limited by guarantee having no share capital.

Other charities detach, from the trustees' report, their legal and administrative details, of which Example 1.2 Tear Fund is one.

Example 1.2 Tear Fund
Legal and administrative details (part) (31 March 1993):

> STATUS
>
> Tear Fund is a company limited by guarantee and registered under the Companies Act 1985, registration number 994339. It is a registered charity, charity number 265464.

Some include the details as a separate note to the accounts, including Example 1.3 Distressed Gentlefolk's Aid Association.

Example 1.3 Distressed Gentlefolk's Aid Association
Note 1: Status of the company (31 March 1993):

> The Distressed Gentlefolk's Aid Association is a company limited by guarantee and not having a share capital.
>
> Ordinary members of the Association are each required to contribute annually. All members, in the event of the Association being wound up whilst they are members or within one year of their ceasing to be members, are required to contribute an amount not exceeding £1 each.
>
> The Association is a registered charity – No. 207812, and is not liable to UK taxation as it has no taxable activities. The Association is, however, unable to reclaim VAT on expenditure incurred.

A minority include it within their accounting policies, such as Example 1.4 Friends of the Lake District.

Example 1.4 Friends of the Lake District
Note 1: Accounting policies (31 December 1993):

> Constitution
>
> The Association is a charity (number 228443) registered under the Charities Act 1960 and is accordingly exempt from taxation. The property of the Association is vested in trustees and the management is through the Executive Committee.

Paragraph 27 of the revised SORP extends these disclosures by recommending that not only should an indication of the nature of the governing instrument be given, but how the charity is, or its trustees are, constituted and that this information be given in, or appended to, the trustees' annual report.

Rather than on its constitutional form, however, whether or not an institution is a charity will depend on what it has been established to do.

1.2.2 'Established for charitable purposes'

As chapter 2 of the White Paper *Charities: A framework for the future* (Cm 694) said:

> 'The starting point for the modern law of England and Wales is found in the preamble to the Statute of Elizabeth I (the Charitable Uses Act, 1601). Guidance on what was to be considered charitable was found there in a list of objects which included:
>
> "Relief of aged impotent and poor people . . . the maintenance of sick and maimed soldiers and mariners, schools of learning, free schools and scholars in universities . . . the repair of bridges, ports, havens, causeways, churches . . . "
>
> and others.
>
> 'For all practical purposes the courts have, for many years, accepted the classification which was made by Lord Macnaghten in 1891 in what has now become well-known as the "Pemsel" case (Income Tax Special Commissioners v Pemsel). This classification (which does not constitute a definition) reads as follows:
>
> "Charity in its legal sense comprises four principal divisions-trusts for the relief of poverty, trusts for the advancement of education, trusts for the advancement of religion, and trusts for other purposes beneficial to the community, not falling under any of the previous heads."

'Lord Macnaghten's classification has largely superseded the 1601 preamble, though in doubtful cases which arise under the head of "purposes beneficial to the community" the courts still refer to the preamble for guidance. The loose framework, which was set by the 1601 preamble and clarified by Lord Macnaghten, has enabled the courts over the years to develop the law in a way which has been sensitive to changing needs whilst maintaining the fundamental principles on which the concept of charity rests.'

From time to time there have been proposals that a definition of charity be formulated and given statutory effect. The White Paper suggested that by:

'(i) listing the purposes which are deemed to be charitable;
(ii) enacting a definition of charity based on Lord Macnaghten's classification; or
(iii) defining "charitable purposes" as "purposes beneficial to the community".'

However, the White Paper reported that:

'The Government considers that an attempt to define charity by any of these means would be fraught with difficulty, and might put at risk the flexibility of the present law which is both its greatest strength and its most valuable feature. In particular, they consider that there could be great dangers in attempting to specify in statute those objects which are to be regarded as charitable.

'Even if it was possible to draw up a list which could command a reasonable measure of agreement it might well lead to the exclusion of trusts which have long been treated as charitable, depriving them of any means of enforcement. A list might be inflexible and quickly outdated by changing public opinion. Listing the details in statute would not evade for long the problems which are inherent in any system of case law. Disputes would undoubtedly quickly arise on which the courts would be asked to adjudicate. There is no reason to believe that a new body of case law would be any less complex than the old.

'. . . Unless it were proposed to preserve the present case law, the incorporation of Lord Macnaghten's classification into statute would throw the law into confusion and uncertainty by depriving the courts of recourse to previous decisions when they were asked to interpret the new statutory provisions. On the other hand, if some form of words were to be found which would successfully preserve the present valuable case law, it is hard to see what the new definition would achieve.

'. . . There would appear, therefore, to be few advantages in attempting to a wholesale redefinition of charitable status–and many real dangers in doing so.'

1.3 Registration

A system of registration was introduced by the 1960 Act, continued, with amendments, by the 1992 Act and, through consolidation, by the 1993 Act. As the White Paper stated:

> 'Contrary to popular misunderstanding, registration does not confer charitable status; this is inherent in an organisation's purpose and trust instrument. Registration does, however, provide conclusive evidence–subject only to correction by the High Court–that an organisation is charitable in law.'

Under s3 of the 1993 Act, a duty is placed on all charity trustees to apply for registration unless the charity is:

(a) exempt;
(b) excepted;
(c) small; or
(d) a place of worship.

1.3.1 Exempt charities

Section 3(5)(a) of the 1993 Act excludes 'exempt charities' from the requirement to register. These institutions generally have some other form of supervision approved by Parliament and *include*:

- the universities of Oxford, Cambridge, Durham and London, including the colleges and halls of the first three;
- the trustees of the British Museum;
- the Church Commissioners and any institution which is administered by them;
- a registered society within the meaning of the Industrial and Provident Societies Act 1965; and
- a registered society or branch within the meaning of the Friendly Societies Act 1974.

Since the 1960 Act, the list of charities exempt from registration has been extended by numerous Acts. A complete list of exempt charities is provided by Sch 2 to the 1993 Act.

Under s4(2) of the 1960 Act, exempt charities were permitted to register voluntarily. This is no longer possible. Section 2(3) and (8) of the 1992 Act effected two changes: firstly, the possibility of registering on a voluntary basis was removed; and, secondly, registration of any exempt charity ceased, automatically, to have effect. These changes were brought into force on 1 September 1992 by the Charities Act 1992 (Commencement No. 1 and Transitional Provisions) Order 1992 (SI 1992 No 1900).

Exempt charities which have previously registered voluntarily might have been somewhat concerned about their loss of registered status and number. But there appears to be no reason why business documents could not contain a statement such as 'We are an exempt charity under Sch 2 to the Charities Act 1993'.

Registered exempt charities wishing to continue to be registered will need to change their status.

1.3.2 Excepted charities

Section 3(5)(b) exempts from registration certain charities by regulation or order.

The following charities have been excepted by regulation:

(a) by the Charities (Exception of Voluntary Schools from Registration) Regulations 1960 (SI 1960 No 2366), all voluntary schools which have no permanent endowment other than the premises of, or connected with, the school;
(b) by the Charities (Exception of Certain Boy Scouts and Girl Guides from Registration) Regulations 1961 (SI 1961 No 1044), funds, not permanent endowments, accumulated for the purpose of local units of the Boy Scouts Association or the Girl Guides Association and which produce an income of more than £15 a year;
(c) by the Charities (Exception from Registration and Accounts) Regulations 1963 (SI 1963 No 2074), property (other than land) held for the purposes of parochial church councils, church trustees and others established to make provision for public religious worship; and charities concerned with the advancement of religion;
(d) by the Charities (Exception of Registration and Accounts) Regulations 1964 (SI 1964 No 1825), certain religious charities where a specified trust corporation takes responsibility;
(e) by the Charities (Exception from Registration and Accounts) Regulations 1965 (SI 1965 No 1056), charities generally concerned with the promotion of the efficiency of any of the armed forces of the Crown; and
(f) by the Charities (Exception of Universities from Registration) Regulations 1966 (SI 1966 No 965), every university which is not an exempt charity.

In the case of the Roman Catholic Church and the Church of Wales, the Commissioners have dealt with the charities vested in diocesan trustees by order, excepting the charities individually (see the 1960 Annual Report of the Commissioners).

1.3.3 Small charities

Section 4(4)(c) of the 1960 Act excluded from registration any charity which had neither a permanent endowment nor the use or occupation of any land and whose income from property did not amount to more than £15 a year.

Section 2(5) of the 1992 Act (now s3(5)(c) of the 1993 Act) amended the last proviso to that sub-section, such that charities 'whose income from all sources does not in aggregate amount to more than £1,000 a year' will not be required to register. This amendment was effected so that charities with a small investment income but a large income from other sources (e.g., fundraising or individual benefactors) would be brought into the supervisory net.

What is 'income' in the phrase 'whose income from all sources does not in aggregate amount to more than £1,000 a year'? Section 96(4) of the 1993 Act provides that such a reference shall be interpreted by reference to the '*gross revenues* of the charity'. And s 96(5) provides that 'the Commissioners may direct that for all or any of the purposes of this Act an institution established for any special purpose of or in connection with a charity (being charitable purposes) shall be treated as forming part of that charity or as forming a distinct charity'. If such a direction were made, income from special trusts would need to be aggregated with that of the charity in determining whether the £1,000 threshold has been exceeded. If so, registration will be compulsory.

The 1993 Annual Report of the Commissioners reported that 12,559 charities were registered in that year. The large increase was attributed to this change. Many of the increased applications were from parent/teacher and home/school associations, pre-school playgroups and women's institutes.

Charities with an annual income of less than £1,000 will still be subject to registration if they have a permanent endowment or use, or occupy, land.

While 'land' includes buildings (this is in s5 of, and Sch 1 to, the Interpretation Act 1978, not in the Charities Acts), there is no definition, nor any guidance notes, of the phrase 'use or occupation of land'. There is some merit, however, in the maxim 'the law does not concern itself with trivialities'. Thus, were a charity to hire a hall for one night of the year (and does not otherwise have the use or occupation of any land), then it is highly unlikely that this situation would be caught by the legislation and require the charity to register. In other words, each case should be considered on its own facts and merits.

As stated on page 7, s3(5)(b) excepts certain scout associations from registration. If they are not excepted, however, and they have the 'use or occupation of any land', for example a scout hut, they will be required to register, regardless of their level of income. This is because they will not be excepted by section 3(5)(c).

Section 3(2) of the 1993 Act continues to allow charities excepted from registration to register voluntarily. Any advantage of registration, however, may be counterbalanced by certain disadvantages. For example, charities excepted by virtue of s3(5)(c) will, *inter alia*, have to submit their accounts (which may be subject to independent examination), annual report and annual return to the Commissioners (see chapter **3**, page 40).

There are provisions allowing existing charities which now fall below the registration threshold to deregister. The Commissioners are required to comply with the request.

Section 3(12) allows the Secretary of State to amend the limit of £1,000 either so as to keep pace with inflation or with a view to extending the scope of the exception provided for.

1.3.4 Places of worship

Provided that places of worship are registered under the Places of Worship Registration Act 1855, they are excepted from registration.

1.4 Declaration of status

Under s5(2) of the 1993 Act (previously s3 of the 1992 Act), registered charities with a *gross income* in their last financial year greater than £5,000 are required to state the fact that they are registered on certain specified business documents. (This provision took effect from 1 January 1993 – SI 1992 No 1900.)

Section 5(2) applies to the following documents:

(a) notices, advertisements and other documents issued by or on behalf of the charity and soliciting money or other property for the benefit of the charity;
(b) bills of exchange, promissory notes, endorsements, cheques and orders for money or goods purporting to be signed on behalf of the charity; and
(c) bills rendered by it and invoices, receipts and letters of credit.

It is regarded as good practice to include the statement on letterheads as well.

The purpose of the provision is to alert the public to the fact that they are dealing with a registered charity (which is subject to the Commissioners' jurisdiction and about which information and accounts may be obtained) and not with a private individual or commercial organisation.

Excepted charities which have registered voluntarily will have to comply with these requirements.

The statement may be in a language as well as, but not instead of, English. It must be clear and easy to read, but otherwise may be printed, rubber-stamped or handwritten. In their booklet 'A trustees' guide to the Charities Act 1992', the Commissioners suggested that the following examples would satisfy the requirement: 'A Registered Charity'; 'Registered Charity No.', followed by the number; 'Registered as a Charity'; or 'Registered with the Charity Commissioners'.

There is no requirement to give the charity registered number, although charities may do so if they wish.

While s68 of the 1993 Act is similar to s5, it is not identical. Section 68 requires that where a company is a charity and its name does not include the word 'charity', or the word 'charitable', the fact that the company is a charity must be stated in English (in legible characters) on certain documents. The documents are very similar to those in section 5 but, unlike that section, include, for example, business letters. It applies to all charitable companies, whether or not registered. And, because it is concerned with *charitable status*, rather than *registered charity status*, it seems charitable companies will need to ensure that their documents comply with both sections.

Under s5(4), trustees and staff of charities who are involved in the issue of any document falling within (a) or (c) above without this statement will be committing an offence and liable, on summary conviction, to a fine. Section 5(5) imposes a similar penalty on any person who signs a document, falling within (b) above, without the necessary statement.

Section 5(6) confers powers on the Secretary of State to amend the limit, of £5,000. (The eighth Deregulation Task Force proposed that the limit be raised to £10,000.)

1.5 Charity names

Prior to the 1992 Act, the Commissioners could not refuse registration on the grounds that the charity had a name similar to, or even the same as, an existing charity.

With effect from 1 September 1992, s4 and 5 of the 1992 Act (now s6 and 7 of the 1993 Act) give powers to the Commissioners to give directions requiring a charity to change its name in certain specified circumstances. These are if:

(a) at the time when the name is entered in the register, the registered name is the same as, or is too like that of, another charity (whether or not registered);
(b) the name of the charity is likely to mislead the public as to the true nature of the purposes or activities of the charity;
(c) the name of the charity includes any word or expression specified in regulations made by the Secretary of State which is likely to mislead the public as to its status;
(d) the name of the charity is likely to give the impression that it is connected in some way with the government, or any local authority, or with any body of persons or any individual, when it is not so connected; or
(e) the name of the charity is offensive.

While any direction in respect of (a) must be given within 12 months of registration, there are no time limits for (b) to (e) inclusive. The powers apply to all charities, whether or not registered (although (a) is specifically concerned with changing the registered name of a registered charity), except for exempt charities which are excluded by s6(9).

Chapter 2 – Trustees, responsibilities, liabilities and insurance

2.1 Introduction

The 1992 Act was a response to the growth of the charity sector and the need for increased accountability. The new requirements for charity accounts, increased controls over fundraising and the strengthened powers of the Commissioners are part of a general initiative to upgrade the regulatory framework within which charities operate. That Act apart, other aspects of the law to which charities may generally be subject are constantly evolving, as a result of which trustees may be unsure whether or not they are acting within the law.

2.2 Who is a 'charity trustee'?

On trust: Increasing the effectiveness of charity trustees and management committees, a report of the NCVO/Charity Commission Working Party on Trustee Training ('the NCVO report'), revealed that 'one of the more striking finds from our survey is how few trustees realise they *are* trustees'. The report attributed this to 'partly a problem of language. In organisations with a "board of trustees", all seemed clear. In organisations with "management committees", most members seemed unclear whether they were charity trustees. In organisations which had incorporated as limited companies, most respondents saw themselves as directors, but not all were clear whether they were trustees as well.'

Section 91(1) of the 1993 Act defines 'charity trustees' as 'the persons having the general control and management of the administration of a charity'. While SORP 2 contained no definition, para 23 of Appendix 1 of its successor contains a definition of 'trustees', which is similar. Paragraph 24 states that 'the status of a trustee is defined in terms of the function to be performed, and not by reference to the title given to any office, or membership of any committee or committees . . . .' Thus, regardless of the constitutional form of a charity, members of the board of directors, or management or executive committee or similar description will be the charity trustees. Persons elected to manage a branch, where it is an integral part of the whole charity, may not be charity trustees. Conversely, some national charities have a structure where their local groups are constituted as independent registered charities. Those in charge will be charity trustees in these circumstances.

'Custodian' (or 'holding') trustees would not fall to be included within either of the above definitions, as they do not actively involve themselves in the management of the administration. Rather, their responsibilities are limited to holding the assets of the charity for safe-keeping and in carrying out the instructions of the charity trustees.

A research report, *The revision of SORP 2 ('Accounting by charities'): A commentary on the exposure draft*, for the CACA, points out that:

> 'The situation with respect to trustees is further complicated by the possibility of special trusts, which are part of the principal charity but sometimes have a separate committee of management. When charities hold events such as Centenary Celebrations, Founder's Days, Carnivals and other festivals, these tend to be run by committees drawn from a wider section of the community than the main trustees of the charity.'

In the light of their responsibilities and liabilities, it is particularly important for all involved to know who the real trustees are. The research report recommends that 'those who are not truly trustees of the charity, could be re- designated as "patrons", "members of advisory committees" and the like. It might also be useful to describe those who are trustees as such-especially in those charities where people bear more traditional titles, such as "fellows", "governors", "bailiffs", "guardians", "brethren" and so on.'

2.3 Who may not be a charity trustee?

The Woodfield Report proposed that persons convicted of any offence 'involving fraud or other dishonesty', or who had previously been removed from trusteeship by the Commissioners, should not be able to be a charity trustee without the Commissioners' consent, in writing.

Sections 72 and 73 of the 1993 Act, which came into effect on 1 January 1993, have implemented these recommendations, but the grounds for disqualification have been widened.

Under s72(1), a person is disqualified from acting as a charity trustee if he:

(a) has been convicted of any offence involving dishonesty or deception (including theft, forgery or fraud);

(b) has been adjudged bankrupt or sequestration of his estate has been awarded and (in either case) he has not been discharged;
(c) has made a composition or arrangement with, or granted a trust deed for, his creditors and has not been discharged in respect of it;
(d) has been removed from the office of charity trustee by order of the Commissioners or by the High Court on the grounds of any misconduct or mismanagement in the charity's administration for which he was responsible or to which he was privy, or which he by his conduct contributed or facilitated;
(e) has been removed under s7 of the Law Reform (Miscellaneous Provisions) (Scotland) Act 1990 (powers of Court of Sessions to deal with management of charities), from being concerned in the management or control of any body; or
(f) is subject to a disqualification order under the Company Directors Disqualification Act 1986 or to an order made under s429(2)(b) of the Insolvency Act 1986 (failure to pay under county court administration order).

Disqualification is, generally, automatic. Disqualified trustees, who may have been appointed lawfully, do not have to take steps to resign or be removed from trusteeship. They should immediately cease to take any further part in the charity's affairs. Under s73(4), the Commissioners may even require the return to the charity of the value of any benefits trustees may have received from the charity while disqualified. However, acts done for a charity while disqualified will not be invalid by reason only of the disqualification (s73(3)).

Section 72(4) allows the Commissioners to waive disqualification either generally or in respect of a particular charity or a particular class of charities, for example in the case of charities working with ex-offenders.

However, a waiver may not be granted in relation to any charitable company if the person is disqualified under the Company Directors Disqualification Act 1986 and has not been granted permission under that Act to act as director of any other company.

Section 73 imposes penalties (either a term of imprisonment or a fine, or both) for acting as a trustee while disqualified. This does not apply to a trustee disqualified on the grounds of (b) or (f) above, as those offences will be dealt with under company law.

Section 72(7) requires the Commissioners to keep a register, which is open to the public, of all persons removed from office by them.

2.4 What are the trustees' responsibilities?

It is important that trustees not only know that they are trustees but, also, have an awareness of their responsibilities in order that they may effectively discharge them. The NCVO report pointed out that many trustees do not understand the nature of their responsibilities, or, if they were aware, do not know how they should be carried out.

The Commissioners have published a leaflet (CC3) 'Responsibilities of charity trustees' and, for ease of reference, the most recent edition is reproduced as the Annex to this chapter.

2.5 Responsibility for preparing the report and accounts

The accounts should include an adequate description of the trustees' relevant responsibilities. (Where such a description is not provided, Auditing Standard 600.3 in SAS 600 *Auditors' reports on financial statements* requires the auditors' report to include one.) The matters to be included will reflect the specific requirements of the reporting entity. Appendix 3 to SAS 600 gives illustrative wording of a description which may be included in company accounts. The wording shown in Example 2.1 as used by Save The Children Fund is typical.

Example 2.1 Save The Children Fund
Report of the Council (extract) (31 March 1993):

Trustees' responsibilities

Company and charity law requires the Council, as trustees and directors, to prepare financial statements for each financial year which give a true and fair view of the state of affairs of SCF, and the results for the period. In preparing the financial statements the trustees are required to:

- select suitable accounting policies and apply them consistently;
- make judgements and estimates that are reasonable and prudent;
- state whether applicable accounting standards have been followed, subject to any material departures disclosed and explained in the financial statements; and
- prepare the financial statements on the going concern basis unless it is inappropriate to presume that SCF will continue in business.

The trustees are responsible for keeping proper accounting records which disclose, with reasonable accuracy at any time, the financial position of SCF

> and enable them to ensure that the financial statements comply with the Companies Act 1985. They are also responsible for safeguarding the assets of SCF and hence for taking reasonable steps for the prevention and detection of fraud and other irregularities.

Some charities, for example SCOPE (formerly The Spastics Society), refer to the Charities Act, as well as to the Companies Act.

This description needs to be adapted, however, for different requirements applicable to different categories of reporting entity. The wording shown in Example 2.2, as used by CAFOD, is typical of an unincorporated entity.

Example 2.2 CAFOD
Report of the trustees (extract) (30 September 1993):

> TRUSTEES' RESPONSIBILITIES IN RESPECT OF THE ACCOUNTS
>
> Under the Charities Act 1993, the Trustees are required to:
>
> (i) ensure that accounting records are kept in respect of the charity, which are sufficient to show and explain all the charity's transactions.
> (ii) prepare in respect of each financial year of the charity a statement of accounts complying with the requirements as to its form and contents as may be prescribed by regulations made by the Secretary of State.

And, because Crosslinks, also unincorporated, does not prepare a statement, the auditors have provided one in their report, as shown in Example 2.3.

Example 2.3. Crosslinks
Auditors' report (extract) (31 December 1993):

> RESPECTIVE RESPONSIBILITIES OF TRUSTEES AND AUDITORS
>
> The trustees are required by Charity Law to keep proper accounting records and to prepare consecutive statements of account. It is our responsibility to form an independent opinion, based on our audit, on those statements and to report our opinion to you.

Neither of the above two statements is particularly informative.

An informative statement is, however, provided by Example 2.4 The Church Commissioners and by the auditors, in accordance with Auditing Standard 600.3, in their report in Example 2.5 Royal National Lifeboat Institution.

Example 2.4. Church Commissioners
Statement of responsibilities of the Church Commissioners (31 December 1993):

Under section 11 (1) of the Church Commissioners Measure 1947, the Church Commissioners shall cause such accounts to be kept as may be required for the due performance and discharge of their functions. The Measure requires the Commissioners to keep a general fund, to which they shall carry all income received in respect of property and funds held by them. Out of the fund are to be discharged all trusts and commitments to which the income is subject and all expenses and obligations falling upon the Commissioners in the due discharge of their functions. The balance on the general fund is available for specified purposes.

Section 3 of the Measure provides for the business of the Commissioners to be transacted by a Board of Governors and the committees constituted under the Measure.

The Assets Committee have, subject to any general rules made by the Board, an exclusive power and duty to act on behalf of the Commissioners in all matters relating to the management of the general fund assets of the Commissioners. They have a duty to recommend to the Board what sums are available for application or distribution by the Commissioners and what sums should be appropriated to reserve and for investment.

The General Purposes Committee shall, subject to any general rules made by the Board, consider and recommend to the Board how to apply or distribute such sums as the Board may have determined to be available for distribution.

In relation to the financial statements, the Board of Governors confirm that:

- where there is no conflict with the terms of the Measure and except where material departures have been disclosed, the financial statements comply with all applicable UK accounting standards and statements of recommended practice and with the accounting requirements of the Companies Acts
- the financial statements give a true and fair view of the consolidated state of affairs of the Church Commissioners and of the consolidated revenue deficit, total recognised gains and losses and consolidated cash flows for the financial year
- suitable accounting policies have been selected and applied on a consistent basis
- reasonable and prudent judgements and estimates have been made
- the financial statements have been prepared on the going concern basis.

The Board of Governors are responsible for keeping proper accounting records which disclose with reasonable accuracy at any time the financial position of the Church Commissioners, for safeguarding the Church Commissioners' assets and for taking reasonable steps for the prevention and detection of fraud and other irregularities.

By order of the Board
P Locke *Secretary*
13 May 1994

Example 2.5 Royal National Lifeboat Institution Auditors' report to the committee of management (31 December 1993):

We have audited the accounts on pages 32 to 36 which have been prepared under the accounting policies set out on page 34.

Responsibilities of Executive Committee
The Charter, the Charities Act 1960 and the Charities (Statement of Account) Regulations 1960 require the Executive Committee to prepare accounts for each financial year. In preparing these accounts, the Executive Committee are encouraged to follow the recommendations outlined in Statement of Recommended Practice No. 2, 'Accounting by Charities' (issued by the Accounting Standards Committee in 1988).

The Executive Committee consider that in preparing these accounts, they have used appropriate accounting policies, consistently applied and supported by reasonable and prudent judgements and estimates.

The Executive Committee are responsible for keeping proper accounting records to enable them to ensure that the accounts comply with the Charities Act 1960 and the Charities (Statement of Account) Regulations 1960. They are also responsible for safeguarding the assets of the Institution and hence for taking reasonable steps for the prevention and detection of fraud and other irregularities.

Responsibilities of auditors
It is our responsibility to form an independent opinion, based on our audit, on those accounts and to report our opinion to you.

Basis of opinion
We conducted our audit in accordance with Auditing Standards issued by the Auditing Practices Board. An audit includes examination, on a test basis, of evidence relevant to the amounts and disclosures in the accounts. It also includes an assessment of the significant estimates and judgements made by the trustees in the preparation of the accounts, and of whether the accounting policies are appropriate to the Institution's circumstances, consistently applied and adequately disclosed.

We planned and performed our audit so as to obtain all the information and explanations which we considered necessary in order to provide us with sufficient evidence to give reasonable assurance that the accounts are free from material misstatement, whether caused by fraud or other irregularity or error. In forming our opinion we also evaluated the overall adequacy of the presentation of information in the accounts.

Opinion
In our opinion the accounts give a true and fair view of the state of the Institution's affairs at 31 December 1993 and of its income and expenditure and cash flows for the year then ended and have been properly prepared in accordance with the provisions of the Charities Act 1960.

Price Waterhouse 24 March 1994

Chartered Accountants
and Registered Auditors
Southampton

In October 1993, the Business Law Committee of the ICAEW issued guidance on reporting on trusts. The guidance, *Occupational pension schemes and other trusts: statement of trustees' responsibilities* (FRAG 22/93), draws attention to the different legal responsibilities that trustees of trusts have in comparison with those of directors of limited companies. It recommends that the wording of the note on trustees' responsibilities should take into account the particular circumstances of each trust, and that it may be appropriate to seek legal advice. Although aimed particularly at pension schemes, the recommendation to seek such advice would, given their wide variety of structure, be equally appropriate (if not more so) to charities. It is understood, however, that there is no current intention to issue companion guidance specifically for charities.

Paragraph 20 of SORP 2 stated that:

> 'The trustees are responsible for the preparation of the annual report and therefore for the form and content of the accounts. They should discharge this responsibility by formally approving and adopting the annual report. The trustees' report and balance sheet should be signed by at least two trustees on behalf of all of them in order to show this approval.'

This compares with s233(1) of the 1985 Act which requires a company's annual accounts to be approved by the board of directors and signed on its behalf by one of them. Section 233(2) requires the signature to be on the balance sheet. And, s234A(1) requires the directors' report to be similarly approved and signed, either by a director or by the secretary.

Although the balance sheet is usually signed by two trustees, the trustees' report, where prepared, is very often signed only by the secretary. Some charities continue to prepare a treasurer's report (see chapter **5**, page 122), which is signed by that person.

Without stating where, para 20 of SORP 2 recommended, also, that the date of approval be disclosed. Paragraph 26 of SSAP 17 *Accounting for post balance sheet events*, requires such approval to be disclosed 'in the financial statements'.

The date of approval is sometimes omitted, either from the balance sheet or from the trustees' report, or both; see, for example, Example 2.6 United Kingdom Band of Hope Union.

Example 2.6 United Kingdom Band of Hope Union
Balance sheet (extract) (31 December 1993):

The financial statements were approved by the board on . . . .

D. Tayler	)	
	)	*Directors*
Miss D. Driver	)	

The notes on pages 7 to 12 form part of these financial statements.

Report of the directors (extract):

AUDITORS

A motion for the appointment of auditors of the company is to be proposed at the Annual General Meeting.

BY ORDER OF THE COMMITTEE

G. Ruston
Executive Director

Date . . . .

MIND, a charitable company, prepares a treasurer's report, but that for its 1993 accounts was neither signed nor dated.

Example 2.7 Guide Dogs for the Blind Association gives the date of approval in the trustees' report, rather than on the face of the balance sheet.

Example 2.7 Guide Dogs for the Blind Association
Report of the Council (extract) (31 December 1993):

The Members of the Council of the Association have pleasure in submitting their Report and the audited Financial Statements of the Association for the year ended 31 December 1993 which were approved by the Council on 29 March 1994.

Paragraph 24 of the ED of the revised SORP proposed that 'each and every trustee' should confirm that this responsibility has been discharged by formally approving and adopting the annual report and accounts. The ED suggested that this could be achieved in one of two ways; either in a meeting or, if the trustees are not all present, in writing. For charities with a substantial number of trustees, this proposal seemed impracticable. Approval at the trustees' meeting, provided it was quorate, should suffice. Acknowledging this, para 30 of the revised SORP recommends that the annual report and accounts be approved by the trustees, as a body, in accordance with their usual administrative procedure, but signed on their behalf by one of the trustees authorised to do so. A copy of the draft accounts should be circulated to all trustees a reasonable time (not specified) before the meeting at which they are to be approved.

However, if any trustee considers that the annual report and/or accounts should not be, or not have been, approved, he should report any concerns which he is unable to resolve with his fellow trustees, and/or with the auditor or examiner, to the Commissioners or other regulator.

Regulation 3(6) requires the balance sheet to give the date on which the accounts were formally approved and signed by one or more of the charity trustees authorised to do so. And, reg 10(1)(c) requires that the trustees' annual report be dated and similarly signed.

2.6 Other financial responsibilities

Trustees have other financial responsibilities. Chapter 7 of the NCVO report stated (*inter alia*) that:

> 'Trustees are responsible for the good administration of the finance of the organisation . . . the importance of sound, effective management information systems cannot be over- stressed . . . budgets and accounts are not just for information, but are the main instrument for direction and control . . . a sound system of internal control is required . . . trustees must be aware of special categories within the funds . . . trustees have a responsibility to maximise returns on investments . . . '.

The importance of effective financial control for all charities was reiterated in the 1993 Annual Report of the Commissioners. Paragraphs 85 and 86 stated:

> 'Effective financial control by the trustees requires a clear understanding that it is they who are responsible for ensuring that the charity's funds are properly applied for its purposes and that proper accounts are prepared each year. This also demands basic accounting disciplines and procedures and, where

appropriate, access to qualified professional advice . . . Without such control procedures, trustees can too easily become isolated from the core financial aspects of their charity with a resulting risk to charity property.

'Comparatively few of the charities we looked at in 1993 had prepared spending plans and budgets at the beginning of each year. Trustees can often be optimistic about finance, but optimism is no substitute for realistic planning, including contingency planning, and regular monitoring of the actual financial situation against the plans. Basic financial planning is essential for even the smallest of charities. More charities are being identified as potentially insolvent with risks to both charitable funds and to the trustees themselves. Insolvency in a charity can often be difficult to identify as well-wishers or grant- makers may be prompted into action to save a charity from financial collapse. Nevertheless, sound budgeting and cash flow management can both prevent such situations arising and help to protect trustees from the consequences of insolvency.'

(Note: A guide to effective internal control in housing associations, *Internal control in housing associations*, was published, in December 1994, by CIPFA and the National Federation of Housing Associations. However, this booklet has since been superseded by the Housing Corporation's Code of Audit Practice which makes greater demands.)

Given their high profile, charities need to regulate themselves in an open and publicly accountable way. Much of the NCVO report is devoted to their governance and accountability (see, also, chapter **4**, page 84).

Some charities already provide disclosures which touch on the concept of governance and accountability. For example, Example 2.8 Leonard Cheshire Foundation's annual report contains a report from the chairman of the audit committee and the Report of the Council of Example 2.9 Save The Children Fund refers to the work of the audit and remuneration committees.

Example 2.8 The Leonard Cheshire Foundation
Report of the chairman of the audit committee (30 September 1993):

The following financial statements relate to the provision of our services in the United Kingdom across the spectrum of care for people with disabilities. The full extent of the work inspired by Leonard Cheshire around the world is not reflected in these statements. The support by 'seed corn' grants and costs of peripatetic personnel to assist in the establishment of services are reported under Grants to Overseas Homes.

Cost of Care

During 1993, some 1,700 people used our residential services either as permanent residents, or for respite or day care, at a cost of £41 million. Local Authorities paid £38.2 million for these services, leaving a deficit of £2.8 million, equivalent to a shortfall for each person of £32 every week.

Our domiciliary services, costing £3.7 million, provided 475,000 hours of care to some 2,500 people in their own homes. Local Authorities paid £3.2 million for these services. The resulting deficit of £0.5 million creates a need for a donation of £1 for each hour of care given.

The total deficit on the provision of care was £3.3 million (£4.2 million in 1992). This reduction in the deficit is due in part to improved funding by the purchasers of our services and also to our constant search for efficiencies and cost reduction.

Voluntary Income

At £9.8 million Voluntary Income is £0.6 million higher than the previous year but this is partly offset by a decrease in Investment Income to £1.5 million from £1.8 million in 1992, largely because of falling interest rates. Whilst the overall position is satisfactory, we are conscious of our dependence on Legacies which represent 67% of our Voluntary Income and without which we would face very serious problems.

During the year four redundant buildings were sold, realising a surplus of £0.7 million.

Expenditure from Charitable Funds

After meeting the deficit on care, Charitable Funds are applied to the costs of administering our services and promoting them to potential users and purchasers. At £1.5 million, this represents only 3% of total expenditure.

The Surplus of £6.3 million has been applied to improving and replacing homes at a cost of £3.4 million, as reported in the Cash Flow Statement. The remainder has been added to Cash on the Balance Sheet. In the previous year the Surplus was £3.9 million, with capital expenditure of £6.3 million, so that over the two years we have applied the totality of funds given to us.

The Future

Reference is made in Note 13 to the level of projected commitment to support our services and to develop new solutions to meet the needs of people with disabilities. Only by a sustained effort to maintain our voluntary support and to identify new supporters and new sources of income can these commitments be met.

Michael Johns

Chairman of the Audit Committee

18th April 1994

Example 2.9 Save The Children Fund
Report of the Council (extract) (31 March 1993):

Organisation
Save the Children is an Association of Members, the business of which is governed by the Council which may exercise all the powers of Association. The Council comprises not more than 20 persons and is responsible for ultimate strategic decisions based upon advice from senior management; it approves budgets and exercises financial control through regular financial reporting. An Audit Committee, appointed by the Council, meets quarterly to consider reports from both the external and the internal auditors. In addition a remuneration committee formed from members of the Council meets annually to determine the salaries of Save the Children's directors.

Day-to-day operational decisions are taken by senior management who coordinate and direct SCF's work in over 50 countries in Africa, Asia, Eastern Europe, the Middle East, Latin America and the Caribbean, and throughout the UK. Save the Children is a leading member of the International Save the Children Alliance, a body which represents and coordinates the activities of 25 autonomous Save the Children organisations around the world.

The names of the members of Council at 31 March 1993 are set out on the inside of the front cover of this report.

Further to the recommendations of The Lambeth Report, Example 2.10 Church Commissioners refer to the strengthening of accountability.

Example 2.10 Church Commissioners
Introduction (extract) (31 December 1993):

STRENGTHENING ACCOUNTABILITY

Steering Group
The Board of Governors has appointed a Steering Group of eight of its members, chaired by the Bishop of Blackburn. The Steering Group is making certain that all the Lambeth Report's recommendations are vigorously pursued through appropriate plans, timescales and actions.

A new Audit Committee
In accordance with the recommendations of the Lambeth Report, we put into place earlier this year an Audit Committee, chaired by Alan McLintock CA, who was a member of the Lambeth Group and is also Chairman of the Central Board of Finance. Other members appointed to date are Derek Fellows FIA, also a member of the Lambeth Group, former Executive Director of the Securities and Investments Board and formerly Chief Actuary to the Prudential Assurance Society, and Viscountess Brentford FCA. Neither Mr McLintock nor Mr Fellows is a Church Commissioner. This Committee, which will report to the Board of Governors, will scrutinise every aspect of the Commissioners' financial management.

The Assets Committee
The Assets Committee was strengthened, as also recommended by the Lambeth Report, by the addition of two experts in property matters, Jeremy Newsum FRICS, Chief Executive of the Grosvenor Estate and Godfrey Richardson FRICS, formerly senior investment partner of Knight Frank and Rutley. We took other steps to reinforce the Committee's existing structure and mechanisms, including the formation of a property sub-group including Mr Richardson, Mr Newsum and Sir Christopher Wates FCA to scrutinise the property element of the portfolio. A similar securities sub-group will be established soon.

Management
In January 1994 we appointed a new Deputy Secretary (Finance and Investment), as recommended by the Lambeth Report, to strengthen our financial management.

2.7 Liabilities and insurance

In the case of liability to third parties in contract, an incorporated charity will enter into contracts, sue and be sued in its own name. In contrast, if unincorporated, creditors contract with the trustees and it will be them from whom they may seek redress.

Whether or not a charity is incorporated, however, all charity trustees will be personally liable for all acts and omissions where a duty of care is owed to third parties. This will be so where there has been a breach of trust, for example, where the charity has purchased investments not authorised by its constitution, where funds have been spent on unauthorised activities, or where the trustees have acted outside of the objects of the charity.

Thus, the sometimes held perception that charity trustees of an incorporated charity are protected from personal liability is something of a myth.

Section 727 of the 1985 Act affords a measure of protection for officers in cases where they may be liable in respect of negligence, default, breach of trust or breach of duty, but have acted honestly and reasonably and where, having regard to all the circumstances of the case, they ought fairly to be excused. Section 61 of the Trustee Act 1925 offers similar protection.

Prior to the 1989 Act, s310 of the 1985 Act provided that certain provisions indemnifying directors were void. The void provisions were generally those for exempting any officer of the company from default, or indemnifying him against default, breach of duty or breach of trust in relation to the company. And, it did not matter whether the provisions were contained in a company's Articles or in any contract with the company, or otherwise.

This last section was amended by s137 of the 1989 Act, such that a company may now take out insurance against those liabilities without that insurance being void. It is understood, however, that this relaxation does not *of itself* permit a charitable company to provide indemnity insurance for its directors. Provision and maintenance of such insurance would confer a personal benefit to trustees. Thus, directors of a charitable company would, generally, be precluded by the company's Memorandum of Association from securing any such benefit. An amendment would, therefore, normally be required to the Memorandum and Articles in order fully to take advantage of this relaxation.

For a charitable company, s64(2) of the 1993 Act requires the Commissioners' consent to any alteration of:

(a) the objects clause in the Memorandum; or
(b) any other provision in either the Memorandum or Articles which directs, or restricts, the manner in which property is used, or applied.

The Commissioners have indicated that they would raise no objection to such an amendment provided that it was limited to covering trustees from personal liability only for acts properly undertaken in the administration of the charity or undertaken in breach of trust but under an honest mistake.

For an unincorporated entity, the provision of indemnity insurance could only be given if there were an express power in its constitution. Such power would need to be approved by the Commissioners.

In their 1990 Annual Report, the Commissioners noted that there was a growing public concern about the extent to which trustees could be held personally liable for the financial consequences of their actions, and whether they could properly insure themselves at the charity's expense against such liabilities. They recognised that potential trustees may be deterred from trusteeship because their personal assets may be at risk due to misjudgment rather than malicious intent. Therefore, the Commissioners agreed, in principle, that, where trustees' liability insurance is in the interests of the charity, the premiums may, in some cases, be paid from charity funds. The Commissioners are anxious to avoid giving the impression that approval for insurance to be taken out will be granted *automatically*. The range of circumstances in which they are likely to agree to such an amendment will, in practice, be quite small. Trustees will need to demonstrate that:

(a) the insurance is in the interests of the charity, and not those of the trustees:
(b) the insurance will be for the benefit of the charity and not to the trustees, even in their capacity as trustees; and
(c) there is a reasonable risk of liability falling on the trustees.

There is no objection, in principle, to a charity insuring against loss to its funds resulting from the acts and defaults of the trustees.

Paragraph 1(d) of Pt IV of the Sch to the Regulations requires the notes to give particulars of the cost to the charity of:

(a) any policies of insurance against loss arising from the neglect or default of any of the charity trustees or trustees of the charity; or
(b) indemnifying the charity trustees, or any of the trustees, for the charity in respect of the consequences of any such loss.

Paragraph 159 of the revised charity SORP recommends that the fact, as well as particulars of the cost, be given.

While the Regulations require disclosure to be given in respect of the purchase of insurance to protect the *charity trustees or trustees for the charity*, the SORP appears to be wider by recommending that it is in respect of the *trustees, employees or agents.*

Paragraph 5A of Sch 7 to the 1985 Act requires that, where the company has purchased or maintained insurance for its officers, that fact should be disclosed in the directors' report. Example 2.11 Nuffield Nursing Homes Trust provides an example.

Example 2.11 Nuffield Nursing Homes Trust
Report of the board of governors (extract) (31 December 1993):

Insurance for Governors and Officers

The Trust has purchased insurance to indemnify its Governors and Principal Officers against liabilities in relation to the Group that may be incurred by them in their respective capacities. The insurance premium relating to them has been reimbursed to the Trust in full by paid officers but the Trust has met the cost of that for the Governors pursuant to provisions adopted by the Members at their last Annual General Meeting with the consent of the Charity Commissioners.

As regards incorporation and trustee liability, the White Paper suggested that the government may consider:

(a) the creation of a new charity structure, fully under the Commissioners' jurisdiction but involving some form of incorporation coupled with limited liability, and tied to model governing instruments; or
(b) provision for the trustee body to be incorporated, and having limited liability, with the charity itself remaining as a charitable trust.

While the 1992 Act took neither course, it did go some way towards the second approach by amending the Charitable Trustees Incorporation Act 1872 so as to facilitate the incorporation of charity trustees, without the benefits of limited liability.

From 1 January 1993 charity trustees have been able to apply to the Commissioners to become incorporated. The incorporated body of trustees has legal personality, is able to hold property, sue and be sued and enter into contracts. Although incorporated, the trustees remain personally liable.

Given the divestment of the Official Custodian, there could be a considerable demand for this, as property may be held in the name of the incorporated body, making it unnecessary for title deeds, share certificates etc. to be constantly changed each time a trustee retires, resigns or is appointed.

During the passage of the Charities Bill, concern was expressed at the current unlimited personal liability of trustees of an unincorporated charity. Although a clause, the object of which was to address this concern, was withdrawn at the Report Stage, a commitment was given 'fully to examine the nature of the existing problem and try to explore the options and implications of addressing it'.

Annex

Responsibilities of Charity Trustees

Introduction

The Charity Commission is often asked to explain what is expected of someone who is appointed to act as a charity trustee. Trusteeship carries legal responsibilities and duties. To be a charity trustee is not a position of honour without responsibility: it requires time, understanding and effort. This leaflet answers some of the more common questions and sets out briefly and simply the duties of charity trustees. It covers such aspects as:

- what is a charity trustee, who can be one, and what personal qualities are needed;
- appointment, length of service and retirement of trustees;
- general principles of trusteeship;
- trustees' duties in relation to charity investments and property;
- trustees' duties in relation to registration, fundraising and accounting;
- liability of trustees, and delegation.

Some expressions used in this leaflet

It may help to explain some of the expressions used in this leaflet. In most cases the rules for running the charity will be set out in a trust deed, a will, a constitution or the Memorandum and Articles of Association of a company. They may sometimes (though not often) be found in a Royal Charter or an Act of Parliament. In any of these cases, except that of a company, there may also be one or more schemes made by the Charity Commission or by the High Court. Whatever form the documents take in any particular case, they are called '**the governing document**' in this leaflet.

'**Permanent endowment**' means property belonging to the charity which can not be expended for the purposes of the charity: usually it is only the income of the property which may be expended for those purposes. A '**permanently endowed**' charity is one which has permanent endowment.

Who are the 'charity trustees' of a charity?

The charity trustees are the people responsible under the charity's governing document for controlling the management and administration of the charity, regardless of what they are called. For instance, in the case of an unincorporated association the executive or management committee are its charity trustees, and in the case of a charitable company it is the directors who are the charity trustees.

Some charities have **custodian** or **holding trustees**, whose function is simply to hold the legal title of the charity's property or investments. Custodian or holding trustees have no role as such in the charity's management. They must act on the instructions of the charity trustees, unless they are told to do something which is in breach of trust.

Can anyone act as a trustee?

No-one under the age of 18 can be appointed as a trustee, and some people are disqualified by law from acting as charity trustees. This includes anyone described in section 72 (1) of the Charities Act 1993. Broadly that covers anyone who has been convicted of an offence involving deception or dishonesty, unless the conviction is spent, and anyone who is an undischarged bankrupt, or who has previously been removed from trusteeship of a charity by the court or the Commissioners, or is under a disqualification order under the Company Directors Disqualification Act 1986. It is an offence to act as a charity trustee while disqualified unless the Commissioners have given a waiver under section 72 (4) of the Charities Act 1993.

What are the qualities needed to be a trustee?

Trustees must be selected for what they can contribute to the charity. They should not be appointed for their status or position in the community alone: this is the function of patrons. Trustees must be able – and willing – to give time to the efficient administration of the charity and the fulfilment of its trusts. They should be selected on the basis of their relevant experience and skills and must be prepared to take an active part in the running of the charity.

What are the first steps that newly-appointed trustees should take?

Trustees can be effective only if they have a sound knowledge of the purposes of the charity, the trusts and procedures which govern the trustees' actions and the nature and condition of the property and resources of the charity. So every trustee (or person asked to be a trustee) should study the governing document or documents of the charity.

If there is any difficulty in obtaining a copy of the governing document, the Charity Commission may be able to help.

New trustees should also take the first opportunity to meet their fellow trustees and anyone else concerned with the administration of the charity and ask about its activities, its funding and the nature and condition of its property.

They should also ensure, where the property of the charity is held in the names of individual trustees (and not in the Official Custodian for Charities or a corporate body), that all the property of the charity is transferred into the names of the people who are the charity trustees at the time.

In addition, they should make sure that they study the latest annual report and accounts of the charity and, where necessary, ask for an explanation of their content and layout.

People who are invited or appointed to be trustees also need to be aware of their duties and responsibilities under trust and charity law. The Commission recommends that every trustee read this leaflet carefully when they are appointed.

Finally, where necessary, new trustees (particularly *ex officio* trustees) should show that they accept their responsibility and duties by signing the minute book.

How often should the trustees meet?

Trustees must meet regularly if they are to administer their charity properly. How often that needs to be will depend on the size and nature of the charity but may sometimes be set out in the charity's governing document.

If the governing document requires the charity to have a certain number of trustees, or specifies a minimum number of trustees who must be present if a meeting of the trustees is to be properly constituted (a quorum), the trustees must ensure that their strength does not fall or, if it does, does not stay below that number. If no such requirements are made in the governing document of the charity, then the number of trustees must be kept up to an effective working strength, having regard to the administrative requirements of the charity and the legal rule (if the governing document does not specify otherwise) that no decision can be taken except by all or a majority of the trustees.

How long does the appointment of a trustee last?

If the governing document does not specify the length of service of a trustee, the appointment continues until the trustee dies or resigns or is removed from office. However, in many cases the governing document says that trustees are to serve for a given period (usually a number of years, or, if the trustee is appointed to fill a vacancy, until the trustee who is replaced would have retired).

Trustees appointed to a local charity by a local authority under section 79 of the Charities Act 1993 are usually appointed for a term of four years.

Can a trustee resign?

Yes, if the governing document says so. The resignation is then handled in the way set out in the governing document. Normally, however, a trustee should not resign unless there will be at least two trustees left after the resignation. If the trustee was appointed by deed there will usually have to be a deed of retirement which may appoint a new trustee or trustees in place of the retiring trustee. A trustee who resigns should ensure that there is someone else willing to be appointed in his place.

Who appoints new trustees?

In many cases the governing document says who is to appoint new trustees. In some cases it says that some people are to be trustees because of an office which they hold. This is often the Vicar of a parish or the Vicar and churchwardens. Sometimes a named person is given the right to say who shall be new trustees. Sometimes different organisations are given the right to appoint representatives.

If the governing document does not say anything about this, the law allows the trustees themselves to appoint new trustees **if** there are enough of them left to take proper decisions (i.e., there is a quorum). A retiring trustee can usually be appointed for a further term of office, but the governing document may in some cases not allow it. This should be checked before a new appointment is made.

If there is any difficulty about appointing new trustees, either because there is no person who has the right to appoint new trustees or because there is not a quorum who can appoint them, the Charity Commission should be told as it has the power to appoint new trustees in those circumstances.

Can trustees be paid for their duties?

Generally, no. Trustees are not entitled to receive any payment out of the charity's property other than reasonable and necessary out-of-pocket expenses which can be met from the charity's income; nor can they directly or indirectly benefit personally from the charity by, for instance, taking a lease of the charity property, borrowing its money or making contracts to do business with the charity. This is a legal rule and breaking it may constitute a breach of trust. A person who commits a breach of trust may have to make good any loss which results to the charity out of their own money. Even if there is no loss, a trustee who makes a profit from dealing with the charity or its property when that is not allowed by the governing document or by one of the rules mentioned in this paragraph, will have to account to the charity for the profit made (i.e., they will have to pay the amount of any such profit to the charity).

There is an exception to this rule where there is an express provision in the governing document but even then any personal benefit must be strictly confined within the terms of the exception. In very special circumstances the Commission may authorise a transaction between the trustees and a trustee personally. If you are in any doubt about this, ask the Commission for advice.

What principles should guide trustees when administering their charity?

The income and property of the charity must be applied for the purposes set out in the governing document and for no other purpose. It must be applied with complete fairness between persons who are properly qualified to benefit from it. If the trustees are allowed a discretion about the use of the charity property but are in some doubt about the proper exercise of that discretion they should ask the Commission for advice.

Trustees must act reasonably and prudently in all matters relating to the charity and must always bear in mind the interests of the charity. They should not let their personal views or prejudices affect their conduct as trustees. They should exercise the same degree of care in dealing with the administration of their charity as a prudent businessman would exercise in managing his own affairs or those of someone else for whom he was responsible.

Where trustees are required to make a decision which affects the personal interests of one of their number, that person should absent himself entirely from any discussion or vote on the matter by his fellow trustees.

What else should charity trustees think about?

Trustees should find out what work is being done by similar charities and voluntary organisations operating in the same area. In some cases this can be done by joining an umbrella charitable association co-ordinating work in a particular field. Trustees should co-operate with other charities and exchange information with them so as to avoid overlapping or duplicating their efforts. They should also work with local authorities and other statutory bodies which provide services similar or complementary to those of the charity.

Charities should not, however, use their resources (unless the governing document clearly permits) to do what is already being done by statutory services financed out of rates or taxes; but they may supplement those services by providing additional benefits beyond the actual statutory provision.

Can the trustees delegate their responsibilities?

The general rule is that trustees must act in person and decisions concerning the charity must be taken by the trustees acting together. They can always invite some of their number to look into particular matters connected with the charity and to make recommendations, but the decision whether or not to act on the recommendations is for the trustees to take together. No single trustee should be allocated a part of the income of a charity or manage any particular aspect alone. In some cases the governing document of a charity may permit the trustees to set up committees with limited powers to carry out particular functions.

A provision in the governing document allowing the employment of a clerk or other officers does not, in itself, authorise the trustees to delegate the administration of the charity to those officers. The trustees of some charities, because of the scale or nature of the work of the charity may, of necessity, have to delegate to employees decisions on day-to-day management matters. But the scope of the delegated authority must be clearly laid down in writing and instructions given for decisions on important matters to be reported to the trustees. The trustees remain legally responsible and must supervise and control the work of the officers.

A person acting as delegate of the trustees should always make clear in dealings with third parties that he is acting in that capacity, and should always record in writing what was agreed in conversation.

Can trustees employ agents?

Yes. Trustees may seek the assistance of professional advisers on technical matters and employ agents or servants to give effect to their decisions. But it is important that where they do so they both retain and exercise overall control of the management of the charity and lay down in writing clear guidelines within which their agents and servants must act. Employees must be engaged under a formal contract of employment.

What are the liabilities of trustees?

If trustees act prudently, lawfully and in accordance with their governing document then any liabilities they incur as trustees can be met out of the charity's resources. But if they act otherwise they may be in breach of trust and personally liable to meet any call on the charity's property arising from their actions, or to make good any loss to the charity. Since trustees must act jointly in administering a charity, they will also be responsible jointly to meet any liability incurred by them or on their behalf.

The Commissioners are able to take proceedings in court for the recovery, from trustees personally, of funds lost to a charity as a result of a breach of trust by the trustees.

Trustees should be particularly careful when entering into substantial contracts or borrowings to ensure that the charity has the means to meet its obligations. If trustees incur liabilities or debts which amount in total to more than the value of the charity's assets they may be sued personally for the difference by the charity's creditors.

Can trustees use the charity's funds to insure themselves against personal liability?

Trustees can, on condition, insure themselves out of the funds of the charity against personal liability arising from acts properly undertaken in the administration of the charity or acts undertaken in breach of trust but under an honest mistake.

The conditions are that the governing document must empower them to do this, and that it must be justified in the interests of the charity (not in the interests of the trustees personally). When deciding whether insurance is justified, trustees should consider the nature of the charity's activities, the degree of risk of personal liability to which the trustees are exposed, the number of trustees, the value of indemnity required, and the cost to the charity of paying the premiums demanded.

Trustees may use the charity's funds to insure the charity against loss to its own funds resulting from the acts and defaults of the trustees.

What duties do trustees have in respect of charity property?

Trustees have the general duty of protecting all the charity's property. They are accountable for the solvency and continuing effectiveness of the charity and the preservation of its endowments. They must exercise overall control over its financial affairs. They should ensure that the way in which the charity is administered is not open to abuse by unscrupulous associates or employees; and that their systems of control are rigorous and constantly maintained.

If the charity owns land, trustees need to know on a continuing basis what condition it is in, if its boundaries are being encroached upon, what can be done with it and how it is or should be used. They should ensure that the land, including any buildings on it, has appropriate and adequate insurance cover.

Money not needed for immediate expenditure should be invested, or deposited to earn interest if expenditure is expected in the near future. Investments should be reviewed periodically to ensure that they remain suitable for the charity's needs. Wherever possible, funds should be placed in a range of investments so as to avoid substantial losses caused by the failure of a single investment or institution. Bank accounts should be controlled by at least two of the trustees. One trustee should not be allowed to operate a bank account alone and a second signatory should never pre-sign blank cheques for countersigning by another.

In particular, trustees should ensure that property which is permanent endowment is preserved and invested in such a way as to produce a good income while at the same time safeguarding the real value of the capital.

Trustees must also ensure that all income due to the charity is received and that all tax and rating relief due is claimed.

What powers do trustees have when investing funds?

The governing documents of some charities make special reference to the trustees' powers of investment. Otherwise these powers will principally be found in the Trustee Investments Act 1961.

The trustees must decide what form of investment will be most suitable for the needs of their charity and obtain skilled advice for this purpose. They should bear in mind the long-term future of the charity as well as the short-term, and try to counteract the effects of inflation on their capital and income.

Leaflet CC32, explaining the 1961 Act and CC14, offering guidance to trustees in selecting and managing the charity's investments, are available from the Commission. The Charities Act 1993 allows for amendments to be made to the investment rules of the 1961 Act, but no amendments have so far been made.

Are there any investments particularly designed for charities?

Yes. The duties of charity trustees may be simplified by contributing money, on proper advice, to a common investment fund. These funds are established specifically to meet the needs of charities and operate on lines similar to a unit trust by providing a wide spread of investments and specialised investment management which smaller charities individually cannot afford. Trustees should look into the advantages that investment in any of these funds may offer.

There are a number of such funds each of which has different objectives. They can take investments only from charities and may have different requirements about minimum investments. The Commission publishes a list of such funds (as leaflet CC15(a)), but does not make any recommendations about which should be selected.

The Charities Act 1993 also allows for the establishment of common deposit funds. These funds are designed to provide charities with the opportunity to deposit their money along with sums belonging to many other charities and so secure a more favourable rate of interest than if they were investing alone. These funds will also be managed by specialised investment managers.

More information about common investment funds and common deposit funds is contained in our leaflet CC15.

What are trustees' duties in relation to fundraising?

Trustees are responsible for ensuring that any fundraising activity carried out by or on behalf of their charity is properly undertaken, and that all funds collected are properly accounted for. Where trustees allow or employ people to undertake fundraising on their behalf, they should ensure that all funds raised are paid into a bank account in the charity's name before deduction of the fundraiser's expenses.

Trustees should always insist on approving both the fundraising methods which will be adopted, and any appeal literature which will be used on their behalf. Where professional fundraisers are employed as agents for the charity, a proper contract should be drawn up. The Commission will be happy to advise on this.

Can trustees dispose of land belonging to the charity?

Generally, yes; but before trustees may sell, lease or otherwise dispose of land or buildings, they will either have to follow a statutory procedure or obtain an order from the Commission consenting to the disposal.

A leaflet (CC28, Disposing of Charity Land) giving guidance to trustees who are considering selling charity property is available from the Commission. Briefly, trustees must instruct a qualified surveyor who acts for them alone to report to them in writing and must follow his advice on the marketing of the property. Trustees may not sell land for less than the best price reasonably obtainable, and their surveyor must confirm that any offer they propose to accept meets this requirement.

Trustees wishing to lease their land for more than seven years must follow the statutory procedure for sales, but there is a simpler procedure for leases for seven years or less.

If in either case trustees are unable to follow the statutory procedure, or they wish to sell land to a person connected with themselves they **must** seek the Commission's consent.

When the property being sold or leased is subject to trusts requiring it to be used for specific purposes of the charity (as an almshouse, for example) the trustees must give public notice of the disposal. They may also need to apply to the Commission for a scheme to give them power to sell such property, and this should be done before the property is put on the market.

Can the charity borrow money on the security of its property?

Generally, yes. But before they mortgage the charity's property trustees must obtain advice from a person with ability in, and experience of, financial matters who has no personal interest in the proposed loan. This person can be a trustee or employee of the charity, and must advise on whether the loan is necessary for the charity, whether the terms are reasonable, and whether the charity will be able to repay the loan on those terms.

Trustees should seek advice in the same way even where the borrowing, such as a temporary overdraft, is unsecured. Trustees who do not seek advice on matters on which they are not themselves experts could be regarded as having acted imprudently and may be personally liable for the consequences.

Is there any requirement for charities to be registered?

Generally, yes. The Charities Act 1993, requires trustees to register charities in England and Wales with the Commission and to give any information needed for the purposes of registration. Any charity which has permanent endowment, or an income from all sources exceeding £1,000 a year, or which uses or occupies land for its own purposes is required to register, though some special classes of charity are excepted or exempted. Leaflet CC21 (Starting a Charity) can be obtained from the Commission.

Once a charity has been registered, the Commission must be told about any changes in the registered particulars or if it ceases to exist or to operate.

While a charity is registered there can be no question about whether or not it is a charity (except for settling the question of whether it should be on the Register). This may well help in obtaining tax and rating relief or in obtaining grants from other charities which can make grants only for charitable purposes.

Every registered charity with an annual income over £5,000 is required to state that it is a registered charity on any appeal documents and on many of its financial documents, such as cheques, invoices and receipts.

Are the trustees required to keep accounts?

New accounting requirements under sections 41 to 49 of the Charities Act 1993 are likely to come into force during 1995, once the Home Secretary has made regulations in connection with the new requirements. The advice below relates to the current requirements under the Charities Acts 1960 and 1985, which apply until then.

Yes. Proper books of account must be kept. Trustees must also prepare consecutive statements of account showing income and expenditure or receipts and payments for periods of not more than 15 months together with a balance sheet relating to the end of the period. The books of account and statements of account must be preserved for at least seven years.

The main legal requirements of the Charities Acts 1960 and 1985 about the keeping of accounts and the trustees' duty to send copies to the Commissioners and to some local authorities are summarised in the Commission's leaflet CC25 Registered charities should submit their accounts to the Commissioners each year.

Preparing accounts is, however, only part of proper financial planning and control. It is also essential to make proper estimates about expected income and expenditure in order to plan ahead effectively.

Must charity accounts be audited?

New requirements for the annual auditing or examination of accounts under sections 43 and 44 of the Charities Act 1993 are likely to come into force during 1995. The advice below relates to the requirements applying before sections 43 and 44 of the 1993 Act are brought into force.

Unless the governing document of a charity specifically requires it, trustees generally are not under a duty to have charity accounts audited professionally. It is reasonable and prudent, however, for trustees to ask some independent person, preferably professionally qualified, to examine and certify the accounts; and where large sums are involved a full professional audit will probably be justified. Auditing expenses can be met out of the charity's income.

Can the trustees change the objects if they no longer serve a useful purpose?

Trustees of charities should regularly review the effectiveness of the trusts of their charity. Sometimes a charity can be made more effective by changes which do not affect the existing trusts but in other cases a change in the trusts themselves may be needed.

The governing documents of some unincorporated charities may contain a power enabling the trustees or members to amend the purposes. In such instances, the required amendment may be made without the intervention of the Commission, subject to the requirements of the governing document and the general law. But in redrawing the objects of the charity, the new objects should be kept close to the original intention of the charity and the purposes of the charity must remain legally charitable.

Any trustees intending to make or propose to the members an alteration are strongly advised to seek the Commission's views before they proceed.

Section 64 of the Charities Act 1993, requires a charitable company to seek the Commission's prior consent to any amendment of the company's objects or provisions relating to the way the company's property must be used. Amendments made without consent will be ineffective.

Sections 74 and 75 of the Charities Act 1993, replace the Charities Act 1985. Trustees of most charities with an income under £5,000 and whose trusts are no longer effective, are able to modify the purposes or administrative provisions of their charity, or to transfer their charity's property to another charity having similar purposes. Trustees of most permanently-endowed charities with an income under £1,000 are allowed to expend the permanent endowment if they believe the income is not large enough to be useful.

Further details can be found in the Commission's leaflet CC44 (Small Charities).

Can a charity be wound up or its assets transferred to another charity?

A charity can only be brought to an end if all its property is expendable and has been disposed of, or if the governing document contains a dissolution or winding up provision, or if sections 74 and 75 of the Charities Act 1993 apply. A provision in the governing document will normally require the assets remaining on dissolution to be passed to a similar charity. The trustees should follow the procedure contained in the dissolution provision closely and send copies of all relevant resolutions to the Commission.

Whenever a registered charity is wound up or ceases to operate because all its property has been spent, the trustees should send a copy of the final accounts to the Commission, with a request to have the charity removed from the Register of charities.

What can be done if a charity is permanently endowed and the governing document contains no winding-up powers?

If a charity is permanently endowed and the governing document contains no power of dissolution the charity cannot usually be wound up. However, if the trustees are satisfied that their charity no longer serves a useful purpose or the purposes for which it was originally established has been fulfilled by other means, the Commission has the power under the Charities Act 1993 to make a scheme to amalgamate the charity with others. In these circumstances the trustees are under a duty to apply to the Commission for a scheme to change the purposes of the charity.

Chapter 3 – The regulatory framework

3.1 Introduction

Sections 41 to 49 of the 1993 Act, and the Regulations made thereunder, herald a daunting new statutory regime for accounting by charities.

The new requirements apply in different ways to charities which are registered, those which are exempt and those which are excepted from registration. In general, charities will now have to maintain proper accounting records and submit, annually, to the Commissioners, accounts, a report and return. For the first time in charity law there is a requirement for most accounts to show a true and fair view and to be audited or subject to some degree of independent scrutiny.

The new regime represents the culmination of many years' debate, which has run parallel to the increasingly visible profile which charities have enjoyed over, in particular, the last decade. The new regime is, thus, no more than commensurate with the important role which charities play in the UK today.

3.2 The 1960 Act

Section 32 required trustees of all charities, whether or not registered, to:

(a) keep proper books of account;
(b) prepare consecutive statements of account, consisting of an income and expenditure account, relating to a period of not more than 15 months' duration, and a balance sheet relating to the end of that period; and
(c) preserve books and statements of account for at least seven years.

There was no general requirement to submit statements of account to the Commissioners. Trustees were required to submit statements of account to the Commissioners on request, however, and trustees of permanently endowed charities, unless excepted, were required to send a statement of account relating to the permanent endowment without any request.

Although the Act contained no general requirement for the accounts of charities to be audited, some trustees were under an obligation, imposed by the trust deed, to have the accounts audited. Under s8, the Commissioners were entitled to order an audit of a charity's accounts (other than those of an exempt charity), but the costs thereof were to be borne by them.

3.3 The impetus for reform

Both the Woodfield Report and that of the Public Accounts Committee (*Monitoring and control of charities*), published in 1988, highlighted charity accounts as a key area of weakness. These reports found that, in spite of the importance of good financial information for supervision and accountability, the requirements for submitting annual accounts to the Commissioners were being 'widely ignored'; only a limited number of accounts were examined each year, and only a small proportion of accounts was professionally audited.

Both the government and the Commissioners fully accepted that the arrangements for submitting and examining accounts needed to be considerably strengthened. Accordingly, the White Paper, published in May 1989, identified, *inter alia*, the regular provision of good-quality financial information by charities as an essential element in their public accountability and an important means for their supervision.

Among the White Paper's proposals were:

(a) a requirement that, in future, all registered charities should submit, annually, statements of account to the Commissioners. Such charities would be required to supplement their statement of account with a trustees' report, modelled on SORP 2, and to provide legal and administrative details of the kind recommended by that SORP;
(b) the introduction of graduated requirements governing the content and audit of accounts; and
(c) a requirement for trustees to make copies of their charity's accounts available to the public on request.

The White Paper was followed by the Charities Bill, which was introduced by the government in 1991. This received the Royal Assent on 16 March 1992.

3.4 The 1993 Act

3.4.1 Overview

What is the regulatory framework?

The following diagram summarises the regulatory framework under the 1993 Act.

Below registration threshold	'Light touch' regime	Independent examination and receipts/ payments accounts	Independent examination & accruals accounts	Audit & accruals accounts
£0	£1,000 aggregate income per year and no permanent endowments or the use or occupation of land	£10,000 gross income or total expenditure per year	£100,000 gross income per year	£250,000 gross income or total expenditure per year
▼	▼	▼	▼	▼

<table>
<tr><td colspan="5">ACCOUNTING RECORDS MUST BE KEPT</td></tr>
<tr><td colspan="3">RECEIPT AND PAYMENTS BASIS OF ACCOUNTS MAY BE CHOSEN</td><td colspan="2">MUST PREPARE ACCOUNTS ON ACCRUALS BASIS</td></tr>
<tr><td colspan="2">THE COMMISSION MAY REQUEST ACCOUNTS</td><td colspan="3">ANNUAL REPORTS AND ACCOUNTS MUST GO TO THE COMMISSION</td></tr>
<tr><td colspan="2">NO EXTERNAL SCRUTINY
AUTOMATICALLY REQUIRED</td><td colspan="2">INDEPENDENT EXAMINATION MAY BE CHOSEN</td><td>MUST BE AUDITED</td></tr>
<tr><td></td><td>ANNUAL RETURN
WILL BE REQUESTED</td><td colspan="3">ANNUAL RETURNS MUST GO TO THE COMMISSION</td></tr>
</table>

When does the regulatory framework come into force?

The Regulations come into force on 1 December 1995* and are binding for accounting periods commencing on or after that date. For financial

* *The consultation on the regulatory framework was completed on 17 May. It is intended to finalise the arrangements and make the Regulations in the summer, to come into effect on this date.*

years commencing earlier, charity trustees may elect to follow the new requirements if they wish. Indeed, they are encouraged to do so.

To which charities does the regulatory framework apply?

The framework applies to different charities in different ways. The following identifies the principal categories of charity, but does not address every possible situation:

(A) NHS charitable trusts

NHS charitable trusts are subject to the 1993 Act. A detailed manual, 'NHS Charitable Funds: A Guide' has been produced, and covers (*inter alia*) the current accounting requirements. It is understood that a further chapter is to be issued in due course on the new requirements contained in the Act.

(B) Friendly and industrial and provident societies

Friendly and Industrial and Provident Societies which are charities and registered with the Registrar of Friendly Societies are exempt charities (Sch 2 to the 1993 Act). The exemption does not extend to a charity administered by such a registered industrial and provident or friendly society, nor to a charity simply because it has a subsidiary which is exempt.

(C) Registered housing associations

Housing associations which are charities and registered with the Housing Corporation (and which are not registered industrial and provident societies and, therefore, exempt) must register with the Commissioners. In order to satisfy the requirements of the 1993 Act, the accounts to be submitted to the Commissioners are those required to be prepared in accordance with the Housing Associations Act 1985 and the Housing Act 1988 and, consequently, the Registered Housing Associations (Accounting Requirements) Order 1992.

(D) Higher education institutions (HEIs)

The Department of Education intends to alert the representative bodies of HEIs in England to the implications for them of the 1993 Act's requirements and to the Privy Council's role in considering applications for exempt status. The Department is reviewing the position of those HEIs which are not yet exempted from registration with the Commissioners.

(E) Common investment (CIFs) and Common deposit (CDFs) funds

The Regulations are not intended to apply to CIFs established under s24 of the 1993 Act, except for those arrangements (usually established as special trusts of a charity) for pooling the investments of a number of charitable trusts under a single trustee body, and CDFs established under s25 of the 1993 Act.

These charities are to be the subject of separate accounting and audit regulations.

(F) Charitable companies
Charities which are companies are subject to the 1985 Act. They are, however, also subject to charity law. Unless they are excepted from registration with the Commissioners and have chosen not to register, they must file an annual report and their own statutory accounts with the Commissioners if their income or expenditure exceeds £10,000, or they are requested to do so by the Commissioners.

(G) Exempt charities
Charities listed in Sch 2 to the 1993 Act are exempt from registration with the Commissioners. They are required to keep accounting records and prepare statements of account under s46(1) and (2), unless they are subject to an alternative statutory regime, e.g., industrial and provident societies.

(H) Excepted charities
Certain charities (see chapter **1**, page 7) are excepted from registration with the Commissioners. Such charities may choose to register, but, if they do, are treated like any other registered charity.

Even if excepted and not registered, the charity must continue to produce annual accounts in exactly the same way as a registered charity, and those accounts will need to be subject to the same audit/independent examination regime, but the charity does not automatically have to file those accounts with the Commissioners. Unless the charity is covered by s3(5)(c), the Commissioners are entitled to request a report and the submission of that report and accounts to them and may investigate that charity.

3.4.2 Accounting

Accounting records

Section 41 requires charity trustees to ensure that such accounting records are maintained, that are sufficient to:

(a) show and explain all the charity's transactions;
(b) disclose, at any time, with reasonable accuracy, the financial position of the charity at that time;

(c) enable the trustees to ensure that any statements of account required by section 42(1) comply with the requirements of the Regulations made thereunder;

and, in particular, to contain:

(d) entries showing, from day to day, all sums of money received and expended by the charity, and the matters in respect of which the receipt and expenditure takes place; and
(e) a record of the assets and liabilities of the charity.

In March 1992 the Council of the ICAEW updated its guidance for members on the interpretation of the obligations of companies to keep accounting records under s221 of the 1985 Act and this is given, for ease of reference, as Annex I to this chapter. In view of the fact that the requirements of that section echo those in the 1993 Act, this guidance should, also, prove useful for charities which are not charitable companies.

Accounting records are to be preserved for six years, although s41(4) permits the Commissioners to agree, in writing, to the records being destroyed or otherwise disposed of should a charity cease to exist. Interestingly, the requirement to keep accounting records for a charity which is not a charitable company appears onerous. Under s221 of the 1985 Act, while a public company must retain its accounting records for six years, a private company, which would include charitable companies, needs only to preserve them for three years. Such companies would be well advised to retain them for the longer period.

Section 41 does not apply to charitable companies, by virtue of their being required to comply with similar requirements in the 1985 Act. Neither does the section apply to exempt charities. Such charities must comply with s46(1) and (2), which requires the charity trustees to keep proper books of account with respect to the charity's affairs and to retain them, together with statements of account, for a period of six years unless the charity ceases to exist and the Commissioners consent, in writing, to their being destroyed or otherwise disposed of.

This section does, however, apply to all excepted charities, whether or not registered.

Duty to prepare accounts

Section 42 introduces new provisions relating to the preparation of annual accounts.

Trustees of charities with a gross income (see below, under ***What is 'gross income' and 'total expenditure'?***) which, in any financial year, does not exceed £100,000 may elect to prepare a simpler form of accounts (confusingly entitled an 'account and statement') comprising:

(a) a receipts and payments account; and
(b) a statement of assets and liabilities.

(See, also, chapter **17**, page 429.)

The trustees of charities whose gross income in any financial year exceeds £100,000 must prepare a 'statement of accounts', the detailed requirements relating to which are laid down in the Regulations. In circumstances where a charity is trading, committed to substantial expenditure or holding significant investments, this method of preparation is advised, even though a charity may need only to prepare accounts on a receipts and payments basis.

Exempt charities are excluded from this provision (s46(1)) but, if not required by another statutory regime (e.g., industrial and provident societies are bound to comply with the Friendly and Industrial and Provident Societies Act 1968 to prepare periodical statements of account), are required to prepare consecutive statements of account consisting of an income and expenditure account of not more than 15 months' duration, and a balance sheet relating to the end of that period.

The section does, however, apply to all excepted charities, whether or not registered.

Statements of accounts – Introduction

Section 42(1) and (2) requires statements of accounts to comply with such requirements as to their form and content as prescribed by the Regulations made by the Secretary of State.

The Regulations make provision as to the form and content of the statements of accounts, including the methods and principles to be used, and information to be provided by way of notes. They also make provision with respect to the financial years of charities, the requirements relating to audit, or examination, of their accounts and the annual reports of charity trustees.

Regulation 3 of, and the Sch to, the Regulations prescribes the form and content of statements of accounts prepared by charity trustees under s 42(1).

The statement of accounts must comprise:

(a) a SOFA, which satisfies the requirements of Pt I of the Sch (reg 3(2)(a); see chapters **4** and **7**);
(b) a balance sheet, which satisfies the requirements of Pt II of the Sch (reg 3(2)(b); see primarily chapters **8**, **9** and **10**); and
(c) by way of notes to the accounts, the information specified in Pt IV of the Sch (reg 3(4); see primarily chapters **6** and **11**).

Statements of accounts – Methods and principles

Regulation 3(3) requires the statement of accounts to be prepared in accordance with the methods and principles specified in Pt III of the Sch.

Paragraph 1(1) of that Part requires the SOFA and the balance sheet to give a true and fair view of, respectively, the financial activities of the charity in, and the state of affairs of, the financial year in respect of which the statement of accounts is prepared. (Prior to this, there was no obligation in charity law, as there is, for example, in company law, for charity accounts to show a true and fair view.)

Where compliance with Pts I, II, or IV of the Sch would not be sufficient for the statement of accounts to give a true and fair view, para 1(2) requires the necessary additional information to be given either in the accounts or in a note to them. If, in special circumstances, compliance with any of those provisions would be inconsistent with the requirement to give a true and fair view, para 1(3) requires the charity trustees to depart from that provision to the extent necessary to give a true and fair view, and to give the reasons for it and its effect in a note to the accounts.

The provisions regarding use of, and disclosures relating to, the true and fair override for charity trustees are the same as those for directors of companies, as set out in s226(4) and (5) of the 1985 Act. (Note: The interpretation of those disclosure requirements by the UITF Abstract 7 *True and fair override disclosures* applies.)

The corresponding figure for the previous year is to be shown throughout the SOFA and balance sheet (para 2(1)).The same applies as regards information contained in the notes (para 1(p) of Pt IV). If not comparable, the corresponding figure must be adjusted and particulars of the adjustment and reasons for it disclosed in the notes to the accounts (para 2(2)). (Note: the adjustment of comparative figures seems to be restricted by the Regulations only to those in the SOFA or balance sheet, and does not appear to extend to those in the notes. This is because para 1(p) of Pt IV of the Sch is less demanding than para 58(2) of Sch 4 to the 1985 Act.)

Paragraph 1(q) of Pt IV requires the notes to the accounts to give a statement as to whether or not the accounts have been prepared in accordance with applicable accounting standards and statements of recommended practice and particulars of any material departure from those standards and practices and the reasons for such departure. Compliance with the SORP is, thus, not mandatory, but charity trustees will be expected to follow its recommendations, which are consistent with accounting and reporting standards.

Information for which there are no figures to be shown both for the current and previous years, should be omitted (paragraph 2(3)).

As regards measurement, para 3 requires the values of the assets and liabilities of the charity to be determined in accordance with the methods and principles for their inclusion in the balance sheet as set out in the revised charity SORP.

Statements of accounts – Special cases

Regulation 4 provides that the form and content of the statement of accounts does not apply to:

(a) a common investment fund established under s24 of the 1993 Act, other than a fund the trusts of which provide for property to be transferred to the fund only by, or on behalf of, a participating charity of which the charity trustees are the trustees appointed to manage the fund. Thus, arrangements for the pooling of investments of a number of charitable trusts under a single trustee body, which will generally be established as special trusts, but may be separately registered, will be subject to the Regulations; and
(b) a common deposit fund established by a scheme under s25 of the 1993 Act.

These charities are governed by separate accounting and auditing regulations (the Charities (Common Investment and Deposit Funds) (Accounts) Regulations 1995 (SI 1995 No . . . .*)).

Charities (other than exempt charities) which are registered housing associations within the meaning of the Housing Association Act 1985 and whose registration has been recorded under s5(3) of that Act are, also, excluded from the Regulations. In order to satisfy the requirements of s42(1), the accounts submitted to the Commissioners will be those prepared in accordance with the regulations made under s24 of the Housing Association Act 1985. At the time of writing, these are the

* *This SI will be issued at the same time as that relating to the Regulations.*

Registered Housing Associations (Accounting Requirements) Order 1992 (SI 1992 No 512) and the Registered Housing Associations (Accounting Requirements) (Wales) (Order) (SI 1992 No 668).

Financial years – How are these determined?

Section 97(1) allows the Secretary of State to make provisions with respect to the determination of a charity's financial year. (Note: These will not apply to charitable companies, as they are subject to s223 of the 1985 Act.) Regulation 5 sets out these provisions.

Financial years are determined by reference to periods, which are calendar-based, and end on the charity's accounting reference date. In order to allow for the use of 52/53 week years, the period can vary by up to seven days either side of that date.

For a charity established before 1 December 1995, its first financial year, for the purposes of the Regulations, will begin immediately after the accounting period for which a statement of accounts was required to be prepared under any statutory provision applicable to it before that date and will end on its accounting reference date (reg 5(2)(a)). Thus, for a charity with an accounting reference date of 31 March, its first financial year will begin on 1 April 1996 and, assuming it is of 12 months' duration, end on 31 March 1997.

For a charity established after 1 December 1995, its financial year will begin on the day established and end with its accounting reference date (reg 5(2)(b)).

Subsequent financial years run from the previous financial year end to the next accounting reference date, plus or minus seven days (reg 5(3)).

Accounting reference dates are determined as follows:

(a) in the first financial year of a charity established before 1 December 1995, such date, not less than 6, nor more than 18, months after the date on which that financial year began;
(b) in the first financial year of a charity established on or after 1 December 1995, such date, not less than 6, nor more than 18, months after the date on which the charity was established; and
(c) in any subsequent financial year, the date which is 12 months after the previous accounting reference date or such other date, not less than 6, nor more than 18, months after the previous accounting reference date.

As regards (c), there are provisions to restrict the frequency with which accounting reference dates may be changed. Such dates cannot be changed unless the immediately preceding two financial years were of 12 months' duration. And, as regards (a) or (c), reg 5(4)(ii) permits trustees to change the accounting reference date only where satisfied that there are exceptional reasons (which are not defined), which must be disclosed in the notes to the accounts (reg 5(4)(ii) and para 1(r) of Pt IV to the Sch).

What is 'gross income' and 'total expenditure'?

'Gross income' is defined in s97(1) as 'gross recorded income from all sources, including special trusts'. This definition is similar, but not identical, to that in respect of 'income', as used in s3(5)(c) (see chapter **1**, page 8). *Gross recorded income*, rather than *gross revenues*, is used, but income from special trusts (broadly, restricted funds) is automatically included within the former term. Other than that, it is not clear if there is any substantial difference between these two terms. The consultation document ('Accounting by charities: Draft regulations') stated that all the incoming resources of a charity are income unless they are permanent or expendable endowment (permanent endowment is capital which may not be expended as income; expendable endowment may be so expended at the trustees' discretion). And 'total expenditure' has not been defined, but will include either payment for fixed assets for use by the charity (e.g., property, equipment etc.), if the accounts are prepared on a receipts and payments basis; or, depreciation of those assets, if prepared on an accruals basis.

3.4.3 Auditing

Audit or independent examination?

Section 43 requires the annual accounts of a charity generally to be audited or independently examined.

If the gross income, or total expenditure, exceeds £250,000 in the year for which the accounts are being prepared, or in the immediately preceding two years, the accounts must be audited by a person who is:

(a) eligible to act as a company auditor under s25 of the 1989 Act (i.e., a registered auditor); or
(b) a member of a body specified under regulations made by the Secretary of State and, under the rules of that body, is eligible for appointment as auditor of the charity.

(Note: Sections 43(2)(b) and 44(1) enable other auditors to be specified in regulations. At the time of writing, the Regulations do not extend the definition of charity auditor beyond those who are registered auditors. It is understood, however, that the DTI is always willing to consider applications from professional bodies wishing to become recognised qualifying bodies under the 1989 Act.)

If gross income and total expenditure are below £250,000 in both the year for which the accounts are being prepared and in the immediately preceding two years, the charity trustees may either have the accounts examined by a suitable qualified independent person, or audited.

What if gross income and total expenditure both exceed £250,000 (this threshold being an increase from £100,000 as originally enacted)? Will an audit still be required? Of course. But, perhaps, this is not as obvious as it seems. On several occasions the government resisted, but eventually conceded to, an amendment, the parliamentary draughtsman claiming that reference to 'gross income or total expenditure' would yield the wrong interpretation unless there were added to it the words 'or both'. This amendment was underpinned by a series of fascinating contributions in the parliamentary debates, personified by those of Lord Allen of Abbeydale and of Lord Simon of Glaisdale. The former commented:

> 'When the noble Earl [Earl Ferrers] explained on Report why he could not accept the amendment the reasons he gave seemed to me so unconvincing and so unlike the noble Earl's persuasive style that I thought I must have misheard. I did not pursue the point then, but when I read Hansard, alas, I found that I had not misunderstood. Perhaps I may read briefly what the noble Earl said:
>
> > "The idea is that if the income is more than £100,000, or if the expenditure is more than £100,000, or if both are more than £100,000, the charity must prepare different forms of accounts. Without the words 'or both' . . .".
>
> 'This is the remarkable part:
>
> > ". . . it might be construed that as both these items have exceeded the limit and not just one item the charity need not be subjected to that regime" [Official Report, 6/2/92; cols 406–407].
>
> 'There seems to be three powerful arguments against that interpretation. The first is that it is contrary to common sense, if that has any relevance to the drafting of a statute. The second is that, to my mind, it introduces a possible ambiguity since it might be thought that the intention, however crudely expressed, was that the income and expenditure added together should exceed £100,000. But thirdly, all the legal opinion that I have received – I have consulted other high legal dignitaries as well as my two eminent noble and learned friends who have added their names to the amendment – is

> unanimous in the view that these words are not necessary' (HL Deb, vol 536, cols 182–3 (25 February 1992))

and those of Lord Simon of Glaisdale were:

> 'My Lords, I am very glad that my noble friend has moved this amendment again because, although these are only two words, they are beyond any reasonable argument unnecessary . . . . I ask the House to think of this situation. At the moment there are five all-rounders contending for three places in the lower middle order of the English test cricket side. Supposing some munificent benefactor said, "I will give £1,000 to any of you who has a batting average over 30 or a bowling average under 20". Two of the five have batting averages over 30 and claim and get the £1,000. Two have bowling averages under 20 and claim and get the £1,000. But the fifth has both a batting average over 30 and a bowling average under 20. What would happen if he were met with the argument, "Oh no, not a penny, I did not say 'or both'"? Such an argument would not only be hooted out of every court of law with derision and execration but out of every cricket pavilion' (HL Deb, vol 536, col 183 (25 February 1992)).

Where a charity's trust deed requires an audit to be carried out, consideration should be given to the intention at the time it was drawn up.

It has been suggested by some commentators that if a charity's governing instrument imposes higher requirements than those in the 1993 Act, the charity need only comply with the latter's requirements. For example, if the trust deed of a charity with an income of less than £250,000 requires an audit, under that Act it might be interpreted as requiring an independent examination. This is not, however, an interpretation which is generally held.

If a charity's trust deed requires the accounts to be audited, but the charity trustees wish to elect (assuming that they are able so to do) for an independent examination to be carried out, they may have the power to vary the trust deed themselves. If they do not, the trustees should obtain the Commissioners' approval.

A lack of clarity of the provisions of the trust deed, or other constitutional document, may highlight other practical problems, e.g., not only in relation to the level of scrutiny required, but by whom that scrutiny should be carried out. This might, also, be important, in the light of the Audit Regulations. It is often the case that trust deeds were drawn up many years ago, when the term 'audit' had a different interpretation, given the then regulatory framework. Accordingly, if an audit is required, trust deeds may not state by whom that audit should be carried out, e.g., by a registered auditor. It is recommended that all trust deeds (and, for that matter, letters of engagement) are revisited and, where necessary, amended to reflect actual requirements, given the new regulatory frameworks which are in place.

A further issue which may raise practical problems is the threshold of £250,000 and its attendant provisions, particularly for any charity which receives large or unexpected donations late in its accounting year or for a charity which is undertaking a major project likely to generate substantial funds and expenditure, possibly over a limited period of time. It may well be that such charities will be caught by this provision in one year, but then revert to having gross income and total expenditure less than £250,000. The accounts will continue to require to be audited for a further two years, which might prove to be expensive.

Section 43 has been amended by s28 of the Deregulation and Contracting Out Act 1994. If a charity's gross income and total expenditure do not exceed £10,000 in a financial year, then, subject to s43(4), the accounts will need neither to be audited nor independently examined. The effect of this amendment has been to introduce a 'light touch' regulatory band and was made as a result of one of the recommendations of the eighth Deregulation Task Force (see, also, chapter **17**, page 430). As a consequence of this, s43(8) has been amended so that the threshold of £10,000 (like that of £250,000), can be altered at any time by the Secretary of State. (Note: It is interesting to note that s43(8) uses the word 'different' rather than 'higher'. Thus, were there to be abuse (e.g., fraud), on a large scale, of the light touch regime, the option is open for the Secretary of State to remove the ability of smaller charities to have this right conferred on them.)

What are the duties of an auditor?

Section 44(1)(b) allows for the Secretary of State to make provisions with respect to the duties of an auditor, including provisions with respect to the form of report (either on the statement of accounts or the account and statement). These duties are provided in reg 6.

(A) The auditors' report – Statement of accounts

Where a statement of accounts has been prepared for a financial year, the auditor must make a report on that statement to the person(s) who appointed him. The report must:

(a) state:
  (i) the name of the charity;
  (ii) the person(s) who appointed him; and
  (iii) his name and address;
  (reg 6(2)(a));
(b) be signed by him and state that he is a registered auditor (reg 6(2)(b)).

(c) be dated and specify the financial year in respect of which the accounts have been prepared (reg 6(2)(c));
(d) specify that it is a report in respect of an audit carried out under s43 and in accordance with the Regulations (reg 6(2)(d)); and
(e) state whether, in his opinion, the statement of accounts complies with the requirements of reg 3 (or, as the case may be, reg 4) and, in particular, gives a true and fair view of the state of affairs of the charity at the end of, and of the financial activities (or income and expenditure) in, the financial year (reg 6(2)(e)).

If the auditor is of the opinion that:

(a) accounting records have not been kept in accordance with s41;
(b) the statement of accounts is not in agreement with those records;
(c) any information contained in the statement of accounts is inconsistent in any material respect with the annual report for the financial year; or
(d) any information or explanations to which he is entitled under reg 8 has not been obtained;

reg 6(2)(f) requires his report to contain a statement of, and of his grounds for forming, that opinion.

There are some noticeable differences between the responsibilities in reg 6(2)(f) and those of auditors under s237 of the 1985 Act.

Firstly, under the 1985 Act, and where applicable, auditors are required to form an opinion as to whether proper returns adequate for their audit have been received from branches not visited by them. There is no such obligation under the 1993 Act for an auditor of a charity with branches.

Secondly, unlike the 1993 Act, the 1985 Act does not require the auditors to give their grounds for forming their opinion (under (a) to (d) of reg 6(2)(f)).

And, thirdly, reg 6(2)(f)(iii) requires any material inconsistency between the statement of accounts and the annual report to be expressed with reference to *the accounts* as this relates to the relevant power in the 1993 Act; the equivalent provision in the 1985 Act is with reference to the *directors' report.*

(B) The auditors' report – Receipts and payments account
Where a receipts and payments account and statement of assets and liabilities have been prepared under s42(3) for a financial year, but an audit has been carried out, the auditor's report must:

(a) state:
    (i) his name and address;
    (ii) the name of the charity; and
    (iii) the person(s) who appointed him;
    (reg 6(3)(a));
(b) be signed by him and state that he is a registered auditor (reg 6(3)(b));
(c) be dated and specify the financial year in respect of which the accounts have been prepared (reg 6(3)(c));
(d) specify that it is a report in respect of an audit carried out under s43 and in accordance with the Regulations (reg 6(3)(d)); and
(e) state whether, in his opinion:
    (i) the receipts and payments account and statement of assets and liabilities are [properly prepared] [in all material respects complete and accurate]*; and
    (ii) the account and statement adequately distinguish any material special trust, or other restricted fund of the charity.
    (reg 6(3)(e)).

If the auditor is of the opinion that:

(a) accounting records have not been kept in accordance with s41;
(b) the account and statement is not in agreement with those records; or
(c) any information or explanations to which he is entitled under reg 8 has not been given;

reg 6(3)(f) requires his report to contain a statement of, and of the grounds for forming, that opinion.

(C) Carrying out investigations for the purposes of the report
Regulation 6(4) requires the auditor to carry out such investigations as will enable him to form an opinion as to the matters specified in paras (e) and (f) of paras (2) or (3) of the Regulation.

(D) 'Whistle blowing'
In keeping with similar arrangements for other regulated bodies (e.g., friendly societies), reg 6(5) places a duty on the auditor, in his capacity as auditor, to inform the Commissioners, in writing, if any matter which he has reasonable cause to believe is, or is likely to be, of material significance for the exercise, in relation to the charity, of the Commissioners' functions under s8 (general power to institute inquiries) or s18 (power

* *To be decided when the final Regulations are published.*

to act for the protection of charities) of the 1993 Act. It has been suggested that this might include the discovery of expenditure not in accordance with the trust deed, material weaknesses in the trustees' control over the charity's affairs, or where insufficient explanations or records are available to enable him satisfactorily to complete the audit.

Such matters may relate not only to the activities or affairs of the charity, but, also, to any institution or body corporate which is a *connected person* of the charity. (Note: 'Connected persons' are more fully discussed in chapter **11**, see page 298.)

This obligation is essential to strengthen accountability and public confidence in charities. It is understood that the Commissioners will respond in a practical and constructive way to information disclosed in this way, and would welcome enquiries from auditors or charities about matters they wish to clarify.

It is understood that the APB is to issue a Practice Note in due course.

(E) Ceasing to hold office
Where an auditor ceases for any reason to hold office, reg 6(6) requires him to send to the charity trustees a statement of any circumstances connected with that cessation which should be brought to their attention or, if there are no such circumstances, a statement to that effect. Except where there are no such circumstances, a copy of any statement must, also, be sent to the Commissioners.

What form does an independent examiner's report take?

Section 44(1)(c) enables the Secretary of State to make provision with respect to the form of report of the independent examiner. This is set out in reg 7.

An independent examiner who has carried out an examination of the accounts in accordance with s43 must make a report to the charity trustees. The report must:

(a) state:
  (i) the name of the charity;
  (ii) the names of the charity trustees; and
  (iii) his name and address;
  (reg 7(a));
(b) be signed by him and specify any relevant professional qualifications or professional body of which he is a member (reg 7(b));
(c) be dated and specify the financial year in respect of which the accounts have been prepared (reg 7(c));

(d) specify that it is a report in respect of an examination carried out under s43 and in accordance with any directions given by the Commissioners under s(7)(b) which are applicable (reg 7(d));
(e) state whether or not any matter has come to his attention in connection with the examination which gives him reasonable cause to believe that in any material respect:
    (i) accounting records have not been kept in accordance with s41;
    (ii) the accounts are not in agreement with those records; or
    (iii) in the case of an examination of a statement of accounts, that statement does not comply with any of the requirements of reg 3, except the requirements specified in para 1 (i.e., the requirement to give a true and fair view) of Pt III of the Sch to the Regulations (reg 7(e)); and
(f) state whether or not any matter has come to his attention in connection with the examination to which, in his opinion, attention should be drawn in order for a proper understanding of the accounts to be given (reg 7(f)).

Where:

(a) any material expenditure or action which appears not to be in accordance with the trusts of the charity;
(b) any information or explanation to which he is entitled under reg 8 has not been given to him; or
(c) in the case of an examination of a statement of accounts prepared under s42(1), any information contained in that statement is inconsistent in any material respect with the annual report of the charity trustees,

reg 7(g) requires his report to contain a positive statement to that effect.

What are the auditors' and independent examiner's rights?
Section 44(1)(d) and (e) enable the Secretary of State to make provision conferring on the auditor, or independent examiner, a right of access to books, documents and other records of the charity. These provisions are set out in reg 8.

Regulation 8(1) provides that an auditor or independent examiner has a right of access to any books, documents and other records (however kept) which relate to the charity concerned and which the auditor, or examiner, considers necessary to inspect for the purposes of carrying out the audit, or examination.

Regulation 8(2) provides that the auditor, or independent examiner, is entitled to require such information and explanations from past or present charity trustees or trustees for the charity, or from past or present officers or employees of the charity, as he considers necessary for the purposes of carrying out the audit, or examination.

Commissioners' powers to require an audit

Where the statutory requirements for the accounts to be audited, or independently examined, have not been complied with within 10 months of the end of the relevant financial year, s43(4)(a) confers upon the Commissioners a power to require an audit of the accounts. In these circumstances, the auditor will be appointed by the Commissioners and the trustees will be personally liable, jointly and severally, for his costs. Only if it appears to the Commissioners that it would not be practical to seek recovery of the costs of the audit from the trustees, will the costs be met from the funds of the charity.

Section 43(4)(b) confers on the Commissioners a power to require an audit of the accounts in circumstances where, although the requirement for an audit does not apply, it appears to them that one would, nonetheless, be desirable. In these circumstances, the trustees may appoint the auditors and, provided the trustees comply with the Commissioners' order, the costs of the audit will be met from the charity's funds.

Dispensation from audit or independent examination requirements in certain circumstances

Section 44(1)(f) allows the Secretary of State to make provision enabling the Commissioners to dispense, in certain circumstances, with an audit, or independent examination, for a particular charity or any particular financial year of a charity. Those circumstances, which are set out in reg 9, are where the Commissioners:

(a) are satisfied that the accounts of the charity are required to be audited in accordance with any statutory provision contained in or having effect under an Act of Parliament which, in their opinion, imposes requirements which are sufficiently similar to the requirements of s43(2) for those requirements to be dispensed with:
(b) are satisfied that the accounts of the charity for the financial year have been audited or examined in accordance with requirements or arrangements which, in their opinion, are sufficiently similar to the relevant requirements of s43 applicable to that financial year for those requirements to be dispensed with;
(c) are satisfied that, in the financial year in question, there has been no

transaction which would be required to be shown and explained in the accounting records; or

(d) consider that, although the financial year of a charity is one to which s43(2) applies, there are exceptional circumstances which justify the examination of the accounts by an independent examiner rather than an audit in accordance with that subsection and the accounts have been so examined,

and where the charity trustees have supplied to the Commissioners any report made to them with respect to the accounts of that charity for the financial year which the Commissioners have requested.

The White Paper suggested that such an exception could be made, for example, where there were corporate trustees, such as the trust companies of the major banks which have their own internal inspections and audit arrangements, or where one of the trustees was a local authority and the accounts were audited by an auditor appointed by the Audit Commission.

Exclusions

These provisions do not apply to:

(a) charitable companies, although s69 retains the powers of the Commissioners, under what was s8(3) and (6) of the 1960 Act, to require the accounts of such a charity to be investigated and audited, but at the cost to the Commissioners;
(b) exempt charities; and
(c) excepted charities which have neither a permanent endowment nor the use or any occupation of any land and whose income is not greater than £1,000 a year and which are not registered (s46(3)). If they register voluntarily, the provisions apply. The provisions do, however, apply to other excepted charities.

3.4.4 Annual reports

Section 45 requires charity trustees to prepare an annual report for each financial year. This is an important document in its own right and will contain a report on the activities of the charity during the year and such other information relating to the charity, or to its trustees or officers, as is prescribed by the Regulations (for further details, see chapter **5**, page 118 and chapter **17**, page 429).

Unless a charity's gross income and total expenditure does not exceed £10,000 in a financial year, trustees must submit the annual report, together with the statement of accounts, or account and statement, together with the auditors', or independent examiner's, report within 10 months of the year end. The Commissioners may grant a longer period where there are special reasons (s45(3)(b)).

Exempt charities and excepted charities which have neither a permanent endowment nor the use or occupation of any land and whose income is not greater than £1,000 a year and which are not registered on a voluntary basis are excluded from this provision (s46(1) and (3)). Other excepted charities which are not registered on a voluntary basis are also excluded, unless the Commissioners specifically request them to prepare and submit an annual report (s46(5) and (6)). In these circumstances, the annual accounts and the report of the auditors, or independent examiner, should be attached.

3.4.5 Public inspection of accounts

Section 47 provides for all annual reports kept by the Commissioners to be open to public inspection at all reasonable times. This will ensure that the public have access to information about registered charities.

Where a person requests, in writing, the trustees of any charity to provide them with a copy of that charity's accounts and pays them a reasonable fee in order to comply with the request, the trustees must comply with the request within two months of receiving it. This provision applies to all charities, including exempt charities. Thus, the accounts of any charity may be obtained by a member of the public which, hitherto, may have been difficult to obtain.

3.4.6 Annual return

Subject to below, s48(1) requires the trustees of all *registered* charities to complete an annual return in the form prescribed by regulations made by the Commissioners and submit it to them within 10 months of the year end. The annual return is necessary to keep the Commissioners' register of charities up to date and to provide information to help the monitoring process for larger charities. The Commissioners have been issuing a range of different annual returns to charities. They are using the experience gained to develop the annual returns to be prescribed under s48 in a way which identifies necessary information without over-burdening charities.

The White Paper indicated that charities will be asked to confirm that details of the charity entered on the register are correct, or to provide details of changes in the charities' trusts and the address of the charity's correspondent.

Section 48(1A), as inserted by s30(3) of the Deregulation and Contracting Out Act 1994, states that these requirements do not apply to registered charities whose gross income and total expenditure do not exceed £10,000 in a financial year. (This implements a further recommendation of the eighth Deregulation Task Force.)

Section 48(3) provides for the Commissioners to dispense with the need to prepare an annual return in the case of a particular charity or particular class of charities, or in the case of a particular financial year of a charity or of any class of charities.

The Secretary of State may, again, amend the figure of £10,000 by substituting a different amount, at any time (s48(4), as inserted by s30(4) of the Deregulation and Contracting Out Act 1994.)

3.4.7 Penalties for non-compliance

Under s49, charity trustees will commit an offence if persistently in default, without reasonable excuse, in:

(a) preparing and submitting annual reports and accounts to the Commissioners;
(b) making available accounts to the public; or
(c) preparing and submitting an annual return.

Such a person will be liable, on summary conviction, to a fine. Persistent failure to supply this information would be evidence of mismanagement and the Commissioners could then institute enquiries.

3.4.8 The 1985 Act versus the 1993 Act

As regards the standard to which accounts should be prepared, subject to scrutiny and by whom, there are some important differences. In some respects, the 1985 Act is more demanding; in others, the 1993 Act.

Standard to which accounts should be prepared and subject to scrutiny

As regards the standard to which accounts are prepared, charity trustees of all charitable companies must prepare a balance sheet which shows a true and fair view of the state of affairs of the charity at the end of its financial year and a SOFA which shows a true and fair view of its financial activities for that year.

The 1993 Act is, however, less demanding. The charity trustees of unincorporated charities whose gross income in a financial year does not exceed £100,000, may elect to prepare a simplified set of accounts, being:

(a) a receipts and payments account, and
(b) a statement of assets and liabilities,

(i.e., an account and statement) rather than a statement of accounts. SSAPs, FRSs and the revised charity SORP do not readily apply to the account and statement, which is not required to give a true and fair view, either of the financial activities of the year or of the state of affairs at the balance sheet date. Where an unincorporated charity's gross income exceeds that figure in a financial year, a statement of accounts must be prepared to give a true and fair view and, thus, complying with SSAPs, FRSs and the revised charity SORP.

Under the 1985 Act, a charitable company will require an audit of its accounts if it does not qualify as a small company, its gross income is greater than £250,000 or if its balance sheet total is greater than £1.4m or, in any event, if it is a parent company or subsidiary undertaking. Under the 1993 Act, an audit will be required if an unincorporated charity's gross income or total expenditure exceeds £250,000, in either a financial year or the immediately preceding two financial years.

Under the 1985 Act, a charitable small company whose gross income is greater than £90,000 but not greater than £250,000 (and where its balance sheet total is not greater than £1.4m) will normally require a report, an audit exemption report, to be prepared in accordance with the specified requirements. Under the 1993 Act, the charity trustees of an unincorporated charity whose gross income or total expenditure exceeds £10,000 but neither in a financial year nor the immediately preceding two financial years does not exceed £250,000, may elect to have its account and statement (or, statement of accounts) examined, by an independent examiner.

In this respect, the 1993 Act appears more demanding. While an unincorporated charity with gross income or total expenditure greater than £10,000 but with gross income of less than £90,000 will require, as a minimum, its account and statement (or, statement of accounts) to be independently examined, a charitable company is exempt from the provisions relating both to audit and to audit exemption reports. Thus, it may be possible for charity trustees to set up a charitable company, hide behind the veil of incorporation and not have that account and statement (or, statement of accounts) subjected to any form of independent scrutiny. It will, however, have to submit the accounts to the Commissioners.

The accounts of unincorporated charities with gross income and total expenditure which do not exceed £10,000 in a financial year will, like those of a charitable company, not normally be subject to any form of independent scrutiny.

The reporting accountant versus the independent examiner

The qualifications required of the persons able to provide an audit exemption report are more demanding than those of persons able to undertake an independent examination.

The Companies Act 1985 (Audit Exemption) Regulations 1994 (SI 1994 No 1935) require the audit exemption report to be prepared by a member of the ICAEW, ICAS, ICAI, CACA or AAPA who, under the rules of the body, either:

(a) holds a practising certificate and is not ineligible, on the grounds of lack of independence, for appointment as a reporting accountant; or
(b) is a registered auditor.

(A) Who is an 'independent examiner'?

An independent examiner is defined in s43(3)(a) as 'an independent person who is reasonably believed by the trustees to have the requisite ability and practical experience to carry out a competent examination of the accounts'.

In accordance with s43(7)(a), the Commissioners have given guidance to charity trustees in connection with the selection of an independent examiner. For ease of reference, that guidance is given as Annex II to this chapter. Charity trustees should take all necessary steps to satisfy themselves that the examiner is independent, has the requisite ability and practical experience to discharge the responsibilities. If charity trustees follow this guidance, they will have taken all reasonable steps to obtain a competent independent examination of their accounts.

(B) Who is an 'independent person'?

For an examiner to be independent, the guidance states that the individual should have no connection with the charity's trustees which might inhibit the impartial conduct of the examination. Whether or not such a connection exists will depend on the particular circumstances, but the guidance lists those persons who, as a minimum, would normally be considered to have such a connection. Those persons are similar to those included within the definition of 'connected person' in Sch 5 (see chapter **11**, page 298). In order for the examiner to be both independent and be seen to be independent, it would be advisable for the persons included within either the Commissioners' guidance or the definition of 'connected person' not to be appointed.

(C) Which persons would have the 'requisite ability'?

During the debates in the House of Lords, the persons, other than accountants, who were thought to have that ability included bank and building society managers and local authority treasurers. At that stage, however, the upper limit for independent examination was intended as £100,000, not £250,000. The Commissioners stress that:

(a) the suitability of an independent examiner; and
(b) the quality both of the independent examiner's credentials and of their evidence,

will depend on the particular circumstances and the size and nature of the charity's transactions.

The Commissioners strongly recommend that where a charity's:

(a) gross assets exceed £1 million; or
(b) gross income exceeds £100,000; or
(c) trustees elect to prepare a statement of accounts in accordance with s42(1),

a qualified accountant should carry out that examination.

And, as regards quality of evidence of those credentials, trustees should consider obtaining references. References should be obtained where a qualified accountant is used and may be judged good practice in any event.

(D) What is 'practical experience'?

Prospective independent examiners should have practical experience which is relevant to the charity. This could be achieved by:

(a) having had an involvement in the financial administration of a charity of a similar nature;
(b) having acted successfully as an independent examiner on previous occasions for such charities; or
(c) relevant practical experience in accountancy or commerce.

(E) Selection procedures

Charity trustees should:

(a) discuss fully with the prospective independent examiner the work of the charity and their expectations;
(b) ensure that the prospective examiner is familiar with:
   (i) the Commissioners' directions to independent examiners and the nature of the report required;
   (ii) where a statement of accounts is prepared, the form and content of the Regulations, the methods and principles with which that statement must be prepared and the revised charity SORP; and
(c) ensure that the letter of engagement recognises and does not limit the examiner's statutory duties.

What is an independent examination and how does it differ from an audit exemption report?

(A) Audit exemption report versus independent examination

Independent examination is a new term introduced by the 1993 Act. It is a less onerous form of scrutiny than an audit and is based on the conceptual approach adopted by the International Standard on Auditing *Engagements to review financial statements.* As there is a fine dividing line between a full audit and no scrutiny at all, the aim has been to find some middle ground.

The examiner is not required to form an opinion as to whether the accounts show a true and fair view. Rather, the objective of the examination is to enable the examiner to state whether, on the basis of procedures carried out, anything has come to his attention that causes him to believe that the account and statement (or, statement of accounts) is not prepared, in all material respects, in accordance with the financial reporting framework. In other words, it is a form of *negative assurance.* Section 43(7)(b) of the 1993 Act enables the Commissioners to give directions, as they consider appropriate, with respect to the carrying out of such an examination. For ease of reference, these are reproduced in Annex III to the chapter.

The examiner should properly plan the work. He should obtain, or update, his knowledge of the charity, its constitution, organisation, activities and accounting systems and of the nature of its assets, liabilities, incoming resources and their application. This information is necessary so that the examiner can design appropriate procedures and make relevant enquiries of the charity trustees.

The examiner should use the same materiality as would be applied were an audit carried out. This is because the judgement as to what is, or is not, material is made by reference to the information on which the examiner is reporting and the needs of those relying on that information, and not on the level of assurance provided.

The examiner's working papers should both record the work done and document matters which are important to support conclusions reached, or statements provided.

The examiner is required to carry out such *procedures and checks* as are necessary to provide reasonable assurance that:

(a) an examination is required and that the requirement for an audit does not apply; and
(b) the charity trustees may properly elect to prepare an account and statement and that a statement of accounts is not required.

These procedures and checks appear more demanding than those in respect of an audit exemption report where the reporting accountant is required to perform such procedures as are necessary to provide a reasonable basis on which to form an opinion on whether, having regard only to, and on the basis of, the information in the accounting records, the company is entitled to exemption from audit. The reporting accountant will accept the information contained in those records and will not attempt to verify further, or substantiate, the basis on which entitlement to the exemption is claimed by the directors (para 9.2 of the SSRA *Audit exemption reports*. Conversely, in order to verify the level to which the accounts should be prepared and subject to scrutiny, the examiner's procedures and checks do not appear to be limited to accepting the information contained in the accounting records. The 'checks' which an examiner might be expected to carry out could, for example, include those relating to cut-off, to ensure that income has not been deferred to a future financial year period to circumvent the preparation of a statement of accounts.

The reporting accountant is required to carry out procedures as are necessary to provide reasonable assurance on which to express an opinion on whether the accounts are in agreement with the accounting records, but not as to whether proper accounting records have been kept. Conversely, the examiner is required to state whether any matter has come to his attention, in connection with his examination, which gives him reasonable cause to believe either that the accounts are not in agreement with the accounting records or that proper accounting records have not been kept. The requirement to keep and maintain proper accounting records is fundamental to the administration, protection and use of funds for the purposes for which they have been given.

An audit exemption report would provide no assurance about that requirement.

The examiner is required to carry out analysis and review procedures of the accounts to identify any unusual items, disclosures or omissions. Where concerns arise, the examiner must seek and obtain satisfactory information and explanations from the charity trustees. If, after making these enquiries, the examiner still has reason to believe that the accounts may be materially misstated, he must carry out additional procedures as are necessary to give that negative assurance.These additional procedures take the form of audit procedures and include the verification of an asset or liability, or the vouching of an incoming resource or application of that resource. Alternatively, those procedures may confirm that a modified report is required.

Where the charity trustees have prepared a statement of accounts, the Commissioners' guidance requires the examiner to carry out the following further procedures. He should:

(a) carry out such procedures as are necessary to provide reasonable assurance that the statement of accounts complies with the requirements (other than that to show a true and fair view) of the Regulations as to their form and content;
(b) review the accounting policies adopted and consider their conformity with fundamental accounting concepts, consistency and appropriateness to the charity's activities;
(c) consider and review the appropriateness of any material assumptions, or financial judgements, made;
(d) enquire of the charity trustees about events subsequent to the balance sheet date which may require adjustment to, or disclosure in, the statement of accounts; and
(e) compare the statement of accounts to any financial references in the trustees' annual report, identify any major inconsistency and consider the significance which such matters may have on a proper and accurate understanding of the accounts.

The additional procedure in (a) differs from that in respect of an audit exemption report. An independent examiner is required to state whether or not any matter has come to his attention which causes him to believe that the statement of accounts does not *comply with* any of the requirements of the Regulations which prescribe the form and content of the statement of accounts. A reporting accountant is, however, only required to state whether the accounts have been drawn up in a *manner consistent with* the specified accounting requirements. The use of the words 'comply with' is to focus on whether the statement of accounts complies with the substance of the legal requirements and not merely on whether it is in the required legal form.

The more onerous requirements imposed on the independent examination are a recognition of greater public expectation, as regards the level of assurance provided of the proper administration of the charity and its funds by the charity trustees. Unless the 1985 Act is changed to provide equivalence, however, it is somewhat ironic that, while the duties placed on an independent examiner are more onerous, the qualifications required of the independent examiner are less.

(B) 'Whistle blowing'
The examiner must inform the Commissioners in writing if, in the course of an examination or while acting in his capacity as an examiner, information or evidence is obtained which gives him reasonable cause to believe such information or evidence to be relevant to the discharge of the Commissioners' functions under s8 (general power to institute enquiries) or s18 (power to act for protection of charities).

(C) Qualifications of the independent examiner's report
The report should contain a clear expression of negative assurance. The examiner should review and assess all conclusions drawn from the evidence obtained as the basis for that expression.

Matters may come to the examiner's attention which cause him to express a qualification, in the relevant part(s) of the report, of the negative assurance provided. For example, reg 7(e)(iii) requires the examiner to state whether, during his examination, a matter has come to his attention which causes him to believe that the statement of accounts does not comply with the requirements of the Regulations. This might be the case where a current asset is stated at cost, rather than at net realisable value, in which case an 'except for' report may be appropriate. Alternatively, there may be circumstances, for example the non-consolidation of a subsidiary, where the matter is so material to the statement of accounts that an 'adverse' statement should be given.

Regulation 7(f) requires the examiner to state whether or not any matter has come to his attention, in connection with the examination, to which, in his opinion, attention should be drawn in the report in order to enable a *proper understanding of the accounts to be reached.* It is difficult to predict to what circumstance, or set of circumstances, this requirement would have particular application and appears more in the nature of a sweeping-up provision.

There may have been a limitation on the scope of the independent examiner's procedures. For example, a limitation of scope may be imposed by circumstances (e.g., where parts of the accounting records have been lost or destroyed). In this circumstance, the independent examiner should express a qualification in the relevant part of his report. Alternatively, a limitation of scope may have been imposed by the directors (e.g., where they refuse to provide information or explanations requested by the independent examiner). In this circumstance, reg 7(g)(ii) requires the independent examiner to make a positive statement to that effect.

The particular position of charitable companies

Unless stated otherwise, charitable companies are excluded from the accounting and auditing requirements, but must comply with the accounting and disclosure provisions in the 1985 Act. Disapplying these provisions to such companies, however, means that they do not have to comply with the Regulations made thereunder and with which other charities would have to comply.

This exclusion raised some concern during the passage of the Charities Bill through Parliament and an amendment was tabled, by the late Lord Benson, at the report stage, the thrust of which was to create a level playing field for charities which are companies and charities which are unincorporated. Any fears, however, were dispelled as Earl Ferrers, for the government, commented:

> ' . . . The anxiety is that the law should not allow charities which choose to become companies to report on their accounting and financial affairs in a less vigorous way than that which is required for unincorporated charities. There is nothing between the noble Lord, Lord Benson, or indeed anyone else, and me on that point.
>
> '. . . I believe that there is an alternative means of achieving our common end. It is to use existing powers in the Companies Act 1985 to create an accounting regime which could be tailored specifically to charitable companies and which would be equivalent to that for unincorporated charities.
>
> 'There are already certain types of company to which the common accounting requirements of company law may not be suited, and the law recognises that. For example, banks and insurance companies prepare their accounts according to a modified regime which is provided by the Companies Act 1985 as amended by the Companies Act 1989. The Secretary of State has power under Section 257 . . . to modify the accounting requirements of that Act in order to establish special accounting regimes for different classes of company. There is no reason in principle why such a modified regime could not be established for charitable purposes.
>
> 'The Secretary of State will consider sympathetically any detailed proposals

> which may be put forward to ensure that charitable companies are subject to accounting provisions which are just as rigorous as those for unincorporated charities.
>
> 'Once the regulations for unincorporated charities have been drafted . . . we shall look carefully at the two sets of requirements to see whether a modified regime for charitable companies would then be desirable. I can assure the noble Lord . . . that I shall be looking at that as a matter of urgency. But he will understand that that cannot be done until the regulations for unincorporated charities have been drawn. If there is found to be a need for that regime, I shall ensure that the two regimes are brought in contemporaneously' (HL Deb, vol 535, cols. 404–405 (6 February 1992)).

As a result of the announcement and concession, the proposed amendment was withdrawn.

It is understood that the DTI intends to consult as to whether or not any amendments are required to the 1985 Act. In view both of the differences highlighted above and in chapter **4** (see page 87) and of the comments made during the parliamentary debates, amendments are inevitable. Specifically but not exclusively, the DTI intends to amend the 1985 Act's provisions so that the trustees' annual report can stand in place of the directors' report, providing that the former includes any items from the directors' report that the DTI decides, after consultation, should be included (see chapter **5**, page 118).

Annex I – Guidance on accounting records

Statement issued in March 1992 by the Council of the Institute of Chartered Accountants in England and Wales for the guidance of members on the obligations of companies to keep accounting records under the Companies Act 1985.

This statement has been settled in consultation with counsel.

References are to the Companies Act 1985 as amended by section 2 of the Companies Act 1989.

1 Section 221 of the Companies Act 1985 obliges all companies to have accounting records satisfying the requirements set out in that section. The term 'accounting records' was introduced by the Companies Act 1976 in recognition of the fact that the term 'books of account' (used in earlier Acts) was no longer apt in the age of computers. Current concern about the incidence of fraud and negligence has directed attention to the need for guidance on the interpretation of this section. No account is taken in this paper of specific requirements of other legislation (eg VAT legislation) in respect of accounting records.

The legal requirements
2 The Act's requirements are as follows:

Duty to keep accounting records

221 (1) Every company shall keep accounting records which are sufficient to show and explain the company's transactions and are such to
a) disclose with reasonable accuracy, at any time, the financial position of the company at that time, and
b) enable the directors to ensure that any balance sheet and profit and loss account prepared under this Part complies with the requirements of this Act.
(2) The accounting records shall in particular contain
a) entries from day to day of all sums of money received and expended by the company, and the matters in respect of which the receipt and expenditure takes place, and
b) a record of the assets and liabilities of the company.
(3) If the company's business involves dealing in goods, the accounting records shall contain
a) statements of stock held by the company at the end of each financial year of the company,
b) all statements of stocktakings from which any such statement of stock as is mentioned in paragraph (a) has been or is to be prepared, and
c) except in the case of goods sold by way of ordinary retail trade, statements of all goods sold and purchased, showing the goods and the buyers and sellers in sufficient detail to enable all these to be identified.

The key requirement is in section 221 (1). Subsections (2) and (3) supplement this.

3 Subsection (4) of section 221 obliges a parent company which has a subsidiary undertaking to which the requirements of subsections (1), (2) and (3) do not apply to take reasonable steps to secure that the undertaking keeps such accounting records as to enable the directors of the parent company to ensure that any balance sheet and profit and loss account prepared under Part VII of the Act complies with the requirements of the Act. Subsections (5) and (6) of section 221 contain penalty provisions.

Contents, form and organisation of accounting records
4 The accounting records should comprise an orderly, classified collection of information capable of timely retrieval, containing details of the company's transactions, assets and liabilities. An unorganised collection of vouchers and documents will not suffice: whatever the physical form of the records, the information should be so organised as to enable a trial balance to be constructed. If, for example, the information is held in a computer database as a subset of a set of wider information, the software should be capable of retrieving the appropriate data.

Preservation of the accounting records
5 Section 222(5) of the Act requires that accounting records, once made, must be preserved for at least 6 years (public companies) or 3 years (private companies). It follows that where programmed instructions and any supporting documentation are needed for retrieval of information in usable form, for example from a computer database, they must be available for the same period, as must any necessary hardware.

Disclosure of the financial position at any time
6 The Act requires that accounting records should be such as to disclose with reasonable accuracy, at any time, the financial position of the company at that time. The words 'at any time' emphasise the obligation to keep accounting records up to date and do not impose an obligation to keep accounting records capable of disclosing the financial position as at any time in the past. The requirement to keep accounting records up to date does not mean that transactions and events must be recorded instantaneously. It is sufficient if they are recorded within a reasonable time. What is a reasonable time depends upon the nature of the business and other circumstances. What, for example, is urgent for a bank, calling for immediate action, may be less so for another business. Records made to disclose the current financial position (including any stock records or memoranda, such as are referred to in paragraphs 10 and 11 below) must be retained for the statutory period.

7 In requiring that the accounting records be sufficient to disclose with reasonable accuracy, at any time, the financial position of the company at that time, the Act recognises that it is not practicable to keep accounting records in such a way as to enable accounts to be prepared giving a true and fair view at every moment during the year. The concept of 'true and fair' is extremely wide and embraces information not necessarily contained within the accounting records themselves.

8 Whether a company is keeping the right kind of accounting records to meet the requirements of the Act is a question of fact to be decided in any particular case. Regard will be had, among other things, to prevailing practice of the time in businesses of the type in question although this consideration will not itself be conclusive.

9 The accounting records should be such as would enable the directors at any time to prepare a reasonably accurate statement of the company's financial position. The accounting records should therefore contain the primary material on which a set of accounts would be based. However, they need not contain whatever additional items of information it would be necessary to know in order to make those accounts true and fair (see paragraph 7 above). The financial position is not limited to the cash position. It comprises the assets and liabilities including items such as those referred to in paragraph 11 below.

10 What is a sufficient record of stocks within the total picture will depend on the circumstances. The materiality of stock and the extent of stock movements are relevant factors. Continuous stock records can provide adequate information when supported by systematic physical checks. The information may, however, require to be supplemented by judgements with respect to realisable value including times of potential realisation and this may require accounting entries to be made, for example by way of memorandum, as indicated in paragraph 11 below. Continuous records are not essential if the stock position can be assessed with sufficient reliability from other accounting records, including in appropriate cases any interim stocktakings. Express requirements with respect to stocks held at the end of financial years are contained in section 221(3), and are discussed in paragraph 16 below.

11 Provisions for such matters as depreciation, bad debts and other losses are often made only at the end of an accounting year. The requirement to disclose the financial position with reasonable accuracy at any time during a financial year will normally be satisfied if a procedure exists to ensure that an adequate record is made and retained – for example by way of memorandum – of any expected loss, liability or contingency material to the assessment of the current position. Such a memorandum would constitute part of the accounting records.

Annual accounts

12 The records must also be such as to enable the directors to satisfy the requirements of the Act with regard to annual accounts, including the notes to the accounts (section 221(1)(b) and section 221(4)).

Cash records to be kept

13 Section 221(2)(a) requires the accounting records to contain entries from day to day of all sums of money received and expended. Accordingly, the accounting records must contain:

(1) the date of transactions;
(2) the sums received and expended;
(3) the matters in respect of which the receipt and expenditure took place.

As noted above, it is not necessary in all cases for entries to be made instantaneously, although they must be made within a reasonable time.

14 It will sometimes be appropriate to record groups of transactions rather than individual transactions (e.g., in the records of the daily cash takings of a shop where a record of individual receipts is not necessary to explain the transactions). Paragraph 17 below sets out the position as regards records of goods sold and purchased.

Assets and liabilities

15 Assets and liabilities must be recorded (section 221(2)(b)). Details must therefore be included of all the company's assets and liabilities such as debtors, creditors, properties and plant. The accounting records must show the dates of transactions.

Stocks

16 Section 221(3)(a) requires that where the company's business involves dealing in goods, statements of stock held at each financial year-end are to be part of the accounting records. 'Statements of stock' is taken to mean a summary supporting the amount included in the annual accounts in respect of stock. It is further required, by section 221(3)(b), that any statements of stocktakings supporting the year-end stock summary are to form part of the accounting records. Any continuous stock records used for that purpose, or if stock is taken physically the original stock sheets, are therefore to be treated as part of the accounting records.

Purchases and sales of goods

17 Where the company's business involves dealing in goods, section 221 (3) (c) requires details of goods sold and purchased, and of individual buyers and sellers, to be recorded. This does not, however, apply to sales by way of ordinary retail trade.

Penalties and disqualification orders

18 Under the penalty provisions in section 221 (5)and(6) non-compliance with section 221 is a criminal offence. In addition, by virtue of section 9 of, and paragraph 4(a) of Schedule 1 to, the Company Directors Disqualification Act 1986, the extent of the director's responsibility for any failure by the company to comply with section 221 is one of the matters to which the court must have regard on an application for disqualification of a director.

Annex II – Draft Charity Commission guidance under s43(7)(a) Charities Act 1993, on the selection of independent examiners

Guidance from the Charity Commissioners to Charity Trustees on the selection of a person for appointment as an Independent Examiner. References to 'sections' are references to sections of the Charities Act 1993.

1 The requirement for an Independent Examiner

1.1 (i) All charities whose income or expenditure is more than £250,000 in the current year or either of the two preceding years must have a professional audit.

(ii) All Charities whose governing instrument requires them to have an audit must do so.

(iii) Charitable companies must follow the provisions of the Companies Act and Regulations made under it.

(iv) Unincorporated charities with an income or expenditure in the current year exceeding £10,000 must have their accounts independently examined, or may choose to have the accounts audited.

1.2 The trustees should take steps to ensure that a competent examination takes place and they will therefore wish to consider most carefully the suitability of a prospective independent examiner.

1.3 Trustees are entitled to pay reasonable remuneration to an independent examiner for services rendered and if they are unable to obtain the services of a competent examiner on a voluntary basis should be prepared to pay such remuneration and regard it as a proper charge on the assets of the charity.

2 The Independent Examiner

2.1 An independent examiner as described in section 43(3)(a) is 'an **independent person** who is reasonably believed by the trustees to have the **requisite ability** and **practical experience** to carry out a **competent examination** of the accounts'.

3 An Independent Person

3.1 For an examiner to be **independent** that individual should have no connection with the charity's trustees which might inhibit the impartial conduct of the examination.

3.2 Whether this connection exists will depend upon the circumstances of a particular charity but the following persons at least will normally be considered to have such a connection.

(a) The charity trustees, or anyone else who is closely involved in the administration of the charity;
(b) a major donor to or major beneficiary of the charity;
(c) a close relative, business partner or employee of any person who falls within sub-paragraph (a) or (b) above.

4 Requisite Ability

4.1 In the House of Lords' debate on the Charities Bill it was stated that 'an independent examiner must obviously be competent for the task that he is to do and he must be familiar with accountancy methods, but he need not be a practising accountant. We have in mind . . . people . . . such as bank or building society managers, local authority treasurers or retired accountants. They would all be suitable as independent examiners.' Nevertheless, at that stage the upper limit for independent examination of a charity was intended as £100,000 income or expenditure in the current or either of the two previous financial years. It is also essential to consider the suitability of an independent examiner with regard to the particular circumstances of each case (see paragraph 4.3, below).

4.2 The quality of evidence of ability which is required will depend upon the size and nature of the charity's transactions. Trustees should consider taking independent references on the capability of the prospective independent examiner to carry out this function.

4.3 It is strongly recommended that trustees of charities with gross assets in excess of £1,000,000 or gross income of more than £100,000 but below the compulsory audit threshold, or of any charity which elects to produce a statement of accounts under section 42(1), select a qualified accountant to carry out the independent examination. When accounts are prepared on the accruals basis an understanding of accountancy principles and accounting standards will be needed, and the skills and experience of a qualified accountant will be desirable when substantial assets are held by a charity.

5 Practical Experience

5.1 Trustees should satisfy themselves that prospective examiners have **practical experience** relevant to the charity in question which might be by virtue of that person having had an involvement in the financial administration of a charity of a similar nature or by having acted successfully as an independent examiner on previous occasions for such charities or by relevant practical experience in accountancy or commerce.

6 Selection Procedures

6.1 Trustees should discuss fully with the prospective examiner the work of the charity and their expectations. They should ensure that the prospective independent examiner is conversant with the Charity Commission directions to independent examiners and the nature of the independent examiners' report prescribed by Regulations under section 44(1)(c); and, where the accounts are prepared under section 42(1), with the Regulations under section 42 as to the form and content of those accounts and the methods and principles in accordance with which they must be prepared, and with the Statement of Recommended Practice on Accounting by Charities.

6.2 Trustees should take all necessary steps to satisfy themselves as to the matters referred to in paragraphs 3 to 5 above.

6.3 Trustees should ensure that any written terms of engagement recognise and do not limit the examiner's statutory duties.

6.4 Trustees who follow these guidelines and gain suitable assurances from prospective examiners and from any referees can be satisfied that they have taken all reasonable steps to obtain a competent independent examination of their accounts for the period in question.

Annex III – Draft general directions of the Charity Commissioners under s43 (7)(b) Charities Act 1993, on the carrying out of an independent examination

These directions set out the essential procedures that must be observed by an Independent Examiner in the carrying out of an examination under Section 43(3)(a) of the Charities Act 1993. References to 'sections' are references to sections of that Act. Compliance with these directions will provide the procedural basis on which an Examiner reports under Regulation 7 of the Charities (Accounts and Reports) Regulations 1995 (in draft).

In carrying out an examination of a statement of accounts prepared under section 42(1) or an account and statement prepared under section 42(3) ('the accounts'), the Examiner shall:

(a) obtain an understanding of the charity's constitution, organisation, accounting systems, activities and nature of its assets, liabilities, incoming resources and application of resources in order to plan the examination procedures appropriate to the circumstances of the charity;

(b) carry out such procedures and checks as are necessary to provide reasonable assurance that an examination is required under Section 43(3) and that section 43(2) (audit) does not apply to the charity, and where accounts are prepared under section 42(3), that the charity trustees may properly elect to prepare accounts under this sub-section;

(c) record the examination procedures carried out, and document matters which are important to support conclusions reached or statements provided in the Examiner's report;

(d) compare the accounts of the charity with the charity's accounting records in sufficient detail to provide a reasonable assurance that the accounts are in accordance with such accounting records;

(e) inspect all accounting records, in order to provide a reasonable assurance that any material or gross failures to maintain the records have been identified;

(f) carry out analysis and review procedures on the accounts to identify unusual items, disclosures or omissions. Where concerns arise from these procedures, the Examiner shall seek explanations and information to explain such items, disclosures or omission from the charity trustees. If, after following such procedures the Examiner has reason to believe that in any respect the accounts may be materially misstated then additional procedures, including verification of the asset or liability or vouching of the item of incoming resource or application, must be carried out;

(g) carry out such procedures as are necessary to provide a reasonable assurance that accounts prepared under section 42(1) conform to regulations as to the form and content of charity accounts;

(h) when accounts are prepared under section 42(1), review the accounting policies adopted and consider their conformity with fundamental accounting concepts, consistency of application and their appropriateness to the activities of the charity. The Examiner shall also consider and review the appropriateness of any material assumptions or financial judgements that have been made in preparing the accounts;

(i) when accounts are prepared under section 42(1), inquire of the charity trustees as to material events subsequent to the year end of the accounts examined which may require adjustment or disclosure in the accounts;

(j) when accounts are prepared under section 42(1), compare the accounts to any financial references in the charity trustees' annual report (if any); identify any major inconsistency and consider the significance such matters will have on a proper and accurate understanding of the charity's accounts;

(k) review and assess all conclusions drawn from the evidence obtained from the examination and consider the implication on the report provided. If the Examiner has cause to make a negative statement on any matter arising from the provisions of Regulation 7(e), or to make a statement on any matter arising from the provisions of Regulation 7(f), then the Examiner shall ensure that the report provided gives a clear explanation of the matter and of its financial effects on the accounts presented together with details of any adjustments or disclosures which the Examiner believes necessary to provide the charity trustees with a proper understanding of the accounts and to ensure compliance with any relevant regulations; and

(l) inform the Charity Commissioners in writing if, in the course of an examination or whilst acting in the capacity of the Examiner of a charity, information or evidence is obtained which gives the Examiner reasonable cause to believe such information or evidence to be relevant to the discharge of the Commissioners' functions under section 8 (general power to institute inquiries) or 18 (power to act for protection of charities).

Chapter 4 – The revised charity SORP and structure and presentation of accounts

4.1 Introduction

It was as long ago as 1981 that *Financial reporting by charities*, a report of a research study by Peter Bird and Peter Morgan-Jones, highlighted the need for greater consistency and clarity in accounting by charities. The study surveyed and evaluated the accounting and reporting practices of charities and found substantial room for improving reporting standards and enhancing comparability of information.

In 1982 the then ASC set up a working party to consider financial reporting by charities. In particular, the working party was asked to explore ways of enhancing the usefulness of charities' annual reports and to examine the possibility of reducing the number of diverse practices of financial accounting and reporting then adopted.

The result was *Accounting by charities: a discussion paper*, published in February 1984. It was a wide-ranging paper which dealt not only with the accounts of a charity, but, also, with the information which should accompany the accounts in the annual report. As Denis Peach, the then Chief Commissioner, explained in the Foreword:

> 'Quite apart from their duty to be accountable for the funds they hold and use, charity trustees will want to work in the light of day and to provide as much information as is practicable and useful to the public they serve and indeed to public at large. Informative and easily-understood accounts – and indeed annual reports – will serve the purpose of averting suspicion and overcoming ignorance and should positively encourage support, not just for individual charities but for charity at large.'

The response to the paper indicated that guidance on how charities should account for the funds they held and use would be welcomed and a proposed SORP, ED 38, was published in late 1985, the recommendations of which were based largely on the conclusions of the discussion paper. This was followed by SORP 2 *Accounting by charities*, in May 1988, the purpose of which was to improve the quality of reporting by charities, to reduce the number of diverse accounting practices adopted and to provide assistance to those responsible for the preparation of charities' annual reports. The recommendations were intended to apply to all charities (except universities), regardless of their constitution, size or complexity and regardless of the reporting requirements, if any, imposed on them.

Why a SORP? The ASC considered that, although many charities were required by law to prepare accounts, only a small minority were subject to detailed requirements on the form and content of accounts or were required to prepare an annual report. The ASC did not seek to impose inflexible accounting practices and standardise formats of presentation on charities. Rather, it believed that, at that time, it was more appropriate to issue guidance which:

(a) left discretion to trustees of each charity to apply the provisions of the SORP according to the character of the charity and the significance of the figures concerned; and
(b) was helpful to the majority of charities in the evolution of their accounting methodology.

4.2 The revised charity SORP*

4.2.1 Background

For five years SORP 2 represented the benchmark for accounting by charities, providing general guidance embodying best practice. But it offered alternative treatment in a number of instances. Experience of working with the SORP had shown that many of the alternatives needed to be eliminated for, as the ED to the revised SORP described, 'the sake of simplicity and consistency'.

Accordingly, in March 1993, the Charity Accounting Review Committee, set up under the auspices of the Commissioners, published an ED of a revised SORP. In framing its proposals, the Committee was mindful not only of the new statutory regime (see chapter **3**, page 40) but, also, of developments internationally, particularly in the United States.

At slightly less than two months, the exposure period was unusually short. In the light of this, some commentators may have found difficulty in giving the proposals the full consideration which they merited. Nonetheless, over 350 responses were received.

* *The consultation on the regulatory framework was completed on 17 May. Final regulations are expected in the summer with a view to their coming into force by December. It is hoped that further revisions to the revised SORP will be avoided. However, that possibility is not ruled out, should the consultation on the whole package render this necessary.*

Having amended the ED to take account of the comments received, the Committee also had discussions with the ASB. This was not to secure the revised SORP's 'franking', as conducted by the ASC, but to be able to append a 'negative assurance statement'. (The ASB's policy for the development of SORPs was originally set out in its Bulletin No 4, issued on 15 October 1990. Its policy and practice on their development were updated in June 1994 – see the ASB Press Notice No 47, issued on 27 June 1994.)

In essence, the ASB's approach is to satisfy itself that any industry body developing a proposed SORP is balanced and representative and conducts the development of its proposals with due process. Although the proposals are not vetted in detail, a 'negative assurance statement' will be issued where the ASB is satisfied that the proposals have been properly developed and do not appear to contain any fundamental points of principle which are unacceptable in the context of current accounting practice or conflict with existing or currently contemplated accounting standards. There is, however, nothing to prevent the proposals from being more stringent.

In its circular of 8 February 1994, the Commissioners reported that discussions with the ASB had been 'more protracted'. This was attributed to the tensions which undoubtedly existed between some elements of the current accounting standards and some of the accounting practices which the Committee felt were appropriate to charities (as opposed to commercial entities.) ' . . . Accounting standards have been developed in a commercial environment, whereas SORP is of course concerned with those entities whose purposes and (often) structures are fundamentally different . . . '. The circular reported, however, that the revised SORP now accorded with current accounting standards and 'respects the difference between charities and commercial entities'. The SORP was granted 'negative assurance' on 13 January 1994.

The final SORP has been considerably amended from the ED. The principal changes are:

(a) in certain circumstances, the SOFA is to be supplemented by a summary income and expenditure account;
(b) the treatment of grants receivable has been made consistent with SSAP 4; and
(c) the rules regarding consolidation have been clarified, to recommend that:
    (i) if a subsidiary's non-charitable trading activity is for the benefit of the charity, its assets and liabilities should be consolidated, on a line-by-line basis in the balance sheet, with its results shown as

a single line entry in the income and expenditure account, together with the disclosure of turnover;

(ii) charitable activities of a subsidiary which are within the objects of the charity should be consolidated on a line-by-line basis; and

(iii) all subsidiaries should, generally, be consolidated, regardless of size criteria.

It is now possible for charitable companies to comply with the revised SORP without being in breach of the 1985 Act. Accordingly, there is nothing to prevent such companies complying with the revised charity SORP when it has been published in final form by the Commissioners and comes into effect. In practice, this means that charitable companies may well be able to comply with the SORP at an earlier stage than unincorporated charities.

4.2.2 Objective

The revised charity SORP, issued on 1 February 1995, provides a new highway code for accounting by charities. It sets out recommendations on the form and content of the annual report and accounts and on the way in which they should be prepared.

In revising the SORP, the Committee's objective has been 'to help improve the quality of financial reporting' (para 12). This has been achieved by reducing the current diversity in accounting practice and recommending comprehensive disclosure, thus increasing the transparency as regards both the accounting policies and assumptions adopted and the charity's activities during the financial year.

Being sophisticated (and, perhaps, somewhat ahead of its time) the revised SORP may not be easy to comply with. But the Commissioners are committed to the need for high standards of accounting by charities. To that extent the revised SORP may prove to be a burden to trustees and their staff. There will be transitional costs, as charities apply the recommendations of the revised SORP, although many of the larger charities should generally have the management information systems in place to meet those recommendations and their costs may not be significantly greater than those for the existing recommendations. The Commissioners have clearly concluded, however, that the overall benefits should justify the costs which the revised SORP may impose.

Nonetheless, the objective of the revised SORP is, also, 'to assist those who are responsible for the preparation of the charity's annual report and accounts' (para 12). The Charity Commission is, in substance, a regulatory department, able to offer a free service to trustees. The

Commissioners have a long record of working with charities. They are able to give a ruling on problems.

While the objectives are undoubtedly laudable, they may be unpalatable, even for the larger charities. Given the diversity of charities and the way they finance themselves, it may not be possible to ensure, in every respect, comparability of accounting methods. Furthermore, a research report, *The revision of SORP 2 ('Accounting by charities'): A commentary on the exposure draft*, for the CACA believed that the disclosures are excessive, especially those relating to the notes to the accounts. Chapter **4** (Overview and recommendations) states (*inter alia*) that:

> 'It is unlikely that general readers will pay much attention to those notes and these requirements could be pruned fairly rigorously, without loss of information to such readers. It may be that the officials of the Charity Commission have other concerns, but it should be remembered that the Charity Commissioners also have powers to demand information through annual returns, which are independent of the content of published reports and accounts of charities.'

It believed that the most effective way of achieving its objective is:

> 'To pay greater attention to matters of "corporate governance" – their administrative structure and regulations. Are there too few or too many trustees to provide proper control of the charity's affairs? Are they aware of their responsibilities? Do they meet sufficiently often to be effective? Do they have effective policies to implement the objectives of the charity? Are the management accounts and reports adequate to show whether the policies are being adhered to? Is there a proper system of budgetary control? Do the trustees know and control the terms under which they accept funds into their trust? Do they have frequent contact with the auditor or independent examiner? . . . . What may be needed is not so much greater disclosure of information in charity accounts but rather some "seal of approval" on those charities . . . because their administrative structure machinery seems adequate – and sufficiently transparent – to secure their reliability. This requires not so much accounting standards as standards of accountability.'

This view has a certain poignancy in the light both of the conclusions of the NCVO report *On trust: Increasing the effectiveness of charity trustees and management committees* (see chapter **2**, page 22) and of the recommendations of the Cadbury Committee on 'The financial aspects of corporate governance'.

4.2.3 Obligation

Paragraph 5 of the revised SORP states that:

'Except for small charities where trustees may elect to prepare a receipts and payment account, the main obligation of the trustees in the preparation of accounts is to give a true and fair view of the charity's financial activities during the year and of its financial position at the end of the year.'

To satisfy this obligation, additional information may be necessary to give that view. Accordingly, and similar to the 1985 Act, para 5 allows the use of the true and fair override:

> 'if a recommendation is incompatible with the obligation to give a true and fair view an alternative accounting treatment will be necessary. Particulars of any material departure . . . the reason for it and the estimated financial effect on the accounts . . . should be given in the annual report and the notes to the accounts.'

As there had been some uncertainty about the extent to which the Commissioners may have wanted to 'enforce' the SORP, their circular of 8 February 1994 outlined their view:

> ' . . . compliance with the provisions of SORP is not an end in itself, and we will not criticise any charity just because it has not followed one or more recommendations of SORP. We may, however, criticise failure to follow SORP if it leads to a distorted, misleading or unclear view of some aspect of the charity's affairs . . . the principal aim of trustees should be to present as clear and accurate a picture as possible of the charity's affairs so that the reader can easily understand what the financial position of the charity is. In general, we believe that this will best be achieved by following the recommendations of SORP and that charities should begin with a *presumption in favour of SORP*, departing from it only where this can be clearly justified in a positive way.'

The principle which holds, therefore, is that, unless the presumption in favour of the SORP can be justifiably rebutted, charity trustees of all charities, regardless of status, when preparing accounts which are required to show a true and fair view, should comply with the SORP's recommendations.

4.2.4 Application

Paragraph 6 states that:

> 'this statement is intended to apply to all charities in the United Kingdom and the Republic of Ireland regardless of their size, constitution or complexity.'

Because it is of generic application only, where a SORP exists for a particular class of charities, para 6 recommends that the trustees adhere to that SORP instead. At the time of writing, such SORPs are:

(a) for registered housing associations, *Accounting by registered housing associations,* issued in February 1994 by the National Federation of Housing Associations;
(b) for common investment funds, *Authorised unit trust schemes,* issued in April 1991 by the Investment Management Regulatory Organisation; and
(c) for Universities, *Accounting in UK universities,* issued in May 1989 by the Committee for Vice-Chancellors and Principals, revised in July 1994 and renamed *Accounting in higher education institutions.*

In presenting their annual results, further education institutions are not required to adopt the higher education SORP but are required to adopt the detailed guidance issued by the Further Education Funding Council. This guidance was issued in 1994 in booklet form and accompanied the circular 94/26 'Sector accounting policies'.

There is, also, an ED of a TR *English anglican cathedral accounts* (FRAG 29/94), issued in November 1994 and prepared by a working party of the Association of English Cathedrals. It is rather odd that it is an ED of a TR* and not of a SORP. Some light on this is shed by its Preface, which states (*inter alia*):

> 'Initially, it was envisaged that the guidance would take the form of a Statement of Recommended Practice (SORP) but the Accounting Standards Board took the view that the subject was not of wide enough application to justify the status of a SORP. As a consequence the Institute of Chartered Accountants in England and Wales agreed to promulgate the guidance, after review by the appropriate committees, in the form of a Technical Release.'

Notwithstanding its form, there appears no reason why the TR, when finally issued, rather than the revised SORP, should not be used by such cathedrals to prepare true and fair view accounts. Indeed, its proposals may have wider application, by being helpful to:

(a) other church bodies for which similar issues are relevant;
(b) those responsible for major Anglican churches which are not of cathedral status; and
(c) similar places of worship for other denominations which may wish to adopt the recommendations.

As reported in chapter **3** (see page 43), NHS charitable trusts are subject to the requirements of the 1993 Act. They must, also, follow the recommendations of the revised SORP. (Each health service body (which administers the trusts) has to complete a proforma set of accounts

* *Further, the due process procedures set by the ASB for SORPs have not been followed.*

which has been designed by the Department of Health. At the time of writing, this does not fulfil all of the revised SORP's recommendations.)

Paragraph 8 states that the revised SORP's recommendations 'should be adapted to meet any statutory requirements relating to the form and content of accounts'. Those requirements would include: the 1985 Act; the Industrial and Provident Societies Acts 1965 to 1978; and, the Registered Housing Associations (Accounting Requirements) Order 1992. Thus, it seems that were, for example, a charitable company to avail itself of the disclosure exemptions afforded by SI 1992 No 2452, any recommended disclosures (e.g., nature of assets – paragraph 208) contained in the revised SORP, which are excluded from disclosure by that statutory instrument, would not have to be provided. However, unincorporated charities still have to provide these disclosures. One possible solution to this problem would be to debar charitable companies from being classified as small and medium-sized companies.

Another example where this adaptation will be necessary is in respect of friendly societies which are exempt charities. In broad terms, there is no reason why such friendly societies should not comply with the recommendations of the revised charity SORP. The recommendations relating to, for example, consolidation will, however, not be applicable. This is because registered friendly societies, i.e., registered under the Friendly Societies Act 1974, are not permitted to have subsidiaries and no friendly society, whether registered or incorporated, can be a subsidiary of another entity. (Incorporated societies, i.e., incorporated under the Friendly Societies Act 1992, may, however, acquire subsidiaries, provided the activities are limited to those set out in Sch 7 to the Friendly Societies Act 1992.) And, compliance with the revised SORP must not compromise full compliance with the statutory requirements placed on such societies by the provisions of the Friendly Societies (Accounts and Related Provisions) Regulations 1994.

4.2.5 Structure and presentation

General

Paragraph 22 states that the accounts should comprise:

(a) a SOFA that shows all resources made available to the charity and all expenditure incurred and reconciles all changes in its funds. The SOFA should consist of a single set of accounting statements and be presented in columnar format if the charity operates more than one fund;
(b) where the charity is required to prepare accounts in accordance with the 1985 Act, or similar legislation, or where the governing

instrument so requires, a summary income and expenditure account (in addition to the SOFA) in certain circumstances;

(c) a balance sheet that shows the assets, liabilities and funds of the charity. The balance sheet (or its notes, see (**e**) below) should also explain, in general terms, how the funds may or, because of restrictions imposed by donors, must be utilised;

(d) a cash flow statement, where required by FRS 1; and

(e) notes explaining the accounting policies adopted as set out in para 35 and other notes which explain, or expand, upon, the information contained in the above accounting statements or which provide further useful information. This will include notes which show an analysis of the figures in the accounts which explain the relationships between them.

Because the SOFA, summary income and expenditure account (where required), balance sheet and cash flow statement (where required) are primary statements, they should be accorded equal prominence in the accounts.

The corresponding amounts for the previous accounting period should be given for figures disclosed in the accounts and in the notes, in accordance with generally accepted accounting practice. Headings should be omitted where there is nothing to report both for the current and preceding financial years (para 95). The duration of the current and corresponding accounting periods should also be shown. (para 23.)

This presentation is a logical extension of the recommendation in para 29 of SORP 2 which stated (*inter alia*):

> 'The accounts and notes should provide information on the charity's fund structure and on the significance of each of the major fund balances. There are a number of different ways in which this information could be presented. For example, the accounts could consist of a single set of accounting statements with columnar or note analysis. On the other hand, separate sets of statements could be produced for each major fund.'

(See chapter **10**, page 270 for the variety of examples currently provided.)

Consequently, although many charities will not have prepared such a document, the content of their existing income and expenditure account, the supporting notes and those to the balance sheet should be in sufficient detail such that the preparation of a SOFA would not be more than a matter of cosmetic restatement.

The new structure is necessary not only to provide the variety of information needed to meet the financial reporting objectives of a charity but, more importantly, to report that information in ways which are relevant, understandable and comparable. These are qualitative characteristics which are described in more detail in draft chapter 2 *Qualitative characteristics of financial statements* of the ASB's Statement of Principles. Classifying and reporting:

(a) items of revenue and expenditure and gains and losses; and
(b) net assets,

based on the existence, or absence, of donor-imposed restrictions and the nature of those restrictions improves the understandability and comparability of the information. Classifying and aggregating items with similar characteristics and separating items with differing characteristics is a reporting practice which, also, enhances the usefulness of the information.

The new structure will provide information which is useful in assessing:

(a) the services a charity provides and its ability to continue to provide those services; and
(b) how trustees discharge their stewardship responsibilities and other aspects of their performance.

The direct beneficiaries of that information are likely to be present and potential donors, members and creditors of charities, which include individuals and foundations. Indirectly, charities and society are likely to benefit from improved information that may lead to more efficient and effective decisions about how resources are allocated. While the revised SORP does not say so explicitly, the structure appears consistent with the ASB's draft chapter 1 *The objective of financial statements.*

The SOFA

In terms of presentation, the main feature, and most controversial change to existing recommendations, is the introduction of a new statement, the SOFA. This is an omnibus statement which, by including all changes to all funds, takes fund accounting to its logical conclusion. Paragraph 69 explained the reasoning behind its introduction:

> 'A traditional income and expenditure account with the distinction between revenue and capital does not always fully explain all the charity's activities whose primary purpose must be the provision of benefit to its beneficiaries rather than the corporate pursuit of gain for the benefit of shareholders. Furthermore, since charities often receive significant amounts of restricted income which can affect the types and level of service they provide, it is

important to consider changes in the amounts of all the resources of the charity. A single accounting statement is now proposed which will analyse all capital and income resources and expenditures and contain a reconciliation of all movements in the charity's funds. Such analysis will be provided by the Statement of Financial Activities, showing total movements on all funds with supporting analysis in the notes of the movements in individual funds.'

Paragraphs 69 to 96 of the revised SORP set out recommendations regarding the form and content of the SOFA. There are, broadly, parallel requirements in Pt I of the Sch to the Regulations.

The form of the SOFA is given in para 73 and reproduced below.

Thus, as well as the total movements, the SOFA shows, in columnar format, for each prescribed heading, the movements in the principal types of fund (i.e., unrestricted, restricted income and endowment). This is the minimum segregation permitted on the face of the SOFA. How-

Description	*Unrestricted funds*	*Restricted income funds*	*Endowment funds*	*Total funds*
Incoming resources before transfers and revaluations- **A**	A	A	A	A
Direct charitable expenditure- **B**	B	B	B	B
Other expenditure- **C**	C	C	C	C
Total expenditure = **B+C**	D	D	D	D
Gross transfers between funds- **E**	E	E	E	(Total = Nil)
Net incoming resources before revaluations and investment asset disposals = **A-D+E**	F	F	F	F
Gains and losses on revaluation and investment assets disposals- **G**	G	G	G	G
Net movement in funds= **F+G**	H	H	H	H
Total funds brought forward- **I**	I	I	I	I
Total funds carried forward = **H+I**	J	J	J	J

ever, there is nothing to prevent a further analysis (e.g., of unrestricted funds, between general and designated funds) where space permits. Movements in all material underlying funds should be analysed in the notes, using the headings from, and reconciling with the figures in, the SOFA (para 81).

Any incoming resource, or application of that resource, can be expanded, as appropriate, to convey the nature of the charity's activities. And, within the three separate sections of incoming resources, direct charitable expenditure and other expenditure, para 96 allows the individual sub-headings to be adapted in order to show a true and fair view of the charity's activities. This adaptation does not, however, extend to any other section of the SOFA.

Paragraph 1 of Pt I of the Sch requires the SOFA to show the total incoming resources and their application, together with any other increase or decrease in the resources during the financial year. And, para 2 requires that information to be analysed by reference to:

(a) the nature of the incoming resources or their application, or other increase or decrease in resources; and
(b) the type of fund to which it relates, in accordance with para 4 – that is, between unrestricted and restricted income funds and capital funds.

(A) Incoming resources before transfers and revaluations
Paragraphs 74 to 76 and 87 to 90 of the SORP set out the recommendations relating to incoming resources before transfers and gains on revaluation and investment asset disposals. Such resources should be summarised, in a manner appropriate to the charity, in the first section of the SOFA. The summary should enable a reader of the accounts to gain an accurate appreciation of the principal elements, but should not be excessively detailed. Where material, the following items should be shown separately:

(a) donations, legacies and similar incoming resources;
(b) grants receivable from government and other public bodies;
(c) investment income;
(d) income from the charity's trading activities; and
(e) other material incoming resources (e.g., net gains on the disposal of fixed assets for charity use).

Supporting analyses may be provided in the notes.

As regards (c), para 128 recommends that the notes to the accounts provide an analysis, similar to that recommended for investment assets (see chapter **8**, page 235), under the following headings:

(a) investment properties;
(b) investments listed on a recognised stock exchange, or ones valued by reference to such investments, such as unit trusts and common investment funds;
(c) investments in subsidiary or associated companies, or in companies which are connected persons;
(d) other unlisted securities;
(e) cash held as part of the investment portfolio; and
(f) any other investments,

together with a further analysis, for each category, of income from investment assets in and outside the UK.

Paragraph 75 of the SORP recommends that the notes analyse endowment fund incoming resources between permanent endowment and expendable endowment. (Note: Para 3 of Appendix 2 states that capital which the trustees have no power to convert into income and apply it as such is permanent endowment, and expendable endowment is capital where the trustees do have that power.)

Paragraphs 121 to 127 deal with the trading activities of a charity. Paragraph 121 identifies those trading activities, covered by s505 of ICTA 1988, the profits of which do not attract income or corporation tax and which a charity may carry out without recourse to setting up a trading subsidiary.

Paragraph 122 covers those permitted occasional trading activities, e.g., jumble sales, gymkhanas etc., covered by Extra-statutory Concession C4. Unless the amounts are 'substantial', the revised SORP recommends that the income from such activities is, 'for the sake of clarity', shown net in the SOFA.

Paragraph 126 covers non-charitable trading, usually put through a subsidiary. The parent charity's accounts will separately recognise and suitably describe all payments (whether by gift aid, covenant etc.) made to it, by that subsidiary, while the subsidiary will account for, and disclose, the results of that trading in accordance with generally accepted accounting principles.

Paragraph 124 recommends that where trading activities of any kind are conducted by, or on behalf of, a charity, the gross, or net, income from each type of trading should be separately shown in the SOFA under the heading 'Trading activities'. Where only the net income is shown, the full trading results should be exploded in the notes. Where a summary income and expenditure account is prepared, the gross income must be shown on the face of the SOFA. Example 3 in Appendix 4 gives that information in a footnote.

(Note: The sale of donated goods is not regarded as a trade. Accordingly, it should not be included under 'Trading activities', but with other voluntary income (para 123)).

Other than incoming resources arising from transfers, gains on revaluation and investment asset disposals, para 3(a) of Pt I requires incoming resources to be divided into:

(a) incoming resources from donors;
(b) income from investment;
(c) income from trading activities:
  (i) which are in furtherance of the charity's objects; and
  (ii) which are for commercial or fund-raising purposes; and
(d) any other material incoming resources.

(B) Charitable and other expenditure
Paragraphs 77 and 91 to 93 of the SORP set out recommendations relating to expenditure. The second section of the SOFA should provide a summary of the main classes of charitable and other expenditure, other than transfers and losses on revaluation and disposal of investment assets, again in a manner appropriate to the charity.

As regards direct charitable expenditure, it may be necessary to disclose separately:

(a) grants payable;
(b) other direct expenditure on charitable objectives, analysed as appropriate;
(c) depreciation or amortisation and losses on disposal of fixed assets used by the charity for its charitable purposes; and
(d) support costs.

For other expenditure, separate amounts should be given for:

(a) fundraising and publicity costs;
(b) administration costs; and
(c) other expenditure,

where those costs do not form part of the direct charitable expenditure.

Paragraph 3(b) of Pt I requires resources expended to be divided into:

(a) expenditure directly relating to the charity's objects;
(b) expenditure in support of charitable activity;
(c) expenditure on fundraising and publicity;
(d) expenditure on the administration of the charity; and
(e) any other expenditure.

Information about costs is, therefore, to be reported by their functional classification, although para 136 of the revised SORP suggests that the natural classification may be given in the notes. (See chapter **7**, page 197 for a further discussion.)

(C) Transfers

All transfers, which should be shown gross, between the principal types of fund should be the next heading (para 78(i) of the SORP and para 3(c) of Pt I of the Sch). Explanations supporting the transfers should be given in the notes.

A sub-total should then be struck for net incoming resources for the financial year (para 3(d) of Pt I of the Sch).

(D) Gains and losses on revaluation and investment asset disposals

Gains and losses on revaluation of all assets and investment asset disposals should come next. Paragraph 78(ii) of the SORP recommends, and para 3(e) of Pt I requires, that gains and losses on revaluation should be analysed between those relating to assets held for charity use and those held for investment purposes. The net gain, or loss, on disposal of investment assets should be separately stated (see, also, para 132).

(E) Net movement in funds

The net incoming resources for the financial year, together with the total of any gains or losses on disposal of revaluation of fixed assets, will produce the net movement in funds for that year (para 79 of the SORP and para 3(f) of Pt I). This net movement should, then, be reconciled to the total funds, as shown in the balance sheet, as follows:

(a) net movement in funds for the year;
(b) total funds brought forward;
(c) total funds carried forward.

(Paragraph 83 of the SORP and para 3(g) and (h) of Pt I.)

As recommended in para 43, this reconciliation should be an integral part of the SOFA.

(F) Material changes in resources applied for fixed assets
Where there has been a material change in the year in the total resources applied for fixed assets for the charity's use, para 86 recommends that the resource implications are explained in a note to the accounts. This note should immediately follow the reconciliation of funds where the change is very large (not defined, but presumably, where the change is so material) in relation to total income or expenditure. The note would take the following form:

(a) the net movement in funds for the year;
(b) the resources used for net acquisitions (or made available from net disposals) of fixed assets for charity use, distinguishing, if material, between assets for charity use for its direct charitable purposes and those for other purposes); and
(c) net movements in funds available for future activities.

(G) What has happened in practice?
Based on the proposals in the ED, Example 4.1 Save The Children Fund, Example 4.2 British Epilepsy Association and Example 4.3 OXFAM, as charitable companies, and Example 4.4 BLESMA (an unincorporated charity) changed the format of their 1993/94 accounts to include a consolidated SOFA, *incorporating* (rather than separately preparing) a consolidated income and expenditure account. Although the proposals in an ED might be held to represent 'best practice', they are issued for comment and may be subject to revision.

The Foreword to Accounting Standards offers some guidance in circumstances where the proposals of a FRED are adopted early. While, perhaps, not entirely appropriate to the early adoption of proposals in an ED of a SORP, the guidance might be regarded as persuasive. Paragraph 32 states that:

> 'Some companies or other reporting entities may wish to provide additional information reflecting proposals in an exposure draft. In the Board's view there are two ways that this can be achieved:
> (a) insofar as the information does not conflict with existing accounting standards, it could be incorporated in the financial statements. It should be remembered, however, that the proposals may change before forming part of an accounting standard and the consequences of a change to the proposals should be considered.
> (b) the information could be provided in supplementary form.'

Although the information is not offered voluntarily it is possible, using

Example 4.1 Save The Children Fund
Consolidated statement of financial activities
(incorporating a consolidated income and expenditure account)
(31 March 1994):

	Notes	Unrestricted funds £'000	Designated funds £'000	Restricted funds £'000	**Totals 31 March 1994 £'000**	*Total 31 March 1993 £'000*
Resources arising						
Voluntary fundraising		26,694	–	8,567	**35,261**	*48,051*
Net profit on trading	1	443	–	–	**443**	*478*
		27,137	–	8,567	**35,704**	*48,529*
Gifts in kind	12	2,906	–	4,344	**7,250**	*19,537*
Grants received	2	–	–	42,328	**42,328**	*42,186*
Investment income	4	1,253	–	399	**1,652**	*2,593*
Gross resources arising in year		31,296	–	55,638	**86,934**	*112,845*
Resources used						
Direct charitable expenditure						
UK and overseas programmes	12	(23,576)	–	(60,702)	**(84,278)**	*(97,816)*
Movement on childcare properties		795	(795)	–	–	–
Project support costs		(5,522)	–	See note 3	**(5,522)**	*(4,773)*
Information and Education		(1,828)	–	See note 3	**(1,828)**	*(1,400)*
		(30,131)	(795)	(60,702)	**(91,628)**	*(103,989)*
Other expenditure						
Fundraising and Publicity		(7,768)	–	See note 3	**(7,768)**	*(7,525)*
Administration		(1,721)	–	See note 3	**(1,721)**	*(1,721)*
Provision for diminution in value		–		–		
of freehold property	5	–	(1,125)	–	**(1,125)**	–
		(9,489)	(1,125)	–	**(10,614)**	*(9,246)*

Example 4.1 Save The Children Fund Consolidated statement of financial activities (incorporating a consolidated income and expenditure account) (31 March 1994): (Continued)

	Notes	Unrestricted funds £'000	Designated funds £'000	Restricted funds £'000	**Totals 31 March 1994 £'000**	*Total 31 March 1993 £'000*
Resources used in the year	3,4	(39,620)	(1,920)	(60,702)	**(102,242)**	*(113,235)*
Transfers						
Transfer from property fund		387	(387)	–	–	–
Transfer from base reserve		4,009	(4,009)	–	–	–
		4,396	(4,396)	–	–	–
Changes in resources (deficit) for the year before valuations		(3,928)	(6,316)	(5,064)	**(15,308)**	*(390)*

Statement of investment gains and movement on total funds:

	Unrestricted funds £'000	Designated funds £'000	Restricted funds £'000	**Totals 31 March 1994 £'000**	*Total 31 March 1993 £'000*
Balance at 1 April 1993	14,414	26,705	18,344	**59,463**	*56,099*
Changes in resources before valuations	(3,928)	(6,316)	(5,064)	**(15,308)**	*(390)*
Net investment gains/(losses)					
–realised	3,648	–	–	**3,648**	*523*
–unrealised	(200)	–	–	**(200)**	*3,231*
Net movement of resources in the year	(480)	(6,316)	(5,064)	**(11,860)**	*3,364*
Balance carried forward 31 March 1994	13,934	20,389	13,280	**47,603**	*59,463*

Example 4.1 Save The Children Fund
Statement of investment gains and movement on total funds (31 March 1994):

	Unrestricted funds £'000	Designated funds £'000	Restricted funds £'000	**Totals 31 March 1994 £'000**	*Total 31 March 1993 £'000*
Represented by					
Tangible Fixed Assets	3,031	8,323	–	**11,354**	*14,230*
Fixed Asset Investments	11,307	12,066	–	**23,373**	*24,627*
Current Assets	12,194	–	13,280	**25,474**	*32,576*
Current Liabilities	(10,320)	–	–	**(10,320)**	*(10,317)*
Provisions for Liabilities and Charges	(2,278)	–	–	**(2,278)**	*(1,653)*
	13,934	20,389	13,280	**47,603**	*59,463*

Example 4.2 British Epilepsy Association
Statement of financial activities (31 December 1993):

	Notes	Unrestricted Funds £	Restricted Funds £	**Total 1993 £**	*Total 1992 £*
Resources arising					
Donations & fundraising	3	670,916	35,293	**706,209**	*567,066*
Legacies received		248,232	10,559	**258,791**	*234,627*
Branch income		128,958	4,713	**133,671**	*44,391*
Interest		1,133	4,027	**5,160**	*12,956*
Rental income		870	–	**870**	*10,220*
Other income		9,400	–	**9,400**	–
Gross resources arising		1,059,509	54,592	**1,114,101**	*869,260*
Resources used					
Direct charitable expenditure					
Information and training	4.1	305,780	9,182	**314,962**	*394,609*
Development	4.2	196,156	3,778	**199,934**	*205,516*
Branch expenditure		49,668	5,000	**54,668**	–
Support costs	4.3	104,675	1,460	**106,135**	*120,748*
Publicity costs		35,935	–	**35,935**	*41,893*
		(692,214)	(19,420)	**(711,634)**	*(762,766)*
Other expenditure					
Fundraising costs		145,500	2,223	**147,723**	*166,505*
Administration costs		111,359	105	**111,464**	*39,193*
Financial charges		83,514	–	**83,514**	*70,223*
		(340,373)	(2,328)	**(342,701)**	*(275,921)*

Example 4.2 British Epilepsy Association
Statement of financial activities (31 December 1993): (Continued)

	Notes	Unrestricted Funds £	Restricted Funds £	**Total 1993 £**	*Total 1992 £*
Resources used in the year		(1,032,587)	(21,748)	**(1,054,335)**	*(1,038,687)*
Changes in resources before transfers and valuations		26,922	32,844	**59,766**	*(169,427)*
Support costs transfer		4,497	(4,497)	–	–
Net movement of resources in the year		31,419	28,347	**59,766**	*(169,427)*

There are no recognised gains and losses other than those passing through the Statement of Financial Activities.

Reconciliation of Funds for the year ended 31 December 1993

	Unrestricted Funds £	Restricted Funds £	**Total 1993 £**	*Total 1992 £*
Balance brought forward at 1 January 1993	457,394	100,155	**557,549**	*1,134,290*
Net movement of resources for the year	31,419	28,347	**59,766**	*(169,427)*
Property revaluations	–	–	–	*(57,314)*
Fixed asset investment written off	–	–	–	*(350,000)*
Balance carried forward at 31 December 1993	488,813	128,502	**617,315**	*557,549*

Included in Unrestricted Funds are monies received towards designated activities of the Association. These include the Epilepsy Helpline, EPDATA, the Epilepsy Liaison project, the National Information Centre and contributions towards the cost of literature publication.

Example 4.3 OXFAM
Consolidated statement of financial activities (30 April 1994):

	Notes	Unrestricted Funds **£'000**	Restricted Funds **£'000**	Endowment Funds **£'000**	Totals 1994 **£'000**	*Totals 1993 £'000*
Incoming Resources						
Donations	3(a)	28,911	2,517	1,132	32,560	*32,117*
Oxfam Shops (net of expenses)	3(b)	13,686	624		14,310	*15,053*
Grants from UK Govt. EU & UN	3(c)	5,945	18,015		23,960	*14,419*
Grants from other Agencies		345	1,532		1,877	*3,167*
Gifts in Kind	3(d)	973	9,907		10,880	*10,393*
Miscellaneous income	3(e)	1,141	0		1,141	*1,696*
		51,001	32,595	1,132	84,728	*76,845*
Net income from trading subsidiary	3(f)	2,070	0	0	2,070	2,208
Total incoming resources		53,071	32,595	1,132	86,798	*79,053*
Resources Expended						
Direct Charitable expenditure						
Grants to Partners	4(a)	23,115	3,706		26,821	*28,386*
Operational Programmes	4(b)	4,896	18,511		23,407	*14,956*
Gifts in Kind	4(b)	973	9,907		10,880	*10,393*
Programme Development & Support	4(c)	12,626	0		12,626	*10,948*
Information, Campaigning & Education	4(d)	4,856	105		4,961	*4,413*
		46,466	32,229	0	78,695	*69,096*
Other expenditure						
Fundraising	2(g)	5,770	149		5,919	*6,373*
Administration	2(g)	1,612	0		1,612	*2,143*
Irrecoverable VAT		363	0		363	*287*
		7,745	149	0	7,894	*8,803*

Example 4.3 OXFAM
Consolidated statement of financial activities (30 April 1994): (Continued)

	Notes	Unrestricted Funds **£'000**	Restricted Funds **£'000**	Endowment Funds **£'000**	Totals 1994 **£'000**	*Totals 1993 £'000*
Total expenditure		54,211	32,378	0	86,589	*77,899*
Transfers between funds	19	(55)	0	55	0	*0*
Surplus/(deficit) of incoming resources for the year	10	(1,195)	217	1,187	209	*1,154*

Statement of total recognised gains and losses:

	Notes	1994 £'000	*1993 as restated £'000*
Surplus/(deficit) as above		209	*1,154*
Prior year adjustment	1	9,242	–
Total gains & losses recognised since last annual report		9,451	*1,154*

Reconciliation of movement on funds:

	Unrestricted Funds **£'000**	Restricted Funds **£'000**	Endowment Funds **£'000**	Totals 1994 **£'000**	*Totals 1993* **£'000**
Funds balances at 30 April 1993	31,541	5,837	357	37,735	*36,581*
Surplus/(deficit) of incoming resources for the year	(1,195)	217	1,187	209	*1,154*
Funds balances at 30 April 1994	30,346	6,054	1,544	37,944	*37,735*

Example 4.3 OXFAM
Reconciliation of movement on funds (30 April 1994): (Continued)

	Notes	Unrestricted Funds **£'000**	Restricted Funds **£'000**	Endowment Funds **£'000**	Totals 1994 **£'000**	*Totals 1993 £'000*
Fund Balances at 30 April 1994 represented by:						
Tangible fixed assets		14,007		1,364	15,371	*16,439*
Investment assets		1,927		180	2,107	*1,960*
Current assets		28,962	6,054		35,016	*34,941*
Current liabilities		(13,901)			(13,901)	*(15,419)*
Long–term liabilities		(649)			(649)	(186)
Total Net Assets at 30 April 1994		30,346	6,054	1,544	37,944	*37,735*
Fund Balances at 30 April 1994 being:						
Endowment Fund				1,544	1,544	*357*
Restricted Fund			6,054		6,054	*5,837*
Programme Guarantee Fund	6(a)	7,197			7,197	*7,926*
Relief & Overseas Aid Fund		3,844			3,844	*3,844*
Capital Fund	6(b)	14,825			14,825	*17,266*
Designated Funds	6(c)	4,480			4,480	*2,505*
		30,346	6,054	1,544	37,944	*37,735*

Example 4.4 BLESMA
Consolidated statement of financial activities
(incorporating an income and expenditure account) (31 December 1993):

	Notes	£	1993 £	*1992 £*
Resources arising				
Appeal income				
General			**233,143**	*267,055*
Legacies			**662,204**	*966,560*
Donations for capital projects			–	*39,000*
			895,347	*1,272,615*
Less amounts received on behalf of branches			**9,207**	*14,182*
			886,140	*1,258,433*
Grants	3		**62,783**	*73,971*
Branch contributions			**8,729**	*29,047*
Total voluntary contributions			**957,652**	*1,361,451*
Residential homes			**724,023**	*662,686*
Investment income (including £1,565 *1992 £1,881* for the Special Hardship Fund)			**569,564**	*479,458*
Other income			**27,281**	*27,072*
Gross resources arising in the year			**2,278,520**	*2,530,667*

Example 4.4 BLESMA
Consolidated statement of financial activities
(incorporating an income and expenditure account) (31 December 1993): (Continued)

	Notes		**1993**	*1992*
		£	**£**	*£*
Resources used				
Direct charitable expenditure				
Residential homes		**1,100,987**		*1,009,999*
Welfare (including *£4,260 1992 Nil* from the Special Hardship Fund)		**284,627**		*242,084*
Rehabilitation		**14,694**		*8,832*
Research		**67,000**		*21,230*
Support costs	4	**112,105**		*141,108*
		1,579,413		*1,423,253*
Other Expenditure				
Fund raising	5	**65,939**		*61,818*
Administration	6	**164,622**		*159,794*
Finance and general expenses	7	**82,233**		*73,485*
Resources used in the year			**1,892,207**	*1,718,350*
SURPLUS ON OPERATIONS			**386,313**	*812,317*
Net investment gains	9		**2,043,977**	*872,299*
TOTAL GAINS AND LOSSES RECOGNISED IN THE YEAR			**2,430,290**	*1,684,616*

Example 4.4 BLESMA
Consolidated statement of financial activities
(incorporating an income and expenditure account) (31 December 1993): (Continued)

Summary of movement of funds:

	General Fund £	Legacy Fund £	Special Hardship Fund £	Capital Fund £	**Totals 1993 £**	*Totals 1992 £*
Resources arising	1,614,751	662,204	1,565	–	**2,278,520**	*2,530,667*
Resources used	1,887,947	–	4,260	–	**1,892,207**	*1,718,350*
SURPLUS/(DEFICIT) ON OPERATIONS	(273,196)	662,204	(2,695)	–	**386,313**	*812,317*
Transfers:						
General fund deficit from legacy fund	273,196	(273,196)	–	–	–	–
Capital fund net fixed asset purchases	(109,938)	–	–	109,938	–	–
Capital fund annual depreciation	93,946	–	–	(93,946)	–	–
	(15,992)	389,008	(2,695)	15,992	**386,313**	*812,317*
Net investment gains	1,349,516	694,461	–	–	**2,043,977**	*872,299*

Example 4.4 BLESMA
Consolidated statement of financial activities
(incorporating an income and expenditure account) (31 December 1993): (Continued)

Summary of movement of funds: (Continued)

	General Fund £	Legacy Fund £	Special Hardship Fund £	Capital Fund £	**Totals 1993 £**	*Totals 1992 £*
TOTAL GAINS AND LOSSES RECOGNISED IN THE YEAR	1,333,524	1,083,469	(2,695)	15,992	**2,430,290**	*1,684,616*
Balances brought forward 1 January 1993	5,218,803	3,919,509	28,726	2,100,407	**11,267,445**	*9,582,829*
BALANCES CARRIED FORWARD 31 DECEMBER 1993	6,552,327	5,002,978	26,031	2,116,399	**13,697,735**	*11,267,445*

Note 1: Accounting policies [part]:

(a) Basis of Accounting

(i) The financial statements of the Association have been prepared using the historical cost convention, except that investments are shown at market value. They are drawn up to reflect the proposed statement of recommended practice number 2 (SORP 2–accounting by charities) and in accordance with other applicable accounting standards.

the information in the 1992 and 1993 accounts of, for example, Save the Children Fund and BLESMA, to construct consolidated income and expenditure accounts for 1993 and calculate what the equivalent surplus (or deficit) would have been. On balance, however, it may have been better, in this circumstance, for both charities to have followed option (b) and prepared a consolidated income and expenditure account, as a primary statement, so as to comply with company and charity law and relevant FRSs, and provided the consolidated SOFA either within the notes or in supplementary form.

As there are no subsidiaries, it is not clear why Example 4.4 BLESMA's SOFA should be described as 'consolidated'.

Since the ED's issue, two other charities which have altered the format of the income and expenditure account, without labelling it a SOFA, are Example 4.5 British Red Cross Society and Example 4.6 Mary Rose Trust. Unlike the other examples, Example 4.6 Mary Rose Trust does not provide a note explaining the change in format. It does, however, analyse its comparative figures on the face of that account across the various funds.

Example 4.5 British Red Cross Society
Income and expenditure account (31 December 1993):

	Notes	General £000	Designated £000	Restricted £000	**Total 1993 £000**	*Total 1992 £000*
Income						
Grants Receivable	3	232	–	12,789	**13,021**	*12,180*
Voluntary Donations		3,151	333	8,129	**11,613**	*11,076*
Legacies Received		5,134	–	–	**5,134**	*4,626*
Supply & Trading Activities		1,846	–	–	**1,846**	*1,333*
Contributions from Branches towards International & Overseas work		913	–	–	**913**	*826*
Investment Income & Interest		421	259	318	**998**	*1,550*
Miscellaneous Income & Rents		957	–	–	**957**	*933*
	5	12,654	592	21,236	**34,482**	*32,524*
Expenditure						
International Disaster Relief & Red Cross Development	4	487	–	17,962	**18,449**	*20,086*
Contributions to International Federation of Red Cross & Red Crescent Societies & International Committee of the Red Cross		590	–	–	**590**	*478*
International Services		1,025	455	–	**1,480**	*754*
UK Operations & Services	4	2,470	888	–	**3,358**	*3,027*
Marketing & Communications		1,723	–	–	**1,723**	*1,354*
Fundraising		1,797	181	1,263	**3,241**	*1,617*
Administrative & Advisory Costs (including irrecoverable VAT)		1,745	8	474	**2,227**	*1,515*
Financial & Central Office Costs		1,044	–	–	**1,044**	*879*

Example 4.5 British Red Cross Society
Income and expenditure account (31 December 1993): (Continued)

	Notes	General £000	Designated £000	Restricted £000	**Total 1993 £000**	*Total 1992 £000*
Supply & Trading Activities		1,768	–	–	**1,768**	*1,141*
	5	12,649	1,532	19,699	**33,880**	*30,851*
Surplus/(Deficit)	2	**5**	**(940)**	**1,537**	**602**	*1,673*

Statement of investment gains & movement of funds:

	Notes	General £000	Designated £000	Restricted £000	**Total 1993 £000**	*Total 1992 £000*
Opening Balance – 1st January		6,363	5,084	8,052	**19,499**	*17,529*
Surplus/(Deficit)		5	(940)	1,537	**602**	*1,673*
Net investment gains – realised	7	1,322	2	–	**1,324**	*297*
Net investment gains – unrealised	7	932	84	–	**1,016**	–
		8,622	4,230	9,589	**22,441**	*19,499*
Transfers	5	(706)	706	–	–	–
Closing Balance – 31st December		7,916	4,936	9,589	**22,441**	*19,499*

Example 4.5 British Red Cross Society
Balance Sheet (31 December 1993):

	Notes	1993 Unrestricted £000	1993 Restricted £000	*1992 Unrestricted £000*	*1992 Restricted £000*
Fixed Assets					
Tangible Assets	6	1,790	–	*1,593*	–
Investments	7	7,635	–	*5,424*	–
		9,425	–	*7,017*	–
Current Assets					
Stocks		559	–	*561*	–
Debtors, Payments in Advance & Accrued Income	8	2,365	840	*1,574*	*853*
Loans & Advances to Branches	9	2,031	–	*1,608*	–
Donated Assets		–	–	–	*92*
Money at Short Notice		766	6,085	*1,515*	*5,998*
Cash at Bank & in Hand		258	2,814	*1,153*	*1,466*
		5,979	9,739	*6,411*	*8,409*
Creditors:					
Amounts falling due within one year	10	(2,469)	(150)	*(1,981)*	*(357)*
Net Current Assets		3,510	9,589	*4,430*	*8,052*
Creditors:					
Amounts falling due in more than one year	11	(83)	–	–	–
		12,852	9,589	*11,447*	*8,052*
Represented by:					
Accumulated General Reserve & Designated Funds		–	–	*11,447*	–
Unrealised Investments Gains		1,016	–	–	–
Other		11,836	–	–	–
Funds held for Restricted Purposes		–	9,589	–	*8,052*
	5	12,852	9,589	*11,447*	*8,052*

Example 4.5 British Red Cross Society
Cash flow statement (31 December 1993):

	Notes	**1993** Unrestricted £000	**1993** Restricted £000	*1992* *Unrestricted* *£000*	*1992* *Restricted* *£000*
Net cash (outflow)/inflow from operations	15	(954)	1,435	*339*	*1,025*
Returns on investment & servicing of finance					
Interest element of Finance Lease		(3)	–	–	–
Investing activities					
Purchase of tangible fixed assets		(385)	–	*(512)*	–
Sale of tangible fixed assets		4	–	*12*	–
Purchase of fixed asset investments		(8,441)	–	*(4,793)*	–
Sale of fixed asset investments		8,570	–	*4,197*	–
Loans to Branches		(741)	–	*(788)*	–
Loan repayments from Branches		318	–	*130*	–
Net cash outflow from investing activities		(675)	–	*(1,754)*	–
Financing					
Capital element of finance lease rentals	17	(12)	–	–	–
(Decrease)/Increase in cash & Short–term Deposits	16	(1,644)	1,435	*(1,415)*	*1,025*

Example 4.6 Mary Rose Trust
Income and expenditure account (31 December 1993):

	Note	1993 Total	1993 Unrestricted Funds	1993 Restricted Funds	*1992 Total*	*1992 Unrestricted Funds*	*1992 Restricted Funds*
Income		£	£	£	*£*	*£*	*£*
Visitor Related		808,661	808,661	–	*815,837*	*815,837*	–
Mary Rose Trading Limited Covenant		90,913	90,913	–	*67,055*	*67,055*	–
Fund raising							
– Permanent building scheme		–	–	–	*65,000*	*65,000*	–
– Visitor Gallery/conservation		346,876	146,876	200,000	–	–	–
– Other		26,864	26,864	–	*82,111*	*70,348*	*11,763*
Miscellaneous		37,156	37,156	–	*68,354*	*68,354*	–
		1,310,470	1,110,470	200,000	*1,098,357*	*1,086,594*	*11,763*
Expenditure							
Direct							
Site Management		419,325	419,325	–	*368,956*	*368,956*	–
Archaeology & conservation		495,988	495,988	–	*491,770*	*491,770*	–
Publicity & promotion		123,990	123,990	–	*164,365*	*164,365*	–
Support costs		78,788	78,788	–	*61,873*	*61,873*	–
		1,118,091	1,118,091	–	*1,086,964*	*1,086,964*	–
Other							
Fund Raising		37,722	37,722	–	*12,356*	*12,356*	–
Administration		157,218	157,218	–	*174,473*	*174,473*	–
		194,940	194,940	–	*186,829*	*186,829*	–
Non recurring							
– Permanent building scheme		40,636	40,636	–	*181,914*	*181,914*	–
– Fund raising consultancy		52,904	52,904	–	*77,567*	*77,567*	–
		93,540	93,540	–	*259,481*	*259,481*	–

Example 4.6 Mary Rose Trust
Income and expenditure account (31 December 1993): (Continued)

	Note	1993 Total	1993 Unrestricted Funds	1993 Restricted Funds	*1992 Total*	*1992 Unrestricted Funds*	*1992 Restricted Funds*
		£	£	£	£	£	£
Total expenditure		1,406,571	1,406,571	–	*1,533,274*	*1,533,274*	–
Operating Deficit	1	(96,101)	(296,101)	200,000	*(434,917)*	*(446,680)*	*11,763*
Interest receivable							
From subsidiary undertaking		4,800	4,800	–	*7,196*	*7,196*	–
Other		4,550	4,550	–	*33,007*	*33,077*	–
		9,350	9,350	–	*40,203*	*40,203*	–
Deficit of income over expenditure		(86,751)	(286,751)	–	*(394,714)*	*(406,477)*	*11,763*
Transfer	10	–	178,342	(178,342)	–	–	–
Interest attributable to designated reserves	11	(3,584)	(3,584)	–	*(28,936)*	*(28,936)*	–
Transfer from designated reserves	11	79,753	79,753	–	*234,901*	*234,901*	–
		76,169	254,511	(178,342)	*205,965*	*205,965*	–
Transfer to reserves		10,582	(32,240)	21,658	*(188,749)*	*(200,512)*	*11,763*
Balance at 1 January 1993		250,682	226,851	23,831	*439,431*	*427,363*	*12,068*
Balance at 31 December 1993		240,100	194,611	45,489	*250,682*	*226,851*	*23,831*

There are no recognised gains or losses in the year other than the profit above. The accompanying accounting policies and notes form an integral part of these financial statements.

Summary income and expenditure account

The summary income and expenditure account is a new requirement. The ED simply replaced that account with the SOFA. By recommending the inclusion of all movements on all funds, including endowments, the SOFA's content went beyond the boundaries of the law to which many charities are subject, in terms of the requirement to prepare an income and expenditure account. Where there are movements on endowment funds either for the financial year or the preceding year, a summary income and expenditure account must be prepared, in addition to the SOFA, by those charities preparing accounts under the 1985 Act, or similar legislation, or where required by the charity's governing instrument.

The form and content of the summary income and expenditure account (which is derived from, and should be cross-referenced to, the SOFA) is dealt with in para 168. That account does not need to distinguish between movements on unrestricted and restricted income funds, but should show separately in respect of continuing operations, acquisitions and discontinued operations:

(a) gross income from all sources, excluding non-charitable trading activities, inter-fund transfers and revaluations of fixed assets;
(b) income from non-charitable trading activities (note: if a net figure is shown, turnover and expenses should be given as an inset);
(c) net gains on disposal of fixed assets belonging to the charity's income funds;
(d) total income, i.e., the sum of (a) to (c) above;
(e) expenditure out of the charity's income funds;
(f) net losses on disposal of fixed assets belonging to the charity's income funds;
(g) total expenditure, i.e., the sum of (e) and (f);
(h) net income, or expenditure, before transfers and disposal of investment assets, i.e., (d) less (g);
(i) net income, or expenditure, before any gain/loss on disposal of investment assets;
(j) gain/loss on disposal of investment assets; and
(k) net income, or expenditure, for the financial year.

Thus, the difference between the content of the summary income and expenditure account and the SOFA would be the *exclusion* of:

(a) all movements relating to capital funds;
(b) unrealised gains and losses on revaluation of assets held in income funds; and
(c) transfers between income funds.

As the SOFA would incorporate the statement of total recognised gains and losses, that statement would not, also, be required to be prepared, but a footnote to that effect should be given. A suitable footnote might be: 'The Statement of Financial Activities incorporates the Statement of Total Recognised Gains and Losses required by FRS 3'.

Where a charity has no movements on endowment funds, neither in the financial year nor in the preceding year, a summary income and expenditure account may be omitted, provided the SOFA is appropriately sectionalised and titled (para 84). In order to comply both with the law and FRS 3, the SOFA should show the unrealised gains and losses on revaluation in a separate section, after a figure struck for net income/expenditure for the year. The SOFA would, accordingly, comprise two parts: an account of income and expenditure; and, a statement of total recognised gains and losses. This latter statement would take the following form:

(a) net income, or expenditure, for the financial year;
(b) net unrealised gains, or losses, on revaluation;
(c) net movement of funds for the financial year;
(d) total funds brought forward; and
(e) total funds carried forward.

Based on its 1994 accounts, Example 4.1 Save The Children Fund will, unlike Example 4.3 OXFAM, not have to prepare a summary income and expenditure account, but will have to reposition net realised gains on investments and retitle some of its headings. Example 4.4 BLESMA will not need to prepare an income and expenditure account, unless required to do so by its governing instrument.

Balance sheet

Paragraphs 171 to 173 state that: 'The assets of a charity should be analysed . . . between fixed assets (including investments and investment properties) and current assets. Liabilities should be analysed between their current and long-term elements. In addition, the assets and liabilities should be analysed in a way that enables the reader to gain a proper appreciation of their spread and character' (See chapters **8**, **9** and **11** for further discussion).

With one exception, these paragraphs retains SORP 2's recommendations. Because they are generally held with the overall intention of retaining them for the continuing benefit of the charity, investments (including investment properties) held for long-term purposes should be classified as a separate category within fixed assets rather than being shown separately on the face of the balance sheet. This presentation is now consistent with that in the balance sheet formats in the 1985 Act.

Paragraph 36(a) of the revised SORP requires that 'the assets and liabilities representing the various funds of the charity should be clearly analysed between the various funds'. Although this aspect of disclosure is more fully discussed in chapter **10** (see page 275), Example 4.5 British Red Cross Society provides this analysis on the face of the balance sheet.

Cash flow statement

Paragraph 210 of the revised SORP recommends that a cash flow statement be prepared for all 'large charities', complying with FRS 1. Unlike the SOFA and reconciliation of funds, there is no recommendation for the cash flow statement to be presented in columnar format, showing the movements in the different types of funds. This creates an asymmetric presentation.

Nonetheless, Example 4.5 British Red Cross Society presents its cash flow statement in this way. (See chapter **12**, page 314 for a further discussion on cash flow statements.)

Chapter 5 – Trustees' annual report

5.1 Introduction

Like directors' reports of commercial organisations, the trustees' annual report forms the main narrative section of the accounts. Unlike commercial organisations, however, many features of a charity's operations, particularly those in respect of voluntary help, donations-in-kind and other intangible income, can be difficult to measure in financial terms. Accordingly, both in terms of accountability and in order to complement the remainder of the accounts, the trustees' annual report should measure the achievement of the charity's objectives not only in quantitative, but also in qualitative, terms, as imaginatively and openly as possible.

The report's completeness and transparency are, thus, prerequisites if the charity's operations and accounts are to be properly understood and appreciated.

5.2 Preparing the trustees' annual report

The charity trustees of all charities, including small charities (para 14, revised SORP), must prepare an annual report. A key change from the recommendation of SORP 2 is that the trustees should prepare the annual report as a separate document (para 26(a)).

Where required, or requested to, charitable companies must send the annual report to the Commissioners, together with annual accounts prepared under the 1985 Act and an auditors' report, or one made for the purposes of s249A(2) of that Act. The directors' report, as prepared under s234 of that Act, will not simply suffice as the trustees' annual report. To be valid as a trustees' annual report, and to avoid the preparation of two separate documents, the directors' report could be expanded to incorporate the additional information recommended by the revised charity SORP and required by reg 10.

The DTI is to issue a consultation document which will propose (*inter alia*) an amendment to the provisions of the 1985 Act such that the trustees' annual report will be able to stand in place of the directors' report. This will be subject to the former including any disclosures from the directors' report that the DTI decides, after that consultation, should be included. In that way, the DTI will disapply any non-essential disclosures.

In the interim, it would seem that the report should be appropriately titled, e.g., 'Trustees' annual report for the purposes of section 45 of the Charities Act 1993 and directors' report for the purposes of section 234 of the Companies Act 1985'.

Paragraph 26(a) of the revised charity SORP recommends that whenever a full set of accounts is distributed, the trustees' annual report is attached.

5.3 Structure and components

Although retaining the structure and principal components recommended by its forerunner, the revised SORP substantially extends the disclosures (given in paras 27–29), which are much more technical than previously. Where there is nothing to report under a particular heading, as may be the case with small charities, those headings may be omitted. Nonetheless, the trustees should include any additional information which is required to be provided by law (for example, see **5.3.4** below for charitable companies).

Paragraph 26 recommends that the trustees confirm that the accounts comply with current statutory requirements and with those of the charity's governing instrument.

5.3.1 Legal and administrative information

Paragraph 19(a) of SORP 2 recommended that legal and administrative details, providing background information on the charity's constitution, be given. Other than those indicating the nature of the governing instrument or legal status (see chapter **1**, page 3), para 21 recommended that such details should include:

'(a) . . . If applicable, the charity registration number and the company registration number . . . ;
(b) the names of the trustees and their nominating body (or other method of appointment or election), the names of the members of any management committee and the names of the principal officers of the charity;
(c) the principal or registered address of the charity;
(d) the names and addresses of any other relevant organisations or persons. This may include the names and addresses of those acting as bankers, solicitors, auditors, and investment or other advisers;
(e) details of any restrictions in the way in which the charity can operate. This should include details of any limitations in the trustees' powers of

investment including, for example, any restrictions imposed by the Trustee Investments Act 1961'.

Example 5.1 Tear Fund provides an example.

Example 5.1. Tear Fund
Legal and administrative details (31 March 1993):

Status

Tear Fund is a company limited by guarantee and registered under the Companies Act 1985, registration number 994339. It is a registered charity, charity number 265464.

Directors

B O Chilver (Chairman)
Rev C R Calver
Rev S L Davies
Dr J Evans
J S Hughesdon
Dr T E Lankester
Mrs S Mitchell
M L Morris
R H Northcott
Professor A M Tomkins

Secretary
D W Adeney

Solicitors

Lewis & Dick
50 Grove Road
Sutton
Surrey SM1 1BT

Auditors
Touche Ross & Co.
Chartered Accountants
Hill House
1 Little New Street
London EC4A 3TR

Bankers

Midland Bank plc

Registered office
100 Church Road
Teddington
Middlesex
TW11 8QE

Section 234(2) of the 1985 Act requires disclosure of the names of the persons who were directors at any time during the year; and s706(2)(a) requires the accounts (among other documents delivered to the Registrar) to show prominently the company's registered number.

Paragraph 27 of the revised SORP extends the recommended disclosures of its predecessor. The names of all of the charity trustees, indicating, when applicable, those who are, also, members of any subcommittee, should be given, together with their method of appointment, or election. Further, a summary of the charity's specific investment powers and its authority (e.g., the governing instrument, Charity Commission order etc.) should now be given.

Regulation 10(2) requires the following to be provided:

(a) the name of the charity, as it appears in the register and any other name by which it makes itself known;
(b) the charity registration number and, if it is a charitable company, the company registration number;

(c) its principal address and, in the case of a charitable company, its registered office;
(d) a description of the trusts of the charity;
(e) the names of the charity trustees and any other person who, at any time during the financial year, was a trustee for, or of, the charity and of any person, or body, entitled to appoint a charity trustee of the charity; and
(f) a description of the charity's organisational structure.

In the case of a particular charity or class of charities, or of a particular financial year of a charity or class of charities, reg 10(3) allows the Commissioners to dispense with the requirement, in paragraph 2(e) above, to give the name of a trustee, where they are satisfied that its disclosure could lead to that person being placed in any personal danger, for example, the trustee of a women's refuge. There is a parallel exemption in para 27 of the revised SORP, but the reason for the omission should be given.

If, in the case of a charitable company, the trustees' annual report also serves as the directors' report, the names of all trustees must be given.

5.3.2 Narrative information

Paragraph 22 of SORP 2 recommended that the trustees' report contain:

> '(a) an explanation of the objectives of the charity and a description of the way in which the charity is organised. The policies that have been adopted in order to try to achieve these objectives should also be explained. If there have been any significant changes in the objectives, organisation or policies since the last report, this should also be made clear. The purpose of this part of the report is to explain what the charity is trying to achieve and how it is going about it;
>
> (b) a review of the development, activities and achievements of the charity during the year. This review should bring the reader up-to-date on the charity's progress and achievements. It should also explain the important events which have occurred during the year and how the charity has responded to them. It will be in this part of the report that information enabling the reader to judge the effectiveness of the charity will usually be provided;
>
> (c) a review of the transactions and financial position of the charity, and an explanation of the salient features of the accounts. This review should enable the reader to appreciate the significance of any surpluses or deficits disclosed in the accounts and the purposes for which the charity's assets are being held. It will also put the charity's current financial position in the context of its future plans and commitments, particularly with regard to on-going items of expenditure, projects not yet completed and obligations not yet met. The purpose of this part of the report is to help ensure that the accounts are properly interpreted.'

Similar disclosures are required by the 1985 Act. Section 234(2) requires the principal activities of the company (and subsidiaries) to be stated, including significant changes during the year; s234(1)(a) requires a fair review of the development of the company (and subsidiaries) during the year; and, para 6(b) of Sch 7 requires an indication of the likely future developments in the business of the company (and subsidiaries).

Paragraph 23 of SORP 2 suggested that other information which, if not included in the accounts, could usefully be provided in the trustees' annual report included 'details of voluntary help, donations-in-kind and other intangible income . . . an indication of the extent to which the charity is dependent upon certain donors and, if the charity was set up to undertake a specific project, cumulative figures on progress of the project'.

Unfortunately, although perhaps predictably, the quality of disclosure varies considerably. The Annex, the British Red Cross Society, to this chapter, provides a highly informative report.

Other charities merely provide a treasurer's report, including Example 5.2 Royal National Lifeboat Institution.

Example 5.2 Royal National Lifeboat Institution
The Treasurer's Statement (31 December 1993):

The RNLI's income has held up well in 1993. Subscriptions and donations for general purposes increased by 8%, an excellent result in a year of tentative economic recovery and impending tax increases. Fewer specific lifeboat appeals in 1993 meant that there was a fall in restricted donations. Legacies totalled a remarkable £46.3 million, including a £6.3 million capital endowment fund from the estate of Mr Roy Barker.

The year saw the completion of the seven-year plan for fast lifeboats referred to on page 11 – on which £57 million has been spent – and the start of the programme for the Severn and Trent classes. With this programme now fully on stream, expenditure on new lifeboats and equipment is planned almost to double in 1994, to about £16 million. With the continuing programme of lifeboat station construction and improvement, we expect to spend a total of £23 million in 1994 on updating the RNLI's fleet and installations. To put the figure into perspective, the replacement cost of the RNLI's operating assets is of the order of £300 million.

It is disappointing that the irrecoverable VAT borne by the RNLI is now approaching £1 million per annum, due mainly to the increased expenditure on modernising and maintaining properties. All property expenditure bears VAT except that on new building construction for the charity's purposes.

During the year a new system was introduced whereby our 1800 financial branches and guilds provide key information and remit funds on a quarterly basis. This has improved management information and increased the Institution's interest earnings by an estimated £25,000 pa. I am most grateful to branch honorary treasurers for their whole-hearted support which has made these benefits possible.

J N C James
Treasurer

While the treasurer's report is an integral part of its annual report and accounts, some charities, including Crosslinks, detached the report from its accounts. Rather than provide a narrative report, others, for example many community organisations, have preferred to give an oral report, later formalised in minutes, at the annual general meeting.

Paragraph 24 of the revised charity SORP requires the trustees' annual report to provide 'a comprehensive review and explanation of the accounts', and that those seeking to interpret the accounts should refer to it. This not only underlines the responsibility of the trustees for their report, but is designed to make them more aware of this.

While retaining the disclosures in SORP 2, the following are new:

(a) the reasons for any *material* (previously *significant*) changes in the objectives or policies since the last report and the reasons for those changes. Alternatively, a statement that there were no changes;
(b) how the charity's funds have been applied and the significance of all material movements in the SOFA;
(c) if materially different from the balance sheet value, the estimated value of assets;
(d) the reasons for, and effect of, any changes in accounting policies;
(e) the performance of any subsidiary and associated undertakings whose results are included in the consolidated accounts or in the notes;
(f) the effects of present and future accounts of any revaluations of fixed assets, other than investments, made during the period;
(g) the nature of any important post balance sheet events;
(h) that any investments held by the charity were acquired in accordance with the powers in the governing instrument;
(i) on a fund-by-fund basis, confirmation or otherwise that the charity's assets are available and adequate to fulfil the obligations of the charity, with specific reference to:
    (i) any likely delays, or shortfalls, in realising those assets in cash; and
    (ii) any commitments or guarantees;
(j) a review of the relationships between the charity and its connected charities and with any other charities and organisations with which it co-operates in the pursuit of its charitable objectives.

Where a charity is established to undertake a specific project, the revised SORP demands greater disclosure: that is, cumulative figures of funding and expenditure to date; estimates of the additional costs; and, the period of time required to complete it.

For charities whose gross income or total expenditure exceeds £10,000 in a financial year, reg 10(1)(a) requires that, in addition to stating the financial year, the report should be a review of:

(a) all activities, including material transactions, significant developments, and achievements, of the charity during the year in relation to its objects;
(b) changes in those activities during the year; and
(c) any post balance sheet events and any likely future developments in those activities.

For charities whose gross income and total expenditure does not exceed £10,000 in a financial year, reg 10(1)(b) requires the report, in addition to stating the financial year, to be a brief summary of the main activities and achievements of the charity during the year in relation to its objects (see, also, chapter **17**, page 430).

5.3.3 Funds held on behalf of others

SORP 2 stated that funds held by a charity as custodian trustee would not usually have fallen within the scope of the annual report. Nonetheless, without stating where such information should be located, it recommended, in para 18, that 'an indication of the extent to which the charity acts as a custodian trustee will need to be provided when explaining the charity's unquantifiable charitable work and the level of its administration expenses incurred'. Example 5.3 NCH Action for Children is one of the many charities which give information about custodian funds.

Example 5.3 NCH Action for Children
Note 11: Associated trusts (31 March 1994):

	Akrill Convalesc. Home £,000s	St Leonards-on-Sea Convalesc. Home £,000s	Mary Yolland Home £,000s	Farningham House for Boys £,000s	Lincoln City and County Home £,000s	Total £,000s
Trust Funds at 1 April 1993	23	656	11	913	58	1,661
Profit on Redemption of Investment	4	–	–	–	–	4
Trust Funds at 31 March 1994	27	656	11	913	58	1,665
Represented by:						
Freehold Land and Buildings	–	–	10	177	–	187
Furniture and Equipment	–	–	1	12	–	13
Investments at Cost	27	656	–	724	58	1,465
	27	656	11	913	58	1,665

As disclosed in note 6(a)(v) and note 7(d) the above assets are held by NCH Action For Children under various trusts. Those associated trusts are not accounted for in the Balance Sheet on page iii. These trusts have common trustees with NCH Action For Children. Certain of the assets are in use by NCH Action For Children and to the extent specified in the Trust Deeds the income is applied for the benefit of NCH Action For Children and is accounted for in the Income and Expenditure Account.

Paragraph 29 of the revised charity SORP states that it is the responsibility of the charity trustees to prepare the annual report and accounts. Accordingly, custodian trustees should make available, to the charity trustees, copies of their records relating to the administration of the charity's funds.

Where a charity is, or its trustees are, acting as custodian trustees, the annual report should:

(a) give a description of the assets which they hold in that capacity;
(b) show how this activity falls within their objects; and
(c) give details of the arrangements for safe custody and segregation of such assets from the charity's own.

In requiring this disclosure, charity trustees not only need to make clear, *but be clear*, what funds do and do not pass through their hands.

The new disclosure might be interpreted as being restricted to *money* funds. Where trustees have taken over responsibility for other assets, e.g., chattels, this could be disclosed in the interests of completeness.

Regulation 10(2)(g) requires to be disclosed a description of any assets held by the charity, or any of its trustees, on behalf of another charity, and particulars of any special arrangements made with respect to such assets and of the objects of the charity on whose behalf the assets are held. Although similar to those recommended by the revised SORP, these disclosures are not identical. For example, while the Regulations require disclosure of the objects of the charity on whose behalf the assets are held, the revised charity SORP requires how the activity falls within the objects of the charity holding the assets.

5.3.4 Other disclosures

In addition to the above disclosures, charitable companies are required to provide further information prescribed by s234 of, and Sch 7 to, the 1985 Act.

Changes in fixed assets

Paragraph 1(1) of Sch 7 requires significant changes in the fixed assets of the company (and subsidiaries) to be stated and commented upon. The quality of disclosure varies, from the informative to a mere reference to the note in the accounts where information on fixed assets and their movements may be located. An example of the former is Example 5.4 Guide Dogs for the Blind Association, and one of the latter is Example 5.5 the British Diabetic Association.

Example 5.4 Guide Dogs for the Blind Association
Report of the Council (extract) (31 December 1993):

2. FIXED ASSETS
The changes in Tangible Fixed Assets during the year are summarised in Note 6 to the Financial Statements. Additions at cost less disposals amounted to £4,032,000 (1992 £5,484,000). The most significant items included in additions related to the provision of a new Small Centre in Southampton, the construction of a School for Rehabilitation Workers at Hillfields, refurbishment of kennels at Bolton Centre, additions and refurbishments at Belfast Centre, and additional staff training facilities at Hillfields.

The market value of the Association's interests in land cannot be ascertained without obtaining professional valuations.

These valuations would be expensive and such expense is considered unwarranted. The Council is of the opinion that, although they would show in total an excess over the book value, such excess would not be significant in the context of the Association's overall financial position.

Example 5.5 British Diabetic Association
Annual Report of the Executive Council (extract) (31 December 1993):

Fixed Assets
The movements in fixed assets during the year are set out in Note 2 to the financial statements.

Market value of land

Paragraph 1(2) requires the difference between the book amount and the market value of land and buildings to be stated, if it is of such significance that, in the opinion of the directors, the attention of members ought to be drawn to it. Example 5.6 Nuffield Nursing Homes Trust offers a good example.

Example 5.6 Nuffield Nursing Homes Trust
Report of the Board of Governors (extract) (31 December 1993):

Fixed Assets

The level of capital investment in the updating of existing and acquisition of new facilities was increased to £25.2 million in 1993 (£21.8 million in 1992) of which the most significant were the acquisition of The Lansdowne Private Hospital in Bournemouth and land near Brighton for the site of a new hospital, both of which will enable the Trust to maintain and improve the services it provides to those towns.

The most recent professional valuation of the hospitals for loan security purposes was undertaken as at 31 December 1991 by Richard Ellis and produced a total value of £103,033,000, excluding moveable furniture and equipment, giving a surplus of £26,685,000 over net book value at that time which has not been incorporated in the Accounts.

Research and development

An indication of the activities (if any) of the company (and subsidiaries) in the field of research and development is required by para 6(c). The main activities of some charities, of which The Institute of Cancer Research is one, are in this field. This charity devotes eight pages (outside of the audited accounts) of its 1992/93 Annual Report to its research sections.

Disabled employees and employee involvement

Paragraph 9(3) requires disclosure of the policy concerning the employment of disabled persons in regard to:

(a) full and fair consideration of applications;
(b) continuing employment and training while employed; and
(c) generally their career development and promotion.

And, para 11(3) requires a description of the action taken during the year to introduce, maintain and develop arrangements aimed at:

(a) systematic provision of employee information;
(b) regular consultations so that views of employees can be taken into account;
(c) encouraging employees' involvement in the company's performance through share schemes or by other means; and
(d) achieving a common awareness of the financial and economic factors affecting the company's performance.

Neither of these disclosures needs to be provided where the number of employees (and disregarding employment outside the UK) does not exceed 250.

Example 5.7 the British Heart Foundation provides a rather terse statement. A more informative disclosure is that provided by Example 5.8 Guide Dogs for the Blind Association. SENSE, while qualifying for disclosure by virtue of its number of employees, did not provide it in its 1993/94 accounts.

Example 5.7 British Heart Foundation
Report of the Council (extract) (31 March 1993):

Employees

The Foundation is an equal opportunities employer and at all times gives full and fair consideration to applications for employment made by disabled persons. The Foundation provides employees with information on matters of concern to them.

Example 5.8 Guide Dogs for the Blind Association Report of the Council (extract) (31 December 1993):

7. EMPLOYEES

The Association actively encourages a policy of staff participation at all levels in the making of decisions which affect the Association's management and future development. An elected staff representative group represents the views of the staff on various matters which affect the welfare and well-being of the staff and they meet senior executives of the Association at least twice a year. A formal grievance procedure can be invoked by any member of staff.

The Association has continued to give full and fair consideration to applications for employment made by disabled persons, having regard to their respective aptitudes and abilities.

The Association's policy includes, where practicable, the continued employment of those who may become disabled during their employment. Equal training facilities are provided for disabled as for other employees in the job function in which they are employed.

Annex – British Red Cross Society

Trustees' report (extract) (31 December 1993):

Introduction

The British Red Cross Society (the Society) has pleasure in presenting the Trustees' Report (pages 3 to 9), and the Audited Financial Statements (pages 10 to 20) of the Central Funds of the Society for the year ended 31 December 1993.

These Financial Statements relate only to funds of the Society which are held centrally. Funds held by its Branches in the United Kingdom and overseas are separately accounted for in the respective Branch accounts and are independently audited. Copies of audited financial statements of the Branches in England and Wales, Scotland, Northern Ireland and the Isle of Man may be obtained on request from the National Headquarters of the Society. During 1993, the Branches received income of £31 million and incurred expenditure of £30 million in carrying out their activities including the provision of a wide range of care services in their local communities.

The central funds of the Society are used primarily for two broad purposes, namely the provision of professional and technical support to the Society's Branches through the Society's staff at National Headquarters and operating regionally and the direct provision of services in the United Kingdom and abroad. A secondary use for central funds is to provide funds, on a loan or grant basis, to Branches.

Legal status

The Society was founded in 1870 and incorporated by Royal Charter in 1908. Supplemental Charters were granted in 1919, 1955 and 1970. Orders in Council have subsequently been made, amending and extending the Charters.

The Trusts and Governing Instruments under which the Society operates comprise the Charters as amended, the Rules of the Society and Policies made from time to time by the Society's governing Council.

Objectives of the British Red Cross Society

The overriding objectives of the Society as set out in its two Charters of 1908 and 1919 respectively are: the furnishing of aid to the sick and wounded in time of war; and the improvement of health, the prevention of disease and the mitigation of suffering throughout the world.

In January 1990, the Society's Council approved the incorporation of these objectives into the following mission statement:

> '*The British Red Cross gives skilled and impartial care to people in need and crisis, in their own homes and in the community, at home and abroad, in peace and in war.*'

In meeting these objectives the Society must have regard to the Movement's seven Fundamental Principles of humanity, impartiality, neutrality, independence, voluntary service, unity and universality.

Organisation (connected charities and companies)

The Society is governed by its Council, which consists of no more than thirty-two Trustee members and which meets four times a year.

The Council, assisted by senior management, is responsible for formulating the strategy and policies for the Society as a whole, including the approval of budgets and the exercising of financial controls through regular financial reporting.

The Society has a National Headquarters in London where its Council and Committees meet and which also houses the office of the Chairman, Director General and the National Headquarters staff (apart from those based regionally). The role of this National Headquarters directorate is to implement the policies laid down by Council and manage on a day to day basis the activities of the Society.

The Society has fifty three local Branches in England and Wales together with Central Council Branches in Scotland, Northern Ireland and the Isle of Man and a Branch or Committee in the Channel Islands and in nine overseas territories.

The Society's Branches consist of Members of the Society and carry out the policies, conform to the directions and observe the rules prescribed by Council although since the early 1960s each Branch in England and Wales, and Northern Ireland has been separately registered with the Charity Commissioners and each, through its Trustee Committee, is responsible for the control and management of its financial and operational activities.

The Society wholly owns Britcross Limited, British Red Cross Events Limited, British Red Cross Trading Limited and British Red Cross Transport Services Limited, subsidiary trading companies incorporated in Great Britain to carry out certain activities on behalf of the Society. The assets and liabilities of these trading companies are not consolidated into the financial statements of central funds on grounds of immateriality.

Trustees' responsibilities

The Council, as Trustees require the Director General to prepare for each financial year financial statements which give a true and fair view of the state of affairs of the Central Funds of the Society and of the results for the period. In preparing the financial statements the Trustees are required to:

- Select suitable accounting policies and apply them consistently;
- Make judgements and estimates that are reasonable and prudent;
- State whether applicable accounting standards have been followed, subject to any material departures disclosed and explained in the financial statements; and
- Prepare the financial statements on the going concern basis unless it is inappropriate to presume that this basis applies.

The Trustees are responsible for ensuring proper accounting records are kept which disclose, with reasonable accuracy at any time, the financial position of the Central Funds of the Society and enable them to ensure that the financial statements comply with the Royal Charter of Incorporation dated 3 September 1908 and its supplementary Charters. They are also responsible for safeguarding the assets of the Central Funds of the Society and hence for taking reasonable steps for the prevention and detection of fraud and other irregularities.

Financial controls

A National Headquarters budget for 1994 which envisages an increase in income generation was approved in December 1993. Actual results during the year will be carefully monitored to ensure timely adjustment if and when considered necessary.

Since the beginning of 1993 monthly financial management reporting from Branches has been introduced, which will enable the financial activities of each Branch to be monitored and interim results for the whole Society to be produced.

Investment powers and restrictions

The Society's investment powers are prescribed in the Supplemental Charter dated 1 July 1955 (as amended by Order in Council of 28 April 1972). Under the principal investment provisions of the Charter, the Society's Trustees are permitted to invest in Trustee investments in the form of government and local authority securities and the shares and fixed interest securities of public companies, investment, financial or unit trusts.

With the approval of the Charity Commissioners, three Common Investment Funds, the Capital, Income and Common Deposit Funds, were established on 1 July 1993 in order to provide a more efficient and cost effective vehicle for managing both the Society's and the Branches' funds. The Society's Trustees realised the centrally held General Fund investment portfolio on 1 July 1993 and invested the proceeds, which included a profit of £1.32 million, in the Common Investment Funds. Currently, 19 Branches also have holdings in the Funds.

Review of developments, activities and achievements

Society Structure

In 1993, one of the major decisions taken by Council was to review the structure of the Society. The objective of the review is to ensure that, in a rapidly changing environment, the Society has the relevant structure to allow it to adapt swiftly to the changes taking place outside of the Society and to remain a major force within the charity sector in the UK and abroad. The review will also be concerned with the need to ensure that the Society's Branches continue to be financially viable, efficient and cost effective.

During 1993, new rules for the Northern Ireland Central Council Branch were approved and the Cumbria Branch of the Society transferred from Region 1 to Region 14. The Government's proposed reform of local authority boundaries has led to consideration of boundary changes for some of the Society's Branches, particularly in Wales for which a working party was set up in 1993 whose proposal to merge Branches into four units was approved, subject to detailed consultation, by Council in December 1993.

Strategic Priorities

After reviewing the Five Year Plan 1992/96, the Society continues to follow the original strategic priorities laid down. These are income generation, profile development, quality assurance, expanding services, recruitment and the support of volunteers. When necessary, the emphasis between the various elements is adjusted.

To develop and improve the Branches' ability to provide the Society's core services within the programmes of emergency response, community services, training, youth and international, a National Strategy developed in 1989 and approved by Council in January 1990, was continued in 1993 with 54 Branches working within its framework. In 1990 a National Strategy Fund was created to assist its implementation and in 1993, just under £1 million was allocated from this fund towards the costs of this initiative. Between January 1991 and December 1993 over £3 million has been allocated.

Following on from the National Strategy, a Working Group was established to focus the activities of the Society and its Branches more clearly and identify the key capabilities required by Branches to allow the delivery of services effectively and to recommend how these should be developed either through the National Strategy or by other means.

Personnel

The Society has continued to develop policies to attract and retain high quality employees at National Headquarters and at Branches. An annual performance review scheme has been introduced from which individual training needs are established and in-house training courses designed to meet these needs are now being run.

The quality of information given to applicants and new employees has been improved in accordance with a more professional approach and employment contracts have been updated. An extensive exercise began in 1993 to update job titles and job descriptions of volunteers and salaried staff at Branches.

United Kingdom Emergency Programme

A review of the Society's war-time and civil disaster role was completed in 1993. The Emergency Planning Officer at National Headquarters has assisted many Branches in reviewing their own emergency response systems.

Communication systems were tested on several occasions such as the Avon Tunnel crash, the floods in Llandudno, N. Wales, and the exercise 'Operation Bold'. A handbook for Branch Emergency Planning Officers with revised procedures for response to disaster occurring in the United Kingdom has been prepared and will be issued in 1994.

Community Programme

Up to fifty different welfare or community care services are delivered by the Society within the Community Programme. They include the core services (first aid cover at public events, medical loan, escort, therapeutic beauty care and hand care) and a range of nationally supported local services (e.g., home from hospital schemes; clubs and day care; holidays for people with disabilities; transport; domiciliary care for frail, elderly persons and people with disabilities; residential care homes and cosmetic camouflage).

In response to changing community care legislation, a contracts unit was established at National Headquarters in 1991 to assist and advise Branches in negotiating service and funding arrangements with local authorities and health authorities. That assistance is now provided through specialist development officers in the Service Development department, with access to financial and legal advice as required. A contracts guide handbook has been issued to Branches.

The Service Development department, together with the Research and Planning department, have set up a number of joint projects to review key services, develop a strategic focus and establish service standards so as to ensure quality. The promotion of good practice and publicity materials will follow.

Training Programme

The Society provides training for its Members in support of the Society's service-giving activities and for the general public in the following areas, First Aid, Community Care, Ambulance Aid, Managing Stress and Crisis, Babysitting and Therapeutic Beauty Care.

Improvements have been made in the materials used in support of many of these training activities, including quality assurance procedures, and a guide for Branches in the marketing of First Aid at Work courses has been piloted.

A new foundation course for Members has been introduced. There is also a new programme of training for the Society's National and Branch Trustees.

The introduction of National Vocational Qualifications (NVQs) has given the

Society a further opportunity to develop its training activities, using in particular a modular format which will ensure the continued relevance of the courses both to Members and the public.

The Society has been preparing to act as host to the Red Cross European First Aid Competition in 1994, when participants from twenty five National Societies will compete for a trophy won in 1993 by the Kent Branch of the British Red Cross.

The Society's Training Centre at Guildford in Surrey continued to provide a venue for many of the Society's conferences and training activities, as well as operating commercially as a training centre for business clients. A small operating surplus of £1800 was generated in the year.

Youth Programme

In 1993, Council approved the recommendations of a report entitled 'Action with Humanity', which identified an exciting new role for Red Cross Youth Members in helping to meet the health and social care needs of other young people. A Five Year Plan for implementation was produced and approved by Council in December 1993.

Membership

Following the approval of a new Volunteering Policy by Council in July 1993 designed to ensure that volunteers working for the Red Cross are given full support, work began on the implementation of the Policy in Branches. This is to be a rolling programme with a review in January 1995.

Effective support and management of volunteers is vital if existing volunteers are to be retained and numbers increased by new people wishing to help the Society.

Volunteer Co-ordinators and others with special responsibility for volunteers have been appointed in twenty Branches, and it is encouraging to note that further Branches are intending to make similar appointments shortly.

Museum and Archives

The Society maintains a Museum, registered with the Museum and Galleries Commission, and archives of historic information relating to its development since its foundation in 1870.

This facility is used by many outside sources as a centre of research and its funding is provided by the Society with, on occasion, grant assistance.

International Programme

The International work of the Society expanded in many ways during 1993. The number of messages exchanged by the International Welfare Tracing Service more than doubled over the previous year and a Family Reunion Service was developed. The work of this section increased dramatically because of the situation in Somalia and former Yugoslavia. In October 1993, the International Director accompanied HRH Princess Alexandra on a visit to

Arolsen, Germany, to view the International Tracing Service, run by the International Committee of the Red Cross (ICRC).

Funds of £9.59 million in hand at the year end and obtained largely from the European Community (EC) and the Overseas Development Administration (ODA), were earmarked for relief and development projects built into a programme of expenditure for 1994.

In addition, over £1 million of goods-in-kind were passed directly to the International Federation of Red Cross and Red Crescent Societies (the Federation), in former Yugoslavia and further substantial programmes funded directly by the ICRC, were run by the Society. In total the International Division of the Society controlled expenditure of over £26 million in the year.

In 1993, the work of the International Division was concentrated on former Yugoslavia and Somalia and, to a lesser degree, in Ethiopia, Angola, Mozambique and Afghanistan. In total the Society was operational in forty four countries. Both the number and quality of its Delegates increased in 1993 and it was the leading donor of personnel to both the ICRC and the Federation. Its Delegates conducted one hundred and seventy two missions which was an increase of over 26% on 1992.

The Development department, which conducts work on rehabilitation and other projects, finalised its strategy and is operational in seven countries. Significant amounts of funding were obtained from private sources, the EC and the ODA.

The workload of the International Law department increased with particular emphasis on supporting the ICRC's campaign to restrict the use of anti-personnel mines and associated issues, and on the dissemination of knowledge of humanitarian law and the Fundamental Principles of the Red Cross Movement to Branches.

The International Director made a number of other visits during 1993 in order to evaluate the Society's input in the major conflict and disaster areas. Several operational visits were made to former Yugoslavia and Somalia with additional visits by the Director to Afghanistan, Pakistan, Hong Kong, Nepal (which included a presentation to HRH The Princess of Wales and the Minister for Overseas Development), Albania (which was also in the company of the Minister for Overseas Development), Kenya, Sri Lanka, Bangladesh and Regional meetings in Beijing.

Fundraising

A broad-based fundraising programme directed at individuals, companies, trusts and foundations and a range of community groups was established. The most successful and cost-effective sources of funds were legacies and direct mail. The effect of the appeal for former Yugoslavia on the programme in 1993 was dramatic. An integrated campaign was set up covering direct mail, press and TV advertising, a TV appeal and one gala event. The database of donors doubled. The number of donations received through gift aid and deed of covenant also increased substantially.

Communications

The Society's communications strategy, devised by the Marketing and Communications department, and assisted by the Society's advertising agency, Abbott Mead Vickers and public relations consultancy, GCI London, was implemented during 1993. It will operate throughout the Society, ensuring that a consistent message relating to Society activities is conveyed across all media.

A new House Style for all the Society's publications was also implemented during 1993, with the assistance of Spencer Landor Design Consultancy.

Red Cross Week 1993 saw the launch of a new identity for the week, and a lapel pin which was piloted in London and Edinburgh. The lapel pin is a highly visible symbol, and tends to lead to higher donations during street collections. The success of the lapel pin was such that an improved version will be introduced nationwide for Red Cross Week 1994.

International Relationships

In 1993, the Society hosted the Statutory Meetings of the International Red Cross and Red Crescent Movement at which its Patron and President HM The Queen addressed the Council of Delegates. The success of these meetings owed much to the dedication of the volunteers which ensured the efficient running of the programme.

At the General Assembly, the Society's Chairman, Lady Limerick, was elected a Vice President of the International Federation of Red Cross and Red Crescent Societies, for a period of four years from October 1993.

The General Assembly also admitted twelve new Societies, increasing the Federation's membership to one hundred and sixty one National Societies.

During the year, Lady Limerick visited the Swedish Red Cross, the Hong Kong Red Cross, the former Yugoslavia, the EC Liaison Bureau and represented the Society on the Federation's Executive Council and attended meetings of the Standing Commission. She also attended the Fourth Asia Pacific Regional Conference in China, accompanied by the Society's International Director and International Adviser.

The Society's Director General, Michael Whitlam, has been involved in the Red Cross Movement's meetings held in Geneva relating to Military Protection, the Federation's Strategic Work Plan, the Group of Twenty Four Co-ordinating Group and the EC Liaison Bureau.

He also visited Iraq, the former Yugoslavia, Kenya, Somalia, and accompanied HRH The Princess of Wales on visits to Nepal and Zimbabwe.

Review of audited Financial Statements for the year

Fixed Asset Movements

Additions (less disposals at net book value) to tangible fixed assets amounted to £0.5 million (1992 £0.51 million) and included the cost of the continuing enhancement of information technology, the addition of seven new vehicles and the replacement of one vehicle, and additions to and the replacement of office equipment.

Depreciation of £0.30 million has been charged in 1993 (1992 £0.24 million).

Loans and Advances to Branches

Loans to Branches for the purchase or improvement of property can be short, medium or long-term spanning five to fifteen years.

New property loans amounting to £541,000 were advanced during 1993 and repayments of £187,000 were received.

Outstanding loans on property at the end of 1993 totalled £1.64 million (1992 £1.28 million), leaving £0.74 million available for granting further loan assistance to Branches. Bank financing for Branch capital acquisitions is being put in place in 1994 to support further Branch activities.

Bridging finance on properties of £6,000 and other emergency loans and cash advances of £317,000 were also outstanding from Branches at the year end.

National Strategy loans outstanding at the year end amounted to £69,000.

Investments

Investment of centrally held funds within the Society's Common Investment Funds amounted to £7.32 million at market value at the year end.

Surplus for the year

Income increased by 6 per cent to £34.48 million (1992 £32.52 million) with increases occurring in all areas with the exception of Investment Income and Interest which fell as the result of less cash on deposit and lower interest rates.

Expenditure increased by 10 per cent to £33.88 million (1992 £30.85 million).

The surplus for the year was £0.60 million (1992 £1.67 million) which when added to realised investment gains of £1.32 million and unrealised gains of £1.02 million increased overall reserves to £22.44 million analysed as follows:-

British Red Cross Society Movements of Funds 1993

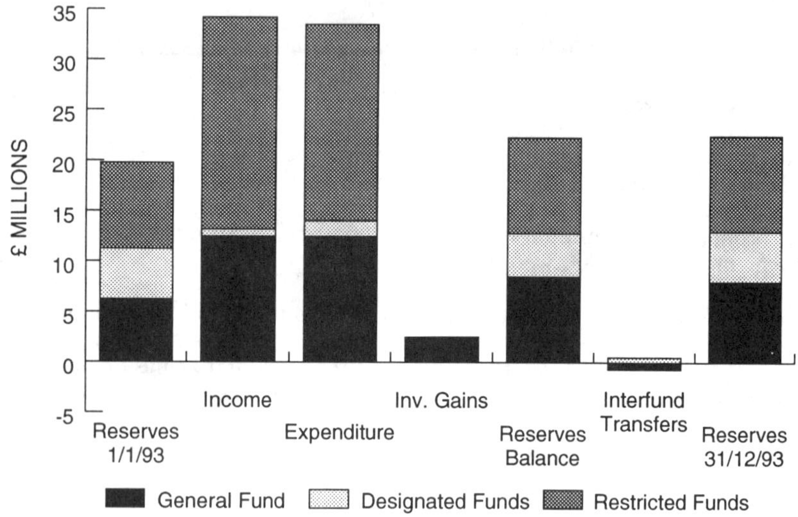

General Fund

The General Fund covers the expenditure incurred by National Headquarters in carrying out its role in respect of the Society's and Branch activities.

In 1993, income increased by 16 per cent to £12.65 million (1992 £10.86 million).

With the exception of investment income and interest which showed a decrease of 10 per cent to £0.42 million (1992 £0.47 million) mainly due to lower levels of cash being available for short-term deposits and lower returns being available on such deposits, all other areas of income showed increases.

As expected, legacies increased by 11 per cent to £5.13 million (1992 £4.63 million), and due to increased fundraising activity, donations by 24 per cent to £3.15 million (1992 £2.54 million) and, in line with the decision of the Society's Quota Committee, contributions from Branches towards International and Overseas work increased by 10 per cent to £0.91 million (1992 £0.83 million).

Partly due to the provision of new First Aid Manuals and the high value resuscitation equipment needed for First Aid at Work courses, supply and trading activities increased by 39 per cent to £1.85 million (1992 £1.33 million). Miscellaneous income and rents increased by 3 per cent to £0.96 million (1992 £0.93 million).

Expenditure increased by 20 per cent to £12.65 million (1992 £10.57 million) and with the exception of UK Operations and Services where there was a decrease of 3 per cent to £2.47 million (1992 £2.54 million) increases occurred in all other areas in line with the priorities set out in the Society's Five Year Plan.

The Society's Statutory and Voluntary Contributions towards the International work of the ICRC and the Federation in Geneva increased by 23 per cent to £0.59 million (1992 £0.48 million) and International Services by 36 per cent to £1.03 million (1992 £0.76 million) due to expanded activity.

In raising public awareness of the Society, and in utilising television advertising for the first time, Marketing and Communication costs increased by 27 per cent to £1.72 million (1992 £1.35 million) and, in anticipation of future income generation, Fundraising costs by 11 per cent to £1.80 million (1992 £1.62 million).

Administrative and Advisory costs, including irrecoverable VAT, increased by 15 per cent to £1.75 million (1992 £1.52 million) while, as budgeted and partly due to increased postal, telephone and copying costs, Financial and Central Office costs increased by 18 per cent to £1.04 million (1992 £0.88 million).

The related costs of supply and trading activities increased by 55 per cent to £1.77 million (1992 £1.14 million).

The surplus on activities amounted to £5,000 which when added to a realised investment gain of £1.32 million and an unrealised gain of £0.93 million increased reserves by £2.26 million from £6.36 million to £8.62 million. Transfers of £0.5 million were made to the National Strategy Fund and £0.23 million to the 125th Birthday Designated Fund. The Branch Fundraising Fund was reduced by a transfer of £0.02 million to General Fund.

Designated Funds

Designated Funds are those set aside from General Funds for particular purposes or projects and, in the main, are used to provide financial assistance, by way of grants or loans, to increase Branch effectiveness and ensure Council policies are implemented and followed.

In 1993, income increased by 84 per cent to £0.59 million (1992 £0.32 million) and expenditure by 151 per cent to £1.53 million (1992 £0.61 million).

Expenditure included support to Branches provided through the National Strategy Fund and the costs of hosting the International Red Cross Movement's Strategic Meetings in 1993.

At the year end the excess of expenditure over income of £0.94 million less investment gains of £0.09 million reduced the opening balances by £0.85 million to £4.23 million which when net transfers from General Fund of £0.71 million, and an inter Designated Fund transfer of £0.13 million from Branch Development Fund to National Strategy Fund, were added resulted in balances of £4.94 million being carried forward into 1994.

Restricted Funds

Restricted Funds are created when donations are made either for particular areas or purposes and which can only be used for that area or purpose. Such donations are usually for international purposes and are expended on disaster and emergency relief in the short term after relevant evaluation.

In 1993, most Restricted income and expenditure was either received in response to, or expended on, disaster and emergency relief and/or development programmes in Somalia, Southern Africa, Sudan, the former Yugoslavia and India.

In 1993, Restricted Fund income decreased marginally by 2 per cent to £21.24 million (1992 £21.57 million) and expenditure by 1 per cent to £19.70 million (1992 £19.98 million). When the excess of income over expenditure of £1.54 million was added to the opening balances of £8.05 million it resulted in balances of £9.59 million being carried forward into 1994.

Projects not yet completed and forward commitments

The commitment to host the European First Aid Competition in 1994 still remains at a maximum expected net cost to the Society of £37,000.

Additionally, the continued implementation of the National Strategy over the next year or two is expected to incur a net cost of approximately £3 million. There are no capital commitments.

All future international project commitments are covered by the relevant Restricted Funds.

General comments

Since the publication of the last Trustees' Report and Accounts of Central Funds, Lord Barnard, having given exceptional service, retired on 31 December 1993 as Vice Chairman of the Society's Council and thereby also ceased to be a member of the Finance Committee. Miss C Dixon-Carter has also retired as a member of the Finance Committee.

The Society expresses its deep appreciation to Lord Barnard and Miss Dixon-Carter for their outstanding contribution and long standing service. Mr Barton ceased to be a Council representative on the Finance Committee in October 1993 but continues as a non Council Member and Mr Wallace became a non Council member of the Finance Committee with effect from March 1993.

Chapter 6 – Accounting policies

6.1 Introduction

By recommending that the accounts should include an explanation of the accounting policies used to prepare them, the provisions of SORP 2 and its successor not only mirror the requirements both of the 1985 Act and of SSAP 2 *Disclosure of accounting policies*, but, more importantly, recognise the basic difficulty of understanding charity accounts.

6.2 SSAP 2 'Disclosure of accounting policies'

The purpose of SSAP 2 is to assist in user understanding and interpretation of accounts by promoting improvement in the quality of information disclosed. It seeks to achieve this by 'establishing as standard accounting practice the disclosure in financial accounts of clear explanations of the accounting policies followed insofar as these are significant for the purpose of giving a true and fair view'.

SSAP 2 develops the standard accounting practice for the disclosure of accounting policies in three stages, by:

(a) describing the four fundamental accounting concepts;
(b) relating these to the development of accounting bases; and then
(c) dealing with the selection of accounting policies.

6.3 Fundamental accounting concepts

Fundamental accounting concepts are the broad basis assumptions which underlie the periodic accounts of business enterprises. Paragraph 2 of the Standard states that 'the use of these concepts is not necessarily self evident from an examination of accounts, but they have such general acceptance that they call for no explanation in published accounts' and, unless there is a clear statement to the contrary, in which case para 17 requires the facts to be explained, there is a presumption that they have been observed. (See, also, para 33 of the revised charity SORP.)

(Note: Where a receipts and payments account is prepared, para 17 of the revised charity SORP states that the only fundamental accounting concept 'assumed will be that of consistency'.)

6.3.1 The going concern concept

Under this concept the enterprise is assumed to be able to continue in operational existence for the foreseeable future. This means, in particular, that the income and expenditure account and balance sheet assume no intention or necessity to liquidate or curtail significantly the scale of operation.

6.3.2 The accruals concept

Under this concept, revenues and costs are accrued (that is, recognised as they are earned or incurred, not as money is received or paid), matched with one another so far as their relationship can be established or justifiably assumed, and dealt with in the income and expenditure account to which they relate. Where the accruals concept is inconsistent with the prudence concept (see below), the latter prevails.

6.3.3 The consistency concept

In terms of this concept, there should be consistency of accounting treatment of like items within each accounting period and from one period to the next.

6.3.4 The prudence concept

Under this concept, revenues and expenses are not anticipated, but are recognised by inclusion in the income and expenditure account only when realised in the form either of cash or of other assets the ultimate cash realisation of which can be assessed with reasonable certainty. Conversely, provision is made for all known liabilities whether the amount of these is known with certainty or is a best estimate in the light of the information available.

Unlike its predecessor, the revised SORP sets out these concepts, in Appendix 2, and, where appropriate, tailors them to reflect both the new structure of accounts and the nature of charities' transactions and business.

6.4 Accounting bases

Paragraph 15 of SSAP 2 defines accounting bases as 'the methods developed for applying fundamental accounting concepts to financial transactions and items, for the purpose of financial accounts, and in particular:

(a) for determining the accounting periods in which revenue and costs should be recognised in the profit and loss account; and
(b) for determining the amounts at which material items should be stated in the balance sheet.'

6.5 Accounting policies

The accounting policies are those accounting bases selected by an enterprise's management which are most appropriate for their own particular circumstances. Thus, accounting policies are defined as 'the specific accounting bases selected and consistently followed by a business enterprise as being, in the opinion of the management, appropriate to its circumstances and best suited to present fairly its results and financial position'.

While SSAP 2 requires disclosure of those accounting policies deemed to be either *material or critical* in determining the profit or loss for the year and in stating the financial position at the year end, paras 31 and 35 of the revised SORP (and its predecessor) recommend disclosure of those polices judged *material.* In both cases, however, the explanations should be clear, fair and as brief as possible. Paragraph 1(a) of Pt IV of the Sch to the Regulations requires a description of the accounting policies of, and accounting assumptions made by, the charity trustees, including any material change in these, the reason for such change and its effect (if material) on the accounts.

Paragraph 33 of SORP 2 set out examples of accounting policies which should be explained. These were:

'(a) the capitalisation and depreciation of fixed assets;
(b) commitments not yet met and the use of designated funds;
(c) determining the amounts at which assets are included in the balance sheet;
(d) donations, legacies and other forms of voluntary income;
(e) grants payable and receivable;
(f) identifying the items to be included within administrative expenses, fund-raising expenses, and publicity expenses;
(g) investment income;
(h) netting off of expenses and related income;
(i) realised and unrealised gains and losses on investments and fixed assets;
(j) stock;
(k) subscriptions for life membership.

> Where a charity is involved in specialised activities, such as research, it is particularly important that the accounting policies adopted to account for these activities are explained.'

These are perpetuated in para 35 of the revised SORP, except that:

(a) as regards (a), the policy has been extended to include valuation;
(b) a policy for (c) has been omitted;
(c) (f) has been expanded to include support costs and recommends that the basis of allocation or apportionment be given;
(d) as well as an accounting policy for investment income, there should be one relating to investment assets, including investment properties;
(e) as regards (a) and (i), the policy should be restricted to assets for charity use.

The 1985 Act requires the policies disclosed to include:

(a) the method for determining the provisions for both depreciation and diminution in the value of assets (para 36 of Sch 4); and
(b) the method of translating foreign currency amounts into sterling (para 58(1) of Sch 4).

Two of the better disclosures are provided by Example 6.1 OXFAM (a charitable company) and Example 6.2 NCH Action for Children (an unincorporated association).

Example 6.1 OXFAM
Note 2: Accounting policies (30 April 1994):

(a) Accounting Conventions
The accounts are prepared under the historical cost convention and in compliance with all relevant Statements of Standard Accounting Practice.

Income is shown as gross except for:

(i) shop income which is shown net after the deduction of direct operating and management expenses. See Note 3(b).
(ii) certain other income raised by fundraising events where direct expenses have been netted off against gross income.

Income is accounted for when received with the exception of income promised for earmarked grants which is shown as soon as it is reliably reported as receivable.

Expenditure is shown as gross except as explained above, and where costs incurred on behalf of the trading subsidiary are recovered therefrom. Accrual adjustments have been made for all known liabilities at the year-end.

Grants to other organisations for relief and development projects are accounted for as and when approved. The value of grants approved, but still to be paid, are included in the Balance Sheet as current liabilities.

Budgets for operational projects managed by Oxfam, are also accounted for when approved but balances unspent at the year-end are treated as designated funds unless they are covered by restricted funds.

The accounts of Oxfam's trading subsidiary company Oxfam Activities Limited have now been consolidated with the accounts of Oxfam in accordance with the latest guidelines. The Statement of Financial Activities includes the net income receivable from the subsidiary company. The taxable profit of the subsidiary is covenanted to Oxfam, so there is no liability to corporation tax. The Balance Sheet of Oxfam alone and that for Oxfam and its subsidiary are both included.

The charity has had to adjust the formats from those prescribed by the 1985 Companies Act to include headings which are relevant to its activities to enable it to show a true and fair view.

(b) Gifts in Kind
Blankets and clothing etc received and given to overseas projects are included in the accounts at market value at the time of export. Goods held pending dispatch are not included in the accounts. Goods which have been dispatched overseas but are not yet distributed from Oxfam controlled stores are included in the value of aid provided and are not included on the Balance Sheet.

Food aid from the World Food Programme for which Oxfam accepts full responsibility for distribution is included in income at its market value and under 'Resources Expended' at the same value.

Example 6.1 OXFAM
Note 2: Accounting policies (30 April 1994): (Continued)

Properties, investments and other fixed assets donated to the charity are included as donation income at market value at the time of receipt and, unless disposed of, are shown as assets on the Balance Sheet at that value.

(c) **Depreciation of Tangible Fixed Assets**
Freehold land is not depreciated.

The cost of other tangible fixed assets is written-off by equal annual instalments over their expected useful lives as follows:

Freehold Buildings	50 years
Leasehold Warehouse	10 years
Leasehold Premises acquired prior to 1 May 1990	5 years
Furniture, Fixtures and Equipment in the UK	5 years
Mainframe Computer Equipment	5 years
Motor Vehicles	4 years
Micro-Computer and Wordprocessor Equipment	3 years
Furniture, Fixtures and Equipment Overseas	3 years

Vehicles and equipment for use in operational programmes are not capitalised but charged in full to 'Resources Expended' when purchased.

Leasehold Properties acquired since 1 May 1990 are amortised on the following basis:

Premium	Period to next Rent Review
Key Money	Period of Lease (max 10 years)
Other Leasehold Costs	5 years

(d) **Stocks**
Bought-in stocks are valued at the lower of cost or net realisable value after making due allowance for any obsolete or slow moving items. Unsold donated items are not included in closing stock since their value is uncertain until sold.

(e) **Foreign Currencies**
Transactions in foreign currencies during the year are translated at prevailing rates. Foreign balance sheet items are translated at the rate of exchange prevailing at the Balance Sheet date.

(f) **Pension Scheme**
The charity operates a Pension Scheme providing benefits based on final pensionable pay. The assets of the scheme, which are held separately from those of the charity, are invested with Insurance Companies. Contributions to the scheme are charged to the Statement of Financial Activities, so as to spread the cost of pensions over employees' working lives with the charity, and are determined by a qualified Actuary.

(g) **Fundraising and Administration Costs**
Fundraising expenses include the salaries and overhead costs of the staff in Area and District Offices throughout the UK and Ireland who

Example 6.1 OXFAM
Note 2: Accounting policies (30 April 1994): (Continued)

promote fundraising events, together with the salaries, direct expenditure and overhead costs of fundraising staff based at Oxfam House.

Administration expenses represent the salaries, direct expenditure and overhead costs of central servicing departments in Oxfam House, such as Corporate Finance, Personnel and Purchasing Departments, net of any appropriate recharge to the operational divisions.

(h) Operating Leases
Rentals applicable to operating leases where substantially all the benefits and risks of ownership remain with the lessor are charged to the Statement of Financial Activities on a straight line basis.

Example 6.2 NCH Action for Children
Note 1: Accounting policies (31 March 1994):

The Financial Statements have been prepared in accordance with applicable accounting standards. The particular accounting policies adopted are described below:

(a) **Accounting Convention**
The financial statements are prepared under the historic cost convention.

(b) **Basis of Consolidation**
The consolidated financial statements have been prepared for the charity and its wholly owned subsidiary, NCH Action For Children Limited. These have not been prepared in prior years as the results of the subsidiary have not been considered to be material.

The Income and Expenditure Account and Cash Flow Statement for the year ended 31 March 1993 and the Balance Sheet as at that date have been restated to include the results of NCH Action For Children Limited for that year.

(c) **Accumulated Funds**
The various accumulated funds represent the following:

Specific Purposes Funds	Legacies and other donations for specific purposes and amounts set aside for specified objects, less amounts expended for these purposes.
Endowment Funds	Funds donated to provide scholarships and income for general purposes.
Legacies Equalisation Account	The aggregate of the surplus/(deficit) of unconditional legacy income over/(under) the average of such income for the past three years.

(d) **Fixed Assets**
Fixed Assets are recorded at cost or, in cases where Fixed Assets have been donated to NCH Action For Children, at valuation at the time of acquisition.

(e) **Depreciation**
In the case of Freehold Buildings, the acquisition cost and any adaptation costs that are considered to add value to the property are treated as the 'core cost'. The remaining adaptation costs are treated as the 'depreciating cost'. No depreciation is charged on the core cost of Freehold Buildings as the maintenance policy for these properties ensures that any depreciation would be immaterial. Depreciating costs are written off over their estimated useful lives (see below).

For the purposes of depreciation, 999 year Leasehold Buildings have been treated as if they were Freehold Buildings. Capital expenditure on other Leasehold Buildings will normally be regarded as a depreciating cost and as such is written off over the estimated useful life (see below).

No depreciation is provided on Freehold Land or the core cost of Freehold Buildings.

Example 6.2 NCH Action for Children
Note 1: Accounting policies (31 March 1994): (Continued)

Depreciation is provided on computer software to write off the cost in the year of acquisition.

Other Fixed Assets are depreciated on a straight line basis over their useful lives which are estimated to be:

Freehold Buildings (depreciating cost)	– 10 years or life of project if shorter
Leasehold Land and Buildings	– 10 years or term of lease if shorter
Plant and Machinery	– 4 and 5 years
Furniture and Equipment	– 5 years
Motor Vehicles	– 4 years

When the currently expected useful life of individual assets is considered to be less than these periods, shorter periods are used.

(f) Voluntary Income and Appeals Expenditure
Voluntary Income represents amounts received and recorded at offices and projects during the year. Except in the case of Charity Shops and fund raising events such as Fetes and Galas, no costs of fund raising have been netted against voluntary income.

Appeals Expenditure represents the direct costs of fund raising and includes the salaries and other direct costs of fund raising staff. Publicity costs directly related to appeals are included in the fund raising costs. Publicity of a more general nature is included in the costs of Information Services.

(g) Fees, Contributions and Grants
These comprise amounts receivable during the year.

(h) Investment Income
Investment Income is accounted for as follows:

(i) Listed and unlisted amounts received during the year;
(ii) Central Finance Board Units distributions in respect of year to 28 February 1994;
(iii) Short term deposits amounts receivable.

(i) Legacy Income
This comprises amounts received during the year.

The amount transferred to/from the Legacies Equalisation Account was calculated upon a 3-year basis, rather than 5 years previously. The net effect of this is to change a transfer to the Legacies Equalisation Account of £34,000 to a transfer from the Legacies Equalisation Account of £461,000 – a difference of £495,000.

(j) Profit on Sale of Fixed Assets
Profit on sale of Land and Buildings is included in the Income and Expenditure Account. Profit on sale of other Fixed Assets is netted

Example 6.2 NCH Action for Children
Note 1: Accounting policies (31 March 1994): (Continued)

against social work expenditure in order to reflect in the project costs the benefit of careful maintenance and use.

(k) Investments
NCH Action For Children's policy is to hold investments primarily in order to generate income for the support of social work over a long-term period. The effect of this policy is that the surplus arising on revaluation at any particular time will not normally be realised. The investments have therefore been stated at cost to their respective funds, if known, or earliest known valuation.

Profits on sales of investments are included in the Income and Expenditure Account with the exception of unrealised profits arising on the transfer of investments between funds which are taken direct to fund accounts.

(l) Foreign Exchange
Assets and liabilities denominated in foreign currencies are translated at year end exchange rates. Exchange differences are included in the Income and Expenditure Account.

(m) Pension Costs
The expected costs of providing pensions, as calculated periodically by professionally qualified actuaries, is charged to the income and expenditure account so as to spread the cost over the service lives of employees in the scheme, in such a way that the pension cost is a substantially level percentage of current and expected future pensionable payroll so long as the age, sex and salary distribution of the membership remains broadly unchanged from its present level.

(n) Value Added Tax
As the majority of NCH Action For Children's activities are classified as exempt or non-business activities for the purposes of Value Added Tax, NCH Action For Children is unable to reclaim all the Value Added Tax which it suffers on its purchases. Expenditure in these financial statements is therefore shown inclusive of Value Added Tax paid.

(o) Voluntary Help and Gifts In Kind
No value has been put on the help received by NCH Action For Children during the year. Individual gifts in kind of significant value have been valued at estimated cost to the donor and included in the Income and Expenditure Account; however there are numerous small gifts that cannot be quantified.

(p) The classification of the Income and Expenditure Account has been altered to present a fairer allocation of overheads. This has necessitated a restatement of comparative amounts.

Less than transparent are many charities' policies for identifying the composition of administrative, fund-raising and publicity expenses. Nonetheless, Example 6.3 Ex-Services Mental Welfare Society's policy is found to be extremely informative.

Example 6.3 Ex-Services Mental Welfare Society
Note 1: Principal accounting policies (extract) (30 September 1993):

(e) **Allocation of expenditure – income and expenditure account**
The Society's Head Office houses the administration, including the accounts department and the national appeals department, together with the welfare office for the London and the South East Region. The offices maintained in Manchester, Cambridge, Alton, Bath, Ayr and Belfast are concerned with regional welfare activities only.

Due to the nature of the Society's activities, the distinction between administration and welfare activities cannot be precisely measured because much of the work undertaken by the administrative staff is directly related to the various welfare activities.

For accounting purposes expenditure is allocated as follows:

Charitable expenditure

All direct expenditure in respect of welfare work in the field and at the homes and the costs of running the homes, including related payroll, office and other costs.

Appeals costs

All direct expenditure including payroll, office costs and mailing expenses.

Publicity

Direct expenditure on advertising in the national press and elsewhere, together with the cost of literature issued by the Society. Publicity is directed towards bringing the specialist services available from the Society to the notice of all those concerned with the welfare of ex-service men and women, as well as for fund-raising purposes.

Administration

All other expenditure not directly allocated above, including financial expenses, pensions to former employees, professional fees and insurances.

Rather than as an integral part of the accounts, some charities, including Barnardo's, present their accounting policies as a separate statement, detached from the notes to the accounts. While this positioning has the advantage of conferring greater prominence to the policies, it conflicts with both SSAP 2 and the revised SORP. Paragraphs 18 of SSAP 2 and 31 and 35 of the revised SORP require, and recommend, respectively, the policies to be displayed 'in the notes to the accounts'. Furthermore, para 36 of Sch 4 to the 1985 Act also requires them to be given in the notes. In these circumstances, the page numbers for the purposes of the auditors', or examiner's, report should include the statement of accounting policies.

SORP 2 encouraged charities to state in their accounts that they had observed its recommendations. While many charities have given this statement, some have not, including the Soldiers' Sailors' and Airmen's Families Association. They were, also, encouraged to disclose any departures from those recommendations with the reasons for such departure.

Where departures are disclosed, they are often not accompanied by a statement of the reasons. For example, Example 6.4 Church Missionary Society disclosed that certain assets acquired by gift or bequest are stated at nominal value, but does not explain why – presumably due to the difficulty in establishing a reliable basis of measurement.

Example 6.4 Church Missionary Society
Note 2: Accounting policies (extract) (31 January 1994):

> ***Accounting convention***
> The accounts are prepared under the historical cost convention, subject to the inclusion of certain assets acquired by gift or bequest at nominal values. Statement of Recommended Practice Number 2 'Accounting by Charities' has been observed in all other respects.

Example 6.5 Royal National Lifeboat Institution has provided the reasons, although that for the non-depreciation of freehold property is invalid (see chapter **16**, page 423).

Example 6.5 Royal National Lifeboat Institution
Note 1: Accounting policies (part) (31 December 1993):

(b) The accounts comply with the Statement of Recommended Practice No. 2, 'Accounting by charities', issued by the Accounting Standards Committee in May 1988, except for the following:

(i) Capital expenditure on the lifeboat fleet, together with certain related operational equipment and buildings, is fully charged to the Income and Expenditure Account in the year in which the expenditure is incurred. Other fixed assets are capitalised at original cost and are subject to depreciation (Note 3).

(ii) No provision has been made for depreciation of freehold property since it is considered that market value is not less than original cost.

Note 2 Lifeboat fleet:

The lifeboat fleet has been written off in the year of purchase in recognition of its unique nature, and in accordance with the accounting policy (Note 1b(i)). The accumulated cost so written off is £78.5 million (1992: £73.6 million). Related shoreworks are also written off in the year of purchase and the accumulated cost so written off in the past five years is £16.8 million (1992: £15.3 million).

Paragraph 35 of the revised charity SORP recommends that the charity trustees explain whether the accounts have been drawn up in accordance with its recommendations.

Accounting policies should be applied consistently throughout the year and from one year to the next. Consistent with FRS 3 *Reporting financial performance*, both the original and revised SORPs permit changes to accounting policies, but only in circumstances where they 'will give a fairer presentation of the transactions or financial position of the charity than the one it replaces'. While the original SORP stated that any changes 'should be disclosed', without further prescription, para 28(c) (iv) (and Appendix 2) of the revised SORP requires this disclosure to be in 'the trustees' report'.

Changes should be accounted for by restating the opening balances of the fund, or funds, involved. The corresponding amounts for the previous year should, also, be adjusted.

Chapter 7 – Income and expenditure

7.1 Introduction

Paragraph 24(a) of SORP 2 stated that the purpose of an income and expenditure account was 'to show the resources made available to the charity and the expenditure incurred . . . during the period'.

This chapter looks at how charities have, historically, presented their income and expenditure accounts and how they have accounted for, and disclosed, different types of income and expenditure and the changes which will need to be made to comply with the revised charity SORP.

7.2 Presentation

Paragraph 58 of SORP 2 allowed trustees to analyse the income and expenditure account 'in a manner appropriate to the charity'. Such analysis, which was not to be excessively detailed, allowed users 'to gain a proper appreciation of the principal elements of income and expenditure'. This approach has permitted charities to display items of income and expenditure in different ways, perhaps reflecting trustees' diverse perceptions both of the role which individual items of income and expenditure play in relation to each other and of the composition of the operating result.

Some charities present both income and expenditure *en bloc,* with or without further differentiation, in calculating a surplus (or deficit) for the year. One such charity is Example 7.1 the British Diabetic Association.

Example 7.1 British Diabetic Association
Group income and expenditure account (part) (31 December 1993):

Income	Notes	1993 £	*1992 £*
Donations	(7)	2,817,032	*2,639,507*
Net income of trading undertaking	(11)	372,023	*171,921*
Legacies		3,371,885	*3,653,793*
Subscriptions		760,690	*658,388*
Professional membership sections		181,067	*151,793*
Dividends and interest		685,054	*900,290*
Sales		282,674	*222,404*
Children's activities		180,398	*142,053*
Other income		34,832	*20,979*
Total Income		8,685,655	*8,561,128*
Expenditure			
Research grants		2,795,141	*2,678,843*
Developmental project grants		42,993	*77,544*
Scientific information service		79,892	*64,792*
Research expenses		109,342	*104,991*
Membership services		1,097,091	*946,782*
Social care		1,193,882	*1,155,859*
Information and education		706,300	*944,234*
Children's activities		688,024	*555,556*
Professional membership sections		284,451	*207,531*
Branches and national conference		228,480	*201,869*
Administration		499,339	*450,720*
Direct fundraising		511,315	*348,914*
Costs of goods sold		171,979	*153,259*
Non-recoverable VAT		74,919	*87,569*
Legal charges	(8)	40,188	*101,041*
Other expenses		18,375	*11,256*
Auditors' remuneration		10,000	*8000*
Total Expenditure		8,551,711	*8,098,760*
Surplus for the year		133,944	*462,368*
Add: Profit on sale of investments		188,601	*352,012*
		322,545	*814,380*

Charities position different categories of expenditure differently. While Example 7.2 Ex-Services Mental Welfare Society deducts indirect expenditure from total income to give a figure available for charitable purposes, followed by the deduction of expenditure in respect of charitable pursuits to produce the operating surplus, Example 7.3 Help The Aged deducts these two types of expenditure in reverse. Alternatively, Example 7.4 the Woodland Trust deducts the cost of woodland management after all income and other expenditure and net movements on funds.

Example 7.2 Ex-Services Mental Welfare Society
Income and expenditure account (part) (30 September 1993):

	Notes	1993 £	1993 £	1992 £	1992 £
INCOME	1(d)				
Appeals income:					
Donations			674,668		*711,083*
Legacies			563,266		*797,119*
			1,237,934		*1,508,202*
Receipts for maintenance of patients			1,643,190		*1,316,257*
Investment income			267,894		*247,653*
Profit (loss) on sale of investments			31,649		*(12,254)*
			3,180,667		*3,059,858*
Special appeal income					
Tyrwhitt House		160,000		–	
Hollybush House		30,420		–	
			190,420		–
TOTAL INCOME (from continuing activities)			3,371,087		*3,059,858*
INDIRECT EXPENDITURE					
Appeals		185,319		*229,879*	
Publicity		151,054		*147,071*	
Administration		182,924		*180,834*	
			519,297		*557,784*
AVAILABLE FOR CHARITABLE PURPOSES			2,851,790		*2,502,074*
CHARITABLE EXPENDITURE					
Homes' running costs		1,802,644		*1,709,704*	
Other welfare costs		242,650		*207,825*	
			2,045,294		*1,917,529*
SURPLUS ON OPERATIONS	2		806,496		*584,545*

Example 7.3 Help The Aged
Income and expenditure account (part) (30 April 1993):

1992 £,000		Notes	£'000
	Income		
30,905	Fundraising Appeals	2	34,954
779	Dividends and Interest	3	370
31,684			35,324
20,913	Distributions	4	25,073
2,546	Direct Charitable Operations	5	2,624
23,459			27,697
8,225			7,627
	Expenditure		
6,973	Fundraising	7	7,212
1,631	Research and Development	8	1,115
483	Administration		571
9,087			8,898
(862)	Operating Deficit		(1,271)

Example 7.4 Woodland Trust
Income and expenditure account (part) (31 December 1993):

		Year ended 31 December 1993		Fourteen months ended 31 December 1992	
	Note	£'000	£'000	*£'000*	*£'000*
INCOME					
Membership subscriptions	1(c)	987		*1,095*	
Legacies		881		*1,173*	
Fundraising		1,889		*1,875*	
Total voluntary income			3,757		*4,143*
Grants for woodland and land purchase	1(d)	741		*739*	
Income from woodland management		634		*612*	
Donated woodland and land	1(f)	140		*637*	
Total contribution from woodland operations			1,515		*1,988*
Invesment income	4	183		*88*	
Contribution from Woodland Trust (Enterprises) Ltd	13	153		*121*	
Sundry income		37		*55*	
Total other sources of income			373		*264*
TOTAL INCOME			5,645		*6,395*
Loss on investments	7		–		*165*
EXPENDITURE					
Supporter recruitment and services	1(g)	413		*549*	
Fundraising	1(h)	461		*581*	
Public Relations/Public Affairs		292		*123*	
Administration and Financial	1(i)	738		*726*	
Depreciation	1(k)	108		*126*	

Example 7.4 Woodland Trust
Income and expenditure account (part) (31 December 1993): (Continued)

	Note	Year ended 31 December 1993 £'000	£'000	Fourteen months ended 31 December 1992 *£'000*	*£'000*
TOTAL EXPENSES (EXCLUSING COST OF WOODLAND MANAGEMENT)			2,012		*2,105*
			3,633		*4,125*
Net movement on funds	12		224		*69*
Balance available for woodland and land acquisition and management			3,857		*4,194*
Cost of woodland management during period	1(j)		(1,935)		*(1,982)*
Balance for period available for woodland and land acquisition, transferred to Capital Fund	12		1,922		*2,212*
Woodland and land acquisition during period	5		1,539		*1,982*

Example 7.5 Guide Dogs for the Blind Association separates out voluntary income from other income. In doing so, rather than combining fundraising expenditure with other expenditure, it has deducted this from voluntary income to form a total for net voluntary income. Linking fundraising income and expenditure in this fashion is seen as being both logical and informative.

Example 7.5 Guide Dogs for the Blind Association
Income and expenditure account (part) (31 December 1993):

	NOTES	**1993**	*1992 Reclassified Page 6,(3)*
NET VOLUNTARY INCOME		**£000**	*£000*
Voluntary Fund-Raising Branches	1a	**2,903**	*4,331*
Donations and Other Income	1b	**3,030**	*3,877*
Legacies		**20,187**	*17,439*
		26,120	*25,647*
Less Fund Raising Expenses		**3,915**	*3,834*
Total Net Voluntary Income		**22,205**	*21,813*

Example 7.6 Dogs' Home Battersea separates out operating income and expenses to produce an operating result. Other, non-recurring, income, e.g., investment income and legacies, is separately identified.

Due to the position of administrative costs and interest, Example 7.7 SENSE has a different meaning for operating result.

Example 7.6 Dogs' Home Battersea
Income and expenditure account (31 December 1993):

	Notes	1993 £	1993 £	*1992 £*	*1992 £*
Operating Income					
Sales and claim-fees for dogs and cats including **£25,844** (1992 – £45,412) vaccination fees on sales		201,500		*227,531*	
Admission charges		20,429		*20,916*	
Receipts from police contracts	11	286,642		*332,056*	
Service charge to Bell Mead Kennels Limited		22,989		*21,500*	
Sundry receipts		36,406		*31,527*	
			567,966		*633,530*
Less: Operating Expenditure					
Kennels and yard –					
Wages and uniforms		935,672		*900,922*	
Food		82,980		*69,941*	
Veterinary salaries and fees		272,120		*243,260*	
Medicine and vaccines		126,110		*169,356*	
Heat, light and water		97,087		*82,616*	
Repairs and upkeep		49,014		*60,610*	
Depreciation of plant and buildings		217,204		*259,269*	
Cost of boarding dogs at Bell Mead		173,460		*132,501*	
Sundry expenses		91,816		*68,311*	
Implants		30,215		*30,734*	
Training		8,515		*16,886*	
		2,084,193		*2,034,406*	
Rent, rates and insurance		42,911		*38,577*	

Example 7.6 Dogs' Home Battersea
Income and expenditure account (31 December 1993): (Continued)

	Notes	1993 £	1993 £	*1992* *£*	*1992* *£*
Administration –					
Salaries and pensions		271,348		*262,195*	
Printing, stationery, postage, telephone and sundries		101,905		*105,506*	
Heat, light and water		6,045		*3,549*	
Auditors' remuneration		9,500		*9,000*	
		388,798		*380,250*	
Motor vans –					
Drivers wages		93,869		*101,493*	
Running costs		16,681		*18,516*	
Depreciation		18,005		*22,097*	
Loss on sale of motor vehicles		3,125		–	
		131,680		*142,106*	
Legal and professional charges		112,357		*80,092*	
Distribution costs of films		1,718		*6,865*	
Donation to UFAW		10,000		–	
			2,771,657		*2,682,296*
Operating Deficit			(2,203,691)		*(2,048,766)*
Other Annual Income					
Income from investments –					
Quoted		1,148,522		*876,092*	
Unquoted		766		*761*	
Bank deposit and other interest		110,991		*284,786*	

Example 7.6 Dogs' Home Battersea
Income and expenditure account (31 December 1993): (Continued)

	Notes	1993 £	1993 £	*1992* £	*1992* £
Donations and subscriptions including covenanted receipt from Bell Mead Kennels Limited of **£5,000** (1992 – £20,000)		144,477		*138,477*	
			1,404,756		*1,300,116*
Deficit of Annual Income over Expenditure for the Year			(798,935)		*(748,650)*
Legacy and Non-Recurring Income for the year					
Legacies	1		2,165,605		*3,693,527*
Profit on sales of investments			189,511		*327,808*
Provision for permanent diminution in value of investment	4		(107,187)		–
Appeal income –					
Toy appeal (income £3,443. less expenditure £3,124)		319		–	
Donations		4,141		*4,137*	
			4,460		*4,137*
			2,252,389		*4,025,472*

All amounts relate to continuing operations.
The company has no recognised gains or losses other than as disclosed in the Income and Expenditure Account.

Example 7.7 SENSE
Income and expenditure account (part) (31 March 1994):

	Note	1994 £	£	£	1993 £
			13,084,321		*9,388,351*
Operating Expenses					
Rehabilitation and Training		7,604,298		*5,617,585*	
Welfare and Information		1,696,525		*1,267,351*	
Education		958,888		*574,009*	
Fundraising		1,038,630		*814,374*	
			(11,298,341)		*(8,273,319)*
Operating Surplus			1,785,980		*1,115,032*
Administrative Expenses	5	(118,888)		*(122,141)*	
Interest payable and similar charges	7	(7,884)		*(4,712)*	
Interest receivable and similar income	6	157,863		*196,868*	
Relating to Restricted and Designated Funds	18	(1,769,170)		*(1,105,122)*	
			(1,738,079)		*(1,035,107)*
Surplus for the year	8		47,901		*79,925*

This limited survey demonstrates the variety of individual forms of presentation. Some charities identify operating result, although there are different interpretations of what constitutes this figure. By subtotalling net resources available for distribution, other charities' (e.g., grant-making charities) presentations seem more like source and application of funds statements. Contrary to the SORP's recommendations, other charities exclude some of their income from the main income and expenditure account. Presumably, the wish is to identify separately results from regular income flows from total incoming resources.

The different forms of presentation, together with the discrete use of sub-totals, serve to highlight trustees' use of different measurement criteria in portraying important features of the income and expenditure account. The form and content of the SOFA, as discussed in chapter **4** (see page 89), will require some charity trustees to rethink the way they both present their income and expenditure accounts and measure the operating result.

7.3 To net or not to net?

Paragraph 61 of SORP 2 explained that:

> 'A minimum of "netting off" of income and expenditure and of assets and liabilities should take place. However, if a charity has received income from, and incurred expenses on, special fund-raising events or activities, it may occasionally be more informative to include only the net figure in the income and expenditure account. Where netting off takes place, the reason for it and, whenever practicable, the "gross" figures should be disclosed in the notes.'

Charitable companies need to observe para 5 of Sch 4 to the 1985 Act which requires that 'Amounts in respect of items representing assets or income may not be set off against amounts in respect of items representing liabilities or expenditure (as the case may be) or vice versa'.

Charities with fundraising events often take advantage of the relaxation to show only the net amount in the income and expenditure account, with gross details exploded in the notes. Example 7.8 Cancer Relief Macmillan Fund and Example 7.9 Multiple Sclerosis Society are two such charities. The latter charity, also, operates a number of holiday homes, which, for accounting purposes, are classified as branches. The operating results are shown net in the income and expenditure account with an analysis, by home, provided in the notes.

Example 7.8 Cancer Relief Macmillan Fund
Note 1: Donations, fundraising and legacies (31 December 1993):

	From local Committees £000	**1993 Total £000**	*From local Committees £000*	*1992 Total £000*
Donations	2,501	**5,155**	*2,323*	*5,212*
Special Fundraising:				
Functions and Special Events	2,189	**2,922**	*1,963*	*3,047*
House to House Collections and Flag Days	427	**478**	*423*	*483*
Raffles	202	**202**	*171*	*171*
	2,818	**3,602**	*2,557*	*3,701*
Less: Direct Expenses	(325)	**(495)**	*(303)*	*(498)*
	2,493	**3,107**	*2,254*	*3,203*
	4,994	**8,262**	*4,577*	*8,415*
Less: Credited to Appeals†	(2,824)	**(4,216)**	*(1,682)*	*(3,493)*
	2,170	**4,046**	*2,895*	*4,922*
Legacies	430	**7,963**	*484*	*7,794*
Less: Credited to Gifts for Specific Purposes*	–	**(1,055)**	*(92)*	*(1,652)*
	2,600	**10,954**	*3,287*	*11,064*

† Income that was, at the request of Committees or donors, credited to a local Macmillan Appeal, is included in the appropriate Building or Nurse Appeal section of these Accounts.

* Legacies that were accepted on the understanding that they may only be used for specific purposes. Of this, £165,000 has been included in Building and Nurse Appeals (1992 – £1,278,000), and £890,000 (1992 – £374,000) has been attributed to other work (see Note 6).

Example 7.9 Multiple Sclerosis Society
Note 4: Fundraising receipts (net) (31 December 1993):

			1993			1992
	Head office	Branches	Consolidated	*Head office*	*Branches*	*Consolidated*
	£	£	£	*£*	*£*	*£*
Income						
General fund raising	220,491	1,675,680	1,896,171	*493,087*	*1,591,694*	*2,084,781*
Flag days and collections	–	776,411	776,411	–	*806,763*	*806,763*
Direct mail	462,910	–	462,910	*468,145*	–	*468,145*
Total fund raising income	683,401	2,452,091	3,135,492	*961,232*	*2,398,457*	*3,359,689*
Expenditure						
General fund raising	269,319	339,886	609,205	*388,071*	*321,939*	*710,010*
Flag days and collections	–	13,212	13,212	–	*14,331*	*14,331*
Direct mail	349,114	–	349,114	*326,167*	–	*326,167*
Total fund raising costs	618,433	353,098	971,531	*714,238*	*336,270*	*1,050,508*
Net fund raising receipts	64,968	2,098,993	2,163,961	*246,994*	*2,062,187*	*2,309,181*

Example 7.9 Multiple Sclerosis Society
Note 7: Respite care centres and holiday homes: (31 December 1993):

(a) The Society operates a total of seven respite care centres and holiday homes, five in England and two in Scotland. For accounting purposes these are classified as branches.
(b) Operating deficits at the respite care centres and holiday homes occurred as follows:

		1993			*1992*	
	Income £	Expend. £	Deficit £	*Income £*	*Expend. £*	*Deficit £*
England						
Brambles – Horley	674,033	972,346	298,313	*569,611*	*886,644*	*317,033*
Helen Ley – Leamington Spa	505,293	791,084	285,791	*429,288*	*695,025*	*265,737*
Kenninghall – Worthing	128,137	217,332	89,195	*151,951*	*215,918*	*63,967*
Orcombeleigh – Exmouth	199,733	344,831	145,098	*196,009*	*318,354*	*122,345*
Woodlands – York	387,122	733,626	346,504	*303,167*	*631,682*	*328,515*
Scotland						
Holmhill – Grantown-on-Spey	90,863	258,074	167,211	*85,333*	*229,885*	*144,552*
Richard Cave MS Home – Leuchie	116,261	206,417	90,156	*104,492*	*183,845*	*79,353*
	2,101,442	3,523,710	1,422,268	*1,839,851*	*3,161,353*	*1,321,502*

Income includes guests fees and expenses, and all donations received by the home; expenditure includes all running expenses but excludes depreciation of £144,449 (1992: £175,338) and audit fees of £8,402 (1992: £8,373).

Some charities, which operate shops selling donated goods, prefer to show the result on a single line on the face of the income and expenditure account, with a breakdown relegated to the notes. One such charity is Example 7.10 OXFAM.

Example 7.10 OXFAM
Note 2: Income (part) (30 April 1993):

	1993 £'000	*1992 £'000*
(b) Oxfam Shops This represents the net income from the sale of donated goods through Oxfam shops:		
Gross Income received by Shops	40,311	*39,709*
Deduct: Expenses of converting donated goods into cash and selling Oxfam Trading goods through Oxfam shops	21,839	*20,814*
Net Shop Income (including earmarked donations)	18,472	*18,895*

Gross income and expenses are based on returns submitted by Oxfam shops. These returns are audited locally. It is not practical for every shop to submit a return in time for incorporation in the annual accounts and the figures are consequently estimates.

Rather than netting off fundraising expenses against voluntary income on the face of the income and expenditure account, like Example 7.5, Example 7.11 Royal National Institute for the Blind has done so in the notes.

Example 7.11 Royal National Institute for the Blind
Note 2: Net voluntary income (31 March 1994):

	1994 £'000	*1993 £'000*
Donations and other voluntary income	7,449	*7,360*
Legacies	18,611	*18,349*
	26,060	*25,709*
Less: fundraising expenditure	5,749	*5,868*
	20,311	*19,841*

Some charities delegate the management of their investment portfolio to outside specialists. While some, for example Example 7.12 Action Research, net off the expenses against the related income, others, for example Example 7.13 Cinema & Television Benevolent Fund, prefer to present the figures gross.

Example 7.12 Action Research
Note 4: Income from fixed assets (31 October 1993):

	1993	*1992*
	£	*£*
Dividends and interest on listed investments (gross or gross equivalent less management charges of £51,350)	955,875	*1,057,112*
Dividends from unlisted investments (see Note 7)	39,760	*48,104*
Short term deposit interest received (gross)	17,756	*72,057*
Profit on sale of investments	1,370,037	*437,036*
	2,383,428	*1,614,309*

Example 7.13 Cinema & Television Benevolent Fund
Consolidated income and expenditure account (part) (31 March 1994):

	1994		*1993*	
	£	£	*£*	*£*
Investment income (Note 10)		1,061,398		*1,143,063*
TOTAL INCOME		1,843,798		*1,907,853*
deduct EXPENDITURE				
Relief granted	867,725		*861,046*	
Glebelands Rest and Convalescent Home (Note 11)	548,590		*484,321*	
	1,416,315		*1,345,367*	
Relief support costs (Note 12)	265,796		*247,798*	
Fund raising and publicity costs	46,675		*46,539*	
Administration costs (Note 13)	210,308		*203,793*	
Investment management fees	73,326		*68,754*	
TOTAL EXPENDITURE		2,012,420		*1,912,251*

The reasons for netting off are seldom disclosed.

Paragraphs 99 and 133 of the revised SORP require, as far as is practicable, all incoming resources to be shown gross. In certain circumstances (e.g., small fundraising events), however, netting off (but not the charity's own staff costs – para 112) is permitted 'for the sake of clarity'. Small fundraising events include the results from permitted occasional trading, e.g., jumble sales, gymkhanas etc., generally for fundraising purposes, provided that the amounts are not substantial. Where netting off takes place, para 133 recommends that the reason and, if material, an estimate of the gross funds raised and the expenditure incurred is disclosed in the notes.

7.4 Income

7.4.1 When should income be recognised?

The revised SORP has changed the emphasis for the recognition of income. Whereas SORP 2 recommended that voluntary income generally be recognised when *received*, its successor requires income to be recognised when it is prudent and practicable to do so. This will usually be when the income is *receivable* or the charity's entitlement thereto becomes *legally enforceable* (para 98).

The fact that an incoming resource may only be used for a restricted purpose should not affect its recognition in the SOFA. In accounting for incoming resources subject to restrictions, however, the revised charity SORP draws an important distinction between restrictions on the purposes for which a resource may be used and conditions which must be fulfilled prior to its receipt, or use, by the charity.

An incoming resource should not be recognised in the SOFA if receipt is subject to preconditions which cannot be satisfied, either at the time of receipt or at a later date. The reasons should be explained in the notes (para 101). On the other hand, preconditions relating to the timing of expenditure could affect the timing of recognition of the related income. For example, where a grant is received in a financial year which precedes that in which the expenditure may be used, its recognition should be deferred to that later period. Thus, an element of income received which clearly relates to a future financial year, e.g., school fees paid in advance or a grant for the purchase of a fixed asset for use by the charity, should be deferred.

However, this does not debar the recognition of restricted income solely on the grounds that the expenditure to which the income relates has not been incurred (para 102). This would be a departure from the accruals concept, since it would prohibit the recognition of that income unless it had been expended in the financial year, but is appropriate for charities because it adopts the matching principle of the accruals concept that in certain circumstances will recognise income only when the expenditure to which it is matched has been incurred. This principle has to be treated with care since strict observance of the concept by a charity could, if taken to an extreme and applied to all income, require that income to be deferred, simply because the charity had not spent it.

7.4.2 Restricted income

Paragraph 38 of SORP 2 stated that:

> '. . . the fact that income is restricted should not affect the manner in which it is accounted for in the income and expenditure account or the timing of its recognition as income. The one exception to this rule is when the restrictions imposed are so onerous that it is impossible to use the income in the way intended. In such circumstances, the income should be carried forward in the balance sheet under the heading "deferred restricted income" and the restrictions involved explained.'

No examples could be found where the restrictions on income were such that they were accounted for and presented as recommended.

As regards presentation, some charities distinguish restricted from unrestricted income on the face of the income and expenditure account, while others do so in the notes. Example 7.14 Royal National Lifeboat Institution is an example of the former, and Example 7.15 Help The Aged of the latter.

Example 7.14 Royal National Lifeboat Institution
Income and expenditure account (part) (31 December 1993):

	1993		*1992*	
	£000	£000	*£000*	*£000*
INCOME				
For general purposes				
Subscriptions and donations	14,197		*13,134*	
Legacies	27,139		*27,937*	
Investment income	5,401		*5,240*	
Profit from trading subsidiaries (*Note 6*)	506	47,243	*372*	*46,683*
For restricted purposes				
Donations	1,728		*2,804*	
Legacies	12,900	14,628	*11,728*	*14,532*
Total Income		61,871		*61,215*

Example 7.15 Help The Aged
Note 2: Fundraising appeals (30 April 1994):

1993 £'000		*£'000*
346	Gifted Housing including loss on realisation of £113,965 (1993 surplus £52,544)	542
1,226	Gifts in Kind (spectacles, clothing etc.) at valuation	1,830
1,188	Covenants	1,306
330	Gift Aid	292
5,129	Legacies	6,596
	Co-Funding from Government and Other Agencies:-	
448	Overseas Development Administration	304
619	Commission of the European Communities	426
152	Other Agencies	254
1,219		984
6,414	Gift Shops – Income	8,620
(5,639)	– Expenditure*	(6,671)
775		1,949
24,741	Field Fundraising and Direct Marketing Proceeds	23,050
34,954		36,549
	of which:-	
18,798	Restricted Income	21,321
16,156	General Income	15,228
34,954		36,549

* Expenditure is made up of direct costs of developing and operating the chain of gift shops.

Paragraph 103 of the revised SORP stresses the importance, to a reader of the accounts, of having a complete understanding of all resources received, regardless of whether they have been recognised in that financial year. Accordingly, the SOFA should include all incoming resources, together with the net change in income deferred to future financial years.

7.4.3 Donated assets

Paragraphs 39 and 40 of SORP 2 stated:

> 'Incoming resources in the form of donated assets should usually be included in the income and expenditure account as soon as they are received. The amount at which they should be included should be a reasonable estimate of their value to the charity. The basis of valuation should be disclosed. This treatment is appropriate regardless of whether the assets were donated for use, sale or distribution.
>
> 'On occasion it may not be practicable to ascertain the value of assets received, in which case their receipt should instead be disclosed in a note to the accounts. If it later becomes practicable to ascertain a value for them, this value should be included in the income and expenditure account as income at the date of valuation. For example, if an asset cannot be valued at the date of receipt but is later sold, the sale proceeds should be included as income at the date of sale. If the amount of assets included in income in a period other than the period of receipt is significant, this fact should be reported and the amounts involved disclosed.'

Both Example 7.16 Tear Fund and Example 7.17 Save The Children Fund have received assets for onward distribution. The former accounts for them on a receipts basis (as stated in its accounting policies), whereas the latter values them only when distributed.

Example 7.16 Tear Fund
Note 5: Gifts in kind (31 March 1993):

During the year ended 31 March 1993, the European Community made a number of allocations of cereals to Tear Fund, and these are detailed below. The total value of £4,455,023 has been shown as 'Gifts in Kind' and a corresponding sum has been included in Project Grant payments.

Grain values are as follows:

			£'000
Ethiopia	1,044	tonnes Wheat	217
Malawi	12,138	tonnes Maize	2,980
Sudan	4,730	tonnes Wheat	983
Zimbabwe	2,790	tonnes Maize	275
			4,455

In addition a payment of £75,997 was received from the European Community as additional support for inland transport costs relating to the project in Malawi.

Example 7.17 Save The Children Fund
Accounting policies (part) (31 March 1994):

> **Gifts in kind**
> Gifts in kind include food, clothing, medical supplies and vehicles. They are valued by officers of Save the Children having regard to market prices when distributed in the field. No value has been placed on stocks of goods as yet undistributed.

More often than not, no value is placed on undistributed assets, for example Example 6.1 OXFAM (see chapter **6**, page 147).

Some charities receive assets for use in their work. While Example 7.18 BEN-Motor & Allied Trades Benevolent Fund has the use of motor vehicles, these are not included in the accounts. Other charities receive investments or other assets from wills, measured at probate value – see Example 7.19 Malcolm Sargent Cancer Fund for Children. Donated assets for use by the charity pose particular accounting problems, which are discussed on page 197 and in chapter **8** (see page 215).

Example 7.18 BEN-Motor & Allied Trades Benevolent Fund
Note 3: Tangible fixed assets (part) (31 March 1994):

> During the period, various motor manufacturers and suppliers donated motor vehicles on a loan basis. At 31 March 1994 the charity enjoyed the benefit of 23 (1993: 25) loaned cars, 3 (1993: 2) loaned mini-buses and 2 (1993: 1) loaned vans. These assets are not shown in the financial statements.

Example 7.19 Malcolm Sargent Cancer Fund for Children
Note 1: Accounting policies (part) (31 March 1993):

> (d) Investments are stated at cost, except in the case of legacies where they are stated at probate value at the date of receipt, less any provisions for permanent diminution in value.

Many of the larger charities operate shops through which they sell donated goods, e.g., clothing. No values are placed on shop stock until sold. Example 7.20 SCOPE (formerly The Spastics Society) is typical.

Example 7.20 SCOPE (formerly The Spastics Society)
Note 1: Accounting policies (part) (5 April 1994):

(g) **Income**
Income is accounted for on an accruals basis except for appeals and donations income which is accounted for when received. Legacies have been credited to the income and expenditure account and bequests in the form of properties or investments have been included at their estimated value at the time of receipt. Donations in kind to the Society's shops are accounted for when they are sold.

Paragraphs 107 and 108 of the revised charity SORP deal with donated assets. Assets given for distribution by the charity should be recognised as income for the year only when distributed. Where there are undistributed assets at the year end, a description of the items involved and an estimate of their value should be given by way of a note to the accounts. Assets given for use by the charity, e.g., property for its own occupation, should be recognised as incoming resources when receivable. Where a gift has been made in kind but on trust for conversion into cash and subsequent application by the charity, the incoming resource should normally be recognised in the financial year when receivable, but in certain cases this will not be practicable, e.g., second-hand goods donated for resale in charity shops. In these cases the income should be included in the financial year in which the gift is sold. In all cases the amount at which gifts in kind are brought into account should be either a reasonable estimate of their value to the charity or the amount actually realised. The basis of any valuation should be disclosed. Where material, an adjustment should be made to the original valuation upon subsequent realisation of the gift.

7.4.4 Donations-in-kind

In respect of this form of income, para 36 of SORP 2 stated:

> 'A charity may receive assistance in the form of donated facilities, voluntary help or beneficial loan arrangements. Such assistance is generally referred to as "intangible income" or "donations-in-kind". Although some intangible income should be included in the income and expenditure account, it will usually be more appropriate to deal with it in the notes to the accounts or in the trustees' report – particularly as its value will often be impossible to quantify. The information disclosed in respect of such income should be sufficient to give a reasonable appreciation of the benefit derived from it.'

Example 7.21 Help The Aged and Example 7.22 Mary Rose Trust provide narrative in the trustees' report, with the latter conservatively estimating the value of the support. Example 7.23 Tidy Britain Group provides monetary details in the notes. Example 7.24 Cancer Relief Macmillan Fund discloses information as an accounting policy.

Example 7.21 Help The Aged
Report of the Board of Trustees (part) (30 April 1994):

Employees and Volunteers
Help The Aged is an equal opportunities employer. All of its employees and volunteers are treated equally, irrespective of their age, sex, ethnic origin, colour, disability or religious faith. The Charity, in conjunction with its employees, operates a democratically elected Joint Consultative Committee.

The Trustees once again wish to record their recognition of the professionalism and commitment of all our staff and volunteers. A key objective was to improve services despite pressure on fundraising and the need to commence rebuilding reserves. Our staff and volunteers responded to this challenge by making our limited funds go even further. Their dedication, enthusiasm and positive approach to opportunities give us every confidence in the future.

Example 7.22 Mary Rose Trust
Report of the Executive Committee (part) (31 December 1993):

Gifts and services in kind
The Committee recognises that gifts and services in kind were an important contributor to the overall financial well-being of The Mary Rose Trust in 1993.

The total value of help in kind including professional services and the invaluable support of the volunteers is conservatively estimated at £250,000 for the year under review. In 1993 additional gifts in kind of equipment and materials worth £308,000 were received, giving a total value of gifts and services in kind of £538,000.

Example 7.23 Tidy Britain Group
Note 7: Benefits in kind (31 March 1994):

The total value of benefits in kind to the Group amounted to £3,051,604 (1993: £3,791,723). Details were recorded by the Group and, where exact values were not available, an estimate was made by Management. Details are as follows:

	1994	*1993*
	£	*£*
Staff and Office Costs	**86,961**	*162,829*
TV and Radio	**2,764,681**	*3,291,615*
Promotions and Public Events	**189,781**	*316,781*
Professional Services	**10,181**	*20,498*
	£3,051,604	*£3,791,723*

In addition to the above, the Group secured an estimated publicity value of £8.8m (1993: £10.2m) from press articles and features which mentioned the Group by name. These estimates are provided for information only and are not reflected in the figures presented in the financial statements.

Example 7.24 Cancer Relief Macmillan Fund
Accounting policies (part) (31 December 1993):

Gifts in Kind
The charity benefits from the many thousands of voluntary hours and unclaimed out-of-pocket expenses contributed by a very large number of supporters. In addition, companies, organisations and individuals have, in many cases, provided the use of facilities, equipment and premises for various activities and meetings without charge. It would be impossible to place a value on all these gifts in kind for which the charity is extremely grateful and without which much of the work undertaken could not be achieved.

In addition, Cancer Relief Macmillan Fund has received the benefit of the services of secondees, and of many items ranging from jumble to pictures, property and shares the value of which is taken to income upon sale or, if retained for investment purposes, at a reasonable valuation.

Sometimes, staff may be seconded to a charity on a part-time basis. In this situation, the charity may need to bear a proportion of staff costs. Example 7.25 Mary Rose Trust is an example. Conversely, a company (or trust) may undertake to pay the salaries of some employees of a charity. In these circumstances, a sensible approach might be to charge the cost of the salaries as an expense, with a corresponding credit to donations.

Example 7.25 Mary Rose Trust
Accounting policies (part) (31 December 1992):

f) Contributions to pension fund
(i) Defined benefit scheme

Certain employees of Portsmouth City Council whose employment costs are charged to the Trust, commensurate with their involvement on Trust activities, participate in a local government superannuation pension scheme. The assets of the scheme are held in a fund independent from the Trust's assets. The contributions payable by the City Council are determined by actuarial valuation using assumptions made by members of the Institute or Faculty of Actuaries. Full actuarial valuations are made regularly at 5 year intervals and contribution levels reviewed. The relevant contributions payable by the Trust to cover the cost of benefits arising from the current service of its employees are included in the income and expenditure account.

The ED to the revised SORP took a more controversial approach to accounting for all donations-in-kind. Paragraph 66 of the ED stated that ' . . . Such intangible income should only be included . . . if the charity would otherwise have to purchase the donated facilities or services. The information disclosed in respect of such income should be sufficient to give a clear appreciation of the benefit derived from it

. . . '. To measure the benefit to a charity of, say, the services of volunteer helpers and include this in the accounts would not only be difficult but highly subjective. Such income may need to be offset by equivalent intangible expenditure, e.g., the extension of free facilities to related causes.

The revised SORP takes a less strict approach. Paragraph 109 still requires intangible income, other than that in respect of voluntary help, to be included in the SOFA, but only if the charity would otherwise have to purchase the donated facilities and where the benefit is both quantifiable and material. An equal and opposite amount would be shown under the appropriate expenditure heading.

Intangible income in the form of voluntary help should be disclosed either in the notes or in the trustees' annual report.

7.4.5 Legacies

SORP 2 recommended that legacies be accounted for on a cash basis. Paragraph 37 stated: ' . . . all legacies (other than those received for permanent endowment) should be included in full in the income and expenditure account as soon as they are received.'

Accounting for legacy income would appear, therefore, to be a relatively uncontroversial matter. But nothing could be further from the truth. There is a variety of accounting practice, perhaps indicative of the unpredictability of the income.

Many charities observe SORP 2's recommendations, including Example 7.26 Mencap.

Example 7.26 Royal Society for Mentally Handicapped Children and Adults (Mencap)
Note 2: Accounting policies (part) (31 March 1994):

> *(g) Legacy and donation income*
> Legacies and donations are credited to the income and expenditure account when they are received.

In order more properly to represent a structured approach to medium-term financial planning, some charities *manage* the income through an equalisation reserve. Having first credited the income and expenditure account, Example 7.27 National Deaf Children's Society credits legacy income to a fund and releases this to income in four equal annual instalments. Example 7.28 Crosslinks directly credits a maximum of

£90,000 to a separate fund and releases this over ten years, any excess being used to finance special projects and credited to income over not longer than three years; Example 6.2 NCH Action for Children (see chapter **6**, page 150) manages such income 'in reverse', but with the same effect. It credits all income to the income and expenditure account and transfers, to an equalisation account, 'the aggregate of the surplus/(deficit) of unconditional legacy income over/(under) the average of such income for the past three years'. While Example 7.27 and Example 6.2 comply with the SORP, Example 7.28 does not.

Example 7.27 National Deaf Children's Society
Note 1: Accounting policies (part) (31 March 1994):

> **1.4 Legacies**
> Legacies are credited to income in four equal annual instalments beginning with the year of receipt.

Example 7.28 Crosslinks
Note 5: Reserves (part) (31 December 1993):

> Legacies, up to £90,000, are credited to the Income and Expenditure Account in equal amounts over ten years. Any amounts received in excess of £90,000 are credited to a Legacies Special Projects reserve to be used for one off projects that might not otherwise have been funded. These legacies are credited to the Income and Expenditure Account as the related expenditure is incurred but over a period not longer than three years. During 1993 £63,600 was used for Special Projects (1992: £46,135) and transferred to the Income and Expenditure account.

Charities which account for legacy income in this way take the view that to include all such income, on receipt, in the income and expenditure account provides a distorted view of such planning. But this fails to account for the income in accordance with its substance, which is that of a windfall gain.

Example 7.29 The National Trust treats legacies as capital receipts and acknowledges, in its accounting policies, that this is a departure from SORP 2.

Example 7.29 The National Trust
Note 3: Accounting policies (part) (28 February 1994):

> **Gifts and Legacies**
> Tied gifts and all legacies have been treated as capital receipts and are disclosed in the Movement of Funds statement. Other gifts have been taken to the Income and Expenditure Account.

Paragraph 106 of the revised SORP requires legacies to be included in income 'unless they are incapable of financial measurement'. Example 7.30 Guide Dogs for the Blind Association will, in future, have to account for its pecuniary legacies. Where the charity has entitlement to material legacies not included in the accounts, that fact and an estimate of the amount receivable should be disclosed in the notes. As confirmed by Example 7.30, providing an estimate of its residuary legacies is a more difficult (if not impossible) task, but the revised SORP does not appear to offer any exceptions from disclosure.

Example 7.30 Guide Dogs for the Blind Association
Note 10: Legacies (31 December 1993):

> As at 31 December 1993 £395,850 was due to the Association in respect of 229 pecuniary legacies. Also 879 residuary legacies had been notified to the Association at that date, against which some payments on account have been received and included in these Financial Statements. The balance outstanding cannot be determined.

7.4.6 Cash collections

Paragraph 41 of SORP 2 stated:

> 'When income has been collected for a charity but has not been received by it by the end of the accounting period, an estimate of the amount not received should in theory be included in the income and expenditure account. Similarly, when some of the charity's income is in collection containers at public premises at the period end, an estimate of the amount in the containers should in theory be included as income. However, because of the practical difficulties which will often be involved, it is not necessary to include such estimates in the income and expenditure account. Whatever treatment is adopted to account for such income should be applied consistently and disclosed.'

Example 7.31 Action Aid is one of the few charities whose accounting policy specifically explains the treatment adopted.

Example 7.31 Action Aid
Note 1: Accounting policies (part) (31 December 1993):

> **1b Income** [part]:
> Income is shown gross with the following exceptions:
>
> Income from the trading subsidiary is the net profit from its operations.
>
> Small sums raised by local fundraising groups in the UK are net of direct expenses incurred by those groups. These groups are autonomous and thus income raised by them is only accounted for when received.
>
> Income is shown in the accounts when collected except for interest and tax recovered from covenants which are shown on a receivable basis.

The revised SORP takes a sensible approach as regards cash collected, to which the charity is legally entitled, but not received at the year end. If considered material, an estimate should be made, based upon a reasoned (e.g., time basis) and consistent apportionment of monies subsequently received. The amount calculated should be shown under current assets, described as 'collections in progress' (paras 13 and 114).

7.4.7 Deposited covenants

Some charities' cash received includes deposited covenants. These are in the form of loans which are paid off over the life of the covenant by being drawn down to satisfy the instalments due under the deed of covenant. In substance, the covenantor has given, up front, all the monies required to be given during the period of the covenant. Advantage to the charity accrues by having immediate access to the funds, while that to the covenantor by being able to claim a deduction from taxable income over the life of the covenant. In accordance with the accruals concept, these monies should be credited to income over the life of the covenant.

In respect of deeds of covenant generally, para 62 of SORP 2 stated:

> 'Income received after deduction of tax at source and income received by deed of covenant should be grossed up for the tax recoverable and this gross figure included in the income and expenditure account. The tax recoverable should be shown as a debtor until the charity recovers the amount involved.'

Paragraph 134 of the revised SORP perpetuates this approach. Example 7.32 Woodland Trust provides a clear example of an accounting policy.

Example 7.32 Woodland Trust
Note 1: Accounting policies (part) (31 December 1993):

p) Deferred Income:

For the preparation of these accounts life membership credit is taken annually for one twentieth of life membership.

Deposited covenants credit is taken annually for the appropriate fraction of the total number of years that the covenant is in existence; the remaining sums are carried forward to be used in future years.

Note 11: Creditors: Amounts falling due after more than one year:

	1993	*1992*
	£'000	*£'000*
Accruals and Deferred income		
Life membership provision	469	*486*
Deposited covenant provision	27	*18*
Payments received on account of future projects	25	*50*
	521	*554*

7.4.8 Life subscriptions

Paragraph 42 of SORP 2 stated:

> 'Life subscriptions purchase for the subscriber facilities or benefits extending over a number of years. In theory a proportion of each subscription received should be allocated to each of the periods for which it is anticipated the subscription will apply. However, rather than undertake lengthy calculations to estimate the appropriate period to use, it is acceptable to use an approximation, perhaps based upon the relationship between the amount of the annual subscription and the amount of the life subscription. The period used should be disclosed.'

Two examples of charities with life subscriptions are Example 7.33 Friends of the Lake District and Example 7.34 The National Trust. While the former releases these to income over 15 years, the latter does so over 10.

Example 7.33 Friends of the Lake District
Note 2: Principal accounting policies (part) (31 December 1993):

(b) Voluntary income, legacies and bequests are recorded when received. Subscriptions are accounted for on a cash basis except subscriptions from life members which are credited as income over a 15 year period. Income from investments is included when it becomes payable.

Balance sheet [part]:

	Note	1993		1992	
		£	£	£	£
Fixed assets					
Tangible assets	3		66,835		*52,235*
Investments	4		612,072		*603,970*
Current assets					
Debtors and accrued income		6,384		*5,033*	
Cash at bank and in hand		3,966		*8,358*	
		10,350		*13,391*	
Creditors: Accruals		2,013		*498*	
Net current assets			8,337		*12,893*
			687,244		*669,098*
Life members subscriptions			(29,139)		*(29,590)*
Designated donations and legacies	5		(43,217)		*(37,402)*
			614,888		*602,106*

Example 7.34 The National Trust
Note 16: Life membership equalisation account (28 February 1994):

Life membership subscriptions are credited to an equalisation account and released over ten years. The movements during the period were:

LIFE MEMBERSHIP EQUALISATION ACCOUNT	14 months to 28/2/94 £'000	12 months to 28/2/94 £'000	*12 months to 31/12/92 £'000*
Balance at start of period	6,519	6,420	*6,387*
Amounts received during period	1,578	1,478	*1,376*
Transfer to Income and Expenditure Account (Note 4)	(1,532)	(1,333)	*(1,244)*
	6,565	6,565	*6,519*

Balance sheet (part):

	Note	28/2/94 £'000	28/2/94 £'000	*31/12/92 £'000*	*31/12/92 £'000*
TOTAL ASSETS LESS CURRENT LIABILITIES			421,749		*361,136*
LESS: LIFE MEMBERSHIP EQUALISATION ACCOUNT	16		6,565		*6,519*
TOTAL ASSETS LESS LIABILITIES			415,184		*354,617*
LESS: TIED FUNDS' ASSETS					
Capital Endowment Funds		226,848		*185,323*	
Defined Purpose Funds		144,425		*129,359*	
Committed Maintenance Fund		26,308		*24,049*	
			397,581		*338,731*
UNTIED ASSETS			17,603		*15,886*
REPRESENTED BY					
General Fund			17,603		*15,886*

With regard to accounting, para 115 of the revised SORP adopts a similar approach. In respect of presentation, the balance carried forward should be included as deferred income under creditors. Both of these charities currently position the unreleased life subscriptions outside of creditors and after a figure struck for total assets less current liabilities. Some reanalysis and repositioning will be necessary.

7.4.9 Grants receivable

Paragraph 43 of SORP 2 sets out the accounting treatment for grants receivable. It stated:

> 'Government and similar grants should be dealt with in accordance with the terms of the grant. Grants made towards the cost of acquiring a fixed asset should be taken to income and expenditure account over the useful life of the asset concerned . . . The amount of the grant still to be taken to income and expenditure account should be shown on the balance sheet as a deferred credit or, where appropriate, included in the relevant fund balance.'

SSAP 4 (Revised) *Accounting for government grants*, like its predecessor, requires grants related to fixed assets to be credited to revenue over the expected useful life of the asset. This may be achieved in one of two ways:

(a) by setting the grant directly against the cost of the asset in the balance sheet, with depreciation being calculated on the net figure; or
(b) by treating the grant as a deferred credit in the balance sheet, and releasing it to income over the life of the related asset to offset the (gross) depreciation charge.

In revising SSAP 4, the ASC considered that both forms of presentation were acceptable and capable of giving a true and fair view. The SSAP went on to say, however, that the CCAB had obtained Counsel's opinion to the effect that the option to deduct government grants from the purchase price or production cost of fixed assets was not available to companies governed by the accounting and reporting provisions of the 1985 Act. Thus, the 'netting' approach would not be available to charitable companies as grant-aided assets would not be stated at the purchase price or production cost. Although other charities could continue to employ either treatment, the 'netting off' approach would create a conflict with the accounting treatment for donated assets (see chapter **8**, page 215), (i.e., such assets would not be shown on the balance sheet).

Example 7.35 BEN-Motor & Allied Trades Benevolent Fund is a charitable company.

Example 7.35 BEN-Motor & Allied Trades Benevolent Fund

Note 3: Tangible fixed assets (part) (31 March 1994):

	Freehold land and buildings £	Furniture fixtures and fittings £	Computer equipment £	Motor vehicles £	**Total £**
Cost					
1 April 1993	11,044,997	1,016,232	109,151	59,409	**12,229,789**
Less Accumulated Grants	(888,863)	(6,806)	–	–	**(895,669)**
	10,156,134	1,009,426	109,151	59,409	**11,334,120**
Reduction in cost accrual	(499,918)	–	–	–	**(499,918)**
Additions	217,170	69,336	980	–	**287,486**
Disposals	(75,307)	–	–	(8,300)	**(83,607)**
31 March 1994	9,798,079	1,078,762	110,131	51,109	**11,038,081**
Depreciation					
1 April 1993	269,923	594,472	95,140	43,527	**1,003,062**
Charged in period	215,998	76,242	13,491	3,886	**309,617**
Disposals	–	–	–	(8,059)	**(8,059)**
31 March 1994	485,921	670,714	108,631	39,354	**1,304,620**
Net book value					
31 March 1994	£9,312,158	£408,048	£1,500	£11,755	**£9,733,461**
31 March 1993	£9,886,209	£414,954	£14,011	£15,882	**£10,331,056**

Grants received in the year were Nil from the Housing Corporation (1993: £72,317).

Rather than carrying the grants as deferred income, they are netted off against the gross cost in determining the amounts shown in the balance sheet. Grant-aided assets continue to be shown gross, in the notes to the accounts, with the total accumulated grants shown separately. For the purposes of calculating depreciation, the accumulated grants are deducted from the gross cost, thereby releasing the grants to income over the lives of the related assets in the form of a reduced depreciation charge. This treatment appears not to satisfy the requirements both of SSAP 4 (Revised) and of the 1985 Act. As para 34 of Pt 4 (Legal requirements in Great Britain and Northern Ireland) of the SSAP states: 'Paragraph 17 of Schedule 4 requires that, . . . , the amount to be included *in the balance sheet* in respect of any fixed assets shall be its purchase price or production cost . . . '. The amounts are not immaterial, but the accounts did not explain that the treatment was a departure from SSAP 4 (Revised) or the 1985 Act.

Prior to 1994, Example 7.36 Barnardo's adopted the same disclosure. In its 1994 accounts, it amended its accounting policy and now classifies unamortised grants as deferred income, within creditors. (Its 1993 accounts were not qualified on these grounds.)

Example 7.36 Barnardo's
Statement of accounting policies (part) (31 March 1993):

GOVERNMENT GRANTS

Regional development grants and other investment grants received are recorded separately and are deducted from the cost of the property to which they relate for the purposes of calculating depreciation (see note 13).

Note 13: Tangible assets (part):

	Properties £'000	Group Equipment & Vehicles £'000	Total £'000
(a) Cost, including gifts at valuation at time of receipt			
At beginning of year			
– as previously reported	86,932	4,857	91,789
– prior year adjustment (note 11b)	(9,740)	–	(9,740)
– as restated	77,192	4,857	82,049
Additions	10,079	3,159	13,238
Disposals	(1,238)	(1,271)	(2,509)
At end of year	86,033	6,745	92,778
(b) Capital grants from statutory authorities (see note 22)			
At beginning of year	3,463		3,463
Further grants in the year	110		110
Repayment	(60)		(60)
At end of year	3,513		3,513

Example 7.36 Barnardo's
Note 13: Tangible assets (part) (31 March 1993): (Continued)

	Properties £'000	Group Equipment & Vehicles £'000	Total £'000
(c) Depreciation			
At beginning of year	16,088	2,310	18,398
Provided during year	3,362	1,562	4,924
On disposals	(418)	(838)	(1,256)
At end of year	19.032	3,034	22,066
(d) Net book value			
At beginning of year			
– as previously reported	67,381	2,547	69,928
– prior year adjustment (note 11b)	(9,740)		(9,740)
– as restated	57,641	2,547	60,188
At end of year	63,488	3,711	67,199

Statement of accounting policies (part) (31 March 1994):

Government Grants

Government grants in respect of capital expenditure are credited to a deferred income account and are released to the income and expenditure account over the expected useful lives of the relevant assets by equal annual instalments.

Example 7.36 Barnardo's
Note 18: Creditors (part) (31 March 1993):

	Group	
	1994	*1993*
	£'000	*£'000*
Amounts falling due within one year:		
Bank overdraft	1,577	*1,489*
Long-term loans (see note 19)	–	*98*
Other taxes and social security costs	2,596	*2,056*
Other creditors	3,162	*3,198*
Accruals	96	*2,833*
Taxation	520	*173*
Trade creditors	276	*174*
Deferred income	3,051	*2,715*
	11,278	*12,736*

By proposing that grants receivable should be included in income in the year of receipt (providing that, for example, any preconditions have been satisfied), the ED of the revised SORP took an approach which conflicted with SSAP 4 (Revised) (to which the ASB requested attention was drawn). An insert to the ED explained the Committee's thinking behind this proposal. A comparison was drawn between the accounting treatment for the purchase of an asset financed wholly, or partly, by a grant and that for a fixed asset donated to the charity:

> 'Grants of money in respect of the purchase of fixed assets may be for the purchase of the asset itself or a contribution to its purchase. The matching treatment of SSAP 4 requires that such money grants are credited to income over the life of the asset concerned. A grant may alternatively be in the form of the asset itself (for example the receipt of a specialised piece of equipment for use in a hospital). In such circumstances the accepted accounting treatment is for the value of the donated asset to be credited immediately on receipt to the income account. The Committee considers that, in substance, there is no difference between these two transactions because in both cases the charity has received an asset for continued use in pursuit of its objectives. The Committee therefore considers that the accounting treatment should be consistent whichever funding route for the receipt of the asset has been followed'.

Thus, because the Committee did not consider that the SSAP 4 approach was appropriate for charities, either for revenue or capital grants, it proposed that all grants should be dealt with, in full, in the SOFA immediately.

Example 7.37 Woodland Trust adopts this form of accounting for grants in respect of woodland and land purchases (its auditors' report is unqualified).

Example 7.37 Woodland Trust
Note 1: Accounting policies (part) (31 December 1993):

d) Grants for woodland and land purchases, tree planting and woodland management which are not repayable, are credited to the Income and Expenditure Account in the year in which they are receivable. This treatment is not in accordance with the relevant Statement of Standard Accounting Practice, but in view of the nature of the Trust's activities and the assets being acquired, it is considered inappropriate to adopt a different treatment for grants received from public bodies than that adopted for donations received for woodland purchase as a result of appeals. Woodland and land purchased is stated in the Balance Sheet at cost.

However, the ED's approach conflicted with the accruals concept. Grants should be recognised in the SOFA so as to match them with the expenditure towards which they are intended to contribute. The proposal ignored the fact that a donated fixed asset is, in substance, outright purchase with a 100% grant and should be accounted for as such in accordance with SSAP 4 (Revised).

In recognition of these arguments, the ED's proposals have been amended in order for the revised SORP to be consistent with SSAP 4 (Revised) (see, also, chapter **4**, page 82, regarding the process by which the ASB gives a 'negative assurance statement').

To be consistent with recognition criteria generally (see page 175), grants should not be included in the SOFA until any preconditions have been satisfied. If there is a likelihood that the grant may be repaid, it should be accounted for, or disclosed, in accordance with the principles which apply to contingent liabilities (see chapter **11**, page 295). Grants for immediate financial support and assistance, or to reimburse previously incurred costs, should be recognised immediately in the SOFA (para 119). Grants restricted to future accounting periods should be deferred and recognised in those future accounting periods.

Thus, where a donated fixed asset is received by a charity, it should be capitalised, when receivable, shown in the SOFA and transferred to a deferred income account. Transfers would be made from that account, in accordance with SSAP 4 (Revised), to offset (all of) the depreciation charge on that asset. This accounting treatment would be consistent with paras 107(b), 102 and 103 respectively. Paragraph 105 recommends that donated fixed assets for a charity's use should, rather than as deferred income, be shown as part of restricted funds, where it is evident that the donor intended the continuing use of the asset.

Paragraph 120 recommends that a description of the sources, by category, of any material grants be disclosed in the notes.

7.5 Expenditure

7.5.1 Classification and allocation of costs

How should costs be classified? Information about costs may be provided by:

(a) functional classification (para 10 of Appendix 1 of the revised charity SORP explains that a 'functional classification' of costs is 'the aggregation of costs incurred in pursuit of a defined purpose (e.g. provision of services to elderly people or counselling), and is achieved by adding together all the costs – salaries, rents, depreciation etc. – relating to that specific activity');

(b) natural classification;
(c) either functional or natural, at the option of the charity; or
(d) both.

Information about expenditure by function is necessary to an understanding of what has been spent on a charity's objects. Requiring that information is, also, a step towards providing information which may be useful in associating a charity's expenses with its accomplishments. Presenting information about expenses by natural classification may be useful in understanding a charity's objects or in assessing its ability to continue to provide services.

In recommending that the following items be separately shown, para 58 of SORP 2 effectively took option (a):

(a) expenditure and grants relating directly to charitable activities;
(b) administration expenses;
(c) fundraising expenses; and
(d) publicity expenses.

Paragraph 59 stated that it was not practicable to produce precise definitions of 'administration expenses', 'fundraising expenses' and 'publicity expenses' or to set out detailed guidance, applicable to all charities. Nonetheless, Pt 2 (Definition of terms) stated that 'administration expenses' comprised:

> 'the costs which are not incurred directly on any charitable activities or projects of the charity and which are not incurred on fundraising activities or publicity';

and 'fundraising expenses' comprised:

> 'costs incurred by a charity in inducing others to make voluntary contributions to it'.

Acknowledging the vagueness of these 'definitions', the SORP recommended that, for the purposes of allocation, the following principles were to be applied:

(a) items of expenditure which involved more than one cost category were to be allocated on a rational basis to the cost categories involved;
(b) expenditure incurred on activities falling directly within one cost category should not be apportioned to any other cost category.

The absence of precise definitions and detailed guidance has allowed charities to develop principles for cost allocation suitable to their own circumstances. While this latitude has had the advantage of allowing charities to report in ways which they believed were meaningful, related to their objects and consistent with their management information systems, it may have had the disadvantage of the adoption of widely differing interpretations. (It should, also, be borne in mind that one charity's direct charitable expenditure may be another's administration costs.) The key, perhaps, was in the further recommendation to provide 'a full description' of the items included within each category and 'of the principles adopted', which were to be consistently applied.

Two of the better disclosures regarding cost allocation are Example 6.3 Ex-Services Mental Welfare Society (see chapter **6** page 153) and Example 7.38 Action Aid.

Example 7.38 Action Aid
Note 5: Central support costs financed from general fund (31 December 1993):

	Note	1993 £'000	*1992 £'000*
Staff costs		4,072	*3,271*
Printing, postage and stationery		1,101	*985*
Advertising		503	*437*
Rent, rates, utilities and telephone		612	*466*
Travel costs		307	*236*
Computer software, maintenance and development		159	*182*
Depreciation of fixed assets		284	*247*
Accountancy and legal fees		151	*82*
Other consultancy costs		314	*184*
General office costs		207	*216*
Bank charges		88	*97*
Repairs and maintenance		183	*225*
Grants		85	*77*
Irrecoverable VAT		260	*172*
Total		8,326	*6,877*
Apportioned as follows	a		
Programme supervision	b	1,180	*1,161*
Publicity, education and research	c	1,218	*909*
Fundraising			
UK	d	3,595	*2,831*
Italy	e	30	–
Total fundraising		3,625	*2,831*
Administration			
UK	f	2,191	*1,787*
Italy	g	112	*189*
Total administration		2,303	*1,976*
Total		8,326	*6,877*

5a Central support expenditure is charged directly to the relevant department wherever possible. The costs of computer services are apportioned to the departments based on estimated usage. The costs of other office services (rent, utilities, building and machinery maintenance etc) are apportioned to departments on an appropriate basis (e.g., area occupied, staff numbers etc).

5b Programme supervision represents the salary and overhead costs of UK based staff who are responsible for the supervision of ACTIONAID's overseas programmes. A small number of grants are made to support other organisations engaged in overseas development activities.

5c Publicity, education and research costs represent the salary and overhead costs of ACTIONAID staff engaged in communications, policy and research work. This work brings the Charity's experience of

Example 7.38 Action Aid
Note 5: Central support costs financed from general fund (31 December 1993): (Continued)

development issues to a wider audience of MP's, government, the education sector and the general public.

5d Fundraising expenditure in the UK represents the costs of sponsorship advertising and general appeals. It includes the salary and overhead costs of staff in fundraising and tax recovery departments in the UK.

5e Fundraising expenditure for the Italian subsidiary undertaking represents the cost of publicity and advertising for Azione Aiuto.

5f Administration expenditure in the UK represents the salary and overhead costs of the service departments: donor support, finance and administration, and personnel.

Auditor's remuneration included in administration expenditure was £36,000 (1992: £30,000) in respect of audit work and £71,000 (1992: £7,000) in respect of consultancy.

5g Administration of the Italian subsidiary undertaking represents the cost of donor support, finance and administration for Azione Aiuto, Italy.

The revised SORP is more prescriptive about what constitutes direct charitable expenditure. Paragraph 92 requires separate disclosure of:

(a) grants payable;
(b) other direct expenditure on charitable objectives, appropriately analysed;
(c) depreciation, or amortisation, of fixed assets used by the charity for its charitable purposes; and
(d) support costs.

Where they do not form part of direct charitable expenditure, fundraising, publicity and administration costs and other expenditure should be shown separately (para 93).

'Support costs' comprise 'all services supplied centrally (either at headquarters or through a regional network) identifiable as wholly or mainly in support of the charity's project work or other direct charitable expenditure' (para 22 of Appendix 1). This would include an appropriate proportion of, for example, finance department, central stores and office accommodation costs. Paragraph 153 recommends that an analysis of all the major items included in support costs is stated separately in the notes to the accounts. This is a new category of cost and recognises that part of the overhead costs may be directly project-related. This represents a change in the treatment recommended by SORP 2, as in the past these costs may have been included within either administration or direct costs.

'Fundraising and publicity costs' comprise 'the costs actually incurred by a charity or by an agent, in inducing others to make voluntary contributions to it' (para 11 of Appendix 1). Such costs will include those in relation to producing advertising and direct mail materials, as well as any remuneration payable to an agent.

Some charities combine publicity costs with those of fundraising, including Example 7.39 Cinema & Television Benevolent Fund. Others show publicity costs separately, for example Example 7.40 Barnardo's, although as an overhead rather than as a direct cost.

Example 7.39 Cinema & Television Benevolent Fund
Consolidated income and expenditure account (part) (31 March 1994):

	1994		*1993*	
	£	£	*£*	*£*
deduct EXPENDITURE				
Relief granted	867,725		*861,046*	
Glebelands Rest and Convalescent Home (Note 11)	548,590		*484,321*	
	1,416,315		*1,345,367*	
Relief support costs (Note 12)	265,796		*247,798*	
Fund raising and publicity costs	46,675		*46,539*	
Administration costs (Note 13)	210,308		*203,793*	
Investment management fees	73,326		*68,754*	
TOTAL EXPENDITURE		2,012,420		*1,912,251*

Example 7.40 Barnardo's
Consolidated income and expenditure account (part) (31 March 1994):

	Note	1994 £'000 Total	*1993 £'000 Total*
Expenditure for Child Care Services			
Child care work in the United Kingdom	4	60,304	*57,418*
Overseas grants	5	1,189	*1,229*
Other Expenditure			
Fundraising costs	6	7,853	*7,817*
Informing the public about our work	7	4,278	*4,030*
Central management services		2,445	*2,438*
Reorganisation costs	8	410	*576*
Total Operating Expenditure		76,479	*73,508*

A change from the proposals of the ED is that publicity costs are, in general, to be combined with fundraising costs. Where publicity costs are a key feature of a charity's charitable effort, however, such costs may be shown under direct charitable expenditure.

'Administration costs' are those which are incurred 'in connection with the management of the charity's assets, organisational (as opposed to project) administration and compliance with constitutional and statutory requirements' (para 1 of Appendix 1) and will comprise, for example, the costs of an audit, trustees' meetings etc. Like support costs, an analysis of the major constituents of administration costs should be provided (para 152).

The following suggestions may be helpful in deciding how costs should be apportioned:

(a) establishment expenses (e.g., rent, rates, light and heat, insurance, cleaning, maintenance of buildings) on a floor area basis;
(b) computer services, telephone, printing, postage, and stationery costs on a usage basis;
(c) personnel and finance costs on a direct staff costs basis.

Whatever basis of allocation is employed, it would be appropriate for the trustees to discuss this with their auditors.

Paragraph 136 recommends that an analysis of expenditure and costs by natural classification be provided in the notes. Some charities already provide an analysis of costs by both functional and natural classification, including Example 7.41 Distressed Gentlefolk's Aid Association.

Example 7.41 Distressed Gentlefolks' Aid Association
Note 7: Operating expenses (31 March 1994):

	Homes £	Counselling Grants & Allowances £	Publicity & Appeals £	Headquarters Administration £	1994 Total £	*1993 Total £*
DIRECT COSTS						
Staff	4,357,536	–	–	–	4,357,536	*4,894,573*
Depreciation	95,176	–	–	–	95,176	*107,800*
Other operating costs	1,981,889	–	–	–	1,981,889	*1,806,803*
Grants and allowances	–	748,736	–	–	748,736	*690,636*
Outside services	–	–	210,676	–	210,676	*341,474*
Refurbishment of existing Homes	607,480	–	–	–	607,480	*2,501,154(3)*
HEADQUARTERS' COSTS						
Staff	153,839(1)	176,377(2)	175,508	404,764	910,488	*996,012*
Depreciation	2,518	2,886	2,872	6,624	14,900	*18,625*
Other operating costs	45,712	52,410	52,151	120,274	270,547	*259,712*
Auditors' remuneration	2,481	2,845	2,831	6,527	14,684	*16,000*
	7,246,631	983,254	444,038	538,189	9,212,112	*11,632,789*

NOTE (1) Includes cost of handling 405 enquiries
(2) Includes cost of counselling some 1052 applicants
(3) Prior year adjustment on change of accounting policy.

The cost of redeveloping and refurbishing existing Homes is now written off as part of Homes operating costs.

	£
Refurbishment of existing homes	2,501,154
Less: Depreciation charged in prior year	(27,810)
Provision for diminution in value charged in prior year	(436,569)
Prior year adjustment per note 14	2,036,775

7.5.2 Expenditure and grants relating directly to the charitable activities

A most important feature of a charity's accounts is the information about its expenditure on projects.

The composition of such costs will differ between charities. For example, a grant-making charity's direct costs will be confined to the grants provided, whereas the direct costs of running a hospice might constitute much of the total expenditure. In view of this lack of uniformity, it would be difficult to compare levels of expenditure on charitable activities between charities. Presentation is, thus, all-important, for maximum advantage to accrue.

SORP 2 was silent as regards the information to be disclosed by grant-making charities. Some charities provided a breakdown of all grants in the year, including the Cystic Fibrosis Research Trust. In its 1992 (but not 1993) accounts, Action Research provided (outside of the audited accounts) a grant policy statement.

In the revised SORP grant-making charities attract greater scrutiny. Paragraph 137 requires that 'material grants made by a charity to one or more institutions should be appropriately analysed and explained either in the Statement of Financial Activities or in the notes to the accounts, or by means of a separate publication referred to in the notes and reconciled to the total amount charged in the accounts'.

What is 'material'? Paragraph 138 states that 'what is material will, to some extent, depend on the size of the grant-making charity and the importance of grant-making to its overall operation'. The ED suggested that disclosure of the 20 largest grants of a charity (provided that they are at least of the value of £1,000), should normally be regarded as material.

NCVO believed that the ED did not go far enough. Its response to the ED stated (*inter alia*):

> 'The Exposure Draft suggests that material grants made by a charity to one or more institutions should be disclosed and supports the disclosure of the twenty largest grants of a charity (provided they are over £1,000). The SORP does not go far enough in the direction of accountability. NCVO believes that the Committee must develop more detailed criteria for small grant making organisations (where small grants under £1,000 will be material); medium sized organisations where the SORP should require disclosure of the largest 250 grants above £1,000; and the largest grantmaking foundations where even greater disclosure could be required . . . '.

Paragraphs 137 and 138 of the revised SORP have gone some way to alleviating these concerns. Grants to *an institution* which, in any financial year, amount in aggregate to £1,000 or more should be regarded as material. Unless contained in a separate publication, disclosure should be limited to the largest 50 grants, or such larger number as may be considered necessary to convey a proper understanding of the charity's grant-making activities.

The name of, and the aggregate amount of grants made in the financial year to, the recipient should be disclosed.

Disclosure is not required:

(a) if, exceptionally, the trustees consider that disclosure of a material grant may prejudice the recipient institution, or the charity's activities. The reasons should be given in the notes; and
(b) where anonymous grants are made. The notes should disclose the total amount given.

In both cases, details of the grants must be disclosed, in writing, to the Commissioners, or other appropriate regulatory body, giving the reasons for non-disclosure, or why the charity is seeking anonymity.

A sensible compromise is the new exception from disclosure in the accounts where a charity, e.g., Cancer Research Campaign, provides a full list of all grants payable in a separate publication to which the accounts refer. No advantage is seen to accrue by repeating this information in the notes to the accounts.

Paragraph 1(k) of Pt IV to the Sch to the Regulations requires the notes to give particulars of any grant made by the charity to another institution, of which any relevant recommended practice requires disclosure. The Regulation, thus, allows for either form of disclosure recommended by the SORP, where that disclosure is required.

The monetary value, and number, of grants to *individuals* need only be shown in aggregate (para 139).

Interest-free loans, or those made on other non-commercial terms, made in furtherance of a charity's objects, should, initially, be accounted for as a debtor, with amounts due after more than one year shown in the notes. The amounts and applicable rate(s) of interest for all such loans should, also, be disclosed in the notes. Provision should be made, within direct charitable expenditure, if the loan is considered not to be, or unlikely to be, recoverable. Where recovery is secured, or the provision is no longer required, the amount should be set off against new provisions and described as 'provisions no longer required' (paras 140 and 141).

Example 7.42 Chartered Accountants' Benevolent Association provides unsecured loans to beneficiaries. These are written off as a form of aid as recovery, although intended, is not enforced.

Example 7.42 Chartered Accountants' Benevolent Association Accounting policies (part) (31 December 1993):

UNSECURED LOANS TO BENEFICIARIES
When appropriate, money is lent to beneficiaries rather than given, it being mutually understood that, while there is no formal charge on assets, the loan will be repaid on realisation of an asset or out of the estate on death. Recovery is intended but as it is not enforceable, loans are written off as a form of aid.

Chapter 8 – Fixed assets

8.1 Introduction

Although not yet progressed further by the ASB, it was the then ASC which, in an attempt to provide a general framework within which enterprises could account for fixed assets, published ED 51 *Accounting for fixed assets and revaluations* in May 1990.

The importance of fixed assets was recognised in paragraph 2 which stated:

> 'Fixed assets often comprise a substantial proportion of an enterprise's total assets and their accounting treatment is, therefore, an important element in the presentation of its financial position. In addition, determining whether expenditure has led to the creation of an asset or whether it constitutes a charge to the profit and loss account can have a significant effect on an enterprise's results for the period.'

This chapter considers the accounting and disclosure of fixed assets, including investments.

8.2 What is a 'fixed asset'?

Section 262(1) of the 1985 Act defines fixed assets as those 'which are intended for use on a continuing basis in the company's activities' and any assets which are not intended for such use are taken to be current assets.

The statutory formats in the 1985 Act give further information as to what is intended as a fixed asset, as shown below.

I Intangible assets

1. Development costs.
2. Concessions, patents, licences, trade marks and similar rights and assets.
3. Goodwill.
4. Payments on account.

II Tangible assets

1 Land and buildings.
2 Plant and machinery.
3 Fixtures, fittings, tools and equipment.
4 Payments on account and assets in course of construction.

III Investments

1 Shares in group undertakings.
2 Loans to group undertakings.
3 Participating interests.
4 Loans to undertakings in which the company has a participating interest.
5 Other investments other than loans.
6 Other loans.
7 Own shares.

But it was ED 51 which seemed to offer a more constructive definition, as follows:

> 'A fixed asset is an asset that:
>
> (a) is held by the enterprise for use in the production or supply of goods and services, for rental to others, or for administrative purposes and may include items held for the maintenance or repair of such assets;
> (b) has been acquired or constructed with the intention of being used on a continuing basis; and
> (c) is not intended for sale in the ordinary course of business.'

(Fixed asset investments, the proposed accounting for which was addressed in the later ED 55, were specifically excluded from the scope of the ED.)

Whereas the 1985 Act formats require fixed asset investments to be displayed as a subset of fixed assets, para 66 of SORP 2 stated that a charity's assets should be analysed in the balance sheet 'between fixed assets, investments (including investment properties) and current assets'. Presentationally, therefore, investments seemed to have been accorded a superior status by the SORP.

By embracing investments, including investment properties, within the general heading of fixed assets, both the Regulations and the revised charity SORP more closely follow the 1985 Act formats.

Paragraph 2(a) of Pt II to the Sch to the Regulations requires the balance sheet to divide fixed assets into:

(a) intangible assets;
(b) tangible assets for use by the charity; and
(c) investments.

Paragraph 1(l) of Pt IV to the Sch requires the notes to provide the following further analysis:

(a) in respect of tangible assets for use by the charity, according to the following categories:
  (i) freehold interests in land and buildings;
  (ii) any other interest in land or buildings;
  (iii) plant and machinery;
  (iv) fixtures, fittings and equipment; and
  (v) payments on account and assets in the course of construction;
(b) in the case of investments, according to the major category of investment; and
[(c) in either case, any material movement in assets during the financial year to which the balance sheet relates.]*

And, para 171 of the revised SORP recommends that the assets are analysed in the balance sheet between fixed assets (including investments and investment properties) and current assets.

8.3 When should a fixed asset be recognised?

Paragraph 66 of ED 51 stated that:

> 'A fixed asset should be recognised on an enterprise's balance sheet when:
>
> (a) it is probable that any future economic benefits associated with the asset will flow to the enterprise; and
> (b) the asset has a cost, and where carried at a valuation, a value that can be measured with reliability'.

In July 1992, the ASB published draft chapter 4 *The recognition of items in financial statements* of its Statement of Principles. It said that an item should be recognised in financial statements if:

(a) the item meets the definition of an element of financial statements (elements of financial statements are assets, liabilities, equity, gains

* *To de decided when the final Regulations are published.*

and losses. 'Assets' are defined in draft chapter 3 *The elements of financial statements* as 'rights or other access to future economic benefits controlled by an entity as a result of past transactions or events');
(b) there is sufficient evidence that the change in assets or liabilities inherent in the item has occurred (including, where appropriate, evidence that a future inflow or outflow of benefit will occur); and
(c) the item can be measured at a monetary amount with sufficient reliability.

The criteria in ED 51 and in the draft chapters of the Statement of Principles are similar. The basic requirements are that there is an expectation of future benefit *and* that the amount at which the asset is to be recorded in the balance sheet can be reliably measured.

8.4 How should fixed assets be measured?

Paragraph 174(a) of the revised charity SORP recommends that fixed assets held for a charity's use should be included in the balance sheet at cost (or valuation), less an appropriate provision for depreciation. And, para 174(b) recommends that fixed assets held for investment purposes be included at market value.

8.5 Fixed assets held for a charity's use

8.5.1 Capitalisation

Paragraph 51 of SORP 2 stated:

> 'All expenditure on the acquisition, production or installation of fixed assets and all receipts of fixed assets by way of gift should be capitalised and included in the balance sheet. This general principle is not affected by the source of finance used to pay for the fixed asset, or the source of finance likely to be used to pay for any future replacement of the asset.
>
> (a) Expenditure on the acquisition, production or installation of fixed assets should be capitalised at the amount expended.
> (b) Fixed assets received by way of gift should be capitalised at the value at which the gift was included in income.
> (c) Fixed assets being capitalised some time after being acquired, for example as a result of a change of accounting policy, should be capitalised similarly at original cost or at the value at which the gift was included in income. However, if neither of these amounts are ascertainable, a reasonable estimate of the asset's current value to the charity should be used'.

In respect of para 51(a), most charities now capitalise expenditure on fixed assets. Nonetheless, there are some exceptions. Some write off certain types of expenditure. Example 8.1 Tidy Britain Group capitalises 'all material expenditure'.

Example 8.1 Tidy Britain Group
Note 1: Accounting policies (part) (31 March 1993):

(*b*) *Fixed Assets*:
 (i) All material expenditure on the acquisition of Fixed Assets is capitalised at the amount expended.

Example 8.2 Cystic Fibrosis Research Trust writes off, on acquisition, all fixed assets, other than freehold property (see, also, chapter **16**, page 423).

Example 8.2 Cystic Fibrosis Research Trust
Note 1: Accounting policies (part) (31 March 1994):

ii) Depreciation
Depreciation is provided on all tangible fixed assets, other than Freehold Property, at a rate of 100% in the year of acquisition.

Some charities write off certain specialised assets. Example 8.3 Institute of Cancer Research: Royal Cancer Hospital writes off 'highly specialised research equipment'.

Example 8.3 Institute of Cancer Research: Royal Cancer Hospital
Note 1: Accounting policies (part) (31 July 1993):

(i) **Accounting Convention** [part]:
The accounts are prepared under the historical cost convention as modified by the valuation of land and buildings and investments to market value, in accordance with applicable accounting standards and comply with the Statement of Recommended Practice 'Accounting by Charities'.

(v) **Equipment**
The purchase of highly specialised research equipment forms part of the Institute's continuous programme of scientific research and is funded out of current income. Consequently the Council considers that the cost of such equipment should be fully written off in the year of purchase.

And, Example 8.4 Royal National Lifeboat Institution writes of its lifeboat fleet, together with certain related operational equipment and buildings.

Example 8.4 Royal National Lifeboat Institution
Note 1: Accounting policies (part) (31 December 1993):

b The accounts comply with the Statement of Recommended Practice No. 2, 'Accounting by charities', issued by the Accounting Standards Committee in May 1988, except for the following:

(i) Capital expenditure on the lifeboat fleet, together with certain related operational equipment and buildings, is fully charged to the Income and Expenditure Account in the year in which the expenditure is incurred. Other fixed assets are capitalised at original cost and are subject to depreciation (Note 3).

Note 2: Lifeboat fleet:

The lifeboat fleet has been written off in the year of purchase in recognition of its unique nature, and in accordance with the accounting policy (Note 1b(i)). The accumulated cost so written off is £78.5 million (1992: £73.6 million). Related shoreworks are also written off in the year of purchase and the accumulated cost so written off in the past five years is £16.8 million (1992: £15.3 million).

While the former two charities make no reference to SORP 2, it is interesting to note the way in which the latter two charities report their policy. While the former states that 'the accounts . . . comply with the Statement of Recommended Practice "Accounting by charities"', the latter states that the accounts comply with SORP 2 'except . . . Capital expenditure on the lifeboat fleet . . . is fully charged to the Income and Expenditure Account in the year in which the expenditure is incurred . . . in recognition of its unique nature . . . '.

Example 8.5 Royal Society for the Protection of Birds capitalises expenditure relating to nature reserves, but does so, firstly, by writing it off as direct charitable expenditure in the income and expenditure account and, subsequently, by adding it back in the notes on the movement of funds. The trustees consider that this accounting treatment 'gives the clearest indication in the income and expenditure account of how funds were applied in the year, whilst still showing in the balance sheet the value of assets entrusted to their safekeeping'.

Example 8.5 Royal Society for the Protection of Birds
Income and expenditure account (part) (31 March 1994):

	1994		*1993*	
	£'000	£'000	*£'000*	*£'000*
Direct Conservation Expenditure				
Species and habitat protection including research	(7,799)		*(7,201)*	
Management of reserves	(4,635)		*(4,335)*	
Publications, films and education	(3,611)		*(3,890)*	
Acquisition of reserves	(2,409)		*(2,545)*	
		(18,454)		*(17,971)*

Note 14: Funds (part):

	1994		*1993*	
	£'000	£'000	*£'000*	*£'000*
Funds at beginning of year		37,326		*36,306*
Surplus/(Deficit) for year		3		*(1,510)*
Calculated after including the following:				
Fixed Asset Movements				
Additions during the year	3,472		*3,864*	
Net book value of disposals	(82)		*(94)*	
Depreciation charge for the year	(1,047)	2,343	*(1,240)*	*2,530*
Funds at end of year		39,672		*37,326*

Consistent with the criteria for recognition is the recommendation in para 51(b) that charities receiving donated assets should capitalise them at the time of acquisition. Example 8.6 NCH Action for Children is typical.

Example 8.6 NCH Action for Children (formerly the National Children's Home)
Note 1: Accounting policies (part) (31 March 1993):
(c) Fixed assets:

Fixed assets are recorded at cost or, in cases where Fixed Assets have been donated to NCH, at valuation at the time of acquisition.

There seems to be some confusion as to whether or not measuring donated assets at a reasonable estimate of their value falls within the historical cost accounting rules, i.e., para 17 of Sch 4 to the 1985 Act requires fixed assets to be measured at purchase price, or production cost. An example of this confusion is provided by Example 8.7 Woodland Trust.

Example 8.7 Woodland Trust
Note 1: Accounting policies (part) (31 December 1993):

a) These accounts have been prepared under the historical cost convention and in accordance with the recommendations set out in the Statement of Recommended Practice No. 2 'Accounting by Charities'.

f) Incoming resources in the form of donated assets have been included in the Income and Expenditure Account and capitalised where appropriate at a reasonable estimate of their value.

This constitutes a departure from the Companies Act 1985 which requires any fixed assets to be valued at their purchase price. This departure is necessary to enable the accounts to reflect the value of donated assets, and to comply with Statement of Recommended Practice No 2 'Accounting by Charities'.

Note 1(f) states that donated assets included in income and capitalised at 'a reasonable estimate of their value' constitutes a departure from the statutory rules which require 'any fixed assets to be valued at their purchase price'. It is difficult to understand what this charity is trying to say. Does this mean that the charity is departing from historical cost in accounting for donated assets in this way? This seems unlikely given that note 1(a) states that 'these accounts have been prepared under the historical cost convention . . . '. If so, however, it is doubtful that this view is correct. The donation has triggered initial recognition. As there is no transaction price, it is necessary to ascribe a historical cost by reference to prices prevailing at the time of the transaction (in this case, the cost is based 'on the average price per acre of woodland and land purchased by the Trust during the relevant financial year'). This is not a departure from, but a variant of, the historical cost rule which arises from the exercise of judgement. (See draft chapter 5 *Measurement in financial statements* of the ASB's Statement of Principles which seems to support this view.) Because the receipt of a donated fixed asset is not seen (wrongly) as, in substance, outright purchase with a 100 per cent grant, there is, also, some confusion regarding accounting for the other side of the transaction (see chapter **7**, page 197).

Having previously written off certain fixed assets, some charities changed their accounting policy following the introduction of SORP 2. Paragraph 51(c) was intended to cater for these circumstances. It recognised that the original cost, or the value at which the gifted asset was included in income, may have been lost in time and, sensibly, allowed for a reasonable estimate of the asset's current value to be used. This relaxation as regards measurement echoes that in para 28 of Sch 4 to the 1985 Act. (This paragraph, also, falls within the section in Sch 4 dealing with the historical cost accounting rules.)

Example 8.8 Royal National Institute for the Blind appears, prior to SORP 2, to have written off its properties in the year of purchase. The 'cost', at the time the accounting policy was changed, was established by a series of valuations, mirrored by a fund entitled 'Property in use by RNIB services'.

Example 8.8 Royal National Institute for the Blind
Note 1: Statement of accounting policies (part) (31 March 1994):
1.2 Fixed Assets [part]:
(a) Property in use by RNIB [part]:

> This represents property used to provide services to visually impaired people. Such properties are included in these financial statements at current use valuation. All properties were valued by Humberts, Chartered Surveyors, between 1 April 1987 and 31 March 1992. Subsequent significant expenditure relating to the implementation of new and improved services has been included at the current use valuation. All other additions have been included at cost.

Paragraph 185 of the revised charity SORP, generally, repeats these capitalisation rules.

If the charity has set up a separate non-charitable company to provide charitable services, the charity's shares in this company should be included here.

8.5.2 Exceptions to capitalisation

Paragraph 52 of SORP 2 stated that:

> 'The only exception to this general principle (of capitalisation) is that a charity need not capitalise a fixed asset which is either:
>
> (a) inalienable (in other words a fixed asset which the charity is prohibited from disposing of) or historic (such as a monument or statue); or
> (b) for which neither a cost nor a market value is available. This should be an extremely rare occurrence: it will usually be possible to determine a reasonable estimate of its cost or value without incurring significant expenditure'.

In affording certain exceptions to capitalisation, SORP 2 recognised the problems which some charities have. The National Trust is one charity which places no value on inalienable property, alienable property deemed by the National Trust to be held for preservation at least in the foreseeable future as permitted under s21 of the National Trust Act 1971, or on chattels held in trust, as those assets are held for preservation purposes and cannot be sold.

Due to the absence of a reliable basis of measurement, historic assets such as cathedrals (see para 77 of the ED of a TR *English anglican cathedral accounts* (FRAG 29/94), issued in November 1994), museums and castles are, similarly, likely to be omitted.

Paragraph 186 of the revised SORP perpetuates these exceptions to capitalisation.

In order to compensate for non-capitalisation, para 52 recommended that a summary of fixed assets not included in the balance sheet but still in use should be given in the *notes to the accounts.* The summary should be sufficient to enable a reader to appreciate their 'age and scale'.

The National Trust provides disclosure in pictorial format of, *inter alia*, miles of coastline protected, acreage owned and under covenant and the number of properties open to the public at a charge in *the commentary which precedes the audited accounts.* Example 8.9 Royal National Lifeboat Institution provides informative details about its fleet in three pages which, also, *precede its audited accounts.*

Example 8.9 Royal National Lifeboat Institution
The lifeboat fleet (part) (31 December 1993):

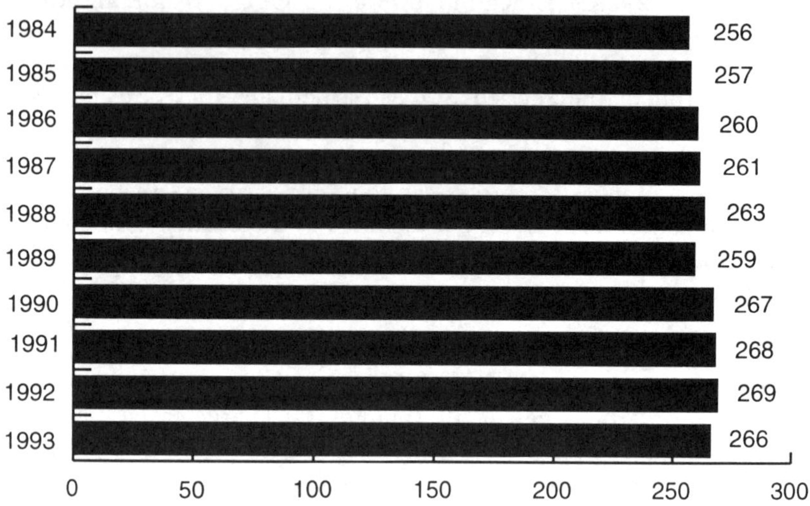

There were 266 lifeboats on station at 31 December 1993 (125 all-weather and intermediate lifeboats and 141 inshore lifeboats) with a further 108 in the relief fleet (30 all-weather and intermediate and 78 inshore).

The fleet was made up of the following classes of lifeboat (extract):

Arun class

Station fleet:	37
Relief fleet:	9
Length:	52ft and 54ft (15.9m and 16.5m)
Speed:	18.2 knots
Range:	330 miles
Introduced:	1971
Last built:	1990
Type:	All-weather

Designed to lie afloat on a mooring at stations requiring a large, all-weather lifeboat. The majority are built of glass reinforced plastic (GRP), although there are three early wood-built boats and one built of steel.

Severn and Trent class lifeboats will eventually replace this class.

Tyne class

Station fleet:	35
Relief fleet:	5
Length:	47ft (14.3m)
Speed:	17.6 knots
Range:	240 miles
Introduced:	1982
Last built:	1990
Type:	All-weather

Example 8.9 Royal National Lifeboat Institution
The lifeboat fleet (part) (31 December 1993): (Continued)

Designed to operate from a slipway, or lie afloat at stations with particular requirements. Propellers and rudders are fully protected. Steel built. The new Severns and Trents will be available for some afloat stations and a new slipway design will be developed before replacement is necessary.

Mersey class

Station fleet:	30
Relief fleet:	7
Length:	38ft (11.6m)
Speed:	17 knots
Range:	140 miles
Introduced:	1988
Last built:	1993
Type:	All-weather

A design providing a fast lifeboat for stations using a carriage-launch. Size and weight determined by the need to launch across beaches, and with fully protected propellers and rudders for beaching. Built of aluminium or fibre reinforced composite (FRC) for light weight and strength. Mersey class lifeboats have now replaced the final traditional lifeboats at carriage-launch stations – the last at the end of 1993.

For the same reasons, as given in para 52 of SORP 2, para 187 of the revised SORP recommends that *information* on fixed assets not capitalised be given. Unless disclosure would 'prejudice the efficient working of the charity', e.g., by materially increasing the risk of the assets' theft or vandalism, it is recommended that the information given should include:

(a) details of the assets' insured value; and
(b) what use is made of them.

8.5.3 Depreciation

The 1985 Act
Schedule 4 requires any fixed asset which has a limited useful economic life to be depreciated, systematically, over that life. Depreciation is to be based on the purchase price, or production cost, (under the historical cost accounting rules), or on the revalued amount (under the alternative accounting rules), less any estimate residual value.

SSAP 12 (Revised)
Having been originally published in 1977 and amended in November 1981, SSAP 12 was revised in 1987. The Standard applies to all fixed assets other than:

(a) investment properties, which are dealt with in SSAP 19 *Accounting for investment properties*;
(b) goodwill, which is dealt with in SSAP 22 *Accounting for goodwill*;
(c) development costs, which are dealt with in SSAP 13 (Revised) *Accounting for research and development*; and
(d) investments which, although not the subject of an accounting standard, were addressed in ED 55 *Accounting for investments*.

Paragraph 15 prescribes the accounting treatment:

> 'Provision for depreciation of fixed assets having a finite useful economic life should be made by allocating the cost (or revalued amount) less estimated residual value of the assets as fairly as possible to the periods expected to benefit from their use. The depreciation methods used should be ones which are the most appropriate having regard to the types of asset and their use in the business'.

Paragraph 23 exempts freehold land from depreciation 'unless it is subject to depletion by, for example, the extraction of minerals' and from being written down unless its value is 'affected by considerations such as changes in the desirability of its location'. Buildings, however, do not enjoy this exemption because they are 'no different from other fixed assets in that they have a limited useful economic life, albeit usually significantly longer than that of other types of assets' (para 24).

SORP 2

SORP 2's recommendations echoed those both of the 1985 Act and of SSAP 12 (Revised). Paragraph 54 stated that:

> 'Most fixed assets depreciate, that is wear out, get consumed, or otherwise suffer a reduction in their useful life through use, the passing of time, or obsolescence. Fixed assets which have a finite useful life should be depreciated. Fixed assets which have an indefinite useful life, such as freehold land, should not be depreciated. This means that:
>
> (a) fixed assets with finite useful lives should be included in the balance sheet at cost (or, if revalued, at a revalued amount) less an appropriate provision for depreciation; and
> (b) fixed assets with an indefinite useful life should be included at cost (or, if revalued, at a revalued amount)'.

Paragraphs 188 to 190 of the revised SORP repeat these recommendations. In general and subject to below, the recommendation to depreciate fixed assets is observed.

Some charities, for example, Example 8.10 Action Aid appear to depreciate freehold land as well as buildings. This may well be because the value of the land is unknown and obtaining such a value is not worth the cost involved.

Example 8.10 Action Aid
Note 1: Accounting policies (part) (31 December 1993):

1d Depreciation of fixed assets
Depreciation is calculated on a straight line basis for the following categories of fixed assets:

Freehold property 25 years
Fixtures and fittings 5 years
Office machinery 5 years

Leasehold properties are commonly written off over the unexpired period of the lease or, if shorter, the useful life of the asset. Where there are rent reviews, any premium paid should be amortised over the period to the next rent review date, see Example 8.11 OXFAM.

Example 8.11 OXFAM
Note 1: Accounting policies (part) (30 April 1993):
(c) Depreciation of tangible fixed assets:

Freehold land is not depreciated.

The cost of other tangible fixed assets is written-off by equal annual instalments over their expected useful lives as follows:

Freehold Buildings	50 years
Leasehold Warehouse	10 years
Leasehold Premises acquired prior to 1 May 1990	5 years
Furniture, Fixtures and Equipment in the UK	5 years
Mainframe Computer Equipment	5 years
Motor Vehicles	4 years
Micro-Computer and Wordprocessor Equipment	3 years
Furniture, Fixtures and Equipment Overseas	3 years

Leasehold Properties acquired since 1 May 1990 are amortised on the following basis:

Premium	Period to next Rent Review
Key Money	Period of Lease (max 10 years)
Other Leasehold Costs	5 years

Some charities explain their policy for accounting for computer software costs. This is not an area on which the standard setters have deliberated. Thus, as might be expected, the policy, where disclosed, varies. While Example 6.2 NCH Action for Children (see chapter **6**, page 151) writes off costs as incurred, Example 8.12 Church Missionary Society writes them off over four years.

Example 8.12 Church Missionary Society
Note 2: Accounting policies (part) (31 January 1994):
Depreciation [part]:

Freehold land and buildings are not depreciated. The trustees consider that this accounting policy results in the accounts giving a true and fair view.

Note 6: Fixed assets [part]:

(d) The net book value of office equipment comprises:

	Depreciation period Years	1994 £	*1993 £*
Office furniture	10	67,729	*80,832*
Typewriters	5	272	*873*
Computer hardware/software	4	54,706	*49,006*
Audio and other equipment	4	4,556	*3,796*
Duplicators and copiers	3	7,915	*7,838*
		135,178	*142,345*

To depreciate or not to depreciate?

Prompted by the issue of an SSAP on accounting for depreciation, a number of industrial and commercial sectors argued against providing for depreciation, in certain circumstances. In order to discuss some of the arguments against providing for depreciation, however, it is first necessary to consider what 'depreciation' is and how it is perceived.

Paragraph 10 of Pt 2 to SSAP 12 (Revised) defines depreciation as:

> 'the measure of the wearing out, consumption or other reduction in the useful economic life of a fixed asset whether arising from use, effluxion of time or obsolescence through technological or market changes.'

This definition takes the view that depreciation is a process of allocation: it is a measure of consumption, whereby the costs (of fixed assets) are charged through the profit and loss account (or its equivalent), over the periods expected to benefit from their use, so as to be matched with the related revenues.

There are those who hold the view, however, that depreciation is a process of valuation. In its response (FRAG 2/92) to the ASB on the review of the standard for major practical problems, the ICAEW called for this (apparent) confusion to be clarified. While it believed that the allocation process was 'the most appropriate', the ICAEW noted that depreciation 'is often seen as a measure of loss of value, not least by the management of many companies unwilling to provide depreciation on certain assets'. Some of the arguments against depreciation are discussed below.

Arguing that depreciation was irrelevant to properties held for investment purposes, the property sector was the first to do so, and successfully. Having secured an initial exemption from the Standard, the ASC issued SSAP 19 *Accounting for investment properties* which, other than for leasehold properties where the unexpired term is fewer than 20 years, requires properties to be carried at current market valuation without provision for depreciation.

Seeing this 'concession', other sectors took up their case. In particular, the brewers did so in 1978 arguing, *inter alia*, that, in order to attract (and retain) customers, they needed to maintain their licensed premises to a high standard. The costs of refurbishment would be charged against revenue each year and, in substance, would represent the charge for depreciation.

While the brewers were unsuccessful, it was acknowledged that the combination of a very long life and high residual values may result in an insignificant amount of depreciation. This argument had become so well established that, when reviewing and revising the Standard, it was recognised in ED 37 which stated (*inter alia*):

> 'In certain very restricted instances it may not be appropriate to charge depreciation in respect of what would normally be a depreciable asset. This would arise only where the asset is maintained to such a standard that:
>
> (a) the estimated residual value is equal to or greater than its net book value; or
>
> (b) its estimated useful economic life is either infinite or such that any depreciation charge would be insignificant.'

Being likened to the opening of a Pandora's box, this was omitted from the revised Standard. The ASC's statement TR 648 *Statement on the publication of SSAP 12 (Revised) "Accounting for depreciation"* which accompanied the revised Standard explained that:

> 'a significant number of commentators expressed concern that the proposal could be open to misinterpretation or misuse. It was believed that it might represent a loophole in the standard, permitting non-depreciation of many types of property, in addition to freehold land and investment properties.'

This statement went on to point out, however, that the general principle of the revised Standard should be applied in all cases, but that there 'may be circumstances where it would not be appropriate to charge depreciation'.

While there was no elaboration of what those circumstances might be, this, clearly, represented a window of opportunity for those sectors which wished to resist applying depreciation. Indeed, it is found to be somewhat ironic that the *omission* of the paragraph, coupled with the later comment, seems to have had precisely the effect that commentators thought its *inclusion* would have.

In its response to the ASB, the ICAEW referred to 'the increasing trend towards the non-depreciation of buildings', which was supported by *Financial Reporting 1991 – 1992 Survey of UK Published Accounts*, the result of which are given overleaf:

As can be seen, of the 300 companies surveyed, 20 per cent did not, for a variety of reasons, depreciate part, or all, of their properties. Disappointingly, the table does not provide a disposition, by sector, of the companies surveyed. Nonetheless, the practice of non-depreciation has mushroomed and has spread to other sectors, not only, for example, to supermarket chains and hotels, but also to *charities*.

Example 8.2 Cystic Fibrosis Research Trust, Example 8.12 Church Missionary Society and Example 8.13 SENSE are three charities which do not. SENSE's explanation is found to be informative.

Example 8.13 SENSE
Note 1: Accounting policies (part) (31 March 1994):
Depreciation [part]:

> No depreciation is provided on freehold buildings. It is Council's policy to maintain these at least to their current standard and to charge to the income and expenditure account the cost of maintenance as incurred. In the opinion of Council the resulting charge would not differ materially from that had the freehold buildings been depreciated.

Example 8.14 MIND does not, also, depreciate its freehold properties on the basis that 'in the opinion of the Council the omission of depreciation does not have a material effect on the accounts'. That may be so, but the cumulative effect may well be material.

Example 8.14 MIND
Note 1: Accounting policies (part) (31 March 1993):
(e) Depreciation and amortisation [part]:

> Depreciation is not provided on freehold properties and in the opinion of the Council the omission of depreciation does not have a material effect on the accounts.

	Large	*Medium*	*Large*	
	Listed	**Listed**	**Unlisted**	**Total**
Number of companies	*100* %	*150* %	*50* %	*300* %
Reasons for not depreciating:				
Depreciation not material	3	2	2	2
Frequently revalued	1	0	0	0
MV exceeds NBV	1	0	0	0
Maintenance standards high	19	12	16	15
No reason given	1	5	2	3
	25	19	20	20
No evidence of non-depreciated buildings	74	78	78	77
No evidence of property fixed assets	1	2	2	2
	100	100	100	100

As regards the lack of depreciation, in expressing their opinion, different positions have been taken by different auditors (see chapter **16**, page 423).

Disclosure

Paragraph 33(a) of SORP 2 (and repeated by para 35 (g) of its successor) recommended that the accounting policy for the capitalisation and depreciation of fixed assets be provided (see chapter **6**, page 145).

Paragraph 22 of SSAP 12 (Revised) requires disclosure of the:

(a) depreciation methods used;
(b) useful economic lives or the depreciation rates used; and
(c) total depreciation charge for the period.

Example 8.11 OXFAM and Example 8.15 Marie Curie Cancer Care are two of the better disclosures.

Example 8.15 Marie Curie Cancer Care
Note 1: Accounting policies (part) (31 March 1993):

(c) Depreciation
Depreciation is not provided on freehold land. Depreciation is provided on all other tangible fixed assets using a straight line basis as follows:

Freehold Buildings Leasehold Buildings	10% per annum until half of the cost has been written off, then 5% per annum
Leasehold Property at 28 Belgrave Square	Over the period of the lease
Leasehold Shops	Over the period of the lease or 10 years whichever is the shorter
Furniture Equipment and Central Computer	20–33⅓% per annum
Motor Vehicles	25% per annum

Depreciation is not provided on the cost of Centres until they become operational.

Paragraph 22(d) of SSAP 12 (Revised) requires to be provided 'the gross amount of depreciable assets and the related accumulated depreciation'. This information is sometimes given explicitly, sometimes implicitly (i.e. by disclosing the value of land and other assets not depreciated). An example of the former is Example 8.16 Nuffield Nursing Homes Trust and of the latter Example 8.17 NCH Action for Children. Some charities, for example the Dogs' Home Battersea, do not provide this information (see its 1993 accounts).

Example 8.16 Nuffield Nursing Homes Trust
Note 9: Tangible fixed assets (part) (31 December 1993):

The gross amount on which depreciation on freehold buildings is being provided is £111,461,000.

Example 8.17 NCH Action for Children (formerly the National Children's Home)
Note 6(a): Tangible fixed assets (part) (31 March 1993):

(ii) Included in Freehold Land and Buildings is Land and Freehold Buildings of £15,857,000 which are not depreciated (1992 £431,000). The effect of the change in method of depreciation referred to in note 1(d) was £286,000 in respect of Freehold Land and Buildings and £39,000 in respect of Leasehold Land and Buildings.

8.5.4 Other disclosures

Disposition of fixed assets
For each of the categories of fixed asset given in the formats, para 42 of Sch 4 to the 1985 Act requires the following to be disclosed:

(a) the amounts at the beginning and end of the year, based on cost or revaluation;
(b) movements during the year, including revaluation surpluses and deficits, additions and disposals; and
(c) the cumulative amount of depreciation at the beginning and end of the year on the basis of cost or revaluation, the charge for the year and that eliminated on disposals.

Example 8.18 Mary Rose Trust provides a good illustration for tangible fixed assets.

Example 8.18 Mary Rose Trust
Note 5: Tangible fixed assets: (31 December 1993):

	Cost				Depreciation and amounts written off				Net book value	
	At 1 January 1993 £	Additions at cost £	Disposals £	At 31 December 1993 £	At1 January 1993 £	Provided in the year £	Disposals £	At 31 December 1993 £	At 31 December 1993 £	*At 31 December 1992 £*
Short-term leasehold premises	1,141,951	1,307	–	1,143,258	969,300	173,958	–	1,143,258	–	*172,651*
Improvement to premises	159,368	–	–	159,368	159,368	–	–	159,368	–	–
Plant and equipment	323,076	–	–	323,076	320,901	2,175	–	323,076	–	*2,175*
Recovery cradle	135,984	–	–	135,984	92,327	9,066	–	101,393	34,591	*43,657*
Conservation equipment	403,594	102,247	–	505,841	378,935	37,529	–	416,464	89,377	*24,659*
Visitors' platform	194,307	102,157	–	296,464	102,906	12,593	–	115,499	180,965	*91,401*
Travelling exhibitions and display equipment	14,340	–	–	14,340	13,403	313	–	13,716	624	*937*
Office furniture and equipment	21,583	700	–	22,283	19,683	2,250	–	21,933	350	*1,900*
Hull turning costs	328,275	–	–	328,275	328,275	–	–	328,275	–	–
	2,722,478	206,411	–	2,928,889	2,385,098	237,884	–	2,622,982	305,907	*337,380*

The depreciation provided in the year of £237,884 (1992 – £217,593) has been charged to the income and expenditure account in arriving at the deficit for the year.

Where there are land and buildings, para 44 of that Sch requires a further analysis between freehold and leasehold properties and, in respect of the latter, an analysis between long and short leasehold properties. Example 8.19 Barnardo's provides an example of this disclosure.

Example 8.19 Barnardo's
Note 12: Tangible assets (part) (31 March 1994):

	Group	
	1994 £'000	*1993 £'000*
g. Freehold and Leasehold Properties		
Freeholds	55,020	*52,357*
Long leaseholds (over 50 years)	7,462	*9,020*
Short leaseholds (50 years and under)	6,380	*4,826*
	68,862	*66,203*

	Group	
i. The above properties are used for:		
Barnardo childcare work	52,155	*50,996*
Leased to other organisations for child care or other community work	190	*185*
Gift shops and warehouses	12,648	*12,659*
Miscellaneous	3,869	*2,363*
	68,862	*66,203*

As para 66 of SORP 2 (and repeated in para 173 of its successor) recommended that assets should be analysed in such a way 'that enables the reader to gain a proper appreciation of their spread and character', similar disclosures would seem appropriate for other charities.

A paper by a group of researchers ('Charity accounting standards: Issues from charity researchers', compiled by the NCVO) suggested that because 'the present SORP does not require any clear distinction to be made between those assets which are employed in the normal course of mission-critical work for the charitable purposes of the charity, and those which are held for investment purposes', the revised SORP should include such a distinction as it is of 'central importance in explaining why charities use their assets as they do'. By recommending that the notes give a further segregation of fixed assets held for charity use between those used for direct charitable purposes and those used for other purposes, para 143 of the revised SORP takes on board this suggestion.

Example 8.19 Barnardo's is one (but not the only) charity which (and informatively, prior to the ED of the revised SORP) provides this information.

Example 8.20 Save The Children Fund began disclosing this information following publication of the ED, but extends the analysis to all fixed assets not only to properties.

Example 8.20 Save The Children Fund
Note 6: Tangible assets (part) (31 March 1993):

	Freehold Property £'000	Short Leasehold Property £'000	Furniture Fixtures & Equipment £'000	Motor Vehicles £'000	Total £'000
The net book value at 31 March 1993 represents tangible fixed assets, used for:					
Direct charitable purposes	2,787	958	193	418	4,356
Other purposes					
Fundraising and charity shops	1,952	1,156	546	263	3,917
Administration offices	2,147	1,630	2,164	15	5,956
	6,886	3,744	2,903	696	14,229

Capitalisation of interest

Paragraph 26(3)(a) of Sch 4 to the 1985 Act allows to be included in the production cost of an asset 'interest on capital borrowed to finance the production of that asset, but only to the extent that it accrues in respect of the period of production'. This is subject to the proviso that the fact and the amount of interest included is disclosed in the notes and Example 8.21 Nuffield Nursing Homes Trust provides these. (Further disclosures were suggested in para 99 of ED 51.)

Example 8.21 Nuffield Nursing Homes Trust
Note 9: Tangible fixed assets (part) (31 December 1993):

Group and Trust

Additions during the year to buildings completed and in the course of construction include capitalised interest of £1,000 (1992 – £739,000) and internal project management costs of £4,000 (1992 – £78,000). The interest charges and internal project management costs capitalised to date are £4,738,000 (1992 – £4,737,000) and £4,739,000 (1992 – £4,735,000) respectively.

8.6 Fixed assets held for investment purposes

8.6.1 Introduction

The extent of the trustees' powers of investment will be conditioned by the trust deed, or other governing instrument. Unless there is a clause to the contrary, trustees will generally have to comply with the restrictions imposed by the Trustee Act 1925 and the Trustee Investments Act 1961 ('TIA'). The TIA extended the investment powers of trustees to include limited investment in equities. Trustees were permitted to split (on a 50:50 basis) their investments into two pools, narrower range and wider range. Narrower range investments broadly consist of government stocks and other fixed interest securities, including convertibles, while the wider range consists of shares satisfying certain conditions.

Although safer, gilts have under-performed equities by approximately 5 per cent pa over the last 30 years. As the report of the eighth Deregulation Task Force stated: 'The loss in under-performance of investments since 1963 has been estimated at £450 million per year'. Thus, what was originally seen as a liberal piece of legislation has turned out to be restrictive and costly. (The restrictions only apply to charities governed by the TIA, as many charities may have wider powers contained in their constitution.)

Sections 70 and 71 of the 1993 Act empower the Secretary of State to make regulations both to vary the 50:50 proportion and for investments of charities so that additional types of investment may be included.

One of the Task Force's recommendations (CA 46) was that:

> 'Home Office/H M Treasury should exercise current statutory powers to significantly widen scope of trustees' investment powers. Section 71 of the Charities Act 1993 and/or Section 12 of the TIA should be used to permit trustees to make certain types of investments which they cannot make under the present system i.e. – to widen the pool of investments from which trustees can make their selection. Section 70, Charities Act *and/or* Section 13, TIA should be used to alter the division of investment funds under the TIA. A division enabling 90% of funds to be invested in the wider-range category using Section 70 is the preferred option'.

The Charities (Trustee Investment Act 1961) Order 1995 (SI 1995 No 1092) has now been made so that the value of the wider-range part of the fund, instead of being equal to the value of the narrower-range part, is three times that value.

The report, also, states that there are already plans 'to bring forward an Order in Council shortly to extend the pool of eligible investments to include instruments in other EU and EEA countries equivalent to those currently permitted in the UK'. Restrictions under the TIA prevent charities investing in trading subsidiaries. Thus, working capital, though needed, cannot be sourced from profit which is covenanted to the parent charity. The government is, also, considering the case for extending the list of eligible investments to include investment in trading subsidiaries.

8.6.2 Presentation

As already stated, SORP 2 recommended that a charity's assets be analysed between fixed assets, investments (including investment properties) and current assets.

In practice, some charitable companies have preferred the presentation of SORP 2, see Example 8.22 the British Heart Foundation, to that of the Act's, see Example 8.23 NCVO.

Example 8.22 British Heart Foundation
Balance sheets (part) (31 March 1993):

	Note	Consolidated 1993 £'000	Consolidated *1992 £'000*	Foundation 1993 £'000	Foundation *1992 £'000*
Fixed assets	10	13,920	*12,866*	13,920	*12,866*
Investments	11	91,911	*72,832*	91,911	*72,832*
		105,831	*85,698*	105,831	*85,698*
Current assets					
Debtors	12	1,519	*1,420*	1,431	*1,506*
Stock of goods held for resale		154	*129*	6	–
Cash on deposit, at bank and in hand		5,367	*2,649*	5,308	*2,615*
		7,040	*4,198*	6,745	*4,121*

Note 11: Investments:

Consolidated and Foundation	General Fund £000	Chairs Maintenance Fund £000	Al Maktoum Lectureship Fund £000	G M Yule Bequest Fund £000	Total £000
Market value					
At 1 April 1992	36,685	35,729	344	74	72,832
Additions	11,741	12,394	329	–	24,464
Disposals	(9,389)	(9,144)	(349)	–	(18,882)
	39,037	38,979	324	74	78,414
Change in market value	6,750	6,714	33	–	13,497
At 31 March 1993	45,787	45,693	357	74	91,911
Represented by:					
Listed investments	44,220	44,130	338	–	88,688
Unlisted investments	118	118	–	74	310
Property	792	790	–	–	1,582
Short-term deposits	657	655	19	–	1,331
	45,787	45,693	357	74	91,911
Historical cost of investments					
At 31 March 1993	37,890	39,377	348	74	77,689
At 31 March 1992	34,598	35,217	342	74	70,231
Analysis of net investment gains (losses)					
Unrealised gains (losses) at 31 March 1993	7,900	6,313	9	–	14,222

Example 8.22 British Heart Foundation
Note 11: Investments (31 March 1993): (Continued)

Unrealised gains (losses) at 31 March 1992	2,087	512	(2)	–	2,597
Change in unrealised gains (losses)	5,813	5,801	11	–	11,625
Realised gains (losses) on disposal	937	913	22	–	1,872
Net investment gains (losses)	6,750	6,714	33	–	13,497

Investment property
For the purposes of giving a true and fair view, the specific requirement of the Companies Act 1985 to provide depreciation on any fixed asset which has a limited useful life has been over-ridden. If the property above was included at its historical cost of £1,747,000, the depreciation charge for the year would have been £28,000.

Example 8.23 NCVO
Balance sheet (part) (31 March 1993):

			1993		*1992*
	Note	£	£	*£*	*£*
Fixed assets					
Tangible assets	6	3,380,076		*3,062,264*	
Investments	7	1,176,454		*1,342,593*	
			4,556,530		*4,404,857*

In effect, paras 192 and 193 of the revised SORP take a portfolio approach to the classification of investments. Because investment assets are generally held with the overall intention of retaining them long term for the continuing benefit of the charity in the form of income and capital gains, an investment should be classified as a fixed asset investment, except where the intention is to realise the investment without reinvestment of the sale proceeds. Current assets are classified by default.

(Note: This is not as strict a classification as that in para 55 of ED 55, which defined a fixed asset investment, with current asset investments forming the residue, as one: 'which is intended to be held for use on a continuing basis in the activities of the enterprise. An investment should be classified as a fixed asset only where the intention to hold the investment for the long term can clearly be demonstrated or where there are restrictions as to the investor's ability to dispose of the investment'.)

Paragraph 66 of SORP 2 recommended that the assets be analysed in a way that enables the reader 'to gain a proper appreciation of their spread and character'.

Although para 173 of the revised SORP repeats this, the recommendation is elaborated upon in para 195. As regards investments, it recommends that the notes show the total value of investments divided between:

(a) investment properties;
(b) investments listed on a recognised stock exchange (or ones valued by reference to such investments, e.g., unit trusts and common investment funds);
(c) investments in subsidiary or associated companies or in companies which are connected persons;
(d) other unlisted securities;
(e) cash held as part of the investment portfolio;
(f) other investments,

distinguishing between assets inside and outside the UK.

If a charity has set up its own non-charitable trading company, any shares which the charity owns in that company should be included under (c).

Paragraph 196 recommends that further information regarding the portfolio's structure be given in the notes. This information should include:

(a) direct and indirect investment in listed securities;
(b) any material investments (i.e., those over 5 per cent by value of the portfolio); and
(c) any material restrictions which might apply to the realisation of an investment.

There is now a specific category for cash held as part of the investment portfolio. This represents cash held by the charity's investment managers, or specifically earmarked by the trustees, for investment. While some charities may have included such cash within current assets, this has had the disadvantage that the balance sheet at the year end is unduly influenced by the policy adopted by the investment managers, and so may have given a misleading picture of the underlying position. Example 8.24 Save The Children Fund separates out the figure and includes it within fixed asset investments.

Example 8.24 Save The Children Fund
Note 7: Fixed asset investments (31 March 1993):

	1993 £'000	*1992* *£'000*
Market value at 1 April 1992	20,829	*15,968*
Acquisitions	12,486	*8,834*
Disposals	(12,441)	*(3,627)*
Net investment gains (losses)	3,753	*(346)*
Market value at 31 March 1993	24,627	*20,829*
Cost at 31 March 1993	19,589	*19,021*
The market value at 31 March represents:		
Investments listed on a recognised stock exchange	23,639	*20,179*
Unlisted investments	22	*22*
Cash held by investment managers awaiting investment	966	*628*
	24,627	*20,829*

Included in the balance sheet of the charity (Note 15) are investments in subsidiary companies costing **£250,000** (1992 – £100).

For fixed asset investments, the 1985 Act requires disclosure of:

(a) the amounts at the beginning and end of the year, based on cost or revaluation;
(b) movements during the year, including revaluation surpluses and deficits, additions and disposals;
(c) the cumulative amount of depreciation or diminution in value at the beginning and end of the year on the basis of cost or revaluation, the charge for the year and that eliminated on disposals.

That Act also requires disclosure of:

(a) the amount relating to listed investments, analysed between those listed on the London Stock Exchange and others;
(b) the aggregate market value of listed investments, if different from the book value, and the stock exchange value if less than the market value disclosed; and
(c) various details (not discussed further here) where an investment is deemed to be 'significant'.

Example 8.22 British Heart Foundation is a good example, although it does not provide a further analysis of listed investments.

Paragraph 67(b) of SORP 2 recommended that 'where funds have been divided into wider and narrower ranges under the powers given to trustees by the Trustee Investments Act 1961, the accounts or notes should indicate the investments allotted to each range'. (This disclosure is perpetuated by para 198 of the revised SORP, but restricts it to the notes.) Example 8.25 BLESMA is a good example of a charity providing this information.

Example 8.25 BLESMA
Note 9: Investments (31 December 1993):

		Total £	Narrow range £	Wide range £
Market value				
At 1 January 1993		8,556,196	2,112,203	6,443,993
Additions		4,705,649	2,597,508	2,108,141
		13,261,845	4,709,711	8,552,134
Sales		(4,009,240)	(2,379,116)	(1,630,124)
Net investment gains		2,043,977	388,346	1,655,631
At 31 December 1993		11,296,582	2,718,941	8,577,641
Add cash awaiting investment		207,096	65,898	141,198
Market value at 31 December 1993		11,503,678	2,784,839	8,718,839
Cost at 31 December 1993		8,277,688	2,440,148	5,837,540
Analysis of investments at 31 December 1993 between funds				
Quoted investments				
Fixed interest	General fund	1,526,696	1,038,271	488,425
	Legacy fund	3,062,174	1,680,686	1,381,488
Ordinary shares	General fund	4,701,822	–	4,701,822
	Legacy fund	1,656,901	–	1,656,901
Other	General fund	109,021	–	109,021
	Legacy fund	214,968	–	214,968
General fund		6,337,539	1,038,271	5,299,268
Legacy fund		4,934,043	1,680,686	3,253,357
Property investment	General fund	25,000	–	25,000
Cash	General fund	138,880	65,898	72,982
	Legacy fund	68,216	–	68,216
General fund		6,501,419	1,104,169	5,397,250
Legacy fund		5,002,259	1,680,686	3,321,573
		11,503,678	2,784,855	8,718,823

New cash for investment purposes and investments received as a donation or legacy are divided as to one third in the narrow range and two thirds in the wide range.

Example 8.26 Army Benevolent Fund provides a different disposition, by extent of the trustees' powers. It might have been informative to explain to what extent their powers were 'limited' and 'extended'.

Example 8.26 Army Benevolent Fund
Note 10: Investments (31 March 1994):

The investment powers of the Fund's Trustees were widened by the Charity Commissioners' Scheme sealed on 18 June 1993, which superseded the earlier Schemes of 29 November 1966 and 7 December 1970. The former requirement to divide investment between the Trust Funds in the following proportions, namely, two-tenths to the Limited Powers Fund, seven-tenths to the Extended Powers Fund and one-tenth to the Unlimited Powers Fund is no longer applicable.

	1994	*1993*
	£	*£*
Cost of investments	15,235,687	–
Limited powers	–	*984,695*
Extended powers	–	*10,470,597*
Unlimited powers	–	*2,115,530*
	15,235,687	*13,570,822*
Market value	20,624,626	*18,551,505*

Where an investment is held within more than one fund, para 197 of the revised SORP recommends that it should be made clear to which funds the investment belongs.

8.6.3 Measurement

Paragraph 68(b) of SORP 2 recommended that investments be stated at cost or market value. Where investments are included at cost, paragraph 68(b) of SORP 2 suggested that the market value be disclosed in the notes. The SORP was silent, however, as to further disclosure, if the accounting were reversed.

Paras 17 and 31(3)(a) of Sch 4 to the 1985 Act also allow fixed asset investments to be measured at cost or market value. Paragraph 31(3)(b), however, allows such investments to be included 'at a value determined on any basis which appears to the directors to be appropriate in the circumstances of the company'. Where adopted, particulars of the method of valuation and the reasons for adopting it must be disclosed in the notes.

Most charities measure their investments at cost, including Example 8.27 NCH Action for Children.

Example 8.27 NCH Action for Children (formerly the National Children's Home)
Note 1: Accounting policies (part): (31 March 1993)

(j) **Investments [part]**
NCH's policy is to hold investments primarily in order to generate income for the support of social work over a long-term period. The effect of this policy is that the surplus arising on revaluation at any particular time will not normally be realised. The investments have therefore been stated at cost to their respective funds, if known, or earliest known valuation.

A minority, including Example 8.28 The National Trust, include them (or some of them) at market value.

Example 8.28 The National Trust
Note 3: Accounting policies (part) (28 February 1994):

ACCOUNTING CONVENTION
The accounts are prepared under the historical cost convention, as modified by the revaluation of investment properties and the annual revaluation of listed investments to market value, and in accordance with applicable accounting standards.

Paragraphs 174(b) and 194 of the revised SORP recommend that investments (including investment properties) be measured at, or at the trustees' best estimate of, market value at the balance sheet date. This is because 'it is considered that market value best represents a true and fair view of the value of these assets to the charity, given the duty of trustees to administer the portfolio of investment assets so as to obtain the best investment performance without undue risk'. As unrealised gains (or losses) are part of the changes in net resources available to the charity during the year, this new recommendation appears consistent with the conceptual approach of the SOFA. In anticipation of this, Example 8.29 Marie Curie Cancer Care has changed its policy and now measures investments at market value.

Example 8.29 Marie Curie Cancer Care
Note 1: Accounting policies (part) (31 March 1993):

(e) Investments
Listed investments are stated at market value. This is a change in accounting policy from previous years when they were shown at cost.
Investment in subsidiary is stated at cost.
Investment income is brought into account when received.

The ED proposed that the cost also be shown, not in the notes, but on the face of the balance sheet. In proposing disclosure in this way, the

Charity Accounting Review Committee seemed to lack the courage of its convictions. This has been rectified by para 194, which recommends disclosure of the cost in the notes.

It is not difficult to obtain market values for listed stocks and shares. (Note: Para 17 of Appendix 1 to the revised charity SORP defines 'market value' as 'the price at which an asset could be, or could be expected to be, sold for or acquired in a public market between a willing buyer and a willing seller. For investments, the market value basis that is to be used in the valuation for the Balance Sheet is defined as the mid-point of the quotation in the Stock Exchange Daily Official List or at a similar recognised market value. For other assets it is the trustees' or valuers' best estimate of such a value.')

Unlike the ED, however, the revised SORP gives some guidance on the methods by which other investment assets should be measured. For shares for which there is no readily identifiable market price or for assets other than shares, para 176 recommends that the trustees adopt a reasonable approach.

Shares in unlisted companies could be valued by reference to underlying net assets, earnings, dividend record etc.

In the rare circumstances where the size, or nature, of a shareholding is such that the market is thought by the trustees not to be capable of absorbing without a material effect on the quoted price, para 178 recommends that the position be summarised in the notes. Where possible, the trustees should give an opinion on how much the market price should be adjusted.

The ED did not state whether investment properties should be professionally valued. For many charities with professionally-managed, large and complex estates the proposal to measure them at market value at the balance sheet date was potentially contentious, as such valuations would be likely to be expensive and might be held not to be an appropriate use of charity funds. In recognition of this, the revised SORP takes a sensible approach. It recommends that trustees obtain valuations from appropriately experienced persons(e.g., qualified valuers) at least every five years, subject only to obtaining advice between valuations as to whether there have been any material movements. Where a charity has a significant portfolio of investment properties, para 177 allows the valuations to be spread over a number of years, i.e., on a rolling basis, so as to temper the effect of their cost.

While the proposal would be consistent with accounting for investment properties generally, it conflicted with para 9 of SSAP 19. In its response to the ED, the ICAEW suggested that 'if it intended that this exclusion should no longer apply, the ASB may wish to issue an amendment to SSAP 19'.

The exclusion from the provisions of SSAP 19 appears to have some effect on whether or not investment properties are subject to depreciation. That is, if investment properties were classed with other investments, no depreciation would appear to be necessary. This is not because investments are excluded from the depreciation rules (although they are excluded from SSAP 12 (Revised) and para 54 of SORP 2, which set out the depreciation rules, only applied to fixed assets). Rather, it is because, generally, they do not have a finite useful economic life. If classed as a tangible fixed asset, however, depreciation would appear to be necessary. This is because para 9 of SSAP 19 excludes from its provisions investment properties owned by charities.

Example 8.30 Church Commissioners for England include investment properties within tangible fixed assets on the balance sheet. Although exempt, they have revalued, in accordance with SSAP 19, those properties and invoked the true and fair view override to justify non-depreciation of freehold properties and leasehold interests with more than 50 (not 20) years unexpired.

Example 8.30 Church Commissioners for England
Note 1: Accounting policies (part) (31 December 1993):

> *Depreciation of fixed assets* [part]:
> In accordance with SSAP 19 no depreciation is charged in respect of freehold properties and leasehold interest with more than 50 years unexpired. This departure from the requirement of the Companies Acts that all property interests be depreciated is, in the Commissioners' opinion, necessary for the financial statements to give a true and fair view. Investment properties are revalued annually and the amount of the revaluation gain or loss attributable by the valuers to depreciation cannot be separately identified; the amount of that gain or loss is taken wholly to capital held for general purposes.

Example 8.22 British Heart Foundation shows investments (including investment properties) as a separate heading below fixed assets on the balance sheet, but invokes the true and fair view override, which confusingly, refers to 'fixed asset', to justify non-depreciation.

8.7 Revaluation of fixed assets

Paragraph 53 of SORP 2 stated:

> 'If a charity revalues some or all of its fixed assets, this fact, together with the date and bases of valuation, should be stated in the notes to the accounts. In the year of valuation, the names and qualifications of the persons responsible for making the valuation should also be disclosed.'

Paragraph 43 of Sch 4 to the 1985 Act requires, where a company revalues any fixed assets, disclosure of:

(a) the years (so far as they are known to the directors) in which the assets were severally valued and the several values; and
(b) in the case of assets that have been valued during the financial year, the names of the persons who valued them or particulars of their qualifications for doing so and (whichever is stated) the bases of valuation used by them.

Additionally, para 33(3) requires to be disclosed the comparable amounts determined under the historical cost convention, or the differences between those amounts and the corresponding amounts shown in the balance sheet.

While these disclosures are similar, they are not identical.

From a review of published accounts, very few charities revalue their fixed assets. This might be due to the concept of asset valuation being more usually linked with commercial organisations. More importantly is that the costs are likely to be prohibitive compared to the benefits and not the best use of funds – see Example 8.31 Barnardo's.

Example 8.31 Barnardo's
Report of Council (part) (31 March 1994):

> **Valuation of Land and Buildings**
> Although some properties would individually realise sums considerably in excess of their book value, others have been purpose-built or specially adapted for a particular use and might not realise their cost. It is therefore not practical to estimate the difference between market value and book value and in view of the fact that the properties are occupied for charitable purposes, Council does not consider the expense of an independent valuation justified.

Example 8.32 MIND does revalue its freehold properties, provides the years in which the revaluation took place and the equivalent historical cost information. Although carried out in years prior to the current year, the bases of valuation, as recommended by SORP 2 (but only required by the 1985 Act in the year of revaluation) are not disclosed.

Example 8.32 MIND
Note 8: Tangible fixed assets (part) (31 March 1993):

Group	Total £	Freehold properties £	Long leasehold properties £	Short-term leasehold property £	Furniture equipment & motor cars £
VALUATION OR COST					
Valuation (1st April 1984)	15,738	–	–	–	15,738
Valuation (31st March 1986, 1987 and 1991)	274,750	274,750	–	–	–
Cost	942,466	28,208	–	170,389	743,869
At 1st April 1992	1,232,954	302,958	–	170,389	759,607
Additions at cost	1,488,990	–	1,250,000	16,801	222,189
	2,721,944	302,958	1,250,000	187,190	981,796
Deduct: disposals	(42,766)	–	–	(2,987)	(39,779)
At 31st March 1993	£2,679,178	£302,958	£1,250,000	£184,203	£942,017
DEPRECIATION AND AMORTISATION					
Aggregate amount provided at 1st April 1992	446,156	–	–	81,177	364,979
Provided in the year	138,992	–	–	8,977	130,015
	585,148	–	–	90,154	494,994
Deduct: Eliminated in respect of disposals	(42,606)	–	–	(2,987)	(39,619)
Aggregate amount provided at 31st March 1993	£542,542	£–	£–	£87,167	£455,375
NET BOOK VALUE					
At 31st March 1993	£2,136,636	£302,958	£1,250,000	£97,036	£486,642
At 31st March 1992	*£786,798*	*£302,958*	*£–*	*£89,212*	*£394,628*

On the historical cost basis the group's freehold properties would have been included at £166,590 (*1992: £166,590*).

Although not incorporated in the accounts, Example 8.33 OXFAM provides details in the fixed assets note of the value at the end of the year and the basis of valuation.

Example 8.33 OXFAM
Note 10: Tangible fixed assets (part) (30 April 1993):

> Oxfam's freehold properties have been revalued at open market value for existing use on 30 April 1993 at £13,006k.

Charitable companies are required by para 1(2) of Sch 7 to the 1985 Act to disclose the difference between the book amount and the market value of land and buildings, if it is of such significance that, in the opinion of the directors, the attention of members ought to be drawn to it (see chapter **5**, page 128).

In view of investments now being classified within fixed assets, and not to be shown as a separate heading, and of an important amendment to the proposal in the ED, the rules relating to revaluations and the attendant disclosures apply to them, as they do to all other fixed assets.

Paragraph 175 of the revised charity SORP continues to recommend that, where a charity revalues its fixed assets, that fact, together with the date and basis of each valuation be given. However, the further disclosure, recommended by SORP 2, that, in the year of valuation, the names and qualifications of the persons responsible for making the valuation be given, is extended to any year in which there is a valuation, but only where the values are determined other than by reference to readily available market prices. If that person is an employee, or trustee of the charity, that fact should, also, be stated.

The difference between the current valuation and the book value should be taken to the SOFA and included within the heading 'gains and losses on revaluation and investments assets disposals'. Paragraph 179 recommends that, where a revaluation takes place, the trustees should refer to it in their annual report. However, there appears to be a conflict with para 28(c)(vi). This recommends that, where there has been a revaluation of fixed assets, *other than of investments*, the effect be given on present and future accounts.

8.8 Permanent diminutions in value

Paragraph 19(2) and (3) of Sch 4 to the 1985 Act and para 19 of SSAP 12 (Revised) both require provisions for permanent diminutions in the value of fixed assets to be charged to and, when no longer required, written back to the profit and loss account.

Paragraph 69 of SORP 2 recommended that:

> 'If an asset suffers a permanent loss (or diminution) in value, the amount at which the asset is carried in the balance sheet should be reduced to the asset's current value by a provision. Where this provision should be charged will depend on the circumstances involved.
>
> (a) If the asset involved is an investment, the provision should be charged to the same place as realised and unrealised losses on investments.
> (b) If the asset involved is a fixed asset, the provision should be charged to the income and expenditure account to the extent that it is not covered by a previous gain on revaluation of that asset. To the extent that it is covered by a previous gain, the provision should be used to reduce the gain by deducting it from the appropriate fund in the balance sheet.'

Example 8.34 Malcolm Sargent Cancer Fund for Children charges provisions against investments to a statement of investment gains.

Example 8.34 Malcolm Sargent Cancer Fund for Children Statement of investment gains (31 March 1993):

		1993 £'000	*1992 £'000*
Net gains on sales of investments		87.3	*147.8*
Release of provision/(Provision) for permanent diminution in value of fixed asset investments		121.6	*(84.4)*
Net investment gains/(losses)	9	208.9	*63.4*

Example 8.35 Distressed Gentlefolk's Aid Association charges provisions against tangible fixed assets as an appropriation of the income and expenditure account.

Example 8.35 Distressed Gentlefolk's Aid Association Income and expenditure account (part) (31 March 1993):

		1993	*1992*
		£	*£*
SURPLUS/(DEFICIT) ON CURRENT ACTIVITIES		1,005,223	*(906,866)*
PROFIT ON SALE OF INVESTMENTS		2,946,713	*1,327,244*
PROFIT ON EXCHANGE OF FOREIGN CURRENCY		238,681	*17,464*
OVERALL SURPLUS		4,190,617	*437,842*
TRANSFERS TO:	Homes appeal	(1,396,000)	*(68,011)*
	Future Development Fund	(2,300,000)	–
	Specific Funds	(1,456)	*(1,083)*
Provision for permanent diminution in value of Halliwell extension	(Note 8)	(436,569)	–
SURPLUS FOR THE YEAR TRANSFERRED TO ACCUMULATED FUND		£56,592	*£368,748*

Paragraph 69 went on to say that provisions for permanent diminutions in value should generally be made on an asset by asset, rather than a portfolio, basis. Example 8.36 Royal Society for the Prevention of Cruelty to Animals is an exception to this rule.

Example 8.36 Royal Society for the Prevention of Cruelty to Animals Accounting policies (part) (31 December 1993):

F Investments
Stocks and shares are included in the accounts at historical cost or donated value. Provisions are made where the market value of investments, on a portfolio basis, is less than historical cost or donated value.

Paragraph 180 of the revised SORP deals with permanent diminutions in value. Such diminutions should be allocated to the appropriate heading (e.g., direct charitable expenditure, fund-raising, administration etc.) in the SOFA. Where the asset has previously been revalued, the diminution should first be deducted from the surplus on that asset, with any resultant balance taken to the SOFA. The amount of the surplus used should, also, be shown in the SOFA, but under the heading 'gains and losses on revaluation and investment assets disposals'.

Paragraph 179 of the revised charity SORP recommends that, where there is a downward revaluation, the accounting process, as indicated in para 180, is reversed. But para 180 deals with *permanent diminutions in value,* not *downward revaluations.* The distinction between a permanent diminution and a downward revaluation in value is blurred. SSAP 12 (Revised) side-steps the issue. Paragraph 20 states that:

> 'This paragraph does not discuss the treatment of provisions for permanent diminutions in value in the case of previously revalued fixed assets.'

Although ED 51 attempted to address this issue, it remains unresolved. Further discussion is beyond the scope of this book. Suffice it to say, this issue arises from a lack of a coherent framework for accounting for fixed assets and, in particular, for the revaluation of fixed assets. The ASB has yet to progress further this issue.

Chapter 9 – Current assets and current and long-term liabilities

9.1 Introduction

In terms of presentation, para 66 of SORP 2 recommended that a charity analyse its assets between 'fixed assets, investments (including investment properties) and current assets' and its liabilities between 'current and long-term liabilities'.

In terms of measurement, sub-paras 68(c) and (d) stated, respectively, that current assets should be 'measured at the lower of cost and net realisable value' and liabilities 'at their settlement value'.

As regards current assets and liabilities, paragraphs 171 and 172 of the revised charity SORP perpetuate these forms of presentation and paras 174(c) and (d) the rules of measurement.

9.2 Current assets

9.2.1 What is a 'current asset'?

For charitable companies, the 1985 Act defines current assets by default. Section 262(1) states that '"fixed assets" means assets of a company which are intended for use on a continuing basis in the company's activities, and "current assets" means assets not intended for such use'.

While there is no equivalent accounting standard in the UK, IAS 13 *Presentation of current assets and current liabilities*, states that:

> 'items are included in current assets on the basis of whether they are expected to be realised within one year or within the normal operating cycle of the enterprise, whichever is the longer'.

9.2.2 Presentation

The statutory formats in the 1985 Act require current assets to be disclosed under the following headings:

I Stocks
1 Raw material and consumables.
2 Work in progress.
3 Finished goods and goods for resale.
4 Payments on account.

II Debtors
1 Trade debtors.
2 Amounts owed by group companies.
3 Amounts owed by undertakings in which the company has a participating interest.
4 Other debtors.
5 Called up share capital not paid.
6 Prepayments and accrued income.

III Investments
1 Shares in group undertakings.
2 Own shares.
3 Other investments.

(Note: Prepayments and accrued income may, alternatively, be shown after current assets, but must still be taken into account in determining net current assets.)

The presentations provided by Example 9.1 British Diabetic Association (a charitable company) and Example 9.2 Royal Society for the Prevention of Cruelty to Animals (a charity incorporated by special Act of Parliament) are typical.

Example 9.1 British Diabetic Association
Balance sheet (part) (31 December 1993):

	Notes	Group		Association	
		1993	*1992*	1993	*1992*
	£	£	£	£	
Current assets					
Stocks of goods for resale		121,841	*135,990*	97,902	*110,990*
Debtors	(4)	499,936	*406,262*	366,353	*264,245*
Cash on deposit at bank and in hand		1,689,315	*1,681,063*	1,689,315	*1,681,063*
Total current assets		2,311,092	*2,223,315*	2,153,570	*2,056,298*

Example 9.2 Royal Society for the Prevention of Cruelty to Animals Consolidated balance sheet (part) (31 December 1993):

	Notes	1993 £'000	*1992 £'000*
Current Assets			
Stocks	6	176	*195*
Donated properties awaiting sale		867	*801*
Debtors	7	2,673	*2,702*
Cash at bank and in hand		2,445	*2,855*
		6,161	*6,553*

Paragraph 2(b) of Pt II of the Sch to the Regulations requires the balance sheet to divide current assets into:

1 Stocks and work in progress;
2 Debtors;
3 Investments; and
4 Cash in hand.

And, paragraph 1(m) of Pt IV of that Sch requires the notes to provide the following further analysis of debtors:

1 Trade debtors;
2 Amounts owed by any institution or body corporate which is a connected person in relation to the charity;
3 Other debtors; and
4 Prepayments and accrued income.

How should current assets due after more than one year be displayed? SORP 2 and its successor are silent on the matter. Like creditors, the 1985 Act requires, for each item comprising debtors, a distinction to be drawn between amounts due within one year and those due after more than one year. This distinction, although disclosed in the notes to the accounts, is, unlike creditors, neither required to be carried through to the total of current assets, nor to the more important total figure of net current assets (or liabilities). Thus, a certain asymmetry exists between the items that the formats require to be classified under current assets and current liabilities.

In July 1992, the UITF published Abstract 4 *Presentation of long-term debtors in current assets*, which dealt with the general question of long-term debtors. It recognised the asymmetry caused by the formats yet, rather surprisingly, ruled that where amounts due after more than one year were 'so material' in the context of the total net current assets, they should be shown separately on the face of the balance sheet (but still within current assets). Where this is not so, it will be satisfactory to continue the practice of displaying the analysis in the notes.

Example 9.3 Tear Fund provides details in the notes of debtors due after more than one year. No examples could be found, however, of charities displaying, on the face of the balance sheet (but still within current assets), debtors due within and after one year.

Example 9.3 Tear Fund
Note 17: Debtors (31 March 1993):

	1993 £'000	*1992* *£'000*
Due within one year:		
Trade debtors	101	*45*
Tax recoverable	192	*167*
Other debtors	182	*129*
Prepayments and accrued income	278	*130*
	753	*471*
Due after more than one year:		
Other debtors	3	*4*
	756	*475*

For charitable companies, where the purchase price of stock differs materially from its replacement value, para 27(3) of Sch 4 requires the amount of that difference to be shown. Although strictly not required to be given, Example 9.4 Nuffield Nursing Homes Trust confirms that there was no significant difference.

Example 9.4 Nuffield Nursing Homes Trust
Note 11: Stocks (31 December 1993):

	Group and Trust	
	1993 £'000	*1992* *£'000*
Raw materials and consumables	3,017	*2,829*

There were no significant differences between the replacement cost and the values disclosed above.

In respect of current (and fixed, see chapter **8** page 236) asset investments, the 1985 Act requires disclosure of:

(a) the amount relating to listed investments, distinguishing between those listed on the London Stock Exchange and those listed on other exchanges;
(b) the aggregate market value of listed investments, if different from the book value(and the stock exchange value, if less than the market value disclosed); and
(c) various details(not summarised further here)where the investment is deemed 'significant'.

9.2.3 Measurement

In terms of measurement, para 68(c) of SORP 2 recommended that current assets be shown 'at the lower of cost and net realisable value'. This is repeated in para 174(c) of its successor. A similar rule exists in para 22 of Sch 4 to the 1985 Act. Example 9.5 United Kingdom Band of Hope Union includes only that amount of cash which it is certain of receiving from the administrators. Although further amounts of interest are receivable, they are omitted from the accounts, on the grounds of prudence, until it is certain they will be received.

Example 9.5 United Kingdom Band of Hope Union
Note 13: Frozen funds (previously held by British & Commonwealth Merchant Bank) (31 December 1993):

> At 31.12.92, The administrator of British & Commonwealth Merchant Bank had committed to make payments to the company of £107,184 and this amount was included as a debtor in the accounts. It was received in March 1993 and represented a final payment of capital and a part payment of interest accruing to 30.8.91.
>
> There remained owing a further £229,680 representing unpaid interest to 30.8.91. Of this £122,496 was received in the year to 31.12.93 and has been included in the accounts.
>
> The balance of the unpaid interest of £107,184 accrued to 30.8.91 was received by the company on 22nd March 1994 and included in the accounts as a Post Balance Sheet adjustment. The unpaid interest accruing from 1.9.91 to 31.10.93 amounting to £99,527 will be included in the accounts as received. It is anticipated that there will be further interest payable for the period after 31st October 1993.

9.3 Current and long-term liabilities

9.3.1 Definitions

Part V of the Sch to the Regulations explains that 'long-term creditor' means an amount falling due after more than one year from the end of the financial year and 'short- term creditor' means an amount falling due within one year.

9.3.2 Presentation

For liabilities, the statutory formats in the 1985 Act require disclosure under the following headings:

1 Debenture loans
2 Bank loans and overdrafts
3 Payments received on account
4 Trade creditors
5 Bills of exchange payable
6 Amounts owed to group undertakings
7 Amounts owed to undertakings in which the company has a participating interest
8 Other creditors, including taxation and social security
9 Accruals and deferred income

The 1985 Act requires amounts falling due within, and after, one year to be shown separately and, in the case of format 1, on the face of the balance sheet.

Paragraph 2(c) and (f) of Pt II of the Sch to the Regulations requires creditors to be divided into those which are short-term and those which are long-term. And, para 1(n) of Pt IV of the Sch requires both short and long-term creditors to be analysed under the following further headings:

1 Loans and overdrafts;
2 Trade creditors;
3 Amounts owed to any institution or body corporate which is a connected person in relation to the charity;
4 Other creditors; and
5 Accruals and deferred income.

For each item included in creditors, para 48(1) of Sch 4 requires disclosure of amounts which are:

(a) payable otherwise than by instalments and which fall due after more than five years; and
(b) payable by instalments, any of which are due after more than five years, and the total of instalments so falling due.

Paragraph 48(2) requires the terms of repayment and rate of interest in each case to be provided. If the number of debts would result in a statement of excessive length, a general indication of terms of repayment and rates of interest will suffice(para 48(3)).

For each item included under creditors, where security has been given for any debt:

(a) the aggregate amount secured; and
(b) an indication of the nature of that security,

are to be disclosed (paras 48(4)(a) and (b)).

Example 9.6 Nuffield Nursing Homes Trust is a good example of a charity providing the disclosures.

Example 9.6 Nuffield Nursing Homes Trust
Note 16: Loans repayable by instalments (31 December 1993):

	Group and Trust	
	1993	*1992*
	£'000	*£'000*
Not wholly repayable within 5 years		
Secured repayable 1994 to 2001	8,000	*8,000*
Secured repayable 1994 to 2000	10,000	*10,000*
Secured repayable 1996 to 2005	12,000	*9,000*
Secured repayable 1999 to 2008	3,000	–
Other loans	–	*160*
	33,000	*27,160*
Wholly repayable within 5 years	139	*345*
	33,139	*27,505*
Included in creditors due within one year	(1,735)	*(226)*
Amounts falling due after more than one year	31,404	*27,279*
Repayable as follows:		
Between 2 and 5 years	12,204	*9,504*
After 5 years	19,200	*17,775*
	31,404	*27,279*

The rates of interest in 1993 varied between 6.4% and 10.8%. The loans are secured by charges on certain assets of the Trust.

While not as demanding as the 1985 Act, para 77 of SORP 2 stated that 'if loans or other liabilities are secured on the assets of a charity then this fact, along with details of the security, should be disclosed in the notes to the accounts'.

Paragraph 208 of the revised SORP, while, broadly, repeating these disclosures, introduces a new recommendation to disclose the proportion the loan, or liability, bears to the present value of the assets mortgaged or charged. This will, clearly, be an important disclosure if the present value of the asset is less than the value of the loan.

Paragraph 1(i) of Pt IV of the Sch to the Regulations requires particulars of any loan or guarantee secured against any of the charity's assets to be shown in the notes.

Paragraph 78 of SORP 2, and repeated in para 209 of the revised SORP, recommend that 'the amounts and interest and repayment terms of all inter-fund loans' be disclosed in the notes. Example 9.7 BEN-Motor & Allied Trades Benevolent Fund provides an example. Although the repayment terms are given, the interest terms are not. Nonetheless, it appears the inter-fund loan is interest free.

That same paragraph also introduces a further new disclosure. Loans made to trading subsidiaries, the security provided, the interest payable and the repayment terms should be separately disclosed in the notes.

Example 9.7 BEN-Motor & Allied Trades Benevolent Fund
Summary of fund balances (31 March 1994):

SUMMARY OF FUND BALANCES

	General Fund £	Town Thorns Capital Appeal £	Permanent Endowment £	Cyclical Maintenance Reserve £	Total £
Balance brought forward 1 April 1993	1,079,020	4,346,679	4,825,113	70,659	10,321,471
Movements in year	64,964	194,670	495,576	14,926	770,136
Balance carried forward 31 March 1994	1,143,984	4,541,349	5,320,689	85,585	11,091,607
Represented by					
Tangible assets	2,663,987	7,069,474	–	–	9,733,461
Investments	129,056	–	3,270,689	–	3,399,745
Current assets	429,774	–	–	–	429,774
Current liabilities	(513,707)	(926,500)	–	–	(1,440,207)
Long term liabilities and provisions	(31,166)	(1,000,000)	–	–	(1,031,166)
Inter Fund loans and transfers	(1,533,960)	(601,625)	2,050,000	85,585	–
Total net assets 31 March 1994	1,143,984	4,541,349	5,320,689	85,585	11,091,607

Note 16: Endowment funds [part]:

On 25 March 1992 the Charity Commissioners approved an order enabling up to £3.8 million to be lent to the General Fund by the Endowment Funds, of which £800,000 was lent during the period (1993: £1,250,000). Annual repayments of £89,130 were due to commence on 31.12.1994 finishing on 31.12.2017.
Since the year end the Management Board have authorised the transfer of a further £1.0 million to the General Fund (total loan £3,050,000) thus increasing the annual repayments to £132,609.

Chapter 10 – Accounting for separate funds

10.1 Introduction

The main purpose of a charity's accounts is to give an overall view of the total resources available to a charity during the period and how those resources have been expended, with the balance sheet showing the position at the year end.

But there are additional requirements for charities. Many receive monies which, either by the donor or by the terms of the appeal, are earmarked for special purposes. Similarly, income generated from assets held in a particular fund may be subject to donor-imposed restrictions as to its use or to the fund to which it belongs. In order to achieve these distinctions between the various funds, the accounting records need to be somewhat sophisticated, tailored to meet the circumstances so that it is known which assets and liabilities are held in which funds. In summary terms, para 24(e) of SORP 2 recommended that charities provide 'details of the movement on, and position of, the various funds'. To be as informative as possible, such details should include a summary of the transactions, assets and liabilities of the main funds under their control, differentiating between restricted, including permanent endowment, funds and unrestricted, including designated, funds.

10.2 What is a 'fund'?

Paragraph 9 of SORP 2 (and para 12 of Appendix 1 to its successor) defined a 'fund' as:

> 'a pool of unexpended resources, held and maintained separately from other pools because of the circumstances in which the resources were originally received or the way in which they have subsequently been treated. A fund will be one of two kinds: a restricted fund or an unrestricted fund.'

10.2.1 Designated funds

Paragraph 12 of SORP 2 defined a 'designated fund' as 'a particular form of unrestricted fund, consisting of amounts of unrestricted funds which have been allocated or designated for specific purposes by the charity itself. The use of designated funds for their designated purpose will remain at the discretion of the trustees.'

While there is no definition in the revised SORP, para 36(d), in effect, repeats this.

Designated funds are not to be confused with restricted funds. While the former are established as a result of a decision of the trustees, which may be later altered, or rescinded, the latter arise either from donor-imposed restrictions or by the terms of the specific appeal.

Designated funds are often employed as buffers to temper the effect on the income and expenditure account of, for example, future maintenance costs of buildings. Example 10.1 BEN-Motor & Allied Trades Benevolent Fund has such a fund for cyclical maintenance.

Example 10.1 BEN-Motor & Allied Trades Benevolent Fund
Note 17: Cyclical maintenance reserve (31 March 1994):

	Lynwood Housing Association £	Alexandra House Hostel £	Birch Hill Sheltered Leasehold £	Town Thorns Sheltered Housing £	12 months to 31 March 1994 Total £	*15 months to March 1993 Total £*
1 April 1993	42,683	8,701	3,832	15,443	70,659	*51,083*
Transfer from/(to) income and expenditure account	7,236	648	(1,169)	8,211	14,926	*19,576*
31 March 1994	£49,919	£9,349	£2,663	£23,654	£85,585	*£70,659*

Paragraph 1 of Appendix 3 to the revised SORP recommends that the precise purpose of such funds is given in the notes.

10.2.2 Restricted funds

Paragraph 10 of SORP 2 (and, broadly, repeated in para 2 of Appendix 3) defines 'restricted funds' as 'funds subject to specific conditions, imposed by the donor (or by the trusts relating to the donation) and binding on the trustees'.

Restricted funds may be restricted income funds, expendable at the discretion of the trustees in furtherance of the charity's pursuits in accordance with the conditions imposed, or they may be capital funds, where the assets are required to be invested, or retained for actual use (e.g., a historic building).

If the trustees use restricted income in a way which is inconsistent with the restrictions imposed, they may be in breach of trust. Accordingly, it is essential that due care is taken to spend from a particular restricted fund only where the trusts so permit. Nonetheless, expenditure may be charged to a restricted fund which is not, at the time, in credit (or in sufficient credit), provided that there is a genuine anticipation of income which can properly be credited to that fund to meet the expenditure. In order to allow for the income not materialising, the trusts of the fund used to finance the expenditure should be sufficiently widely drawn to permit that expenditure.

Expenditure charged to an unrestricted fund should not, subsequently, be recharged to a restricted fund, simply in order to increase the amount of that fund.

Where restricted income has been temporarily invested, prior to being used for a suitable charitable purpose, any income derived from the investment should be added to, and form part of, the restricted income fund in question. Unless a specific purpose has been declared by the donor for the application of the income, in which case such income will be restricted income, income derived from the investment of capital funds may be applied for the general purposes of the charity.

The power may be conferred upon the trustees to convert capital funds into expendable income. Were such a power to be exercised, the relevant funds would become restricted or unrestricted income, depending on whether or not the trusts permit expenditure for any of the purposes of the charity, or only for specific purposes.

Paragraph 28 of SORP 2 stated that the treatment of movements on funds other than permanent endowment funds, should 'not be affected by the type of fund involved'. Thus, both restricted and unrestricted income (and expenditure) should be included in the income and expenditure account at the same time. Net restricted income (or expenditure) which forms part of the surplus (or deficit) for a year should be transferred to the relevant restricted fund.

In practice, both the accounting for, and the disclosure of, restricted income and expenditure has differed.

By presenting its income and expenditure account in columnar form, Example 10.2 Boys' Brigade analyses both its restricted and unrestricted income and expenditure across the various funds.

Example 10.3 Royal National Lifeboat Institution separates out restricted and unrestricted income (but not expenditure) on the face of the income and expenditure account, and explains in the notes how the net surplus is attributed to each fund.

Example 10.4 SENSE combines restricted and unrestricted income and expenditure in the income and expenditure account and makes a net transfer to restricted and designated funds.

And, Example 10.5 SCOPE (formerly The Spastics Society) credits, and debits, income, and expenditure, to restricted funds, without first passing through the income and expenditure account.

Example 10.2 Boys' Brigade
Income and expenditure account (31 March 1993):

	Notes	General Fund £	Special Appeal Fund £	Centenary Appeal Fund £	Other Special Funds £	Resource Centre £	Total £	*1992 Total £*
Income								
Annual Contributions		542,412	–	–	–	–	542,412	*246,920*
Supplies and Resource Centre Sales	3 & 18	761,126	–	–	–	15,299	776,425	*711,496*
Training Centres		198,846	–	–	–	–	198,846	*208,164*
Grants	4	81,004	–	–	–	15,201	96,205	*84,160*
Profit on disposal of fixed assets/investments		9,320	20,144	12,970	–	–	42,434	*73,910*
Donations		64,469	–	1,039	98,196	–	163,704	*135,223*
Legacies		91,972	–	–	–	–	91,972	*128,798*
Investment Income and Interest	5	35,055	9,365	9,630	3,342	–	57,392	*120,484*
Permanent Endowment Funds		5,663	–	–	–	–	5,663	*7,146*
		1,789,867	29,509	23,639	101,538	30,500	1,975,053	*1,716,301*

Example 10.2 Boys' Brigade
Income and expenditure account (31 March 1993): (Continued)

	Notes	General Fund £	Special Appeal Fund £	Centenary Appeal Fund £	Other Special Funds £	Resource Centre £	Total £	*1992 Total £*
Expenditure								
Grants to Battalions and Districts		94,451	–	7,950	–	–	102,401	*141,369*
Subscription/payment to World Conference	19 & 21	7,000	–	–	22,727	–	29,727	*42,747*
Supplies & Resource Centre cost of sales	3 & 18	497,037	–	–	–	7,455	504,492	*499,557*
Training Centres		166,918	–	–	–	–	166,918	*184,273*
Administration – Supplies	6	158,606	–	–	–	–	158,606	*167,414*
– General	6	969,656	–	–	–	–	969,656	*1,031,882*
– Resource Centre	6	–	–	–	–	14,418	14,418	*20,537*
Sundry Special Fund Expenditure		–	–	–	29,668	–	29,668	*6,049*
Major Building Maintenance		(4,335)	–	–	–	–	(4,335)	*50,000*
		1,889,333	–	7,950	52,395	21,873	1,971,551	*2,143,828*
(Deficit)/Surplus for the Year		(99,466)	29,509	15,689	49,143	8,627	3,502	*(427,527)*
Transfers	7	22,070	(29,509)	9,216	(1,777)	–	–	–
		(77,396)	–	24,905	47,366	8,627	3,502	*(427,527)*
Funds at 1 April 1992		1,730,545	156,715	244,245	53,797	14,491	2,199,793	*2,627,320*
Funds at 31 March 1993		1,653,149	156,715	269,150	101,163	23,118	2,203,295	*2,199,793*

Example 10.3 Royal National Lifeboat Institution
Income and expenditure account (part) (31 December 1993):

	1993		*1992*	
	£000	£000	*£000*	*£000*
INCOME				
For general purposes				
Subscriptions and donations	14,197		*13,134*	
Legacies	27,139		*27,937*	
Investment income	5,401		*5,240*	
Profit from trading subsidiaries (Note 6)	506	47,243	*372*	*46,683*
For restricted purposes				
Donations	1,728		*2,804*	
Legacies	12,900	14,628	*11,728*	*14,532*
Total Income		61,871		*61,215*

Note 7: Movement on funds (part):

	At 1 January 1993 £000	Income and Expenditure Account £000	Statement of Investment Gains £000	Endowment funds movements £000	*At 31 December 1993 £000*
Endowment	757	–	–	6,584	*7,341*
Restricted	17,386	5,305	–	–	*22,691*
Property	7,884	1,560	–	–	*9,444*
General	122,580	7,265	33,768	–	*163,613*
Total funds	148,607	14,130	33,768	6,584	*203,089*

Example 10.4 SENSE
Income and expenditure account (part) (31 March 1994):

	Note	£	1994 £	£	*1993 £*
Operating Surplus			1,785,980		*1,115,032*
Administrative Expenses	5	(118,888)		*(122,141)*	
Interest payable and similar charges	7	(7,884)		*(4,712)*	
Interest receivable and similar income	6	157,863		*196,868*	
Relating to Restricted and Designated Funds	18	(1,769,170)		*(1,105,122)*	
			(1,738,079)		*(1,035,107)*
Surplus for the year	8		47,901		*79,925*

Example 10.5 SCOPE (formerly The Spastics Society)
Statement of movement on reserves (part) (5 April 1994):

The Group	General Fund	Designated Funds	Restricted Funds: Schools, Centres & Others	Restricted Funds: SOS	Total
	£000	£000	£000	£000	£000
Balance on 6 April 1993	20,500	771	1,599	2,339	25,209
Reclassification of funds	3,110	(771)	–	(2,339)	–
Surplus for year	2,653	–	–	–	2,653
	26,263	–	1,599	–	27,862
Specific funds movements in year					
Income	–	–	1,336	–	–
Expenditure	–	–	(1,127)	–	–
Net surplus on specific funds transferred from general fund	(209)	–	209	–	–
Balance at 5 April 1994	**26,054**	**–**	**1,808**	**–**	**27,862**

Apart from movements in permanent endowment funds being accounted for separately, Example 10.2's presentation is very similar to the SOFA. But, the latter three charities will all need to change the way they account for, or disclose, all of the movements in restricted funds.

10.2.3 Permanent endowment funds

Paragraph 11 of SORP 2 (and, broadly, repeated, in para 7 of Appendix 3 to the revised SORP) defines a 'permanent endowment fund' as 'a particular form of restricted fund in that the fund must be held permanently, although its constituent assets may change from time to time'.

The concept of 'permanence' does not, however, necessarily mean that the assets held in the endowment fund cannot be exchanged, although, in some cases, the trusts will require the retention of a specific asset, e.g., a historic building, for actual use. What it does mean is that the fund cannot be used as if it were income, i.e., to make payments or grants to others. Where assets held in a permanent endowment fund are exchanged, their place in the fund must be taken by the assets received in exchange. Paragraph 7 of Appendix 3 to the revised SORP states that 'exchange' may simply mean 'a change of investment', but it may, also, for example, mean 'the application of the proceeds of sale of permanent endowment land and buildings in the purchase or improvement of other property'.

Rather than passing through the income and expenditure account, para 26 of SORP 2 recommended that increases and decreases (which will now appear in the SOFA) in these funds should be taken directly to the relevant fund in the balance sheet.

Example 10.6 Boys' Brigade is one charity with permanent endowment funds. It provides a separate note of the movements and explains to what extent the income is restricted.

Example 10.6 Boys' Brigade
Note 20: Permanent endowment funds (31 March 1993):

Income arising on the capital comprised in the Cave Allen Legacy, the 1st London Company Fund and the MacRobert Trust is available towards expenditure in accordance with the donor's direction.

		Balance 1 April 1992 £	Investment Income £	Expend £	Balance 31 March 1993 £
Cave Allen Legacy (Upkeep of grave and balance 50 : 50 to London District and Boys' Brigade)		13,443	1,013	1,013	13,443
1st London Company (50 : 50 London District and Boys' Brigade)		26,907	2,031	2,031	26,907
MacRobert Trust (Brigade training)		54,863	4,141	4,141	54,863
Total		95,213	7,185	7,185	95,213
Balance of Funds at 31 March are represented by					
Quoted investments	(Note 9)	55,890			27,471
Debtors	(Note 11)	626			450
Cash at bank	(Note 12)	40,607			68,781
Creditors	(Note 13)	(1,910)			(1,489)
		95,213			95,213

10.3 Fund structure

In recognising the importance of providing information about both the structure of a charity's funds and the significance of each of the major fund balances, SORP 2 hinted, perhaps unconsciously, at the more coherent framework recommended by its successor. It acknowledged that this information could be presented in a variety of ways. Paragraph 29 suggested that:

> '. . . the accounts could consist of a single set of accounting statements with columnar or note analysis. On the other hand, separate sets of statements could be produced for each major fund.'

The decision as to the most appropriate form of presentation was conferred on the trustees, having regard both to the complexity of the fund structure and to the need to avoid confusion between the movements on the various funds.

Within the new framework, the importance of providing information about the structure and significance of each of the charity's funds, and the discretion afforded to trustees to choose the most appropriate and informative way of achieving this, is repeated in para 41.

Example 10.7 The National Trust is one of the few charities which, prior to the ED's issue, was preparing its accounts generally in columnar form. Note 2 to the accounts explains their form. Although the income and expenditure account is not presented in columnar form, the cash flow statement and its notes are. So, although not ideal, it is possible to recalculate, for most headings, how that account would have been presented in such form.

Example 10.7 The National Trust
Note 2: Form of the accounts (28 February 1994):

The Provisions of the Statement of Recommended Practice for Charities issued by the Accounting Standards Committee in May 1988 are followed except in the treatment of tied gifts, legacies and accumulated investment income. In view of the nature of the Trust's activities, these are treated as capital receipts.

The accounts comprise four principal statements supported by notes. These statements are:

INCOME AND EXPENDITURE ACCOUNT

This identifies the Trust's funding requirement in the year and summarises its principal sources of income and the major categories of expenditure.

BALANCE SHEET

This summarises the working assets which are used by the Trust to achieve its objective of preserving places of historic interest or natural beauty.

MOVEMENT OF FUNDS

This is the capital account. It shows how the funding requirement identified on the Income and Expenditure Account is met from capital receipts and identifies movements for each of the main categories of funds.

CASH FLOW STATEMENT

This shows for each category of fund how the net cashflow from operating activities and investment income is used to finance capital projects and fixed assets. The resulting cash outflow is met from legacies, gifts and grants.

The National Trust's accounts are a consolidation of some 1,900 individual funds. These divide into four distinct categories which are defined as follows:

GENERAL FUND

The General Fund is the free fund of the Trust. It is not tied as are the other funds for use on a particular property or in a particular area or for some other defined purpose.

The General Fund has to provide for the net deficit of all properties that have an inadequate income of their own to meet the cost of their maintenance, improvement and management. It has to pay for the general administration of the Trust, for servicing the membership and for publicity and fundraising. It has also to meet the Trust's requirement for working capital and the cost of tangible fixed assets.

Example 10.7 The National Trust
Note 2: Form of the accounts (28 February 1994): (Continued)

COMMITTED MAINTENANCE FUND

The Committed Maintenance Fund has been established to pay for General Fund capital projects, after allowing for grants and other contributions. The balance at the end of the year equates to the estimated future costs on projects which had commenced prior to the year end and the expenditure planned for the forthcoming year.

Appropriations are made to the fund from the General Fund legacies approved for transfer by the Finance Committee and the General Fund.

DEFINED PURPOSE FUNDS

Defined Purpose Funds include gifts and legacies which have been given or bequeathed to the Trust to be used in accordance with the wishes of the donors or their representatives. Both the capital and the income may be spent. The use of these funds is generally restricted to the maintenance, improvement and management of specific properties or to the purchase of a specific property or a property in a named locality. Until they are spent the funds are invested in stocks, shares, deposits and property.

CAPITAL ENDOWMENT FUNDS

These relate to properties and chattels held for preservation. Many of the properties held for preservation have been endowed, mostly by the donors and occasionally by others. The endowments have been given to the Trust on condition that the capital will not be spent and consist of farms and other property and of stocks, shares and deposits. They are used only for the purpose of earning income to pay for the upkeep, improvement and management of the property or properties to which they relate. In some cases any income then remaining may be used for general or defined purposes of the Trust.

The three latter categories are referred to as "Tied Funds".

By giving only totals in the income and expenditure account and balance sheet, Example 10.8 Royal Society for the Prevention of Cruelty to Animals prefers to display the breakdown by fund by way of note.

And, Example 10.9 Army Benevolent Fund is one (but not the only) charity which shows the total net assets relating to each of its special funds on the face of the balance sheet. These totals are mirrored by equivalent fund balances, with the movements during the year given in the notes. In effect, this presentation creates a balance sheet within the main balance sheet.

Example 10.7 The National Trust

Movement of funds (28 February 1994):

	Note	Total £'000	General £'000	Committed Maintenance £'000	Defined Purpose £'000	Capital Endowment £'000
FUNDS AT START OF PERIOD		354,617	15,886	24,049	129,359	185,323
DRAWINGS FROM FUNDS	22	(27,074)	(4,253)	(14,230)	(8,241)	(350)
CONTRIBUTION TO COMMITTED MAINTENANCE FUND	22	–	(3,082)	3,082	–	–
FUNDS FROM OTHER SOURCES						
Capital grants		2,570	–	–	–	2,570
Sales of leases and freeholds		3,939	–	–	2,658	1,281
Appeals and tied gifts	7	3,773	–	–	3,641	132
Legacies		25,227	–	13,407	11,669	151
Accumulated investment income	5	506	–	–	419	87
		363,558	8,551	26,308	139,505	189,194
REALISED AND UNREALISED MOVEMENT IN INVESTMENTS	5	51,626	(121)	–	17,840	33,907
TRANSFERS	23	–	9,173	–	(12,920)	3,747
TOTAL FUNDS AT CLOSE OF PERIOD		415,184	17,603	26,308	144,425	226,848
TOTAL FUNDS ARE REPRESENTED BY						
Tangible fixed assets		14,144	14,144	–	–	–
Investments		391,881	7,097	26,308	131,628	226,848
Net current assets		15,724	2,927	–	12,797	–
Life membership equalisation account		(6,565)	(6,565)	–	–	–
TOTAL ASSETS		415,184	17,603	26,308	144,425	226,848

Example 10.7 The National Trust

Cash flow statement (28 February 1994):

	Note	Total £'000	General £'000	Committed Maintenance £'000	Defined Purpose £'000	Capital Endowment £'000
NET CASH INFLOW/(OUTFLOW) FROM OPERATING ACTIVITIES	17A	(9,904)	7,513	3,082	(14,087)	(6,412)
RETURNS ON INVESTMENTS AND SERVICING OF FINANCE						
Investment income received		21,537	1,514	–	10,127	9,896
NET (PURCHASES)/SALES ON INVESTMENT PORTFOLIO	17B	(11,848)	(8,921)	–	4,691	(7,618)
TRANSACTIONS OF A CAPITAL NATURE						
Payments to acquire properties for preservation		(7,051)	–	–	(7,051)	–
Capital works and projects		(41,601)	(15,734)	(14,230)	(11,637)	–
Receipts from sales of leases and freeholds		3,939	–	–	2,658	1,281
Receipts of capital grants		2,570	–	–	–	2,570
		(42,143)	(15,734)	(14,230)	(16,030)	3,851
Payments to acquire fixed assets		(4,220)	(4,220)	–	–	–
Receipts from sales of fixed assets		211	211	–	–	–
NET INFLOW/(OUTFLOW) FROM TRANSACTIONS OF A CAPITAL NATURE		(46,152)	(19,743)	(14,230)	(16,030)	3,851
NET CASH OUTFLOW BEFORE FINANCING		(46,367)	(19,637)	(11,148)	(15,299)	(283)
FINANCING						
Receipts of legacies		25,227	–	13,407	11,669	151
Receipts of appeals and tied gifts		3,773	–	–	3,641	132
Receipts of grants and special donations		18,720	16,814	–	1,906	–
		47,720	16,814	13,407	17,216	283
INCREASE/(DECREASE) IN WORKING CASH BALANCE	17B	1,353	(2,823)	2,259	1,917	–

Example 10.8 Royal Society for the Prevention of Cruelty to Animals Consolidated income and expenditure account (31 December 1993):

	Notes	1993 £'000	1993 £'000	*1992 £'000*	*1992 £'000*
SPECIFIC ACTIVITIES					
Income	1		7,871		*8,411*
Expenditure	1, 2		(31,241)		*(28,936)*
OPERATING DEFICIT			(23,370)		*(20,525)*
ADMINISTRATION AND SUPPORT COSTS	2	3,561		*3,173*	
OTHER EXPENDITURE	2	247		*198*	
			(3,808)		*(3,371)*
			(27,178)		*(23,896)*
ADMINISTRATION AND SUPPORT INCOME		484		*285*	
OTHER INCOME					
Voluntary:					
Legacy Income		19,933		*23,846*	
Contributions and Donations		1,217		*744*	
Subscriptions		221		*202*	
Investment Income	3	4,042		*3,623*	
NET TAXATION		–		*2*	
			25,897		*28,702*
EXCESS OF (EXPENDITURE)/INCOME TRANSFERRED (FROM)/TO ACCUMULATED FUNDS	15		(1,281)		*4,806*

Example 10.8 Royal Society for the Prevention of Cruelty to Animals
Note 15: Analysis of funds (part):

ANALYSIS OF FUNDS Income and Expenditure Account	General fund £'000	Wyndham Cottle bequest £'000	Overseas fund £'000	Animal help fund £'000	Hadow bequest £'000	Minor funds £'000	Regional funds £'000	Permanent fund £'000	Animal Centre funds £'000	RSPCA Trading Limited £'000	Total 1993 £'000	*Total 1992 £'000*
SPECIFIC ACTIVITIES												
Income from Activities	7,623	–	57	–	–	1	3	–	414	247	8,345	*8,704*
Less Interfund Contributions	4	(15)	–	(69)	(307)	–	(83)	(4)	–	–	(474)	*(293)*
Net external income	7,627	(15)	57	(69)	(307)	1	(80)	(4)	414	247	7,871	*8,411*
Expenditure	(30,591)	–	(147)	(7)	–	(6)	(352)	(1)	–	(137)	(31,241)	*(28,936)*
OPERATING (DEFICIT)/SURPLUS	(22,964)	(15)	(90)	(76)	(307)	(5)	(432)	(5)	414	110	(23,370)	*(20,525)*
ADMINISTRATION AND SUPPORT COSTS	(3,551)	–	–	–	–	–	–	–	–	(10)	(3,561)	*(3,173)*
OTHER EXPENDITURE	(247)	–	–	–	–	–	–	–	–	–	(247)	*(198)*
	(26,762)	(15)	(90)	(76)	(307)	(5)	(432)	(5)	414	100	(27,178)	*(23,896)*
ADMINISTRATION AND SUPPORT INCOME	484	–	–	–	–	–	–	–	–	–	484	*285*
OTHER INCOME												
Voluntary:												
Legacy Income	19,799	–	41	–	–	2	91	–	–	–	19,933	*23,846*
Contributions & Donations	600	–	–	–	–	–	187	430	–	–	1,217	*744*
Subscriptions	221	–	–	–	–	–	–	–	–	–	221	*202*
Investment Income	3,207	13	54	–	284	8	–	–	–	–	3,566	*3,056*
Deposit Income	385	1	9	23	9	–	42	5	–	2	476	*567*
–												
Trading Company	102	–	–	–	–	–	–	–	–	(102)	–	–
NET TAXATION	–	–	–	–	–	–	–	–	–	–	–	*2*
BALANCE AVAILABLE FOR FUTURE OPERATIONS TRANSFERRED (FROM)/TO ACCUMULATED FUNDS	(1,964)	(1)	14	(53)	(14)	5	(112)	430	414	–	(1,281)	*4,806*

Example 10.9 Army Benevolent Fund
Balance sheet (part) (31 March 1994):

	Notes	1994	*1993*
		£	*£*
FUNDS EMPLOYED			
Grants Equalization	7	746,378	*1,657,946*
General	2, 8	14,780,448	*12,628,808*
Northern Ireland Special Relief Fund	12	885,943	*807,960*
Sir Jules Thorn Account	13	4,904	*4,860*
Falklands Account	14	1,605,365	1,589,522
The Sumner Bequest	15	–	*20,232*
The Gulf Trust	16	7,940	*23,212*
		18,030,978	*16,732,540*

Note 14: Falklands fund [formerly Falklands account]:

The South Atlantic fund made an advance of £250,000 in 1982 to the Army Benevolent Fund to deal with minor cases arising from the Falklands Campaign. This was known as the Falklands Account. On closure of the South Atlantic Fund, its unallocated funds were distributed to King George's Fund for Sailors, the Royal Naval Benevolent Trust, the Army Benevolent Fund and the Royal Air Force Benevolent Fund. The assets of the Falklands Account already held by the Army Benevolent Fund, with the distribution from the South Atlantic Fund, together formed the Falklands Fund, which is "ring-fenced" as a separate Fund to meet the needs of Falklands beneficiaries at least until 31 December 2002 and indefinitely thereafter, unless and until the Trustees of the Army Benevolent Fund determine that it can reasonably be concluded that special reasons no longer exist for maintaining a separate Falklands Fund, when its assets may be subsumed into their General Funds. Thereafter, the needs of Falklands beneficiaries will be met by payment from the General Funds.

Example 10.9 Army Benevolent Fund
Note 14: Falkland Fund (formerly Falklands account): (Continued)

	1994	*1993*
	£	*£*
ASSETS EMPLOYED		
Investments at cost (market value £1,768,484: 1993 – £1,645,503)	1,557,713	*1,555,556*
Debtors	15,090	–
Amount owed by the Army Benevolent Fund	32,562	*33,966*
	1,605,365	*1,589,522*
FUNDS EMPLOYED		
General Fund balance at 1 April 1993	1,589,522	*93,681*
Distribution from South Atlantic Fund	–	*1,437,543*
Donations received from the public	60	–
Interest and dividends (a)	95,856	*41,415*
Gain on sale of investments	–	*83,453*
	1,685,438	*1,656,092*
ASSISTANCE		
Grants paid	(81,033)	*(16,316)*
Loans made (b)	960	*(50,254)*
General Fund balance at 31 March 1994	1,605,365	*1,589,522*

(a) Interest and dividends earned from the Falklands Account investments formed part of the investment income recorded in the Income and Expenditure Account of the main Army Benevolent Fund. With the creation and "ring-fencing" of the Falklands Fund, all interest and dividends earned from the Falklands Fund investments form part of the income of that Fund.

(b)

	1994	*1993*
	£	*£*
Loans made to ex-servicemen and/or dependants		
Amount due to the Falklands Fund at 1 April 1993	50,254	*51,134*
Loan instalments repaid	960	*880*
Amount due to the Falklands Fund at 31 March 1994	49,294	*50,254*
Provision made by charging loans, net of repayments, to the Falklands Fund in the year in which made	(49,294)	*(50,254)*
	–	–

10.4 Reconciliation and analysis of funds

(A) Reconciliation of opening and closing funds
Regardless of the form of presentation, para 30 of SORP 2 recommended that the accounts, or notes, contain 'a reconciliation of the total opening funds . . . to the total closing funds, showing the income less expenditure . . . from the income and expenditure account and details of all other movements on the funds during the period'. This reconciliation should be analysed 'between the major funds of the charity'. Example 10.7 The National Trust provides an example.

Paragraph 43 of the revised charity SORP recommends that the SOFA should provide a reconciliation (see, also, chapter **4**, page 94) of the opening and closing balances on all of the funds of the charity, which should be analysed between unrestricted and restricted and, in the latter case, between income and capital (i.e., endowment) funds. Further analysis of, and details concerning, individual funds (i.e., in the case of endowment funds, between permanent endowment and expendable endowment) should be relegated to the notes. Any restricted funds in deficit should be separately disclosed. These analyses and details will show that the charity trustees have accounted for the proper administration of individual funds, in accordance with their terms.

(B) Analysis of the total amount of assets and liabilities
Paragraph 67 of SORP 2 recommended that there should be an analysis between the major funds of 'the total amount of the assets less liabilities'. It is important to be able to distinguish between the assets and liabilities held in the different funds in order to maintain the integrity of those funds. Profits on disposal of assets will form part of the fund in which each asset is held. Unrealised profits should be treated similarly. Unrealised losses, provisions for depreciation (where the asset has a finite useful life) and permanent diminutions will reduce the value of the fund in which the assets are held. Example 10.10 SENSE is a good example.

An example of allocation of assets (in this case, investments) based on unit-trust principles is provided by Example 10.11 Cambridge University Catholic Association.

The importance of segregating assets and liabilities and income and expenditure between restricted and unrestricted funds is, perhaps, personified by the problems experienced by Example 10.12 War on Want. These are explained, in lengthy detail, in the Chief Executive's report in its 1991 accounts.

The disclosure recommended by para 67 is perpetuated in para 36(a) of the revised charity SORP.

(C) Are the resources held in an appropriate form?
It is important to provide an indication as to whether or not sufficient resources are held in an appropriate form to enable the funds concerned to be applied in accordance with restrictions imposed. Thus, funds which are to be spent in the short-term need to be matched with assets and investments of a short-term nature. If a fund which has to be applied in the short term is represented by assets which cannot reasonably be expected to be realised in the short term, the charity may not be able to apply its funds, as directed.

This disclosure was not specifically recommended by SORP 2, although the principle was recognised and discussed in Appendix 1. Paragraph 36(a) of the revised charity SORP, however, recommends that the notes indicate whether or not sufficient resources are so held, but not what action is being taken by the charity trustees, or what the consequences (if any) might be, if assets are not held in that form.

(D) Realised and unrealised elements
Because many charities do not revalue their fixed assets or investments, the funds will generally not contain any unrealised element. Nonetheless, para 30 went on to recommend that the amount of each fund be analysed 'between the amount that is realised and the amount that is unrealised'. See Example 10.10 SENSE.

This particular disclosure does not appear in the revised SORP. In view of the fact that investment assets must be shown at market value, the reason for its omission is unclear.

(E) The nature and purpose of each fund
Paragraph 30 of SORP 2 recommended that 'the nature and purpose of each major fund' be provided. Where disclosed, the position of this information differs. Example 10.7 The National Trust gives it in a separate note, entitled 'Form of the accounts'; Example 10.9 Army Benevolent Fund, in the note allocated to each fund; and, Example 10.13 NCH Action for Children, in its accounting policies.

Example 10.10 SENSE
Note 23:Analysis of fund balances between the net assets (31 March 1994):

Fund	Regional Funds	National Funds	International Funds	Total Designated & Restricted Funds
Designated and Restricted Funds:	£	£	£	£
Fixed Assets	4,742,241	–	–	4,742,241
Investments	1,613,050	581,586	26,984	2,221,620
Net Current Assets	–	481,902	–	481,902
Total	6,355,291	1,063,488	26,984	7,445,763
Realised Amounts	6,320,768	1,063,488	26,984	7,411,240
Revaluation Reserve	34,523	–	–	34,523
Fund Balance	6,355,291	1,063,488	26,984	7,445,763

	General Fund	Grand Total
Unrestricted Funds	£	£
Fixed Assets	1,563,169	6,305,410
Investments	–	2,221,620
Net Current Assets	228,233	710,135
Total	1,791,402	9,237,165
Realised Amounts	1,511,585	8,922,825
Revaluation Reserve	279,817	314,340
Fund Balance	1,791,402	9,237,165

Example 10.11 Cambridge University Catholic Association
Note 2: Investment pool (part) (30 June 1993):

(a) Individual funds hold units in the Association's investment pool as follows:

	At 30/6/92	Purchased/ (Sold) in Year	At 30/6/93
Laffan Mass Fund	11	–	11
Endowment Fund No 1	6,915	–	6,915
Endowment Fund No 2	8,622	(2,000)	6,622
Stopp Fund	5,434	–	5,434
	20,982	(2,000)	18,982

Income from interest and dividends and realised surpluses have been allocated to the various funds' income accounts on the basis of units held at the beginning of the year.

Example 10.12 War on Want
Chief Executive's Report (part) (31 December 1991):

The 1991 accounts show a remarkable turnaround in the affairs of War on Want. The significant improvement in War on Want's financial affairs is the result of the Council of Management's careful and painstaking work in re-establishing War on Want and of the continued loyal support of members, donors and fellow charities. The Council of Management are resolved to continue their efforts to further strengthen the charity so as to effectively pursue the objects for which it was set up.

It is important to put this achievement within context. In March 1990 War on Want was brought to the brink of liquidation with reported debts of over £1.6 million. In July 1990 an Extraordinary General Meeting of the members of the charity agreed that work should proceed on a rescue proposal which would allow War on Want's unique work to continue.

In November 1990 the proposal entitled 'Beyond Survival' was put to an Extraordinary General Meeting of the members of the charity. It outlined steps to be taken to address the severe financial and administrative problems which had beset the charity. . . . Stringent financial controls were approved and put in place, overheads were drastically reduced and War on Want began to operate with a staffing complement of seven.

In March 1991 the Charity Commissioners published their Inquirers' Report. Although the report was severely critical of War on Want it did find inter alia that 'during the period covered by the review War on Want arranged many worthwhile projects in difficult and very needy parts of the world. Funds totalling over £30 million from various public and private sources were received and expended between 1984 and 1989'.

The Inquirers' Report attributed the main reason for War on Want's potential insolvency to its intermingling of restricted and general fund monies. The Commissioners therefore asked the charity to conduct a tracing exercise to identify all restricted funds received from 1985 to 1990 which had not been spent on the purpose for which they were given.

This exercise was carried out by the charity's new auditors, Moores Rowland, in October 1991 and their findings were incorporated in the audited accounts for the period ended 31 December 1990. Moores Rowland found that War on Want's internal bookkeeping system was essentially sound. However, they found that some direct project expenditure and costs had not been deducted from the appropriate restricted funds and that the charity had not made an administrative charge on many of these funds in accordance with its stated accounting policy. The auditors reported that although at 31st October 1991 there remained restricted fund commitments of £167,000, the charity had overspent on its overall restricted fund projects by over £500,000, this overspending being funded by the general fund.

The Moores Rowland report confirmed the findings of the Charity Commissioners' Inquiry that War on Want had suffered a serious loss as a result of the intermingling of its general fund and restricted funds. It also confirmed that for this reason War on Want's accounts for the years ending 1985 to 1989 were 'materially misstated'.

Example 10.13 NCH Action for Children (formerly the National Children's Home)
Note 1: Accounting policies (part) (31 March 1993):

(b) Accumulated Funds

The various accumulated funds represent the following:

Specific Purposes Funds	Legacies and other donations for specific purposes and amounts set aside for specified objects, less amounts expended for these purposes.
Endowment Funds	Funds donated to provide scholarships and income for general purposes.
Legacies Equalisation Account	The aggregate of the Surplus/(deficit) of unconditional legacy income over/(under) the average of such income for the past five years.

Paragraph 43 of the revised charity SORP repeats this disclosure. And, para 1(b) of Pt IV of the Sch to the Regulations requires the notes to contain a description of the nature and purpose of all *significant* funds of the charity.

(F) Funds retained by subsidiaries
A matter not addressed in SORP 2 is the disclosure, in consolidated accounts, of funds, other than those used for charitable purposes, retained by subsidiaries. Paragraph 42 of the revised charity SORP recommends that these be disclosed separately, under an appropriate heading, e.g., 'non-charitable trading funds'.

10.5 Transfers and allocations

SORP 2 offered some recommendations as regards transfers and allocations.

Paragraph 31 recommended that:

> 'When disclosing details of movements on the major funds, transfers should be shown separately from allocations to designated funds. Furthermore:
>
> (a) material transfers and allocations of income received to designated funds should be separately disclosed, without aggregation or netting off, and should be accompanied by a narrative explanation of the nature and objective of the transfer or allocation;
> (b) transfers and allocations should, if they are to be included in the income and expenditure account, be shown separately from, and beneath a sub-total of, the income and expenditure for the period.'

Other than for (b), these recommendations are repeated in para 44 of the revised SORP.

Paragraph 1(g) of Pt IV to the Sch to the Regulations requires the notes to give an itemised analysis of any material movement between any of the restricted funds of the charity, or between a restricted and unrestricted fund, together with an explanation of the nature and purpose of each of those funds.

Chapter 11 – Other disclosures

11.1 Introduction

This chapter considers the following:

(a) capital and charitable commitments and the use of designated funds;
(b) contingent liabilities and guarantees;
(c) transactions with trustees and connected persons;
(d) trustees' and employees' emoluments;
(e) auditors' and independent examiners' remuneration;
(f) ex-gratia payments;
(g) leasing;
(h) pension costs; and
(i) post balance sheet events.

11.2 What is a 'liability'?

For commercial organisations, expenditure is not usually incurred until consideration for that expenditure, i.e., goods or services received, has passed. For charities, however, such an exchange for consideration does not normally arise in respect of expenditure and grants relating to direct charitable activities. Nonetheless, the charity may still have an obligation, to make a transfer of value to a third party, which should be recognised.

A 'liability' is defined in para 16 of Appendix 1 to the revised SORP as:

> 'a claim against an accounting entity which:
>
> (a) is expected to be settled by the entity parting with assets or in some way losing an economic benefit; and
> (b) results from past transactions or events; and
> (c) embodies a present duty or responsibility to one or more other entities that entails settlement at a specified or determinable future date, on the occurrence of a specified event, or on demand; and
> (d) results from a duty or responsibility which obligates the entity either legally, or practically, because it would be financially or otherwise operationally damaging to the entity not to discharge the duty or responsibility.

A moral obligation – such as results from the making of a non-contractual promise – does not create a liability unless it meets the definition above.'

Because of the need to satisfy *all* conditions, the definition affords a degree of flexibility to those charities which either fund future commitments from future income streams or are under a moral, but not legal, obligation to meet them.

Paragraph 144 recommends that a liability should be recognised, in full, as soon as the obligation arises and, if material, disclosed in the notes.

11.3 Capital and charitable commitments and the use of designated funds

Paragraph 50(3) of Sch 4 to the 1985 Act requires charitable companies to disclose the aggregate or estimated amount of:

(a) capital expenditure contracted for, insofar as not provided; and
(b) capital expenditure authorised by the directors, but not contracted for.

Regardless of the charity's constitution, disclosure of capital commitments is common. While most allocate a separate note for this information, for example Example 11.1 Royal Society for the Prevention of Cruelty to Animals, some, including Example 11.2 Ex-Services Mental Welfare Society, prefer to include the details within the fixed assets note.

Example 11.1 Royal Society for the Prevention of Cruelty to Animals
Note 11: Capital commitments (31 December 1993):

	1993 £'000	*1992* *£'000*
Contracted	2,439	*1,176*
Authorised but not contracted	1,031	*1,004*

Included in Operating Properties (Note 4) and Capital Commitments contracted for are amounts of £1,152,000, (1992 £1,506,000) and £1,130,000, (1992 £941,000) respectively relating to assets in the course of construction.

Example 11.2 Ex-Services Mental Welfare Society
Note 3: Tangible fixed assets (part) (30 September 1993):

	1993	*1992*
CAPITAL COMMITMENTS		
Authorised but not contracted	£60,000	*£295,000*

In respect of charitable commitments and the use of designated funds, paras 74 and 75 of SORP 2 stated that:

> 'Particulars of all material commitments in respect of specific charitable projects, whether they are legally binding or not, should be disclosed in the accounts. These particulars should include the amounts involved, when the commitments are likely to be met, and the movements on commitments previously reported. Particulars of all other material legally binding commitments should also be disclosed'; and

> 'Commitments can be dealt with either by disclosing them in a note to the accounts or by using designated funds to represent committed unrestricted funds. If designated funds are used, they should be disclosed separately from restricted funds and appropriately described.'

Paragraph 50(4) of Sch 4 requires disclosure of all other commitments which have not been provided for and which are relevant to assessing the state of the charitable company's affairs.

In accordance with para 75, Example 10.1 BEN-Motor & Allied Trades Benevolent Fund (see chapter **10**, page 260) employs designated funds for commitments in respect of cyclical maintenance.

But it is in relation to grant commitments where disparity seems to lie. Paragraphs 74 and 75 needed to be considered with para 57 which stated (*inter alia*):

> ' . . . grant should be recognised in the income and expenditure account when its payment becomes due. An implication of this is that commitments which extend beyond the end of the accounting period and grants which fall to be paid in future accounting periods should be charged in future income and expenditure accounts.'

Example 11.3 Cancer Relief Macmillan Fund complies with SORP 2's recommendations.

Example 11.3 Cancer Relief Macmillan Fund
Accounting policies (part) (31 December 1993):

Commitments
Provision is not made in the Income and Expenditure Account for future liabilities in respect of Grant commitments

Details of the Commitments in respect of such Grants at the Balance Sheet date are set out in Note 21.

Note 21: Commitments [part]:

A-Charitable Grants	1993 £M	*1992 £M*
At 31 December 1992	28.3	*25.8*
Further Commitments during the year	29.0	*14.4*
Expended during the year	(17.1)	*(11.9)*
At 31 December 1993	40.2	*28.3*
less contributions from third parties received & receivable	(4.3)	*(4.8)*
	35.9	*23.5*
Expected to be payable: within one year	15.7	*11.5*
between one and five years	20.2	*12.0*
	35.9	*23.5*

In practice, however, a number of grant-making charities have chosen not to follow these recommendations. Rather, the charity trustees have taken the view that, as they are committed to paying the grant, even if over a period of years, the liability should be accrued for, and in full.

Example 11.4 CAFOD charges, to the income and expenditure account, project commitments in the year in which they are approved by the Management Committee. When the payments are made, they are deducted from the liability and do not pass through the income and expenditure account. Commitments not disbursed at the balance sheet date are shown as a separate caption on the face of the balance sheet and added to current liabilities. Note 1(d) explains that the accounting policy is a departure from SORP 2 (with which the auditors appear to concur). Details of when the commitments are likely to be met are not provided. And Example 11.5 Cystic Fibrosis Research Trust provides, in full and as a liability, for all authorised grants for the following year (with the general fund balance held against commitments after that date). The grants pass through the income and expenditure account, together with the opening and closing appropriations. This does not, also, strictly

Example 11.4 CAFOD
Note 1: Accounting policies (part) (30 September 1993):

(d) Project allocations

These are charged to the income and expenditure account when they have been approved. Project allocations approved, but not disbursed at the balance sheet date, are carried forward as project commitments in the balance sheet. This does not comply with SORP 2 which recommends that grants which fall to be paid in future accounting periods should be charged in future income and expenditure accounts. The Trustees' policy is to recognise the cost of CAFOD's commitments in the year in which each commitment is made in order to ensure that there is adequate liquidity to meet these liabilities.

Note 16: Project commitments:

	Balance at 1st Oct 1992 *£*	Allocated in year £	Disbursed in year £	Balance at 30th Sept 1993 £
From general income				
Overseas:				
Development grants	*2,930,170*	5,214,059	4,774,999	3,369,230
Emergency overseas	*5,540*	307,974	305,623	7,891
Development education	*220,344*	1,407,084	1,306,562	320,866
Project preparation	–	754,682	754,682	–

Example 11.4 CAFOD
Note 16: Project commitments: (Continued)

	Balance at 1st Oct 1992 £	Allocated in year £	Disbursed in year £	Balance at 30th Sept 1993 £
From restricted income				
Overseas:				
Development grants	*9,920*	2,746,845	2,738,626	18,139
Emergency grants	*5,084,360*	7,295,990	6,278,394	6,101,956
Bishop Hitchen Memorial fund	–	374	374	–
Caritas consortia	*1,270,068*	1,235,796	1,616,531	889,333
	£9,520,402	£18,962,804	£17,775,791	£10,707,415

(a) The balance of project commitments from restricted income represents those amounts received from donors for specified purposes or regions which had not been remitted at the balance sheet date.
(b) The balance of project commitments from general income represents amounts allocated from general income to specific projects by the Executive Committee which had not been remitted at the balance sheet date.
(c) The development education fund represents unspent amounts allocated for development education in accordance with the accounting policies.

Example 11.5 Cystic Fibrosis Research Trust
Income and expenditure account (part) (31 March 1994):

	Notes	1994 £	1994 £	*1993 £*	*1993 £*
FUNDS AVAILABLE FOR APPROPRIATION					
For the year			2,726,000		*3,010,062*
Brought forward from the previous year	3		2,930,833		*3,483,366*
			5,656,833		*6,493,428*
SUPPORT EXPENDITURE					
Family and adult support services		235,219		*218,372*	
Branch, regional and group support		163,418		*160,991*	
Research support		97,006		*94,430*	
Conferences		24,896		*36,098*	
Association of Cystic Fibrosis Adults		61,295		*50,112*	
		581,834		*560,003*	
GRANTS	14				
Research		1,127,814		*1,712,693*	
Cystic Fibrosis Clinical Fellowships		557,096		*589,295*	
Development of Cystic Fibrosis Centres		347,965		*700,604*	
		2,032,875		*3,002,592*	
APPROPRIATION FOR GRANTS FOR THE YEAR ENDING 31 MARCH 1995					
Research		1,345,000		*1,223,000*	
Cystic Fibrosis Clinical Fellowships		124,000		*500,000*	
Development of Cystic Fibrosis Centres		724,000		*450,000*	
		2,193,000		*2,173,000*	
TOTAL GRANTS AND SUPPORT EXPENDITURE			(4,807,709)		*(5,735,595)*

Example 11.5 Cystic Fibrosis Research Trust
Balance sheet: (part) (31 March 1994):

	Notes	1994 £	1994 £	*1993* *£*	*1993* *£*
CURRENT LIABILITIES					
Funds appropriated for grants in 1994/95		2,193,000		*2,173,000*	
Grants awaiting claim		322,340		*590,657*	
Creditors and accrued charges	8	183,020		*177,681*	
			(2,698,360)		*(2,941,338)*

Note 2: Grants authorised:

Grants authorised by the Trust cover projects for two or three year periods from the date the grant is taken up. The accounts make provision for grant commitments up to 31 March 1995. The general fund balance of £849,124 is held against commitments in respect of specific projects arising from authorised grants after that date. At 31 March 1994 these commitments amounted to approximately £1,150,000.

Note 3: Funds available for appropriation:

Funds brought forward from previous year were disclosed as:

Funds appropriated for grants	2,173,000
General fund	757,833
	£2,930,833

comply with SORP 2, but the accounts contain no reference to compliance, or otherwise, with the SORP.

Some charities, with small or no surplus funds, enter into future commitments on the basis of expected future income streams and are, therefore, able fully to comply with SORP 2's recommendations. If they were required to accrue for such commitments, the balance sheets might show a negative position which might prejudice their ability to raise future income.

Paragraphs 199 to 201 of the revised SORP deal with commitments. Commitments which are legally binding should be accrued for.

Charitable commitments are liabilities where the trustees have promised financial support to a recipient as part of a binding commitment. Where the amount is payable by instalments, the full amount should be accrued in the financial year in which the commitment is entered into. Future instalments should be analysed in the balance sheet between those due within one year and those due after more than one year. Paragraph 200 recommends that particulars of all material charitable commitments accrued should be provided in the notes. Those particulars include:

(a) the amount accrued in the year;
(b) when each payment is likely to be made; and
(c) the movement on any previously accrued commitment.

For those charities which fund future commitments from future income streams and, thus, not liabilities (as defined), the revised SORP affords a degree of flexibility. If not accrued for, particulars of all material commitments in respect of specific charitable projects should be disclosed in the notes. Those particulars should include:

(a) the amounts involved;
(b) when the commitments are likely to be met; and
(c) the movements on commitments previously reported.

In addition, para 145 recommends that the relationship between the expected income and expenditure is explained. Promises of support which are not binding on the charity trustees are not usually liabilities, but 'intentions'. Paragraphs 146 and 201 of the revised SORP recommend that, where the trustees have decided to incur the expenditure out of existing unrestricted funds, they should account for such intentions by the use of designated funds. The designated fund should be separately disclosed as part of unrestricted funds and clearly explained in the notes.

Paragraph 146 recommends, also, that the notes give the trustees' reasons for setting up the fund.

If there is a related recognisable asset, para 148 recommends that this be shown and the relationship explained.

If a later event makes redundant the recognition of a liability, it should be written back in the SOFA against the heading used to recognise the initial liability. If material, the release of the liability should be separately disclosed and a clear explanation given in the notes.

11.4 Contingent liabilities and guarantees

Unlike its successor, SORP 2 did not specifically deal with contingent liabilities.

Paragraph 18 of SSAP 18 *Accounting for contingencies* requires, for all contingent gains and losses requiring disclosure, the notes to contain:

(a) the nature of the contingency;
(b) the uncertainties which are expected to affect the ultimate outcome; and
(c) a prudent estimate of the financial effect, made at the date on which the accounts are approved by the board of directors, or a statement that it is not practicable to make such an estimate. In the case of a contingent loss, the amount should exclude any amounts accrued and any component where the possibility of loss is remote.

For charitable companies, para 50(2) of Sch 4 to the 1985 Act requires disclosure of:

(a) the amount or estimated amount of any such liability;
(b) its legal nature; and
(c) whether any valuable security has been provided by the company in connection with that liability and, if so, what.

Example 11.6 NCH Action for Children provides an example.

Example 11.6 NCH Action for Children
Note 10: Contingent liabilities (31 March 1994):

> Certain grants received in respect of property alterations and improvements and equipment attach conditions whereby amounts could be repayable in the event of the relevant property or equipment being sold or ceasing to be used for the stated purpose. At 31 March 1994 these grants amounted to £1,526,000 (1993 – £1,526,000).
>
> Out of this total £914,000 (1993 £914,000) relates to property and equipment where the conditions of the grant continue to be fulfilled. The remainder, £612,000 (1993 £612,000), relates to 3 properties which have ceased to be used in accordance with the conditions prescribed. However it is not possible at this stage to quantify any sums which might become repayable.

Paragraphs 203 to 207 of the revised charity SORP deal with contingent liabilities. In general, the provisions are consistent with SSAP 18. There are, however, some differences. For example, while para 16 of SSAP 18 requires the disclosure of a material contingent loss not accrued for except where the possibility of loss is 'remote', para 205 of the revised SORP requires disclosure unless the possibility of loss is 'extremely remote'. Where a prudent estimate of the financial effect of a contingent loss not accrued for cannot be made, para 18(c) of SSAP 18 requires 'a statement *that* it is not practicable to make such an estimate', but para 207 of the revised SORP requires a statement *why* it is not practicable. The revised charity SORP does not deal with contingent gains.

Like the 1985 Act, para 1(o) of Pt IV of the Sch to the Regulations requires the following to be disclosed in the notes for each contingent liability:

(a) its amount, or estimated amount;
(b) its legal nature;
(c) whether any valuble security has been provided by the charity in connection with that liability and, if so, what.

Where material, para 76 of SORP 2 required 'guarantees given by the charity, and the conditions under which liabilities might arise as a result of guarantees', to be disclosed in the notes. Example 11.7 Barnardo's provides an example. Paragraph 202 of the revised SORP repeats this disclosure.

Example 11.7 Barnardo's
Note 22: Commitments (part) (31 March 1994):

a. Republic of Ireland

The Council have entered into a Deed of Guarantee with the Council of Barnardo's Republic of Ireland Limited whereby financial support by way of grants covering a rolling four year period is assured. At 31 March 1994, this Guarantee covers a total commitment estimated at £3.8 million (1993 – £4.4 million).

11.5 Transactions with trustees and connected persons

Paragraphs 79 and 80 of SORP 2 stated:

> 'Particulars, including the amounts involved, of any transaction, contract or other arrangement between a charity and any of its employees or trustees, or persons connected with them, should be disclosed in the notes to the accounts if the transaction, contract or other arrangement is likely to be significant to the user of the accounts. Employees' contracts of employment are an example of contracts which will not usually be significant to the user'; and

> 'Particulars of any relevant connection of the trustees or officers of a charity (for example, as trustees or officers of charities with which the reporting charity works) should also be disclosed.'

In very broad terms, these recommendations are similar to those in Sch 6 to the 1985 Act regarding disclosure of directors' transactions. These latter rules are extremely complex and a discussion of them is beyond the realm of this book. Suffice it to say that, from a survey of published accounts, only one positive statement could be found – Example 11.8 Woodland Trust.

Example 11.8 Woodland Trust
Note 3: Directors' emoluments (part) (31 December 1993):

> Mr R H Trafford is a consultant with Stones which is one of three firms of solicitors the Trust uses to undertake its legal work.

Negative statements vary from the simple statement that 'no trustee has or has had during the year a significant interest in any contract with the company' (either in the trustees' report or in the notes), to a statement of what interest subsists together with the trustees' opinion that they do not consider the interest to be material – see Example 11.9 Ex-Services Mental Welfare Society.

Example 11.9 Ex-Services Mental Welfare Society
Note 2: Surplus on operations for the year (part) (30 September 1993):

> No member of the management committee received any remuneration for their services during the year, nor had any beneficial interest in any contract with the Society during the year.
>
> Mr D.B. Bailey is a director in Hichens Harrison & Co. Plc., who provide stockbroking services to the Society on normal business terms. The Management Committee do not consider that this represnets a material beneficial interest in the contract.

Paragraph 154 of the revised SORP recommends that, where a charity enters into a transaction, contract or other arrangement with a connected person, the amounts involved and terms and conditions should be disclosed in the notes. Paragraph 156 points out that transactions, whether direct or indirect, involving trustees personally should always be regarded as material. Unlike the 1985 Act, there are no *de minimis* provisions regarding disclosure.

Who is a 'connected person'? Regulation 2 states that a 'connected person' is to be interpreted in accordance with Sch 5 to the 1993 Act. That Sch states that a 'connected person' is:

(a) a charity trustee or trustee of the charity;
(b) a person who is the donor of any land to the charity, whether the gift was made on or after the charity's establishment;
(c) a child (including a stepchild or illegitimate child), grandchild, parent, grandparent, brother or sister of any such trustee or donor;
(d) an officer, agent or employee of the charity;
(e) the spouse (including a person living with another as that person's husband or wife) of any person in (a) to (d);
(f) an institution which is controlled:
    (i) by any person within (a) to (e);
    (ii) by two or more persons, taken together; or
(g) a body corporate in which:
    (i) any connected person in (a) to (f) has a substantial interest; or
    (ii) two or more such persons, taken together, have a substantial interest.

For the purposes of (f), a person controls an institution if he is able to secure that the affairs of the institution are conducted in accordance with his wishes.

And, for the purposes of (g), a connected person has a substantial interest in a body corporate if the person, or institution:

(a) is interested in shares comprised in the equity share capital of that body of a nominal value of more than one-fifth of that share capital; or
(b) is entitled to exercise, or control the exercise of, more than one-fifth of the voting power at any general meeting of that body.

Section 97(1) of the 1993 Act states that an 'institution' includes 'any trust or undertaking'.

The rules which are set out in Pt I of Sch 13 to the 1985 Act apply, as they do for the purposes of s346(4) of that Act. And, 'equity share capital' and 'share' have the same meaning as in that Act.

This definition is, broadly, the same as that in para 6 of Appendix 1 to the revised SORP.

Paragraph 1(e) of Pt IV of the Sch to the Regulations requires to be disclosed in the notes particulars of any transaction undertaken in the name of, or on behalf of, the charity in which any person connected with the charity has a material interest.

And, para 1(h) of that Pt requires to be disclosed the name of any institution, or body corporate, which is a connected person, together with a description of the nature of the charity's relationship with that institution, or body corporate, and of its activities, including, where material, its turnover and net profit, or loss, for the corresponding financial year and any qualification in an auditor's report on its accounts.

11.6 Trustees' and employees' emoluments

Paragraph 81 of SORP 2 stated that:

> 'If some or all of the trustees have received remuneration from the charity or have been reimbursed by the charity for expenses which they have incurred, this fact and the amounts involved should be disclosed in the notes to the accounts. An indication of the type of expenses reimbursed should also be provided. If no remuneration was paid or no expenses reimbursed, this should be reported.'

This disclosure is extended by paras 157 and 158 of the revised SORP to include remuneration received, directly or indirectly, or from a company 'controlled' by the trustees. If relevant, the source of the remuneration should, also, be disclosed. As regards expenses, the notes should, also, indicate the number of trustees reimbursed.

In general, a review of published accounts suggests that trustees do not receive remuneration*, only out-of-pocket expenses – see Example 11.10 Royal Society for the Protection of Birds.

Example 11.10 Royal Society for the Protection of Birds
Note 6: Staff costs (part) (31 March 1994):

> No remuneration is paid to the members of the Society's Council. Travelling expenses incurred by them on Council business are reimbursed.

In note 10 to its 1994 accounts, SENSE stated that 'As required by the Charities Acts, members of Council receive no remuneration', while, in note 23 to its 1994 accounts, SCOPE (formerly The Spastics Society) stated 'In accordance with the articles of association the members of the Executive Council do not receive any remuneration from the Society'.

Paragraph 82 of SORP 2 (and, broadly, reiterated by para 160 of its successor) states that:

> 'The total emoluments (i.e., remuneration and benefits-in-kind) paid to employees during the accounting period and the average number of employees during the period should be disclosed in the notes to the accounts.'

Example 11.11 British Red Cross Society provides a good example.

* *See the Annex to Chapter 2, page 32, for a summary of charity trustees' responsibilities in this respect.*

Example 11.11 British Red Cross Society
Note 12: Staff emoluments and trustees expenses (part) (31 December 1993):

	Total 1993 £000	*Total 1992 £000*
Total staff emoluments for the year were as follows:		
Salary Costs	5,841	*4,375*
National Insurance Costs	543	*382*
Pension Costs	268	*117*
	6,652	*4,874*

	1993 Full Time Nos.	1993 Part Time Nos.	*1992 Full Time Nos.*	*1992 Part Time Nos.*
The average number of individuals employed by the Society during the year was as follows:				
UK Operations	59	16	*53*	*16*
International (employed in UK)	56	1	*31*	*2*
Public Affairs	70	8	*55*	*10*
Finance	42	15	*40*	*14*
Personnel	9	2	*4*	*2*
Management and Advisors	5	6	*4*	*6*
	241	48	*187*	*50*
International (Employed overseas)	68	–	*41*	–
	309	48	*228*	*50*

Charitable companies are required to observe para 56 of Sch 4 to the 1985 Act. In addition to the above, this requires:

(a) the average number of persons employed within each category; and
(b) if not disclosed in the profit and loss account, the aggregate amounts relating to:
  (i) wages and salaries paid or payable in the year;
  (ii) social security costs incurred on their behalf; and
  (iii) other pension costs incurred.

Although repealed by the 1989 Act, Example 11.12 Mary Rose Trust provides details of higher-paid employees' emoluments. Paragraph 161 of the revised SORP recommends such disclosure, within bands of £5,000 from £30,000 upwards. In the light of the relaxation afforded by that Act, an explanation for the resurrection of the disclosure would have been helpful. If the income and expenditure account covers a period that exceeds 12 months, the bands still remain as multiples of £5,000. Trustees may wish to give, as additional information, the amounts in bands on an annualised basis.

Example 11.12 Mary Rose Trust
Note 3: Staff costs and employees (part) (31 December 1993):

The number of employees whose emoluments exceeded £30,000 were as follows:

	1993	*1992*
£40,001 – £45,000	1	*1*

11.7 Auditors' and independent examiners' remuneration

SORP 2 made no mention as regards disclosure of auditors' remuneration.

Charitable companies are, however, required, by s390A(3) of the 1985 Act, to disclose such remuneration, including expenses.

Disclosure of amounts paid to the company's auditors and to their associates in respect of other services is required by SI 1991 No 2128. Companies which qualify as small or medium-sized are, however, exempt from this requirement.

Paragraph 162 of the revised SORP requires separate disclosure in the notes of remuneration payable to the charity auditor or independent examiner in respect of:

(a) audit and independent examination services; and
(b) other services such as taxation advice, consultancy, financial advice and accountancy.

Whether or not intentional, the revised SORP, as drafted, requires a further analysis of fees in respect of other services across the various sub-headings.

Where consolidated accounts are prepared, the amounts to be disclosed are those for the group.

Paragraph 1(j) of the Sch to the Regulations requires the notes to disclose particulars of any remuneration paid to an auditor, or independent examiner, for auditing, or examining, the accounts, together with similar particulars of any remuneration paid for other services rendered.

11.8 Ex-gratia payments

A new disclosure is that recommended by paragraph 164 of the revised charity SORP. The total amount, or value, of any:

(a) payment; or
(b) non-monetary benefit; or
(c) other expenditure of any kind; or
(d) waiver of rights to property to which a charity is entitled,

which is made, not as an application of funds or property for charitable purposes, but in fulfilment of a compelling moral obligation, should be disclosed in the notes.

Where the trustees require the authority of the Court, the Attorney General or the Commissioners, para 165 recommends disclosure of the nature and date of the authority for each such payment.

11.9 Leasing

Many charities are party, generally as lessees, to lease and hire purchase contracts. They are, thus, required to comply with the accounting and disclosure requirements of SSAP 21 *Accounting for leases and hire purchase contracts.*

Where the leases are finance leases (or hire purchase contracts with similar characteristics), SSAP 21 requires the following disclosures:

(a) the accounting policy;
(b) total of gross amount and accumulated depreciation for each major class of asset. Alternatively, if this information is combined with owned assets, the net amount included in the overall total may be given;
(c) net obligations split between amounts payable in the next year, in two to five years inclusive and after five years. Alternatively, this may be shown as gross obligations with future finance charges deducted from the total. The net obligations analysis may be combined with other obligations and liabilities;
(d) aggregate finance charges for the year;
(e) aggregate depreciation charged for the year;
(f) commitments existing at the balance sheet date when, at the date, neither has the asset been brought into use, nor have rentals began to accrue.

Where the leases are operating leases, SSAP 21 requires disclosure of:

(a) the accounting policy;
(b) total operating rentals charged, analysed between those in respect of hire of plant and machinery and others;
(c) payments committed to be made for (i) land and buildings and (ii) other leases. Both amounts should be further analysed between those expiring:
    (i) within one year;
    (ii) in the second to fifth years inclusive; and
    (iii) in over five years.

The 1985 Act has certain disclosure requirements which affect leases. Paragraph 53(6) of Sch 4 requires the amount charged to revenue in respect of sums payable for the hire of plant and machinery. This requirement will be satisfied by providing the information in (d) and (e) in relation to finance leases and (b) in relation to operating leases.

Paragraph 50(5) of the same Sch requires particulars of commitments which (i) have not been provided for and (ii) are relevant to assessing the state of the company's affairs. This requirement will normally only apply to operating leases.

Net obligations of finance leases will have to be split between amounts payable within, and after, one year for the purposes of the formats.

Example 11.13 BEN-Motor & Allied Trades Benevolent Fund is a good example of a charity which provides many of the disclosures relating to finance leases. SENSE, also, has finance leases.While (a),(c) and (d) are

Example 11.13 BEN-Motor & Allied Trades Benevolent Fund
Note 2: Accounting policies (part) (31 March 1994):

(h) Leasing contracts
Instalments on operating lease contracts are charged to the income and expenditure account when they become payable. Assets purchased under finance leases are capitalised and the corresponding lease commitments are shown as obligations to the lessor in the balance sheet. The interest element of the lease payment is charged to the income and expenditure account evenly over the period of the lease.

Note 3: Tangible fixed assets (part):

Computer equipment with a net book value at the year end of Nil (1993: £18,862) has been purchased under a finance lease. The depreciation charge for the year was £12,239 (1993: £21,076).

Note 9: Creditors: amounts falling due within one year:

	31 March 1994 £	*31 March 1993 £*
Bank loans (note 11)	926,500	*865,792*
Bank overdraft (note 12)	85,302	*188,720*
Interest free loans (note 14)	8,431	*40,038*
Obligations under finance leases (note 15)	17,408	*15,449*
Creditors and accruals	332,288	*797,749*
Other taxes and social security costs	70,278	*69,462*
Bentrade Limited (note 20)	–	*27*
	£1,440,207	*£1,977,237*

Note 10: Creditors: amounts falling due after more than one year:

Bank loan (note 11)	1,000,000	*2,000,000*
Obligations under finance leases (note 15)	–	*10,997*
Loan advance by Housing Corporation (note 13)	31,166	*31,166*
	£1,031,166	*£2,042,163*

Example 11.13 BEN-Motor & Allied Trades Benevolent Fund
Note 15: Obligations under finance leases: (31 March 1994):

	31 March 1994 £	*31 March 1993 £*
The net obligation under finance leases is repayable as follows:		
in one year or less	18,633	*18,634*
between one and five years	–	*18,633*
	18,633	*37,267*
Less finance charges allocated to future periods	(1,225)	*(10,821)*
	£17,408	*£26,446*

provided in its 1993/1994 accounts, (b) and (e) are not. (Note: Examples of commitments under (f) above could not be found.)

Example 11.14 Nuffield Nursing Homes Trust provides an example of disclosures for operating leases.

Example 11.14 Nuffield Nursing Homes Trust
Note 24: Operating lease commitments (31 December 1993):

	Group 1993 £'000	*1992 £'000*	Trust 1993 £'000	*1992 £'000*
Next year's commitments under operating leases expire as follows:				
Property				
Less than 1 year	17	–	17	–
After 5 years	746	*757*	541	*577*
	763	*757*	558	*577*
Plant and machinery leases				
Less than 1 year	267	*22*	267	*22*
Between 2 and 5 years	1,243	*1,130*	1,243	*1,130*
After 5 years	103	*116*	103	*116*
	1,613	*1,268*	1,613	*1,268*

So, too, does Example 11.15 Royal Society for the Prevention of Cruelty to Animals, but does not provide comparative figures, as required.

Example 11.15 Royal Society for the Prevention of Cruelty to Animals
Note 12: Operating lease commitments (31 December 1993):

At 31 December 1993 the Society was committed to making the following payments during the next year in respect of operating leases:

	Motor vehicles and equipment £'000
Leases which expire:	
Within one year	289
Between two and five years	1,193
	1,482

11.10 Pension costs

Charities with a legal or contractual commitment under a pension scheme must comply with the disclosure requirements of SSAP 24 *Accounting for pension costs.* These disclosures are extensive.

For a defined contribution scheme, para 87 requires disclosure of:

(a) the nature of the scheme;
(b) the accounting policy;
(c) the pension cost charge for the year; and
(d) any outstanding or prepaid contributions at the balance sheet date.

Example 11.16 United Kingdom Band of Hope Union provides the disclosures.

Example 11.16 United Kingdom Band of Hope Union
Note 1: Accounting policies (part) (31 December 1993):

(e) Pension Scheme
The company operates a defined contributions scheme. The assets of the scheme are held separately from those of the company in an independently administered fund. The pension cost charge represents contributions payable by the company to the fund.

Note 3: Staff costs (part):

	1993	*1992*
Their total remuneration was:		
Wages and salaries	198,073	*174,679*
Social Security Costs	19,157	*18,416*
Other pension costs	7,513	*7,880*
	£224,743	*£200,975*

In relation to a defined benefit scheme, para 88 requires disclosure of:

(a) the nature of the scheme;
(b) whether it is funded or unfunded;
(c) the accounting policy and, if different, the funding policy;
(d) whether the pension cost and provision (or asset) are assessed in accordance with the advice of a professionally qualified actuary and, if so, the date of the most recent formal actuarial valuation or later formal review used for this purpose. If the actuary is an employee or officer of the reporting company, or of the group of which it is a member, this fact should be disclosed;
(e) the pension cost charge for the period together with explanations of significant changes in the charge compared to that in the previous accounting period;
(f) any provisions or prepayments in the balance sheet resulting from a difference between the amounts recognised as cost and the amounts funded or paid directly;
(g) the amount of any deficiency on a current funding level basis, indicating what action, if any, is being taken to deal with it in the current and future accounting periods;
(h) an outline of the results of the most recent formal actuarial valuation or later formal review of the scheme on an ongoing basis. This should include disclosure of:
    (i) the actuarial method used and a brief description of the main actuarial assumptions;

(ii) the *market* value of the scheme assets at the date of their valuation or review;
(iii) the level of funding expressed in percentage terms;
(iv) comments on any material actuarial surplus or deficiency indicated by (iii) above;

(i) any commitment to make additional payments over a limited number of years;
(j) the accounting treatment adopted in respect of a refund made in accordance with the provisions of paragraph 83(of the Standard), where a credit appears in the accounts in relation to it;
(k) details of the expected effects on future costs of any material changes in the charity's pension arrangements.

One of the better disclosures is provided by Example 11.17 Royal Society for the Prevention of Cruelty to Animals.

Example 11.17 Royal Society for the Prevention of Cruelty to Animals
Note 2: Expenditure (part) (31 December 1993):

(d) Pensions
The Society operates a final salary (ie a defined benefit) pension scheme for its permanent employees. The assets of the scheme are held separately from those of the Society. This fund is under the control of a trustee which invests it in a wide range of Stock Exchange securities.

The Society pays contributions to the fund in order to provide security for existing pensions and the accrued benefits of members. The pension scheme guarantees pension increases in line with rises in the Retail Prices Index (subject to a maximum of 5% pa) to pensions in payment, in excess of the Guaranteed Minimum Pension, but higher increases have recently been granted from the surplus in the scheme.

The pension cost charge for the year ended 31 December 1993 was £599,000, (1992 £545,000). This allows for a reduction of £693,000 in respect of the amortisation of a surplus which is being recognised over 11 years – the average remaining service life of members.

The pension cost charged is determined by qualified actuaries who are partners of Bacon & Woodrow, consulting actuaries. The pension cost for 1993 is based on information received for the most recent valuation of the scheme which took place as at 31 March 1991. The assumptions which have the most significant effect on the pension cost are those relating to the rate of return on investments and the rates of increase in pay levels, pensions and equity dividends. For the assessment of pension cost for 1993 the projected unit valuation method together with the following actuarial assumptions were adopted:

Rate of return on investments	$8\frac{1}{2}$% pa
Rate of increase in pay levels, including promotional increases	7% pa

Example 11.17 Royal Society for the Prevention of Cruelty to Animals
Note 2: Expenditure (part) (31 December 1993): (Continued)

Rate of pension increases	5% pa
Rate of increase in equity dividends	4% pa

Members retiring are assumed to be replaced by new entrants so that the average age of the membership remains constant.

An accrual of £135,000, (1992 prepayment £25,000), is included in the consolidated balance sheet which represents the shortfall of the amount paid by the Society into the pension scheme over the accumulated pension cost.

The market value of the scheme's assets at 31 March 1991 was £24.1 million. On the assumptions used to calculate the pension cost, the actuarial value of assets at that date represented 126% of the value of the members' accrued benefits. The accrued benefits include all benefits for pensioners and other former members as well as benefits based on service completed to date for active members allowing for future pay rises. The excess of assets over liabilities has arisen because recent investment performance has been better than assumed. The Society's contributions to the scheme in 1993 amounted to £439,000, (1992 £406,000).

In his 1993 budget statement, the Chancellor of the Exchequer announced a reduction in the rate at which pension funds can recover the tax credit attached to UK dividends. The consulting actuaries have recommended that the impact of this change should be assessed at the next actuarial review of the scheme. Accordingly, these financial statements do not recognise any additional cost which may arise from the change in rate of tax credit.

For Example 11.18 Church Commissioners the funding of clergy pensions is one of their main concerns. The Lambeth Report, published in July 1993, was highly critical of the Commissioners' asset management. An article in March 1994's *Accountancy* stated (*inter alia*):

> '. . . A dozen years ago, the church – innocent of any actuarial assessment of what the long-term cost might be – launched a programme of radically improving the, admittedly pitiful, clergy pension. The Commissioners went on paying . . . Rash investment policies, combined with the precipitous property slump of recent years, have sadly depleted their assets. Now, it is clear that pensions will swallow a greater and greater part of the Commissioners' income for many years. Indeed, on pessimistic projections, that income might eventually be insufficient to cover the basic pension commitment, let alone top up clergy pay . . . '.

One of the report's key findings was that the Commissioners had taken on commitments to finance clergy benefits that exceeded their financial capacity and that consideration needed to be given to a separate pension fund with independent trustees.

Example 11.18 Church Commissioners
Introduction (extract) (31 December 1993):

Future funding of clergy pensions
A major issue the Church is facing is the way in which pensions should be provided in future. There is no current threat to the payment of clergy pensions as our investment income is more than adequate to meet our pension obligations for some time to come. However, the cost of pensions is continuing to rise and there is a risk that, if no action is taken, pensions might, in the long term, use up all or most of our income.

The Lambeth Group drew attention to this possible danger and, as a matter of urgency, we are considering carefully with the Pensions Board what steps may be necessary to deal with this potential long-term problem.

Note 1: Accounting policies (part):

Pensions
Payments made under the main clergy and staff pension schemes are charged against the general fund income of the Commissioners. In neither case is there a fund separately invested and distinct from the Commissioners' corporate property. The funding arrangements for pensions are under review in the light of the Lambeth Report. The extent of the applicability to the staff pension scheme of SSAP 24, which requires an employing organisation to base the charge in the accounts on the accruing pension liability for its current employees, will be reconsidered following that review.

Example 11.18 Church Commissioners
Note 10: Clergy pensions:

	1993 £m	*1992* *£m*
Pensions to clergy	39.2	*36.1*
Lump sum payments on retirement and on death in service	9.4	*8.4*
Pensions to clergy widows and children	18.7	*17.3*
Pensions to deaconesses and licensed lay workers	1.2	*1.2*
Housing subsidies	0.9	*0.9*
	69.4	*63.9*

The main clergy pension scheme is an unfunded scheme which currently provides benefits based on years of service and the stipend of those in active service in the previous year. As detailed in the Lambeth Report, on 31 December 1992 the past service liability was computed by a qualified actuary at £1,148m. The principal assumption was that the rate of return on investments would exceed the rate of stipend and pension increases by 3.0 per cent p.a. The Commissioners have no power to make an actual appropriation of capital for this purpose.

Part of the pensions liability in respect of deaconesses and licensed lay workers who retired before December 1988 is met from a separate funded scheme.

11.11 Post balance sheet events

SORP 2 did not deal specifically with post balance sheet events.

SSAP 17 *Accounting for post balance sheet events* requires, for each event, the following to be disclosed in the notes:

(a) the nature of the event; and
(b) an estimate of the financial effect, or a statement that it is not practicable to make such an estimate.

What appears to be a wider disclosure requirement is that in para 6(a) of Sch 7 to the 1985 Act, whereby the directors' report must provide particulars of any important events affecting the company and/or of its subsidiaries which have occurred since the end of the year.

Example 11.19 Tidy Britain Group
Note 25: Post balance sheet events (31 March 1993):

> On the 1st March 1993 a company limited by guarantee was formed, with members assuming a maximum liability of £1 each. The Company remained dormant until 31st March 1993 and on 1st April 1993 took over the existing activities, assets and liabilities of the Group. The registered number of the new company is 2796148.
>
> The Charity Commissioners have accepted the incorporation and have re-registered the Group with a new charity number 1018496. The tax exempt status of the Group is not affected.

Example 11.19 Tidy Britain Group provides an example of a post balance sheet event given in the notes (as well as within its legal and administrative details, which fall outside of the directors' report).

Paragraph 28(c)(viii) of the revised charity SORP recommends, and reg 10 (1)(b) requires, except for charities whose gross income and total expenditure do not exceed £10,000 in a financial year, that the trustees' annual report gives the nature of any post balance sheet event.

Chapter 12 – Cash flow statements

12.1 Introduction

In accordance with SSAP 10 *Statements of source and application of funds*, SORP 2 recommended that charities prepare a source and application of funds statement. SSAP 10, however, suffered from many criticisms; indeed, between 1975 and 1989 it was twice considered for revision, although no changes were made. Developments internationally requiring the preparation of cash flow statements prompted first the ASC to issue ED 54 in July 1990 and, subsequently, the ASB to publish, 15 months later, its first financial reporting standard, FRS 1 *Cash flow statements*. Paragraph 212(a) of the revised charity SORP requires the preparation of a cash flow statement, complying with FRS 1.

In its draft chapter 1 of its Statement of Principles, the ASB states that the objective of financial statements is 'to provide information about the financial position, performance and financial adaptability of an enterprise that is useful to a wide range of users in making economic decisions'. The draft chapter indicates that information concerning cash flows of an enterprise is useful in providing the user with a basis to assess its ability to generate cash and its needs to utilise those cash flows. The revised charity SORP is, perhaps, less forward-looking: para 210 states that 'the object is to show the cash generated and absorbed (received and used) by the charity in the accounting period'.

As the cash flow statement is considered to be a 'primary statement', it should be accorded the same prominence in the accounts as the SOFA and, where prepared, the summary income and expenditure account.

FRS 1 was mandatory for accounting periods ending on or after 23 March 1992, although earlier adoption was encouraged.

12.2 Exemption

Charities, whether or not incorporated under the Companies Acts, are exempt from FRS 1 if they satisfy the 'small company' limits for the purposes of, *inter alia*, filing abbreviated accounts with the Registrar.

Example 12.1 War on Want draws the reader's attention, in the accounting policies, to the fact that a cash flow statement has not been prepared on these grounds. Other charities, for example, United Kingdom of Band Hope Union, take advantage of the exemption, but do not provide the reason why.

Example 12.1 War on Want
Note 1: Accounting policies (part) (31 December 1992):

> Cashflow statements:
>
> No cashflow statement is prepared for the current year as the company qualifies for the small company exemption.

Although para 210 and Appendix 2 of the revised SORP perpetuate this exemption, this appears inconsistent with, for example, the recommendation to prepare consolidated accounts regardless of the size of the group.

12.3 Format of cash flow statements

Paragraph 12 of FRS 1 requires the cash flow statement to list the inflows and outflows of cash and cash equivalents for the period under the following *standard headings*:

(a) operating activities;
(b) returns on investments and servicing of finance;
(c) taxation (unlikely to apply to charities);
(d) investing activities; and
(e) financing.

The headings should be presented in that order, showing a total for each and a total of the net cash inflow, or outflow, before financing. Except in those rare circumstances where the presentation would not be a fair representation of the activities of the charity, the cash flow statement should disclose separately, where material, the individual categories of cash flows under those standard headings. In those circumstances informed judgement should be used to devise an appropriate alternative treatment. The cash flow classifications may be further divided to give a fuller description of the activities of the charity, or to provide segmental information.

While no presentation may necessarily be seen to be right or wrong, the examples in this chapter serve to illustrate the thought which charity trustees have devoted to presenting the cash flow statements in the most informative way, given the nature of their activities.

12.3.1 Operating activities

Cash flows from operating activities are, in general, the cash effects of transactions and other events relating to operating, or trading, activities. FRS 1 states that the cash flow from such activities represents the net increase, or decrease, in cash and cash equivalents resulting from the operations shown in the income and expenditure account in arriving at operating profit.

Paragraph 16 of FRS 1 permits operating cash flows to be reported in one of two ways: either by the 'direct method' or by the 'indirect method'. The direct method reports operating receipts and payments, including, in the case of charities, cash receipts from fundraising, donations etc. and cash payments in respect of beneficiaries and on behalf of employees, which, when aggregated and netted, produce net cash flow but do so by adjusting, in the form of a reconciliation, the operating result for, for example, depreciation, accruals and prepayments and other items which do not affect cash.

Paragraph 212(b) of the revised SORP suggests that the direct (i.e., gross) method may be the more suitable approach for most charities. A review of published accounts, however, reveals that most charities prefer the indirect method, of which Example 12.2 British Leprosy Relief Association is typical.

Example 12.2 British Leprosy Relief Association
Cash flow statement (31 December 1993):

	Note	1993 £	1993 £	*1992* £	*1992* £
Net cash (outflow) inflow from operating activities	18		(363,439)		*10,381*
Returns on investments and servicing of finance					
Interest received		40,004		*69,415*	
Dividends received		21,922		*24,448*	
Interest paid		(3,431)		–	
Net cash inflow from returns on investments and servicing of finance			58,495		*93,863*
Investing Activities					
Payments to acquire fixed asset investments		(371,524)		*(275,656)*	
Payments to acquire tangible fixed assets		(193,044)		*(118,897)*	
Receipts from sales of fixed asset investments		348,356		*361,629*	
Receipts from sales of tangible fixed assets		26,800		*34,350*	
Net cash (outflow) inflow from investing activities			(189,412)		*1,426*
Net cash (outflow) inflow before financing			(494,356)		*105,670*
Financing					
Loan received		70,000		–	
Loan repayments		(6,341)		–	
Net cash inflow from financing			63,659		–
(Decrease) increase in cash and cash equivalents	19		(430,697)		*105,670*

Example 12.3 Cinema & Television Benevolent Fund is one of the few examples of the direct method.

Example 12.3 Cinema & Television Benevolent Fund
Consolidated cash flow statement (31 March 1994):

1993 £	*1993* £		1994 £	1994 £
		Operating activities		
	201,666	Cash received from fund raising	136,052	
	563,124	Cash received from donations and other income	646,348	
	1,143,063	Cash received from investments	1,061,398	
	(653,053)	Cash paid to and on behalf of employees	(674,249)	
	(379,609)	Cash payments to suppliers	(382,223)	
	(861,046)	Cash paid to and on behalf of beneficiaries	(867,725)	
14,145		Net cash inflow/(outflow) from operating activities		(80,399)
		Investing activities		
	(6,052,128)	Purchase of investments	(3,320,965)	
	6,162,601	Sale of investments	3,472,502	
	(883,208)	Purchase of property	(433,398)	
	(3,870)	Purchase of fixtures and fittings	(46,805)	
	–	Sale of car	3,700	
(776,605)		Net cash outflow from investing activities		(324,966)
(762,460)		Net cash outflow before financing		(405,365)
(762,460)		Decrease in cash and equivalents		(405,365)

Paragraph 17 of FRS 1 requires the information provided by the indirect method to be given in *all* circumstances. Where only the indirect method information is given, the FRS shows the reconciliation in a note to the cash flow statement, with the statement itself starting with 'Net cash inflow from operating activities'.

A charity may choose to add the information given by the direct method and, where the benefits to users outweigh the costs of obtaining the information, para 70 of the FRS encourages this.

Where information is given in accordance with the direct method, the examples in the FRS position this on the face of the cash flow statement with the indirect method reconciliation given by way of note.

Example 12.2 British Leprosy Relief Association does not, as with most charities using the indirect method, offer, voluntarily, the direct method information. Example 12.3 The Cinema & Television Benevolent Fund, while using the direct method, does not provide the indirect method reconciliation as a note (the auditors' report is unqualified).

As was reported in chapter **8** (see page 213), the Royal Society for the Protection of Birds capitalises fixed assets in accordance with the SORP, but does so by writing off additions generally as direct charitable expenditure in the income and expenditure account and adds them back (with an adjustment for depreciation) in the notes on the movement of funds. The reconciliation of operating deficit to the net cash inflow from operating activities, see Example 12.4, adjusts for these movements with additions to fixed assets subsequently being classified under investing activities.

Example 12.4 Royal Society for the Protection of Birds
Notes to the cash flow statement (part) (31 March 1994):

(a) **Net Cash Inflow from Operating Activities**	£000	1994 £000	£000	1993 £000
Operating surplus/(deficit)		3		(1510)
Net capital expenditure included in operating surplus/(deficit)		3,393		3,770
		3,396		2,260
Profit on sale of tangible assets		(175)		(43)
Income from investments		(845)		(893)
Movement in working capital:				
Stocks Decrease/(Increase)	130		(113)	
Debtors (Increase)/Decrease	(468)		45	
Creditors Increase	947	609	491	423
		2,985		1,747

Grant-making charities need to decide where to show grants paid. Whereas Example 12.5 Action Research shows these on the face of the cash flow statement below a figure struck for total cash inflow, Example 12.6 Cystic Fibrosis Research Trust prefers to incorporate these within the figure for 'net cash outflow from operating activities'.

Example 12.5 Action Research
Cash flow statement (part) (31 October 1993):

	1993 £	1992 £
INVESTING ACTIVITIES		
Purchase of investments	(5,365,087)	(6,606,539)
Purchase of tangible fixed assets	(169,978)	(168,109)
Sale of investments	7,155,000	8,235,569
Sale of tangible fixed assets	58,753	66,810
Net cash inflow from investing activities	1,678,688	1,527,731
Total cash inflow	4,628,946	3,646,034
Cash outflow: Grants paid	(4,611,664)	(4,027,955)

Example 12.6 Cystic Fibrosis Research Trust
Note 12: Notes to the cash flow statement (part) (31 March 1994):

(i) Reconciliation of operating surplus to net cash outflow from operating activities

	1994	*1993*
	£	*£*
General fund		
Net funds raised	2,401,671	*2,702,383*
Support expenditure	(581,834)	*(560,003)*
Grants	(2,032,875)	*(3,002,592)*
	(213,038)	*(860,212)*

12.3.2 Returns on investments and servicing of finance

These are receipts resulting from the ownership of investments and payments to providers of finance and include interest and dividends. Also, included is the interest element of finance lease rentals and interest capitalised. Excluded are those items required to be classified under other headings. Example 12.7 Nuffield Nursing Homes Trust provides an example.

Example 12.7 Nuffield Nursing Homes Trust
Consolidated cash flow statement (part) (31 December 1993):

	1993		*1992*	
	£'000	£'000	*£'000*	*£'000*
Net cash inflow from operating activities (note 19)		20,748		*18,466*
Returns on investments and servicing of finance				
Interest received	285		*49*	
Interest paid	(2,197)		*(2,811)*	
Interest element of finance lease rentals payments	(260)		*(429)*	
Dividend received from associated undertaking	6		*5*	
Net cash outflow from returns on investments and servicing of finance		(2,166)		*(3,186)*
Net cash flow before investing activities		18,582		*15,280*
Investing activities				
Purchase of tangible fixed assets (note 20)	(24,364)		*(21,028)*	
Sale of tangible fixed assets	255		*296*	
Purchase of short-term investments	–		*(176)*	
Sale of short-term investments	211		*15*	
Net cash outflow from investing activities		(23,898)		*(20,893)*
Net cash outflow before financing		(5,316)		*(5,613)*
Financing				
Increase in accumulated fund	287		*550*	
New medium term loans	6,000		*5,500*	
Repayment of loans	(366)		*(240)*	
Capital element of finance lease rental payments	(808)		*(795)*	
Net cash inflow from financing		5,113		*5,015*

Note 20: Purchase of tangible fixed assets:

	1993	*Group* *1992*
	£'000	*£'000*
Additions to tangible fixed assets (note 9)	25,231	*21,814*
Capitalised finance leases included in additions to tangible fixed assets	(19)	*(626)*
Capitalised interest included in additions	(1)	*(739)*
Decrease/(increase) in capital creditors	(847)	*579*
	24,364	*21,028*

12.3.3 Investing activities

These cash flows will include those related to the acquisition or disposal of any fixed asset or current asset investment.

Cash flows include receipts from:

(a) the sale or other disposal of fixed assets;
(b) the sale of investments in subsidiary undertakings net of any balances of cash and cash equivalents transferred as part of the sale;
(c) sales of investments in other entities with separate disclosure of divestments of equity-accounted entities; and
(d) repayment or sales of loans made to other entities by the charity or of others' debt (other than cash equivalents) which were purchased by the charity.

Cash outflows include:

(a) payments to acquire fixed assets;
(b) payments to acquire investments in subsidiary undertakings net of balances of cash and cash equivalents acquired;
(c) payments to acquire investments in other entities with separate disclosure of investments in equity-accounted entities; and
(d) loans made by the charity and payments to acquire debt of other entities(other than cash equivalents).

Example 12.2 British Leprosy Relief Association is typical.

The figure shown as payments to acquire fixed assets may differ from that shown in the notes to the accounts as additions to fixed assets. This may be due, in part, to movements in creditors relating to fixed assets – see Example 12.7 Nuffield Nursing Homes Trust.

FRS 1 is silent as regards the position of grants received for the purchase of fixed assets. While some charities, for example Example 12.8 Barnardo's, classify them as investing cash flows, others, including Example 12.9 BEN-Motor & Allied Trades Benevolent Fund, classify them as part of financing.

Example 12.8 Barnardo's
Consolidated cash flow statement (part) (31 March 1994):

	Note	1994 £'000	1994 £'000	*1993 £'000*	*1993 £'000*
Investing Activities					
Purchase of tangible fixed assets		(8,889)		*(13,238)*	
Purchase of investments		(27,145)		*(16,886)*	
Sale of tangible fixed assets		1,635		*1,357*	
Sale of investments		33,140		*22,469*	
Repayment of loan by associated charity		–		*100*	
Capital grants received		–		*110*	
Capital grants repaid		–		*(60)*	
Net Cash Outflow from Investing Activities			(1,259)		*(6,148)*
Net Cash Inflow/(Outflow) Before Financing			581		*(1,195)*
Financing					
Repayment of long term loans		(150)		*(134)*	
Net Cash Outflow from Financing	24b		(150)		*(134)*

Note 24: Notes to the consolidated cash flow statement [part]:

b. Analysis of changes in financing during the year

	1994 £'000	*1993 £'000*
Long term loans		
Financing at beginning of year	150	*284*
Cash outflow during year	(150)	*(134)*
Financing at end of year	–	*150*

c. Analysis of the balances of cash and cash equivalents as shown in the balance sheet

	1992 £'000	*Change in 92/93 £'000*	1993 £'000	Change in 93/94 £'000	1994 £'000
Cash at bank & in hand	*759*	*333*	1,092	201	1,293
Short-term deposits	*6,173*	*(454)*	5,719	318	6,037
Bank overdraft	*(281)*	*(1,208)*	(1,489)	(88)	(1,577)
	6,651	*(1,329)*	5,322	431	5,753

Example 12.9 BEN-Motor & Allied Trades Benevolent Fund Cash flow statement (part) (31 March 1994):

	12 months to 31 March 1994		*15 months to 31 March 1993*	
	£	£	*£*	*£*
FINANCING				
Repayments of amounts borrowed	(939,292)		*(556,084)*	
Capital grants received	–		*72,318*	
		(939,292)		*(483,766)*

ANALYSIS OF CASH AND CASH EQUIVALENTS AS SHOWN IN THE BALANCE SHEETS	31March 1994	31 March 1993	Change in period
	£	*£*	£
Cash on deposit at bank and in hand	82,645	*29,477*	53,168
Overdraft	(85,302)	*(188,720)*	103,418
Endowed cash	595,004	*270,188*	324,816
	592,347	*110,945*	481,402

Like the Royal National Lifeboat Institution, The National Trust writes off, on acquisition, certain assets, including inalienable property held for preservation. Unlike that charity, however, it adds back these costs in the reconciliation of operating profit to net cash flow from operating activities and treats them as cash outflows from investing activities under the heading 'Transactions of a capital nature' – see Example 10.7 (chapter **10**, page 274).

12.3.4 Financing

Financing cash flows comprise receipts from, and repayments to, external providers of finance of amounts in respect of principal amounts of finance.

Financing cash flows include:

(a) receipts from the issue of shares or other equity instruments;
(b) receipts from the issue of debentures, loans, notes and bonds and from other long and short-term borrowings(other than those included within cash equivalents).

Financing cash outflows include:

(a) repayments of amounts borrowed (other than those included within cash equivalents);
(b) the capital element of finance lease rental payments;
(c) payments to reacquire or redeem the charity's shares (unlikely to apply);
(d) payments of expenses or commissions on any issue of shares, debentures, loans, notes, bonds or other financing.

Example 12.7 Nuffield Nursing Homes Trust is, again, typical.

12.4 Major non-cash transactions

Paragraphs 212(d) and 43 of the revised SORP and FRS 1 respectively require all material transactions not resulting in movements of cash or cash equivalents of the charity to be disclosed in the notes to the cash flow statement, if such disclosure is necessary for an understanding of the underlying transactions. This would include the inception of a finance lease. However, Example 12.10 SENSE has included this under financing, with the purchase of the related fixed asset under investing activities.

Example 12.10 SENSE
Cash flow statement (part) (31 March 1994):

	1994		*1993*	
	£	£	*£*	*£*
FINANCING				
Additional lease purchase contracts	62,079		*4,155*	
Repayment of lease purchase contracts	(34,383)		*(29,939)*	
Net cash inflow/(outflow) from financing		27,696		*(25,784)*

Fixed assets donated to a charity would, also, be classified as a non-cash transaction and, if material, disclosed. No examples could be found, presumably on the basis that they were immaterial. Nonetheless, Example 12.11 The Royal Society for the Prevention of Cruelty to Animals includes, in the cash flow statement itself, donated assets with investing activities, with the other side of the entry being in net cash outflow from operating activities.

Example 12.11 Royal Society for the Prevention of Cruelty to Animals
Consolidated cash flow statement (part) (31 December 1993):

	1993 £'000	1993 £'000	*1992 £'000*	*1992 £'000*
Investing activities				
Purchase of investments	(9,568)		*(28,638)*	
Legacy and donated investments received	(86)		*(740)*	
Purchases of tangible fixed assets	(4,115)		*(3,208)*	
Legacy and donated fixed assets received	–		*(400)*	
Receipts from disposals of investments	11,385		*26,458*	
Receipts from disposals of tangible fixed assets	683		*581*	
		(1,701)		*(5,947)*
(DECREASE) IN CASH AND CASH EQUIVALENTS		(1,845)		*(316)*

12.5 Reconciliation with balance sheet figures

Paragraph 212(e) of the revised SORP and para 44 of FRS 1 require the movements in cash and cash equivalents and the items shown within the financing section of the cash flow statement to be reconciled to the related items in the opening and closing balance sheets. The reconciliation must disclose separately for both cash and cash equivalents and for financing items the movements resulting from cash flows, differences arising from changes in foreign currency exchange rates and other movements. Paragraph 84 of FRS 1 points out that these reconciliations are provided so as to facilitate the use of both cash flow and balance sheet information in assessing the liquidity, viability and financial adaptability of the charity. Example 12.8 Barnardo's provides this information.

12.6 Comparatives

Paragraph 212(f) of the revised SORP and para 45 of the FRS require comparatives to be provided for all items in the cash flow statement and such notes thereto as are required. This requirement should extend to the notes reconciling the balance sheet figures, i.e., the analyses of changes in cash and cash equivalents and in financing. While Example 12.8 Barnardo's provides this information, many charities do not, including Example 12.9 BEN-Motor & Allied Trades Benevolent Fund.

12.7 Review of the functioning of FRS 1

As stated in its Bulletin 46, the ASB invited comments on the functioning of FRS 1, as part of its post-issue review process.

As FRS 1 had been standard for accounting periods ending on or after 23 March 1992, preparers and users had had two years of experience in applying the Standard and evaluating the information provided. It should have been possible, therefore, to distinguish continuing issues relating to the Standard from those arising from unfamiliarity on its initial implementation.

While the ASB welcomed suggestions for improving any aspect of FRS 1, it was particularly interested in receiving comments on:

(a) the definition of cash and cash equivalents and the treatment of short-term investments;
(b) the format of the cash flow statement and, in particular, whether any changes in presentation could assist understanding of the Standard, for example by providing a reconciliation to net debt;
(c) the classification of items in the cash flow statement and whether amounts should be shown gross or net or both; and
(d) the scope of the Standard.

As a result of the review, the ASB may identify opportunities to improve the Standard. If so, the aim is to publish proposals in draft for public comment in the summer of 1995.

Chapter 13 – Consolidated accounts

13.1 Introduction

A question arises as to whether or not a charity should prepare consolidated accounts in respect of all entities which it controls.

Many of the larger charities have subsidiaries, some of whose activities are fundamentally different from those of their parents. In those circumstances, there has been some debate in recent years as to whether or not consolidation is appropriate. In looking at this question, it is necessary to revisit the position both before and after the introduction of the 1989 Act and to consider developments since.

13.2 The 1960 Act

In charity law, every charity was a separate entity, governed by its particular charitable trusts. The concept of one charity having control of another and creating a parent/subsidiary relationship was not recognised.

13.3 SORP 2, SSAP 14 and the 1985 Act

SORP 2 contained the following criteria for determining whether or not subsidiaries should be consolidated. Paragraph 72 stated:

'A charity may have one or more subsidiary companies.

'(a) The activities of a subsidiary may not be fundamentally different from those of the charity. For example, the subsidiary may be an investment-holding company; it might be concerned solely or largely with fund-raising; or it might be the vehicle used to undertake the charitable activities of the charity. If a charity has such a subsidiary or subsidiaries, it should prepare consolidated accounts for itself and its subsidiary or subsidiaries. Separate accounts for the charity itself should still be prepared.

'(b) If a subsidiary undertakes activities which are fundamentally different from those of the charity, for example if it is a trading company, it will not be appropriate to consolidate its accounts with those of the charity. Instead, the investment in the subsidiary should be treated in the same way as other investments are treated. A summary of the transactions, assets and liabilities of the subsidiary, together with an explanation of its activities and their relevance to the charity, should be disclosed in the notes to the accounts. As an alternative to providing a summary of its subsidiary's transactions, assets and liabilities, the charity may if it wishes include the accounts of the subsidiary within its annual report.'

These recommendations were similar (but not identical) to those in the 1985 Act (before amendment) and SSAP 14 *Group accounts* (before amendment and later withdrawal).

Section 229(3)(d) of the unamended Act stated that group accounts *may* exclude a subsidiary if the company's directors were of the opinion that (*inter alia*) the business of the holding company and that of the subsidiary were *so different* that they could not reasonably be treated as a single undertaking. (This was subject to the proviso that the directors obtained the approval of the Secretary of State to exclude the subsidiary.) In circumstances where group accounts were not prepared, or where a subsidiary was excluded from the group accounts, para 69 of Sch 4 required, subject to specified exceptions, certain disclosures to be given in the notes to the holding company's (or, where prepared, consolidated) accounts.

In contrast to the Act's requirements, SSAP 14 set out various situations, including the above, where it *required* a subsidiary to be excluded from *consolidation*, and also set out the accounting treatment that was to be followed in these circumstances. In the case of a subsidiary excluded on the grounds that its activities were dissimilar, para 23 of SSAP 14 (as unamended) required the subsidiary to be included using the equity method of accounting. The group accounts were to include the separate accounts of the subsidiary, together with certain other prescribed information.

13.4 The 1985 Act (as amended by the 1989 Act)

Changes, originating from the EC Seventh Company Law Directive, in relation to group accounts, were introduced by the 1989 Act. Group accounts now had to be in the form of consolidated accounts; other forms no longer being permitted.

In relation to who had to prepare group accounts, changes were made to the definitions of parent and subsidiary and, throughout, references are now to 'parent undertakings' and 'subsidiary undertakings'. In determining whether one undertaking is a subsidiary of another, the main shift of emphasis was from ownership to control. By widening these definitions, many of the so-called off-balance sheet vehicles now had to be consolidated. These vehicles had been an artificial device, typically controlled by the parent but kept outside of the previous definition. Their widespread use had had the effect of undermining the value of consolidated accounts.

Although, perhaps, not consciously aimed at the charity sector, the purpose of the amendments was to close possible loopholes to prevent such vehicles from not being consolidated, while at the same time ensuring that bodies which quite rightly should not be consolidated, are not consolidated.

Changes were, also, made to the rules about when consolidated accounts were required and when members of a group could be left out of consolidated accounts.

13.4.1 How are parent and subsidiary undertakings defined?

In summary, an undertaking is a parent undertaking to a subsidiary undertaking if:

(a) it holds a majority of the voting rights in the subsidiary undertaking;
(b) it is a member of the subsidiary undertaking and has the right to appoint or remove a majority of its board of directors;
(c) it has the right to exercise a dominant influence over the subsidiary undertaking by virtue of:
 (i) provisions contained in the subsidiary undertaking's Memorandum or Articles; or
 (ii) a control contract;
 (Note: it is not necessary for the parent undertaking to be a member of the subsidiary undertaking in this case);
(d) it is a member of the subsidiary undertaking and controls, alone, pursuant to an agreement with other shareholders or members, a majority of the voting rights in the undertaking; or
(e) it has a participating interest in the undertaking and:
 (i) it actually exercises a dominant influence over it; or
 (ii) it and the subsidiary undertaking are managed on a unified basis.
 (Note: A 'participating interest' is an interest held by an undertaking in the shares of another undertaking which it holds on a long-term basis for the purpose of securing a contribution to its activities by the exercise of control or influence arising from, or related to, that interest. A holding of 20 per cent or more of the shares of an

undertaking is presumed to be a participating interest, although this presumption may be rebutted.)

As with the previous law, subsidiaries include sub-subsidiaries.

13.4.2 What are the requirements governing the preparation of group accounts?

The 1985 Act exempts a parent undertaking from preparing consolidated accounts if:

(a) the parent undertaking is a wholly-owned subsidiary undertaking and its immediate parent undertaking is established under the law of a member state of the European Union. Exemption is conditional on compliance with certain further conditions set out in s228(2);
(b) the parent undertaking is a majority-owned subsidiary and meets all the conditions for exemption as a wholly-owned subsidiary undertaking set out in s228(2) as well as the additional conditions set out in s228(1)(b);
(c) all of the parent undertaking's subsidiary undertakings are permitted or required to be excluded from consolidation by s229; or
(d) the group is small or medium-sized and is not an ineligible group, as defined in s248. A group is ineligible if any of its members is a public company, a banking institution, an insurance company, an authorised person under the Financial Services Act 1986, or a body corporate which has power under its constitution to offer its shares or debentures to the public and may lawfully exercise that power.

It is this last exemption which is likely to be of most relevance to parent charities.

13.4.3 Exemptions on the grounds of size from the requirement to prepare group accounts

Prior to the 1989 Act, small and medium-sized groups were required to prepare group accounts, but were permitted to modify these group accounts delivered to the Registrar. The 1989 Act no longer provides for the filing of modified group accounts. Section 248 permits a parent company not to prepare group accounts for a financial year if the group qualifies as small or medium-sized (and is not an ineligible group). Thus, parent companies of such groups which had previously filed such accounts now had to file either unmodified group accounts or, if they satisfied certain criteria for exemption and did not elect voluntarily to prepare group accounts, no group accounts at all.

The criteria (as raised by SI 1992 No 2452) for determining whether a group is small or medium-sized are:

	NET	GROSS
Small group:		
Turnover	£2.8m	£3.36m
Balance sheet totals	£1.4m	£1.68m
No of employees	50	50
Medium-sized group:		
Turnover	£11.2m	£13.44m
Balance sheet totals	£5.6m	£6.72m
No of employees	250	250

Unlike the provisions for individual companies, there is no requirement to adjust the turnover limit in respect of an accounting period which is less, or more, than a year in length. 'Gross' means without eliminating intra-group transactions, while 'net' means the converse; and a company may satisfy the relevant requirement on either basis. There is no requirement to use the same basis for both turnover and balance sheet totals.

There is no distinction between the exemptions available to a small or medium-sized group; if the necessary criteria are met both small and medium-sized groups are exempt from the requirement to prepare group accounts. Although it is obvious that small groups will, also, qualify as medium-sized groups, the two sets of criteria are relevant for the purposes of ascertaining whether a parent company qualifies as small or medium-sized for disclosure exemptions relating to its individual accounts. In order to do so, the group which it heads must fall within the appropriate criteria set out above. Thus, a parent company cannot be treated as qualifying as a small company, unless the group as a whole qualifies as a small group. Similarly, a parent company cannot be treated as qualifying as a medium-sized company, unless the group qualifies as a medium-sized group.

The figures for each subsidiary undertaking are those included in its accounts for the relevant financial year, that is:

(a) if its financial year ends with that of the parent company, that financial year; and
(b) if not, its financial year ending last before the end of the financial year of the parent company.

If these figures cannot be obtained without disproportionate expense or undue delay, the latest available figures may be used.

In deciding whether the criteria are satisfied, all subsidiary undertakings must be taken into account, even if the group is entitled to exclude some of them from consolidation.

A group will qualify as small or medium-sized in relation to a financial year if the following qualifying conditions are satisfied:

(a) in the case of the parent company's first financial year, in that year;
(b) in the case of any subsequent financial year, in that year and the preceding year.

A group will be treated as qualifying as small or medium-sized in relation to a financial year if:

(c) it qualified in relation to the previous financial year under (a) or (b) above or (d) below; or
(d) if it was treated as so qualifying in relation to the previous year by virtue of paragraph (c) and the qualifying conditions are met in the year in question.

The effect of these provisions is that a single miss will not disqualify, but two consecutive misses will.

If the directors of a parent company propose to take advantage of the exemption afforded by s248, it is the auditors' duty to provide them with a report, which must be 'attached' to the individual accounts, stating whether, in their opinion, the company is entitled to the exemption. AG 503 *Reports by auditors under company legislation in the United Kingdom* took the view that it was preferable for the report to be included as an additional opinion in the audit report under s235 on the individual accounts. With effect from 17 October 1994, Practice Note 8 superseded AG 503. Example 6 gives the new report to be provided. An italicised note to the example states that: 'The Act requires the report to be attached to the company's individual financial statements. This may be done by presenting the report on a separate page or by putting it on the same page as the auditors' report on the individual financial statements.'

The Act sets out the disclosure requirements for parent companies not required to prepare consolidated accounts (s231 and Sch 5, Pt I). In particular, para 1(4) requires to be disclosed the grounds on which the parent undertaking is exempt from preparing consolidated accounts.

Example 13.1 Dogs' Home Battersea, a charitable company, is one parent charity which has taken the advantage of the exemption.

Example 13.1 Dogs' Home Battersea
Note 1: Accounting policies (part) (31 December 1993):

(a) Basis of accounting

The financial statements have been prepared under the historical cost convention and in accordance with applicable accounting standards. The Dogs' Home has taken advantage of the exemption conferred by Section 248 of the Companies Act 1985 from the requirement to prepare group accounts and, accordingly, these financial statements present information in respect of the Home, as an individual undertaking, rather than as a group.

So, too, has Example 13.2 Mary Rose Trust. Informatively, this charity includes the trading company's accounts as an appendix.

Example 13.2 Mary Rose Trust
Note 2: Mary Rose Trading Limited (part) (31 December 1993):

The Trading Company's accounts have not been consolidated with those of the Trust under the provisions of Section 249 of the Companies Act 1985. However, it is the opinion of the Executive Committee that the equivalent information is more readily appreciated by the inclusion of the Trading Company's accounts as an appendix to the Trust's financial statements.

13.4.4 What are the conditions permitting, or requiring, subsidiary undertakings to be excluded from consolidation?

Generally, all subsidiary undertakings are to be included in the consolidation. There are, however, five exceptions, four of which are permissive and one prescriptive.

A subsidiary undertaking *may* be excluded from consolidation where:

(a) its inclusion is not material in determining whether a true and fair view is given. However, two or more undertakings may only be excluded if they are not material, taken together;
(b) severe long-term restrictions substantially hinder the exercise of the rights of the parent over the assets or management of the undertaking;
(c) the information necessary for the preparation of consolidated accounts cannot be obtained without disproportionate expense or undue delay;
(d) the interest of the parent is held exclusively with a view to subsequent

resale and the undertaking has not previously been included in the consolidated accounts prepared by the parent.

The fifth exception is a requirement that a subsidiary undertaking *must* be excluded from consolidation where:

(e) its activities are so different from those of other undertakings to be included in the consolidation that its inclusion would be incompatible with the requirement to show a true and fair view.

The Act stresses that this requirement does not apply 'merely because some of the undertakings are industrial, some commercial and some provide services, or because they carry on industrial or commercial activities involving different products or provide different services'.

Many subsidiary companies covenant up to their parent the profits earned during the financial year. In doing this, they tend to revert, in substance, to 'shell companies'. Consolidation may, thus, be circumvented on the grounds of immateriality. (Note: FRS 2 *Accounting for subsidiary undertakings*, see page 344, does not deal with this situation, para 78 stating that because the Standard deals only with material items, no special mention is required for that exclusion permitted by the Act.)

A number of parent charities have taken the opportunity not to consolidate on these grounds. However, the level of disclosure not only differs but, in some cases, seems excessive.

Example 13.3 Help The Aged provides a note informing the reader of the turnover and amount covenanted to the charity by each subsidiary. And, Example 13.4 Cancer Relief Macmillan Fund devotes a whole page to providing a summary of the subsidiary's income and expenditure account and balance sheet.

Example 13.3 Help The Aged
Note 27: Group Undertakings (30 April 1993):

All subsidiary undertakings are wholly owned and incorporated in England.

The principal subsidiary undertakings are as follows:

	Share Capital £'000	Reserves £'000
HelpAge Limited	67	(3)

The principal activity of HelpAge Limited is the sale of Christmas cards and other merchandise by mail order catalogue. The profits of the company are covenanted to the charity. For the year ended 30th April, 1993, the turnover of the company amounted to £2,363,443 (1992 £2,324,461) and the covenant to the charity was £242,280 (1992 £417,047). The value of the shareholding in Helpage Limited is considered to be not less than £67,100, the amount at which it is included in the charity's investments.

Help the Aged (Trading) Limited	10	–

The principal activity of Help the Aged (Trading) Limited is fundraising via commercial events and sponsorship together with the sale of sports merchandise. The profits of the company are covenanted to the charity. For the year ended 30th April, 1993, the turnover of the company amounted to £51,124 (1992 £23,445) and the covenant to the charity was £6,170 (1992 £2,620). The value of the shareholding in Help the Aged (Trading) Limited is considered to be not less than £10,000, the amount at which it is included in the charity's investments.

Example 13.4 Cancer Relief Macmillan Fund
Note 5: Subsidiary companies (31 December 1993):

Cancer Relief Macmillan Fund has three wholly-owned subsidiary companies, none of which is a charity. All are registered in England, and the appropriate Reports have been filed with the Registrar of Companies. Two of these companies, Macmillan Events Limited and Macpac Education Limited, were incorporated during 1993, each with paid up ordinary share capital of £2. Neither company undertook any trading activity before 31 December 1993 or incurred any liabilities or entered into any commitments.

Cancer Relief (Sales) Limited sells Christmas cards and gift items and holds events to raise funds for the charitable purposes of Cancer Relief Macmillan Fund. It has a covenant with the Charity to pay over the whole of its taxable profits each year: the amount paid over in 1993 including Income Tax recoverable was £87,526 (1992 – £ 176,000). The amount due from the subsidiary at 31 December 1993 was £47,000 (1992 – £36,000). Cancer Relief (Sales) Limited also pays interest on its loan from Cancer Relief Macmillan Fund. Its Board comprises three employees of Cancer Relief Macmillan Fund who receive no remuneration in respect of their duties on behalf of Cancer Relief (Sales) Limited.

A summary of the results of Cancer Relief (Sales) Limited for the year to 30 June 1993 is shown below. Its year end of 30 June was chosen as the point of lowest activity allowing for settlement of the previous year's Christmas trading before commitments are made for the following year, and its Accounts have not been consolidated with those of the Charity on the grounds of immateriality. The auditor's report contained no qualifications.

Example 13.4 Cancer Relief Macmillan Fund
Note 5: Subsidiary companies (31 December 1993): (Continued)

PROFIT AND LOSS ACCOUNT

	1993 £000	*1992* *£000*
Turnover on sale of goods	469	*461*
Cost of Sales	(369)	*(348)*
Gross profit on sale of goods	100	*113*
Income from Events and Royalties	51	*137*
Costs	(22)	*(30)*
Overall gross profit	129	*220*
Management charge, payable to Cancer Relief Macmillan Fund	(16)	*(16)*
Other operating charges	(22)	*(27)*
	91	*177*
Interest payable to Cancer Relief Macmillan Fund	(4)	*(1)*
Bank interest receivable and similar income	2	*3*
Net Profit on Ordinary Activities	89	*179*
Amount payable and covenanted to Cancer Relief Macmillan Fund	(87)	*(176)*
Profit for the year	2	*3*
Deficit Brought Forward	(1)	*(4)*
Surplus/(Deficit) Carried Forward	1	*(1)*

SUMMARISED BALANCE SHEET at 30 JUNE 1993

Current Assets		
Stocks	44	*62*
Debtors	22	*32*
Cash	15	*16*
	81	*110*
Creditors: Amounts falling due within one year	(75)	*(106)*
Net Current Assets	6	*4*
Creditors: Amount falling due after more than one year		
Loan from Cancer Relief Macmillan Fund	(5)	*(5)*
	1	*(1)*
Capital and Reserves		
Share Capital (2 ordinary shares of £1 each)	–	–
Profit and Loss Account (deficit)	1	*(1)*

Investments in subsidiary companies, with a total cost of £6, are included in Other Investments in Note 16.

Although para 72(b) of SORP 2 recommended that a summary of the transactions, assets and liabilities of excluded subsidiaries should be provided, this would seem not to extend to those where the figures are not material.

But it is the exception in (e) which would appear to have the most relevance to charities and it is this which is considered further in the light of subsequent developments.

13.5 ASB Interim Statement: 'Consolidated accounts'

In December 1990, the ASB issued an interim statement, *Consolidated accounts* ('the Statement'), the objective of which was to give timely guidance on the interpretation of certain of the changes made by the 1989 Act for the preparation of group accounts, and to make consequential changes to both SSAPs 1 (Revised) and 14, *Accounting for associated companies* and *Group accounts* respectively. For the purposes of consistency with the commencement dates of the relevant provisions of the Act, the Statement was effective for accounting periods commencing on or after 23 December 1989.

Paragraph 2 of the Statement made an important point. Incorporating references to the guidance in both SSAPs 1 and 14 had the effect of giving the guidance itself the force of an accounting standard. Accordingly, by virtue of para 2 of the then Explanatory Foreword to Accounting Standards, its guidance was to be applied to the accounts of all parents whose purpose was to give a true and fair view of the financial position and of profit or loss (or excess of income over expenditure, or vice versa) for the period, whether or not the parents were incorporated, and report, under the Companies Acts.

The Statement argued that the value of the information provided about a group by its consolidated accounts depended on the extent to which the information about the group was complete. The information was complete if all the undertakings which were part of the group were included in the consolidation. Thus, a subsidiary undertaking could be excluded from consolidation only 'in exceptional circumstances'.

In order to assist preparers identify exceptional cases where it was inappropriate to consolidate a subsidiary undertaking, the Statement discussed the circumstances under which the Act allowed or required a subsidiary undertaking not to be included in the consolidation. The following extracts relate to its guidance in respect of subsidiary undertakings with different activities:

> 'Section 229(4) of the Act requires that subsidiary undertakings be excluded from consolidation "where the activities of one or more subsidiary undertakings are so different from those of other undertakings to be included in the consolidation that their inclusion would be incompatible with the obligation to give a true and fair view". This does not apply "merely because some of the undertakings are industrial, some commercial and some provide services, or because they carry on industrial or commercial activities involving different products or provide different services". Because consolidated information can be further analysed in the notes or on the face of the primary statements, it is exceptional that the activities of a subsidiary undertaking should so differ from those of other undertakings included in the consolidation that including that subsidiary in the consolidation would be incompatible with the obligation to give a true and fair view.'

And:

> 'The circumstances under which a subsidiary undertaking's activities are so different that its inclusion in the consolidated accounts would be incompatible with the obligation to give a true and fair view are so exceptional that the Board considers it misleading to link them with any particular contrast of activities. Unless, exceptionally, there are conclusive grounds for believing that the inclusion of a subsidiary undertaking in the consolidated accounts is incompatible with showing a true and fair view of the group, all subsidiary undertakings, whatever their activities, should be consolidated with the group. The grounds for considering that the inclusion of such a subsidiary undertaking would not be compatible with the true and fair view should be explained in a note to the accounts.'

The Statement implicitly acknowledged that the effect of consolidating the parent and its subsidiary undertakings may have obscured useful information about the different undertakings and activities included in the consolidation. Accordingly, para 23 encouraged parent undertakings to give segmental analysis to provide users with useful information on the different risks and rewards, growth and prospects of different parts of the group.

Applying this guidance to charities, there would seem to be few (if any) subsidiary undertakings which should, or could, have been excluded from consolidation on these grounds. Because of the apparent conflict with the recommendations of SORP 2 (that is, that non-charitable trading subsidiaries whose activities are fundamentally different should not be consolidated), however, it is this particular exception which has caused a certain amount of controversy. Moreover, this controversy seems to have been fuelled by seemingly conflicting positions taken by auditors.

As a result of the 1989 Act and the Statement, a number of charities changed their accounting policies and consolidated their non-charitable trading subsidiaries. Two charities which did this were Save The Children Fund and Malcolm Sargent Cancer Fund for Children, although not in the first (but the second) accounts to which the new guidance applied. It is not clear why this delay occurred. Neither charity's accounts were qualified on the grounds of non-compliance with the new rules.

Rather than consolidating non-charitable trading subsidiaries, some charities continued the practice of providing information about these by way of note. One was Example 13.5 Barnardo's and this practice attracted a qualified report from its auditors.

Example 13.5 Barnardo's
Report of Council (part) (31 March 1992):
Charity accounts and the Companies Act 1989:

The Companies Act 1985 (as amended by the Companies Act 1989) requires companies to consolidate the accounts of subsidiary undertakings with those of their parent. This requirement is subject to exceptions on grounds of immateriality or if the activities are so different that their inclusion would be incompatible with the need to give a true and fair view.

Previously charities constituted as companies limited by guarantee, of which Barnardo's is one, were not required to consolidate these activities. Indeed, paragraph 72(b) of the Statement of Recommended Practice for Charities (SORP 2) expressly states it is not appropriate to consolidate the accounts of a non-charitable trading subsidiary with those of the charity and recommends the treatment which Barnardo's has heretofore adopted.

The Council of Barnardo's believes that SORP 2 correctly recognises where the public interest lies in disclosing the stewardship of charitable monies. It regards this particular paragraph of SORP 2 as an important means of reinforcing the accountability of charity trustees by recognising the inappropriateness of consolidating activities which if done by the charity itself would be unlawful. It also believes that the true and fair exemption from consolidation should and does apply to the accounts prepared by such a charity. The auditors disagree. They consider the requirements for exemption are not met merely because some undertakings are charitable and some non-charitable. Furthermore, they consider SORP 2 should be amended to take into account the new requirements of the Companies Act 1985.

Last year Council decided to continue the practice previously adopted of compliance with SORP 2 (there having been no statement from the Accounting Standards Board that SORP 2 required amendment) and to accept an audit report qualification. Other major charities reporting on accounts ending after 23 December 1990 have taken this view without receiving an audit report qualification.

The accounts for the current year have been presented in the same format as for the previous year and the auditors have accordingly qualified their audit

Example 13.5 Barnardo's
Report of Council (part) (31 March 1992):
Charity accounts and the Companies Act 1989: (Continued)

report for a second time. The results, assets and liabilities of all subsidiary undertakings are set out fully in Note 12 to the accounts.

Statement of accounting policies (part):
Basis of preparation of financial statements:

Consolidated accounts have not been prepared by virtue of the exemption under Section 229(4)Companies Act 1985 as in the opinion of Council the nature of charitable activity is so fundamentally different from the non-charitable trading activity of the wholly owned subsidiary undertakings that to include them would not give a true and fair view of the affairs of the charity. Furthermore, fuller disclosure is made by showing the accounts of the subsidiary undertakings separately as required by the Statement of Recommended Practice No. 2 (SORP 2). Accordingly the group accounts comprise the accounts of Barnardo's together with the additional information contained in Note 12 to the accounts. In the opinion of Council the group accounts satisfy the requirements of Statement of Standard Accounting Practice 14 (Group Accounts) and comply with the Companies Act 1985 and SORP 2.

Report of the auditors to the members

We have audited the accounts on pages 6 to 14 in accordance with Auditing Standards.

The Companies Act 1985 requires consolidated accounts to be presented, incorporating the accounts of the trading subsidiaries. We do not consider that the activities of the subsidiaries are so different from those of the company that their inclusion in consolidated accounts would be incompatible with the requirement for those accounts to give a true and fair view. Accordingly, in our opinion the exemption given by section 229(4) of the Act, referred to in accounting policy (ii) on page 13, is not available.

In our opinion, the accounts give a true and fair view of the state of affairs of the company at 31 March 1992 and of its result and cash flows for the year then ended and, except for the omission of consolidated accounts as mentioned above, have been properly prepared in accordance with the Companies Act 1985.

Ernst & Young
Chartered Accountants
Registered Auditor
London
21 July 1992

In their report, the Council of Barnardo's commented that 'other major charities reporting on accounts ending on or after 23 December 1990 have taken this view without receiving an audit report qualification'. Specifically but not exclusively, neither Action Aid, in its 1991 accounts (31 December) nor SENSE in its 1992 (31 March) accounts, both charitable companies, consolidated their non-charitable trading subsidiaries.

Conversely, the Army Benevolent Fund has a trading subsidiary, the activities of which are fundamentally different and, although not a charitable company, reports in true and fair terms. These accounts were not consolidated but, interestingly, its auditors, being those of Barnardo's, did not qualify their report.

So, it seems that, historically, not only have conflicting positions been taken by different auditors, but also by the same auditors.

13.6 FRS 2 'Accounting for subsidiary undertakings'

In July 1992, the ASB published FRS 2. Except for the paragraphs relating to joint ventures and those dealing with amendments to SSAP 1, the FRS superseded both SSAP 14 and the Statement. Its provisions applied for all accounting periods ending on or after 23 December 1992.

Like the Statement, the FRS is drafted to be consistent with the 1989 Act. Although it perpetuates the guidance, given in the Statement, on dissimilar activities, para (xii)(b) of *The development of the Standard* states:

> 'The explanation dealing with subsidiary undertakings whose activities are so different that consolidation is incompatible with the obligation to give a true and fair view now states explicitly that the contrast between . . . profit and not-for-profit undertakings is not sufficient of itself to justify non-consolidation.'

Thus, if its forerunner did not say so explicitly, the FRS requires consolidation of all subsidiaries. If necessary, information about a group's different activities may be exploded segmentally in the notes.

This approach is consistent with international trends. In the United States, SFAS 94 *Consolidation of All Majority – owned Subsidiaries*, issued in 1987, made it no longer possible to exclude a subsidiary from consolidation because of 'non-homogeneous' operations and, in 1989, the IASC changed its approach. Under IAS 3 *Consolidated financial statements* it was possible to exclude, from consolidation, those subsidiaries which undertook dissimilar activities. This was no longer permitted by its successor, IAS 27 *Consolidated financial statements and accounting for investments in subsidiaries.*

In its 1992 accounts, Example 13.6 Action Aid changed its accounting policy and now consolidates its non-charitable trading subsidiary. In its 1993 accounts so, too, did Example 13.7 Barnardo's (without a murmur of objection in its annual report).

Example 13.6 Action Aid
Note 1: Accounting policies (part) (31 December 1992):

ACTIONAID has for the first time in 1992 prepared consolidated financial statements which incorporate the results of its subsidiaries, ACTIONAID Trading and Promotions Limited in the UK and Azione Aiuto in Italy.

These financial statements are prepared in accordance with Statement of Recommended Practice No 2 'Accounting by Charities', and applicable Accounting Standards with the exception of Financial Reporting Standard No 2 'Accounting for Subsidiary Undertakings.' The net profit of ACTIONAID's trading subsidiary, ACTIONAID Trading and Promotions Limited, has been incorporated into income for the reasons explained in note 1c below.

1c Treatment of trading subsidiary

The net operating profits of the trading subsidiary, ACTIONAID Trading and Promotions Limited, have been incorporated into consolidated income. The Trustees consider that full consolidation of gross income and expenditure of the trading subsidiary would be inappropriate because its activities are fundamentally different from the activities of the Charity.

The full operating results of the trading subsidiary have been disclosed in note 2d.

The balance sheet of the trading subsidiary has been consolidated for the first time in 1992 and prior year comparatives adjusted accordingly. The adjustment to funds brought forward at 31 December 1991 is shown in note 12.

1d Treatment of Italian subsidiary

The full results of ACTIONAID's subsidiary in Italy, Azione Aiuto, have been consolidated for the first time in 1992 and prior year comparatives adjusted accordingly. The adjustment to funds brought forward at 31 December 1991 is shown in note 12.

Example 13.6 Action Aid
Note 2: Income (part):
Net profit of trading subsidiary

This represents the net profit earned by ACTIONAID Trading and Promotions Limited, a wholly owned trading subsidiary whose profits are annually covenanted to ACTIONAID. The full operational results are given below:

	1992 £'000	*1991 £'000*
Turnover	487	*308*
Cost of sales	311	*207*
Gross profit	176	*101*
Distribution costs	7	*16*
Administration costs	77	*39*
Trading profit	92	*46*
Covenantable to ACTIONAID	111	*61*
Retained in subsidiary	(19)	*(15)*

Example 13.7 Barnardo's
Statement of accounting policies (part) (31 March 1993):

Basis of Consolidation
The consolidated accounts of the Group incorporate the accounts of the Company and its subsidiary undertakings, all of which were made up to 31 March.

Conversely, Example 13.8 SENSE and Example 13.9 Army Benevolent Fund continue not to consolidate (and do not receive a qualification). In the former example, perhaps the figures are not material; but this is not stated.

The application of the clear requirements concerning consolidation has not been fully addressed within the charity world.

Example 13.8 SENSE
Note 15: Investments (part) (31 March 1994):

The Association has a subsidiary company, Helping Sense Limited, of which it holds 100 per cent of the ordinary share capital. Helping Sense Limited is a company registered in England, its principal activity consists of retail sales through Christmas mail order catalogues and telemarketing. It trades in order to raise funds for the Association.

The results of Helping Sense Limited have not been consolidated due to its activities being so dissimilar from those of the Association.

Example 13.9 Army Benevolent Fund (31 March 1994)

The Army Benevolent Fund has a subsidiary, The Army Benevolent Fund Trading Co. Limited, which undertakes trading activities. As these activities are fundamentally different from the activities of the Charity, consolidated accounts have not been prepared. The ABF Trading Co Limited has its registered offices at, and operates from, the headquarters of the Charity. Its principal activities are the purchase from manufacturers of Army Benevolent Fund artefacts and Christmas Cards, which are then sold to the public, the underwriting of stocks and shares and the organization and presentation of theatrical shows and other events. Any profits earned are passed to the Charity by means of a deed of covenant. The Controller, National Enterprises Secretary and Finance Secretary of the Charity sit on the board of the ABF Trading Co Limited, but receive no additional remuneration for so doing. A summary of the ABF Trading Co Limited's transactions and financial position, extracted from the audited accounts, is set out below:

(a) PROFIT AND LOSS ACCOUNT
For the year ended 28 February 1994

	1994	*1993*
	£	*£*
TURNOVER	81,891	*897,054*
Cost of sales	53,750	*554,487*
GROSS PROFIT	28,141	*342,567*
Administration expenses	(4,741)	*(5,639)*
Other operating income	7,696	*9,911*
	31,096	*346,839*
Bank interest receivable	92	–
Bank interest payable	(257)	–
PROFIT BEFORE CHARGING COVENANTED PAYMENT	30,931	*346,839*
COVENANTED PAYMENT	30,931	*346,839*

(b) BALANCE SHEET
As at 28 February 1994

CURRENT ASSETS		
Stocks	4,108	*4,719*
Debtors	1,385	*4,090*
Cash	19,058	–
	24,551	*8,809*

Example 13.9 Army Benevolent Fund (31 March 1994) (Continued)

	1994	*1993*
	£	*£*
CREDITORS: amounts falling due within one year		
Trade creditors	1,350	*6,953*
The Army Benevolent Fund	23,198	*1,853*
	24,548	*8,806*
NET CURRENT ASSETS	3	*3*
CAPITAL		
Called up share capital	3	*3*

It was not until its 1992 (31 December) accounts that Example 13.10 Church Commissioners prepared consolidated accounts. The Church Commissioners' finances were described in an article ('An epitaph to speculation') in *Accountancy* (March 1994, pages 36 to 39), which stated (*inter alia*):

> 'Unencumbered, as a registered charity, by the Companies Act, the Commissioners failed to produce consolidated accounts until last year, though many subsidiary companies were set up to undertake property developments. Close to £600,000 of interest on the Commissioners' loans to subsidiaries was capitalised in the subsidiaries' accounts but counted as income in the Commissioners . . . . A misleading impression was being created of income which, in fact, was replicated by an obligation in the subsidiary company. By not consolidating the accounts, it created this misleading impression about the amount of income available . . . that is illegal . . . . More serious in its extent was the practice of subsidiaries charging the Commissioners management fees (likewise charged to their capital accounts) while their profits were booked to the Commissioners as income. Between 1984 and 1988, about £7 million of fictitious income was created in this way. . . the Commissioners would have been better advised to have consolidated their accounts earlier than in fact they did . . . '.

Example 13.10 Church Commissioners
Note 1: Accounting policies (part) (31 December 1992):

(a) Basis of accounting [part]:

Consolidated accounts have been prepared for the first time this year although in former years the interests in and income of group and associated undertakings were included in the accounts of the Commissioners without any formal consolidation being done.

The consolidated accounts include the accounts of subsidiary undertakings made up to 31 December. Where entities become or cease to be subsidiaries during the year the group general fund income includes profit for the period during which they are subsidiaries. The group general fund income includes the group's share of the profit of the partnerships and associated undertakings and the balance sheet includes the group interest in partnerships and associated undertakings at the book value attributable to net tangible assets.

The corresponding figures for 1991 have been restated accordingly.

While this clearly represents an extreme case, the failure to consolidate subsidiaries generally may allow the accounts to portray a more attractive position than is the case.

In accordance with the latest proposals OXFAM (a charitable company) has consolidated, in its 1994 accounts, its non-charitable trading subsidiary (its audit report had not previously been qualified).

13.7 Accounting for, and disclosure of, subsidiaries excluded from consolidation

Where a subsidiary is excluded from consolidation on the grounds of different activities, para 18 of Sch 4A to the 1985 Act requires it to be equity accounted. As these subsidiaries' results would be covenanted up to the parent charity, this requirement would, broadly, appear to be satisfied. This does not appear to be the case, however, with Example 13.8 SENSE. Apart from the details given in note 15, no further details are offered and the investment is stated in the balance sheet at its cost, of £100.

Paragraphs 1,2,3 and 5 of Pt I of Sch 5 to the 1985 Act require the following information to be disclosed for each subsidiary:

(a) its name;
(b) (i) if it is incorporated outside Great Britain, its country of incorporation;

   (ii) if incorporated inside Great Britain, whether it is registered in England and Wales or Scotland;
   (iii) if unincorporated, the address of its principal place of business;
(c) the identity of each class of shares held by the parent and the proportion of the nominal value held;
(d) the aggregate amount of its share capital and reserves as at the end of its financial year and of its profit or loss for that year;
(e) any qualifications in the auditors' report on its accounts for financial years ending with or during that of the parent; and
(f) any note, or saving, contained in such accounts to call attention to a matter which, the note or saving apart, would properly have been referred to in such a qualification.

(Note: The information in (d) is not required if the subsidiary is equity accounted and that in (e) and (f) need only be disclosed if the matter is not covered by the consolidated accounts and is material from the point of view of the parent's members.)

Example 13.8 SENSE only provides details for (a), (b) and (c).

Additionally, para 22 of FRS 2 requires a parent undertaking not preparing consolidated accounts to state that its accounts present information about it as an individual undertaking and not about its group. And, para 31(d) requires, for subsidiaries excluded because of different activities, their separate accounts to be included in the consolidated accounts. 'Summarised information may be provided for undertakings that individually, or in combination with those with similar operations, do not account for more than 20% of any one or more of operating profits, turnover or net assets of the group . . . .'. Example 13.8 SENSE does not provide the information required.

Paragraph 72(b) of SORP 2 recommended similar disclosure to that in para 31(d) above. Example 13.9 Army Benevolent Fund provides these disclosures.

13.8 The revised charity SORP

Unlike the 1985 Act, the 1993 Act and the Regulations made thereunder do not set out provisions relating to consolidation. This responsibility is conferred on the revised charity SORP.

It is important to appreciate that it is the entity accounts of a parent charity which are paramount. Charity trustees have an obligation to ensure that the charity's activities are conducted in accordance with its objects in the most efficient and effective way. The concept of one charity having 'control' of another appears to be in conflict with this obligation.

In order to show a true and fair view of the state of affairs and activities of the parent charity and its subsidiary(ies) as a whole, para 56 perpetuates the recommendation, in para 72(a) of SORP 2, that the parent's individual accounts, as well as consolidated accounts, are prepared.

13.8.1 What is a 'subsidiary undertaking'?

A 'subsidiary undertaking' is defined in para 20 of Appendix 1.

> '"Subsidiary undertaking" in relation to a charity means, subject to what is said below, any entity in which the charity or its trustees hold or control the majority of the voting rights, or have the right to appoint or remove a majority of the board of directors or trustees. For a fuller definition, reference should be made to sections 258 and 259, Companies Act 1985.
>
> '"Subsidiary undertaking" will, for the purposes of these recommendations, not include a body which is itself established as a charity, except as mentioned in paragraph 54; subject to that, paragraphs 45–53 deal with accounting for multicellular charities'.

The SORP's definition of a subsidiary undertaking is based on that in the 1985 Act, to which reference should be made, if necessary.

13.8.2 When should a subsidiary undertaking be consolidated?

Paragraphs 54 and 55 discuss whether or not consolidated accounts should be prepared. The SORP distinguishes between subsidiary undertakings used for charitable purposes and those which are not.

Paragraph 2 of Appendix 1 (which defines branches for the purposes of the SORP) states that FRS 2 expressly disapplies its requirements where they are not consistent with a particular statutory framework. Thus, charitable bodies, including separate legal entities, which are controlled by other charitable bodies will not normally be subject to the requirements of that Standard as they will be treated as 'special trusts' under the 1993 Act or will be the subject of a direction under s96(5) that they should be treated as part of the main charity for accounting purposes. That is, the main charity and the charitable body will, in substance, be treated *as one*. The question of consolidation does not arise since the 'branch' results etc. will be included within the reported results of the main body.

This is one area which some charities may be able to explore further. For example, consolidated accounts are currently prepared of all NHS charitable trusts administered by a particular health service body. From 1996/97, each trust, as a registered charity – the Commissioners are contacting all bodies in order to register all their charitable funds – will be required to prepare separate accounts, complying with the 1993 Act and the revised charity SORP.

A significant increase in work is likely to result as a typical health service body may administer a substantial number of trusts, but there appear to be a number of possible ways in which this may be reduced. If, for example, each body were to set up an umbrella charity, under which all funds would be defined as 'special trusts', only that umbrella charity would need to be registered with the Commissioners. Each body would then have to submit only one set of accounts. Although current legislation permits this, it cannot be applied retrospectively. However, it is understood that action is being taken to remove this restriction.

If both the parent and subsidiary undertakings are charitable companies, consolidated accounts should be prepared, in accordance with the 1985 Act.

If a non-charitable subsidiary undertaking is used to carry out the parent's charitable purposes, consolidated accounts should be prepared. Other subsidiary undertakings may carry out trading activities, typically solely or mainly of a fundraising nature, which are not of a directly charitable nature. Any profits are passed up, usually by way of covenant, to the parent charity. In this circumstance, para 55 recommends that consolidated accounts be prepared in all cases.

Consolidated accounts should be prepared regardless of the size of the charity group. Thus, even if a group would fall to be classified as a small or medium-sized group under the 1985 Act, it would not be able to avail itself of the exemption afforded by that Act from preparing group accounts. This more stringent requirement imposed on parent charities may herald the future exclusion of charitable companies from being classified as small or medium-sized.

13.8.3 How should subsidiary undertakings be accounted for?

Paragraphs 62 to 66 set out the recommendations regarding the method of consolidation.

The approach to consolidation in the SOFA (and, where prepared, the summary income and expenditure account) depends on whether or not the subsidiary undertaking is used for charitable purposes. The aim has been to segregate those activities of a directly charitable nature from those that are not. Regardless of the method of presentation in the SOFA etc., however, the assets and liabilities of all subsidiaries should be consolidated on a line-by-line basis in the balance sheet, in the traditional way (para 66).

Subsidiary undertakings used for charitable purposes should be consolidated on a line-by-line basis in the SOFA (and, where prepared, summary income and expenditure account). Such subsidiaries will include those which carry out activities which are capable of being carried out by the parent charity, such as primary purpose trading.

For subsidiary undertakings used for non-charitable purposes, it is not appropriate to consolidate the results on a line-by-line basis. Rather, the results of the charity group are best presented by segregating and summarising the results of the non-charitable trading activity on the face of the consolidated SOFA and, where prepared, summary income and expenditure account (para 64). Where the trading activity is not material, its results may be shown as a single line entry. However, the degree of summarisation appropriate depends on the individual circumstances and the size and importance of the trading activities. (Note: Where a summary income and expenditure account is, also, prepared, para 168(b) recommends that, where the results are shown net, the turnover and expenses are shown as an inset.) Nonetheless, in all cases where summarised information is provided, the full profit and loss account headings and amounts should be given in the notes.

13.8.4 If consolidated accounts are not prepared, what disclosures are required?

Because of the overriding requirement to prepare accounts which show a true and fair view and that, as stated in para 56, the purpose of consolidated accounts is to present that view, the circumstances when such accounts will not be prepared are likely to be rare. Where that is the case, however, the trustees should explain why in the notes.

Apart from the disclosures where the true and fair view override is used, that note should, also, give the aggregate amount of the total investment of the charity in subsidiary undertakings and, for each subsidiary, give:

(a) its name;
(b) particulars of the charity's shareholding or other controlling interest;
(c) how its activities relate to those of the charity;

(d) if material, the aggregate amount of its capital and reserves at the end of the financial year;
(e) if material, a summary of its turnover and expenditure, and its profit, or loss, for the year;
(f) particulars of any qualifications contained in the auditors' report and any note, or reservation, in those accounts to call attention to a matter which, apart from that note or reservation, would properly have been referred to in such a qualification (para 59).

Paragraph 60 stresses the importance of the presentation. It should be sufficiently detailed to distinguish the assets, liabilities and transactions of the charity from those of its subsidiary(ies) and that the turnover and result of the subsidiary(ies) are clearly stated. Examples of those headings that should be separately disclosed include expenditure for charitable purposes (including support costs), fundraising and publicity costs, and administration costs.

13.8.5 Accounting for associated undertakings

Paragraphs 67 and 68 deal with accounting for associated undertakings.

If a charity has a participating interest (as defined by s260 of the 1985 Act) in a company:

(a) if consolidated accounts are prepared, the value of that interest should be measured according to the equity method of accounting. A note should disclose the name of the company and particulars of the charity's shareholding or other interest; or
(b) if consolidated accounts are not prepared, a note to the accounts should, for each such interest, state:
    (i) its name;
    (ii) particulars of the charity's shareholding or other interest;
    (iii) if material, the aggregate amount of its capital and reserves at the end of the financial year; and
    (iv) if material, its turnover and net result for the year.

Chapter 14 – Accounting for branches

14.1 Introduction

Apart from a diversity of purpose, charities have a diversity of structure.

Some charities have local branches which form part of the registered charity, with one charity number. If the charity is a company incorporated under the Companies Acts, s221 requires the charity to obtain returns from its branches and incorporate these in the national accounts. Such branches will need to comply with s5 of the 1993 Act and state the fact that they are a registered charity on, *inter alia*, all notices, advertisements, cheques, invoices and receipts (see chapter **1**, page 9).

Others may have local groups, which are constituted as registered charities and run on autonomous lines. They are subject to compulsory registration with the Commissioners, under s3 of the 1993 Act, if, broadly, they either use or occupy land, have permanent endowment or have gross income of more than £1,000 p.a. from any source. They will have their own accounts and their own body of trustees.

Some charities may have a mix of local branches and autonomous groups.

Who accounts for what? It is extremely important that charity trustees recognise and account for all subsidiary charitable funds, special trusts and branches it controls because the relevant income and expenditure thresholds (see, for example, chapter **3**, page 42) identified in the 1993 Act relate to those of the charity *as a whole, including its special trusts and controlled branches*. Because many charities do not neatly fall into one category or another, this is a complex area of accounting. It is understood that, for certain circumstances, the Commissioners will be providing further guidance to charity trustees.

14.2 What is a 'branch'?

(A) SORP 2
Paragraph 8 stated that:

> 'A charity is an institution established for charitable purposes only. Where the institution is involved in more than one activity, operates more than one fund, or is not centralised into one unit of operation, the term is used in this statement to incorporate all those activities and funds which fall within the scope of a single instrument (or instruments supplemental to the main instrument) and any further endowments held within the terms of the original instrument.'

This was a very basic definition, which was largely unhelpful to those charities with complex structures. Not surprisingly, practice has varied. For example, the British Diabetic Association included 'donations and payments made to the Association by Branches' in its 1991 accounts, but not 'the transactions reflecting their own activities and their balances'. Similarly, Cancer Research Campaign did not include, in its balance sheet, the 'assets and liabilities of local committees'. Conversely, in its 1992 accounts, Save The Children Fund, with some 800 branches throughout the UK, stated, in its Report of the Council, that 'the Accounts cover all activities controlled by the Fund in the United Kingdom and abroad'.

(B) The revised charity SORP
In recognition of accounting for branches being a complex area, para 2 of Appendix 1 gives more guidance on what is a branch for the purposes of the SORP.

Branches are entities, or administrative bodies, which are established to conduct:

(a) a particular facet of the charity's business: or
(b) the main business of the charity in a particular geographical area.

They may or may not be separate legal entities.

A 'branch' is:

(a) part of the administrative machinery of the main charity; or
(b) a separate legal entity administered by, or on behalf of, the main charity and whose funds are held for specific purposes within the general purposes of the main charity. 'Legal entity' includes a trust or unincorporated association formed for a charitable purpose, e.g., a school prize fund; or

(c) a separate legal entity, not falling within (b), which the Commissioners have directed, under s96(5) of the 1993 Act, should be treated as part of the main charity.

Charitable bodies controlled by other charitable bodies will usually be treated as 'special trusts' under the 1993 Act or will be the subject of a direction under s96(5) that they should be treated as part of the main charity for accounting purposes. That is, for accounting purposes they will be treated *as one*. The concept of consolidation is not relevant since, by their nature, they will already have been accounted for within the main charity's accounts. This is one area which some charities may wish to explore further (see also chapter **13**, page 351).

Paragraph 2 suggests that some of the characteristics of a branch are that it:

(a) uses the name of the main charity within its title;
(b) exclusively raises funds for the main charity and/or for its own local activities;
(c) uses the main charity's registration number to receive tax relief on its activities;
(d) is perceived by the public to be the main charity's local representative;
(e) receives support from the main charity through advice, publicity materials etc.

Other questions might be: what are the consequences of the branch closing? where do the funds go? The test which appears to apply is to what extent the branch is autonomous.

'Branches' within a multicellular structure, which have a level of constitutional and administrative autonomy requiring them to be treated as separate accounting entities, will not be regarded as branches.

The Appendix clarifies that branches do not include groups of people who occasionally gather together to raise funds for one or a number of different charities and special interest groups which are affiliated to a particular charity, but do not themselves undertake charitable activities, including fundraising.

National charities with local 'branches' may need to review their constitutional structures. If the local branches are controlled by the 'parent' and not autonomous, all branch transactions and assets and liabilities should be reflected in the 'parent's' accounts. (Where branches operate locally, it may still be best practice to publish separate local accounts.)

In anticipation of these provisions, Example 14.1 British Diabetic Association changed its policy and now incorporates the transactions, assets and liabilities of its branches.

Example 14.1 British Diabetic Association
1992 Annual Report (extract):

> Branch activities
>
> In the past, the published accounts have included only the donations from the Branches and Voluntary Groups made to the Central Office. It has been decided that as we all form part of the same Association, it is only proper that the activities of these groups should be represented in the accounts and thereby give a comprehensive picture of the Association's national strength. This move also ensures we are complying with the best practice as required by the Charities Act.

Note 1: Accounting policies (part) (31 December 1993):

> The financial statements . . . consolidate the results of the Association and its branches, and its subsidiary undertaking, BDA Trading Limited.

Example 14.2 Cancer Research Campaign, while acknowledging that it will need to change its policy, has not yet done so.

Example 14.2 Cancer Research Campaign Annual Review 1992–93 (extract):

> However, there is one aspect of the revised SORP 2 which will change the way in which the Campaign produces its accounts. This is in the accounting treatment of local committee activity. At present local committees' transactions are not included in the Campaign's accounts in detail and the money they remit to the Campaign is included net of costs as with other donations.
>
> The regulations will change this, if, as expected, they follow the revised SORP 2, which effectively recommends that all local committee transactions should be reflected in the charity's own accounts whether or not the funds were received by the charity during the year in question. Similarly, all assets and liabilities at the year end of the committee should be incorporated into the charity's own Balance Sheet. With well over one thousand local committees, compliance with these provisions would mean an increase in the accounting effort required, both by local committees and at Headquarters. The regulations have yet to come into force, but they are expected to be law by June 1994. However, the Campaign will be taking steps to introduce these and any other recommended improvements as early as possible and certainly by January 1994.

Note 1: Accounting policies (part) (31 December 1993):

> *Local committees*
>
> Assets and liabilities of local committees are not included in the Campaign's balance sheet.

(C) How should branches be accounted for?

Paragraph 48 of the revised SORP recommends that all branch transactions, assets and liabilities should be accounted for *gross* in the main charity's accounts, unless the figures, in aggregate, are not material.

Funds raised by a branch for the general purposes of the main charity should be accounted for as unrestricted funds in the main charity's accounts. Funds raised for specific purposes of the main charity should, however, be accounted for as restricted funds. Funds held for the general purposes of the branch, which is a separate charity, should usually be accounted for as restricted funds (para 49).

14.3 Other branches and connected charities

14.3.1 Other branches

Local groups constituted as registered charities and run on autonomous lines will have their own accounts and body of charity trustees. The role of the national body may be limited to providing support, advice, training etc. Current practice has been, generally, not to consolidate, or aggregate, their figures with those of the national charity (see Example 14.3 Royal Society for the Prevention of Cruelty to Animals and Example 14.4 British Red Cross Society), although it might be argued that they should have been (see below). Consideration may, also, need to be given to the requirements of FRS 5 *Reporting the substance of transactions.*

Example 14.3 Royal Society for the Prevention of Cruelty to Animals Accounting policies (part) (31 December 1993):

B Consolidation

These accounts consolidate only the funds administered by the Society's headquarters and Trading Company. The assets, liabilities, income and expenditure of branches are not included, except to the extent that:

(i) Branches made contributions towards the cost of regional operations borne by headquarters.
(ii) Headquarters has made loans and non-recoverable grants to branches.
(iii) Headquarters has paid to branches legacies, subscriptions and donations due to them.

Each branch is required to produce separate audited accounts annually in relation to the funds it administers. The branches are separately registered charities and prepare their own accounts.

Example 14.4 British Red Cross Society
Note 1: Accounting policies (part) (31 December 1993):
(a) Scope and basis of accounting (part):

The financial statements do not include the results, assets and liabilities of the Society's Branches which as separate registered charities produce their own accounts for filing with the Charity Commission. Land and buildings of the branches which are vested in the name of the Society as custodian trustee are similarly not included.

Example 14.5 National Deaf Children's Society states, rather vaguely, that regional associations are not incorporated 'in accordance with the . . . constitution'.

Example 14.5 National Deaf Children's Society
Note 1: Accounting policies (part) (31 March 1994):

1.9 Regional associations
In accordance with the Society's constitution, the financial statements do not incorporate the accounts of the regional associations.

The litmus test, of whether there is sufficient autonomy, may be obscured in circumstances where there is a mix of independence and control. For example, local groups may use the national charity number for, for example, fundraising purposes but, in all other respects, may be autonomous. This appears to be the case with Example 14.6 Multiple Sclerosis Society where its branches are 'autonomous and have control over the conduct of their affairs but are covered by the Society's registration as a charity'. Nonetheless, the branches are consolidated on the grounds that the Council believes 'that a more complete and fair view of the Society's activities is provided'.

Example 14.6 Multiple Sclerosis Society
Consolidated income and expenditure account (31 December 1993):

Notes		Head office	Branches	1993 Consolidated	*Head office*	*Branches*	*1992 Consolidated*
	Ordinary income						
	Legacies	3,687,987	1,089,110	4,777,097	*3,740,532*	*957,143*	*4,697,675*
3	Donations & subscriptions	1,795,187	2,575,445	4,370,632	*1,938,982*	*2,452,200*	*4,391,182*
4	Fund raising (net receipts)	64,968	2,098,993	2,163,961	*246,994*	*2,062,187*	*2,309,181*
	Voluntary income	5,548,142	5,763,548	11,311,690	*5,926,508*	*5,471,530*	*11,398,038*
	Investment income	980,444	678,235	1,658,679	*1,057,877*	*930,707*	*1,988,584*
	Net profit from sale of investments	368,652	87,784	456,436	*531,311*	*17,559*	*548,870*
		6,897,238	6,529,567	13,426,805	*7,515,696*	*6,419,796*	*13,935,492*
	Expenditure						
15b	Research	3,141,555	305,694	3,447,249	*2,344,874*	*262,337*	*2,607,211*
6	Welfare	2,733,603	3,300,592	6,034,195	*2,834,252*	*3,204,508*	*6,038,760*
	Advertising & publicity	1,028,545	–	1,028,545	*1,377,247*	–	*1,377,247*
8	Fund raising administration	351,000	160,000	511,000	*327,000*	*147,000*	*474,000*
	MS News and Messenger	171,263	–	171,263	*164,164*	–	*164,164*
8	Establishment & administration	212,568	161,367	373,935	*140,971*	*147,487*	*288,458*
9	Depreciation	38,537	731,748	770,285	*39,462*	*703,873*	*743,335*
	International Federation	39,969	–	39,969	*36,159*	–	*36,159*
		7,717,040	4,659,401	12,376,441	*7,264,129*	*4,465,205*	*11,729,334*

Example 14.6 Multiple Sclerosis Society
Consolidated income and expenditure account (31 December 1993): (Continued)

Notes		Head office	Branches	1993 Consolidated	*Head office*	*Branches*	*1992 Consolidated*
	(Deficit)/surplus of ordinary income	(819,802)	1,870,166	1,050,364	*251,567*	*1,954,591*	*2,206,158*
	Transfers between branches and head office						
10	Net transfers to head office	830,540	(830,540)	–	*832,723*	*(832,723)*	–
11	Head office expenditure on Woodlands Respite Care Centre	(4,625)	4,625	–	*(107,339)*	*107,339*	–
		825,915	(825,915)	–	*725,384*	*(725,384)*	–
	Surplus after transfers between branches and head office	6,113	1,044,251	1,050,364	*976,951*	*1,229,207*	*2,206,158*
15a	Transfers (to)/from research reserve	(1,029,898)	185,531	(844,367)	*(540,987)*	*(229,237)*	*(770,224)*
17a	Transfers (to) restricted funds	(93,238)	–	(93,238)	*(148,010)*	*(150,741)*	*(298,751)*
16	**(Deficit)/surplus for the year**	(1,117,023)	1,229,782	112,759	*287,954*	*849,229*	*1,137,183*

All income and expenditure is derived from continuing activities.

Example 14.6 Multiple Sclerosis Society
Report of the Council (part) (31 December 1993):

Accounts

The Society's consolidated accounts for 1993 appear on pages 4 to 17 and the Honorary Treasurer's Report on page 2.

The Society's branches, associations, respite care centres and holiday homes are autonomous and have control over the conduct of their affairs but are covered by the Society's registration as a charity and are subject to the Rules for Branches set out in the Society's Charter of Constitution. The accounts consolidate the results of these branches, associations, respite care centres and holiday homes.

Note 1: Accounting policies (part):

(b) The accounts include the assets, liabilities and funds, and the income and expenditure of the Society's branches including associations, respite care centres and holiday homes and are compiled from audited accounts and returns supplied by branch treasurers.

Details of the number of branch and association accounts consolidated in these accounts appear in note 2.

Note 2: Branches and associations:

The Society's Charter of Constitution requires that the branch annual accounts must be audited by a person who is independent of the branch and who is a qualified member of either the Institute of Chartered Accountants or The Chartered Association of Certified Accountants and by a registered auditor if the branch income exceeds £100,000.

A total of 2 branches (1992: 17) and 7 associations (1992: 6), failed to submit accounts in time for inclusion in these consolidated accounts. In accordance with previous practice the consolidated balance sheet includes the assets, liabilities and funds appearing in the last annual accounts submitted by each of these defaulting branches.

Example 14.6 Multiple Sclerosis Society
Note 2: Branches and associates: (Continued)

A summary of the branch returns included in these accounts appears below:

			1993			*1992*
	Branches	Associations	Total	*Branches*	*Associations*	*Total*
Audited or independently inspected	361	5	366	*339*	*9*	*348*
Not independently inspected	8	8	16	*6*	*5*	*11*
Accounts not submitted	2	7	9	*17*	*6*	*23*
Total	371	20	391	*362*	*20*	*382*

14.3.2 Connected charities

In order for a reader to gain a full appreciation of the scope of a charity's activities, the annual report and accounts should provide information about charities with which it is connected.

SORP 2

Paragraphs 70 and 71 of SORP 2 set out some criteria for determining whether a charity was connected, what information should be given for each of them and how such charities should be accounted for.

Although a description rather than a definition, para 70 identified connected charities as having the following characteristics:

(a) common trustees;
(b) unity of administration; and
(c) common, parallel or related objects and activities.

This might be the case where a charity has a number of local groups which have separate constitutions (see above).

Paragraph 71 stated that:

> 'If the reporting charity is connected to other charities, information about the other charities' activities and resources should be included in its annual report. This information should include:
>
> (a) particulars of the connected charities, including principal contact addresses and the nature of the relationship between the charities; and
> (b) particulars of any material transactions between the charities.'

Example 14.7 British Leprosy Relief Association provides this information.

Example 14.7 British Leprosy Relief Association
Note 5: Connected charity (31 December 1993):

> The Association is connected by virtue of common objects and activities to the 'LEPRA Society of India' (hereafter called LEPRA India). LEPRA India is a registered charity, Charity Registration number 474 of 1989 under the Andra Pradesh Public Societies Registration Act 1350 Fasli and having its offices at Plot No 17, Krishnapuri Colony, Beside Yellamma Temple, West Marredpally, Secunderabad 500-026, India.
>
> The Chairman of the Association's Executive Committee and of its Medical Advisory Board, plus the Secretary of LEPRA UK are ex-officio members of the Management Committee of LEPRA India. LEPRA India determines its own policies governing its leprosy control and related work in India and is free to raise funds in India in future; but currently, and for the foreseeable future, LEPRA India is dependent on the Association for its funding support under a mutually agreed annual budget. Funds and asets sent by the Association to LEPRA India are therefore written off as operational grants.
>
> During the year, the Association made grants to LEPRA India totalling £437,292 (1992, £592,127).

Paragraph 71 went on to say that one way in which the relevant information could be given was to aggregate the accounts of the charity with those of its connected charities, and to disclose the basis of preparation.

The revised charity SORP

Paragraph 5 of Appendix 1 states that 'connected charities' are those which have:

(a) common, parallel or related objects and activities; and either have:
(b) (i) common control; or
    (ii) unity of administration.

Because of the need to satisfy either (b)(i) or (ii), rather than both, this is a wider definition than that in SORP 2.

Common control exists if the same person(s):

(a) has the right to appoint a majority of the charity trustees; or
(b) holds a majority of the voting rights in the administration,

of both, or all, of the charities.

Paragraphs 50 to 53 set out the disclosures recommended for charities connected with the main charity. They do not prescribe how to account for them (unlike para 71 above).

Paragraph 51 recommends that the annual report includes:

(a) the names of the connected charities, principal contact addresses and the nature of the relationship; and
(b) particulars of any material transactions,

between the charities.

Where the reporting charity is an 'umbrella organisation' for a number of connected charities, para 52 considers it sufficient to:

(a) state how many there are;
(b) describe the areas in which they operate;
(c) explain how they can be contacted; and
(d) give particulars of any material transactions between them.

For (b), as regards para 51, and (d), as regards para 52, it is not clear what those 'particulars' might be as they are not prescribed. Presumably they would be similar to those for directors under Sch 6 to the 1985 Act.

Chapter 15 – Summarised accounts

15.1 Introduction

Summarised accounts have become a regular feature of UK financial reporting. But they are not confined to those companies reporting under the Companies Acts. As the Introduction to the ED of the revised SORP pointed out, many charities now issue such accounts for one purpose or another, in addition to their full accounts. Conceptually, however, their issue appears at odds with the ASB's draft chapters of its Statement of Principles.

In 1991, the ASB issued draft chapters 1 and 2 respectively *The objective of financial statements* and *Qualitative characteristics of financial statements* of its Statement of Principles. Paragraph 38 of draft chapter 2 (which, according to para 8 of the Introduction to the Statement of Principles, applies equally to not-for-profit organisations) states that:

> 'An essential quality of the information provided in the financial statements is that it should be presented in such a way that it is readily understandable to users. For this purpose, users are assumed to have a reasonable knowledge of the business and economic activities and accounting and a willingness to study the information with reasonable diligence. Information about complex matters that should be included in the financial statements because of its relevance to the economic decision-making needs of users should not be excluded merely on the grounds that it may be too difficult for certain users to understand . . . .'.

That their introduction has contributed to the quality of financial reporting might, therefore, be open to question.

15.2 What are 'summarised accounts'?

(A) The 1985 Act

In implementing the EC Fourth Company Law Directive, it was the 1981 Act which introduced the concept of 'abridged accounts'. This concept has been continued by the 1985 (through consolidation) and the 1989 Acts, although, in the latter case, with different terminology; that is, the term 'non-statutory accounts' has replaced the term 'abridged accounts'.

'Non-statutory accounts' are any balance sheet or profit and loss account that a company publishes that relates to, or purports to deal with, any financial year, but that does not qualify as full individual accounts or full group accounts in respect of that financial year (s240(5)). For this purpose, a company publishes a balance sheet or a profit and loss account whenever it publishes, issues or circulates it (or makes it available in any other way for public inspection) with a view to its being read by the public generally or by any class of members of the public.

(B) SORP 2

Paragraph 7 of SORP 2 recognised that many charities published 'simplified accounts' within their annual report or included extracts from their annual report in other publications. No definition was offered nor, in view of their diversity of purpose, was it practicable to provide detailed recommendations on their preparation. Nonetheless, para 7(c) did state that they should be 'a fair summary of the full accounts. This means that they should contain information on both the income and expenditure and the balance sheet and that they should be based on the principles set out in SORP 2.'

(C) What is happening in practice?

For charitable companies, Example 15.1 London Lighthouse provides both an income and expenditure account and balance sheet, with a treasurer's report.

Example 15.1 London Lighthouse
Annual report 1993 (extract) (31 March 1993):

Treasurer's report

Income

The financial year 1992/93 was, in monetary terms, a successful one. Our main source of income continued to be statutory funding, with health service support for the Residential Unit forming a substantial part of our total income. The 'fostering' arrangement continued to work well: within this, North West Thames Regional Health Authority is designated as the primary health service purchaser of Lighthouse services, acting on behalf of the other Thames regions for contracting purposes. Additional contributions were received from the London Boroughs Grants Committee and London boroughs.

The current funding 'split' on operating activity is 72 per cent statutory funding to 28 per cent from non-statutory sources, including charitable trusts, corporate support, individual donations and income from events. The total raised from non-statutory sources in 1992/93 was £1,433,940.

Expenditure

Over 500 individuals received at least one direct service. With services ranging from 291 Residential Unit users to 7,000 recorded attendances at classes, service costs per user vary from service to service. Whilst some are very staff intensive, other services involve extensive deployment of volunteers without whom the 'real' costs would be substantially greater.

Balance sheet (reserves)

Due to a healthy operating surplus, Lighthouse reserves grew from £4,872,910 to £5,909,099. Most of this growth was represented by an increase in liquid funds.

Much of the year's surplus was designated for future capital expenditure, designated funds increasing from £467,829 to £1,409,963 with the intention of creating a capital endowment. However, in the challenging contract environment of 1993/94, we may be called upon to utilise some of these reserves to fund revenue costs.

Example 15.1 London Lighthouse
Annual report 1993 (extract) (31 March 1993): (Continued)

Treasurer's report (Continued)

Looking to the future

The 1993/94 financial year is the last in which the 'fostering' arrangement will operate. In addition a review of Section 64 funding will result in a taper from 1995/96, reducing this source of funding by £50,000 annually. Lighthouse is therefore reviewing its present funding split and aims to increase support received from non-statutory sources. The introduction of an organisational strategic plan, development of quality standards, and continued vigilance to identify efficiency savings and maximise income all aim to strengthen the organisation financially.

Peter Commins
Treasurer
November 1993

Abridged accounts for the year ended 31 March 1993

Balance sheet – 31 March 1993

	1993		*1992*	
	£	£	£	£
Fixed assets				
Tangible fixed assets		4,449,156		*4,347,082*
Current assets				
Stocks	10,131		*11,419*	
Debtors	652,281		*329,711*	
Cash at bank and in hand	1,106,581		*413,652*	
	1,768,993		*754,782*	
Creditors: amounts falling due within one year	308,530		*226,994*	
Net current assets		1,460,463		*527,788*
Total assets less current liabilities		5,909,619		*4,874,870*

Example 15.1 London Lighthouse
Annual report 1993 (extract) (31 March 1993): (Continued)

Abridged accounts for the year ended 31 March 1993
Balance sheet – 31 March 1993 (Continued)

	1993 £	1993 £	*1992* *£*	*1992* *£*
Creditors:				
amounts falling due after more than one year				
Convenanted loans		520		*1,960*
		5,909,099		*4,872,910*
Funds and reserves				
Restricted funds		4,475,423		*4,393,232*
Designated funds		1,409,963		*467,829*
General fund		23,713		*11,849*
		5,909,099		*4,872,910*
Income and expenditure account for the year ended 31 March 1993				
Income				
Voluntary income				
Grants receivable		3,682,163		*2,683,517*
Donations and gifts		1,141,296		*676,592*
		4,823,459		*3,360,109*
Other income		292,644		*238,405*
Total income		5,116,103		*3,598,514*
Expenditure				
Indirect expenditure				
Management services	1,199,944		*1,315,813*	
Fundraising	211,864		*115,839*	
Depreciation	128,581		*275,104*	
		1,540,389		*1,706,756*

Example 15.1 London Lighthouse
Annual report 1993 (extract) (31 March 1993): (Continued)

Income and expenditure account for the year ended 31 March 1993 (Continued)

Income available for charitable expenditure		3,575,714		*1,891,758*
Direct charitable expenditure				
Residential services	1,554,883		*1,226,416*	
Education and training	209,005		*164,253*	
Centre and community-based work	868,369		*573,218*	
		2,632,257		*1,963,887*
		943,457		*(72,129)*
Operating surplus (deficit) for the year				
Interest receivable	78,664		*38,245*	
Interest payable	(472)		*(515)*	
		78,192		*37,730*
Exceptional item				
VAT		14,540		*50,000*
Surplus for the year before transfers and appropriations		1,036,189		*15,601*
Transfers and appropriations				
Net expenditure in respect of restricted funds		(71,151)		*222,404*
Transfers to designated funds		(953,174)		*(235,000)*
Net surplus for the year		11,864		*3,005*

The accounts set out on these pages are abridged versions of the company's full accounts, which have been filed with the Registrar of Companies, and on which the company's auditors, Buzzacott & Co, reported without qualification on 6 December 1993.

The full audited accounts together with the auditors' report can be inspected at the registered office of London Lighthouse on request.

While Example 15.2 Guide Dogs for the Blind Association provides an income and expenditure account, both in traditional format and pictorially, but without a balance sheet or any narrative, Example 15.3 British Diabetic Association goes one stage further by providing accompanying narrative.

Example 15.2 Guide Dogs for the Blind Association 1993 Annual review (extract) (31 December 1993):

Financial summary 1993

The figures on this page are an abridged version of the full accounts on which the auditors gave an unqualified report. Copies of the full document are avaiable on request from GDBA, Hillfields, Burghfield, Reading, RG7 3YG.

Income and Expenditure Account for the year ended 31 December 1993

	1993	*1992*
NET VOLUNTARY INCOME	£000	*£000*
Voluntary Fund-Raising Branches	2,903	*4,331*
Donations and Other Income	3,030	*3,877*
Legacies	20,187	*17,439*
	26,120	*25,647*
Less Fund Raising Expenses	3,915	*3,834*
Total Net Voluntary Income	22,205	*21,813*
DIRECT CHARITABLE EXPENDITURE		
Guide Dog Applications	1,443	*961*
Dog Breeding and Training	8,391	*7,922*
Guide Dog Owner Services	8,746	*8,004*
Rehabilitation and Other Support Services	3,358	*3,116*
Training of Staff and Rehabilitation Workers	1,876	*1,710*
Research and Development Projects	1,343	*901*
	25,157	*22,614*
OTHER EXPENDITURE		
Administration and General (1992 includes relocation expenditure of £407,000)	2,072	*2,397*
	27,229	*25,011*
DEFICIT before Investment Income	(5,024)	*(3,198)*
Investment Income	6,414	*6,297*
SURPLUS FOR THE YEAR transferred to General Fund	1,390	*3,099*

Statement of Investment Gains for the year ended 31 December 1993

GAINS ON REALISATION OF INVESTMENTS transferred to General Fund	9,832	*3,879*

Example 15.2 Guide Dogs for the Blind Association 1993 Annual review (extract) (31 December 1993): (Continued)

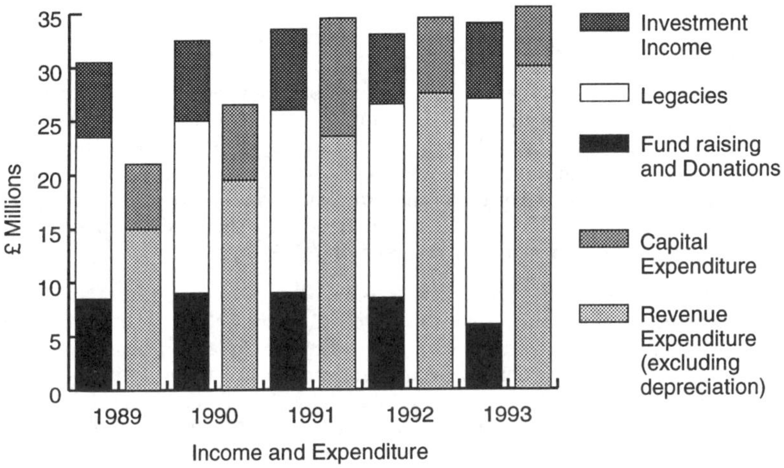

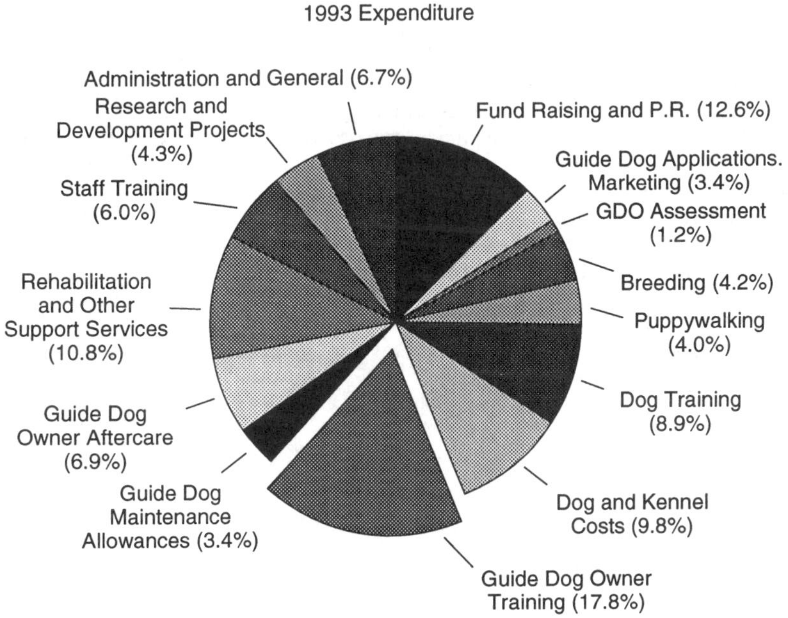

Example 15.3 British Diabetic Association Annual report (extract) (31 December 1993):

Accounting notes

General Comment

The year to 31 December 1993 has been another very difficult year for the charity sector. Despite this, the Association has achieved an increase in total income of £125,000 or 1.5 per cent over the previous year: against this, expenditure has increased by £453,000 or 5.6 per cent over 1992. The overall result was a surplus of income over expenditure for the year of £134,000 which, when added to the profit on the sale of investments of £188,000, led to a transfer to reserves of £322,000.

These figures reflect the tremendous generosity of our members and supporters both individual and corporate: we are extremely grateful for this vital help in enabling us to increase our funding of an ambitious research programme and in the higher levels of spending on social care and membership services. Meanwhile the continued maintenance of firm financial discipline will ensure the long term growth and success of the Association.

- Total income over the last five years has risen by 46 per cent enabling the Association to greatly increase the research programme into the causes and treatment of diabetes and provide direct and practical help to both our members and the wider diabetic community.
- Total income for the year was almost £8.7m of which £6.2m – or over 71 per cent – came from legacies and donations illustrating the extent to which the Association continues to rely on such voluntary sources.
- Total expenditure of over £8.5m includes main items of expenditure of just over £3m on research and £3.2m on social care, membership services, children's activities and branches. Administration costs were again held at 6 per cent of total expenditure.
- Total donations are up 6.7 per cent on the last year at £2.8m and this reflects the enthusiasm and commitment of our local branch network of over 400 groups and our individual and corporate members and supporters.

Example 15.3 British Diabetic Association Annual report (extract) (31 December 1993): (Continued)

Total Income and Expenditure over the last 5 years (£'000s)

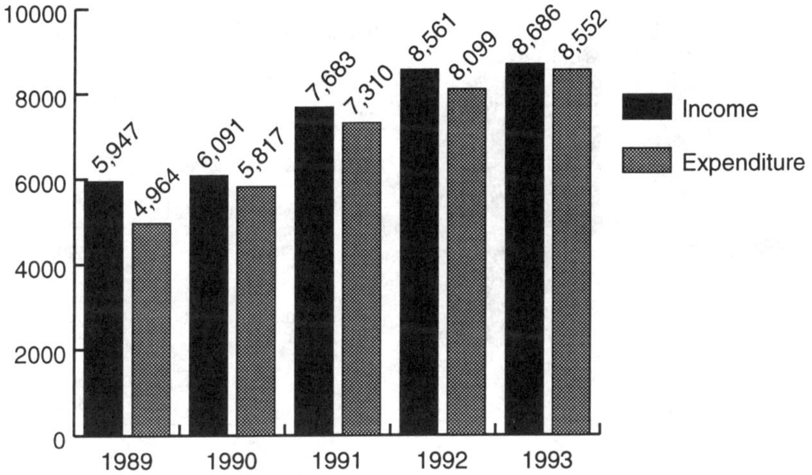

Total Donations (£'000s)

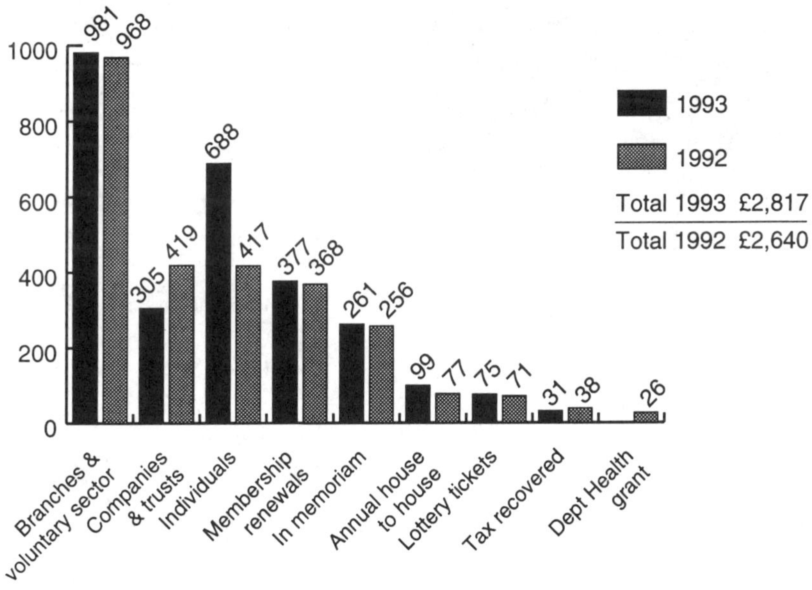

**Example 15.3 British Diabetic Association
Annual report (extract) (31 December 1993): (Continued)**

Total Income 1993 by Category

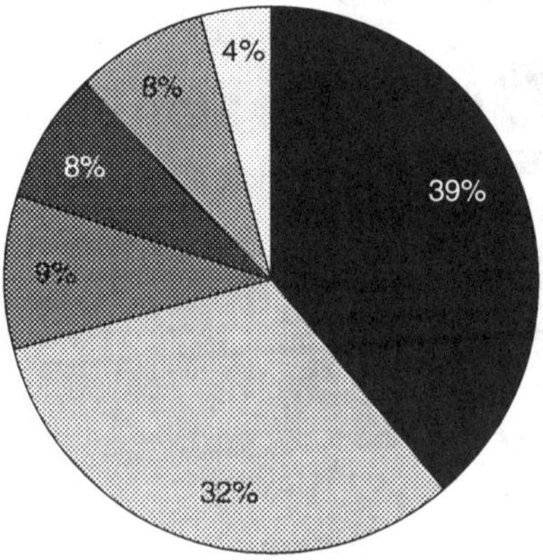

	£'000s
Legacies	3,372
Donations	2,817
Subscriptions	761
Dividends & Interest	685
Net Income Trading Company, Sales & Other Income	690
Professional Members Section & Childrens Activities	361
Total	8,686

Total Expenditure 1993

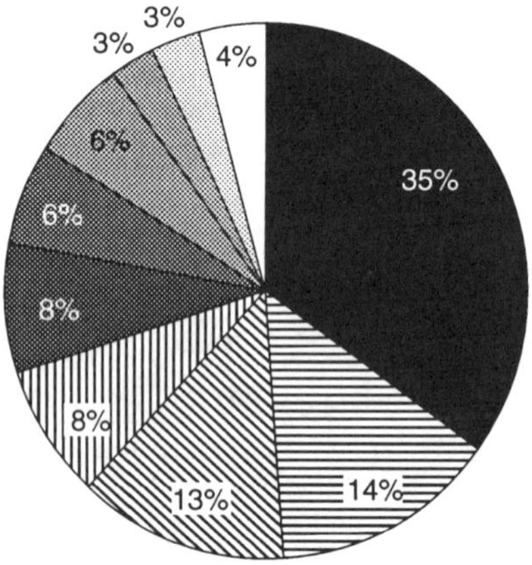

	£'000s
Research	3,028
Social care	1,194
Membership Services	1,097
Information & Education	706
Children's Activities	688
Direct Fundraising	511
Administration	499
Professional Members Section	285
Branches & National Conference	229
Cost of Goods Sold, Legal Charges, Non-recoverable VAT & Other Expenses	315
Total	8,552

Example 15.3 British Diabetic Association
Annual report (extract) (31 December 1993): (Continued)

The Cost of Caring

- We rely on voluntary contributions for 71 per cent of our income
- Over the past year our expenditure has increased: we are spending more in real terms on the things that matter – care and research – and our administration costs are consistently low
- Over the past five years there has been an increase of 46 per cent in our total income
- In 1993 a small surplus was recorded, which was added to our reserves. We currently hold sufficient reserves to cover 15 months' expenditure. Our ambitious plans for 1994–1998 include considerable expenditure on both Care and Research which will require continued support from all sectors

For charities not companies incorporated under the Companies Acts, whereas Example 15.4 Soldiers' Sailors' & Airmen's Families Association provides an income and expenditure account and balance sheet, together with pictorial information and narrative, Example 15.5 Royal National Institute for the Blind provides details only of income and expenditure, although with some accompanying narrative.

Example 15.4 Soldiers' Sailors' & Airmen's Families Association
Report of Council 1993 (extract) (31 December 1993):
General Fund Balance as at 31st December 1993

	1993		1992	
	£	£	*£*	*£*
CAPITAL ACCOUNTS				
Accumulated Fund Balance at 1st January		15,870,955		*16,065,522*
Add net deficit on Income & Expenditure Account		(102,934)		*(194,567)*
		15,768,021		*15,870,955*
Central Office Property Maintenance & Equipment Reserve		610,852		*610,852*
		16,378,873		*16,481,807*
REPRESENTED BY				
FIXED ASSETS				
Freehold Properties	6,183,399		*5,895,505*	
Furniture, Fittings & Equipment	500		*500*	
Motor Cars	16,116		*16,290*	
		6,200,015		*5,912,295*
INVESTMENTS		8,151,960		*8,109,014*
CURRENT ASSETS				
Investment in Subsidiary Companies	20,000		*20,000*	
Debtors	504,620		*558,881*	
Cash in hand and at bank	2,766,724		*3,584,658*	
	3,291,344		*4,163,539*	

Example 15.4 Soldiers' Sailors' & Airmen's Families Association
Report of Council 1993 (extract) (31 December 1993): (Continued)
General Fund Balance as at 31st December 1993 (Continued)

	1993		*1992*	
	£	£	*£*	*£*
LESS CURRENT LIABILITIES				
Trust Funds	220,782		*197,302*	
Other Charities	690,047		*647,433*	
Creditors	353,617		*858,306*	
	1,264,446		*1,703,041*	
NET CURRENT ASSETS		2,026,898		*2,460,498*
		16,378,873		*16,481,807*

Financial review

During 1993 SSAFA received £5,026,476 from other Charities and this amount was paid in financial casegrants during the year.

An additional £367,716 was paid in casegrants from SSAFA Funds and the joint Branch network found and expended £1,524,444 for Forces Help Society cases.

The total benevolence administered by SSAFA/FHS of £6,918,636 represents a small decrease from 1992 but is forecast to increase substantially in future years.

No account has been taken of the considerable amounts of grants and benefits which are obtained for our clients and paid direct to them.

Strenuous efforts have been made to contain operating costs and in 1993 Management and Branch Administration costs have decreased.

Income from donations, fund-raising and legacies saw a fall but it is hoped that a national advertising campaign in Summer 1994, which should regenerate funds for future campaigns, will reverse the position in years to come.

Example 15.4 Soldiers' Sailors' & Airmen's Families Association Report of Council 1993 (extract) (31 December 1993): (Continued) Financial review (Continued)

The deficit for the year was £102,934. Council are seeking to ensure that all Association money is available to be put to use where needed, but as work expands, deficits are forecast to increase and fund-raising efforts nationally and locally are required to turn these deficits to a surplus.

H B Singer, Honorary Treasurer

AUDITOR'S STATEMENT

In our opinion the Income and Expenditure Account and Balance Sheet set out above are consistent with the full Annual Accounts for the year ended 31st December 1993. We have issued an unqualified Audit Report on the full Annual Accounts.

The extracts from the full Accounts do not contain sufficient information to allow for a complete understanding of the result for the year and state of affairs of the Charity.

71 Mark Lane
London EC3R 7RD

DRURY THURGOOD & CO
Chartered Accountants

9th June 1994

Example 15.4 Soldiers' Sailors' & Airmen's Families Association Report of Council 1993 (extract) (31 December 1993): (Continued)

General Fund Income and Expenditure Account for the year ended 31st December 1993

	1993		*1992*	
INCOME	£	£	*£*	*£*
Contributions				
From Public Funds	6,884,029		*6,274,933*	
From Service Funds				
and Other Charities	5,196,768		*5,299,492*	
Donations	736,852		*749,501*	
Fund Raising Events	460,640		*488,497*	
Legacies	576,156		*794,295*	
Investment Income	731,695		*792,743*	
		14,586,140		*14,399,461*
EXPENDITURE				
Costs incurred on behalf				
of Public Funds	6,875,188		*6,253,344*	
Casegrants paid				
From SSAFA Funds	367,716		*394,876*	
On behalf of Other Charities	5,026,476		*5,133,288*	
Welfare Service	959,741		*954,118*	
Appeals	384,383		*289,679*	
Press & Publicity	421,284		*400,417*	
Management & Branch Administration	525,380		*554,015*	
Branch Organisation & Recruitment	245,970		*235,772*	
Training	431,304		*410,333*	
Housing & Resettlement	297,707		*305,494*	
		15,535,149		*14,931,336*

Example 15.4 Soldiers' Sailors' & Airmen's Families Association Report of Council 1993 (extract) (31 December 1993): (Continued)

General Fund Income and Expenditure Account for the year ended 31st December 1993 (Continued)

	1993		1992	
	£	£	£	£
DEFICIT		(949,009)		*(531,875)*
Surplus on Sales of Investments		546,075		*115,569*
Balance available before adjustment for extraordinary items		(402,934)		*(416,306)*
Extraordinary items		300,000		*221,739*
BALANCE FROM ACCUMULATED FUND		(102,934)		*(194,567)*

Example 15.4 Soldiers' Sailors' & Airmen's Families Association Report of Council 1993 (extract) (31 December 1993): (Continued)

HANDLING COST PER CASE TO SSAFA

Figures not adjusted for inflation

STRENGTH OF VOLUNTEER NETWORK

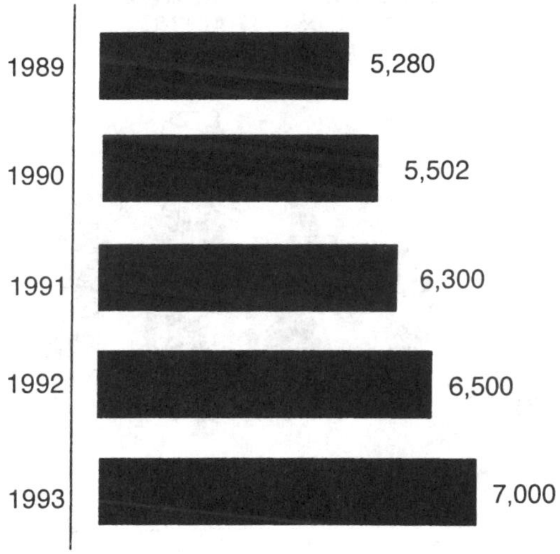

Example 15.4 Soldiers' Sailors' & Airmen's Families Association Report of Council 1993 (extract) (31 December 1993): (Continued)

CASEWORK/FRIENDSHIP VISITS BY VOLUNTEERS
Figures for last five years by service

	1989	1990	1991	1992	1993
Royal Navy	9,186	10,212	11,734	14,022	13,248
Army	45,433	50,473	54,883	54,204	53,522
RAF	10,256	11,684	12,856	14,108	14,730
Total	64,875	72,369	79,473	82,334	81,500

VOLUNTEERS AND SERVICE WIVES
ATTENDING NATIONAL TRAINING
COURSES/CONFERENCES

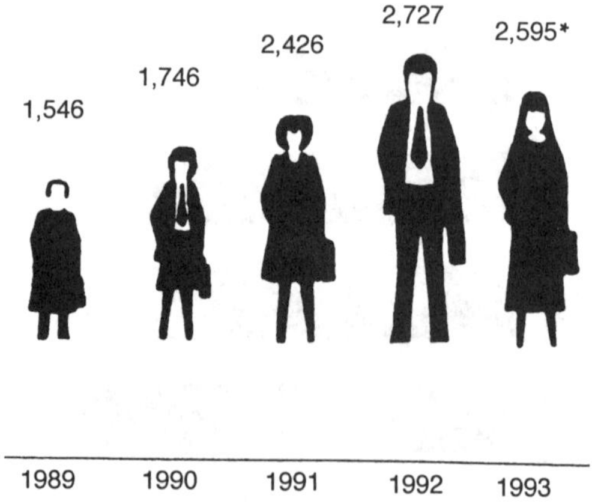

* *No Annual Conference held in 1993*

Example 15.5 Royal National Institute for the Blind Annual review 1993/94 (extract) (31 March 1994):

Our finances in 1993/94

At a time of continuing economic difficulty, it is cheering to be able to report that we increased our expenditure on services to blind and partially sighted people. We spent £45.7 million on service provision, an increase of £4.5 million on the previous year. Some of the 60-plus services we now offer are long-standing, developed over time to reflect the needs of the people we serve; others are brand new.

We invested £1.6 million on two capital projects completed during the past year. The RNIB Springfield Centre near Glasgow, referred to on page 13 of the review, was finished during the year. A highly innovative scheme, it was largely funded through a very successful appeal in Scotland. At RNIB Vocational College in Loughborough we opened new student accommodation specially designed for people with impaired sight. Much of the funding for this was also raised locally.

Our income from Government, other public sources and fees of £21.4 million was topped up by £2.6 million investment income, plus a marvellous £20.3 million from our generous supporters who include individuals, trusts and companies. We balanced the books by withdrawing £1.4 million from reserves. Our policy on keeping only modest reserves is explained in the full accounts, available on request.

As part of RNIB's tax planning arrangements, we made a pre-payment to a wholly-owned company which will purchase fuel on our behalf. It is very said that charities have to consider such tax planning in order to maximise their hard-won resources.

My heart-felt thanks go to all the supporters, volunteers and staff who make our work possible. This year over 100,000 blind and partially sighted people benefited directly from our work. We have now set ourselves the monumental task of doubling that number by the end of the century. We need friends now more than ever.

With my thanks to you all,

Jack Dunn
Honorary Treasurer

Example 15.5 Royal National Institute for the Blind
Annual review 1993/94 (extract) (31 March 1994): (Continued)

Expenditure in 1993/94

Access to information	**£10.7 million**

Braille, Moon and print publications, Talking Book Service, audio services.

Education and training	**£13.9 million**

Three Sunshine House Schools, Rushton Hall School, Condover Hall School, New College Worcester, Redhill College, Education Support Services, Student Support Services, Physiotherapy Support Services, information and advisory services for parents and teachers.

Employment services	**£6.1 million**

Vocational College, Employment Network, Employment Rehabilitation Centres.

Social and residential services, products and shops	**£8.6 million**

Social services including the Benefit Rights and Information Service, four residential care homes, Garrow House, three holiday hotels, subsidised equipment, Resource Centres and advisory services.

Services for the public and professionals	**£5.2 million**

Information and training services on multiple disabilities, Health Services Unit, training for rehabilitation workers, Social Services Consultancy, research into blindness, information services.

Central administration	**£1.2 million**

Committee and central administration costs to support our service provision.

Total expenditure	**£45.7 million**

Income in 1993/94

Donations, legacies, and investment income	£22.9 million
Fees, grants and sales	£21.4 million
Total income	£44.3 million
Transfer from reserves	£1.4 million

The above figures are a summary of our financial position in 1993/94. If you would like a copy of the full accounts (on which the auditors gave an unqualified report) please contact the Director of Finance and Administration at our London office.

(D) The revised charity SORP
Unlike both SORP 2 and the ED, para 21 of Appendix 1 of the revised SORP contains the following description:

> '"Summarised accounts" means accounts derived from the full annual accounts of the charity in any year and expressed in any form purporting to be or to represent a Balance Sheet, Statement of Assets and Liabilities, Statement of Financial Activities, Statement of Income and Expenditure or Statement of Receipts and Payments'.

Regardless of the intended circulation of any summarised accounts, the full trustees' annual report and accounts should always be prepared. Paragraph 25 recommends that the summarised accounts should not only be a fair, but also an accurate, summary of the full accounts.

15.3 What statement is required to be given?

(A) The 1985 Act
If a charitable company publishes such accounts, s240(3)(as amended by SI 1994 No 1935) requires a statement to be appended, indicating:

(a) that they are not the company's statutory accounts;
(b) whether statutory accounts dealing with any financial year with which the non-statutory accounts purport to deal have been delivered to the Registrar;
(c) whether the company's auditors have made a report under s235 on the statutory accounts for any such financial year or, if no such report has been made, whether the company's reporting accountant has made a report for the purposes of s249A(2); and
(d) whether any auditors' report was qualified or contained a statement under ss237(2) or (3) (accounting records or returns inadequate, accounts not agreeing with records and returns or failure to obtain necessary information and explanations) or whether any report made for the purposes of s249A(2) was qualified; and

it must *not* publish, with the non-statutory accounts, either the auditors' report, under s235, or that for the purposes of s249A(2).

A company which does not comply with the requirements for the publication of non-statutory accounts and any officer who is in default will be liable to a fine (s240(6)).

(B) SORP 2
Paragraph 7(b) merely stated that simplified accounts should contain a statement explaining that they are not the full accounts and that they are not audited.

(C) What is happening in practice?
Once again, practice varies. Example 15.6 Boys' Brigade complies fully with the requirements.

Some charities, however, do not give all the required statements. For example, Example 15.2 Guide Dogs for the Blind Association does not give a statement relating to (b) and Example 15.7 Save The Children Fund, statements for (c) and (d).

Example 15.6 Boys' Brigade
Annual report (part) (31 March 1993):
Abridged accounts (part):

> These accounts are not the full statutory accounts, which have been prepared and audited and which have been delivered to the Registrar of Companies. The report of the auditors upon the statutory accounts was unqualified in the context of Companies Act 1985 Section 225 (3)(d) which is not relevant to this company.
>
> A complete copy of the audited accounts and annexed reports may be obtained on application to the Director of Finance, The Boys' Brigade, Business Centre, Alington Road, St Neots, Cambridgeshire, PE19 2RD.
>
> September 1993.

Example 15.7 Save The Children Fund
Annual report 1993–94 (extract) (31 March 1994):

> A full set of the annual report and accounts – which were approved on 28 July 1994 – have been submitted to the Charity Commissioners and the Registrar of Companies and can be obtained from Save the Children, 17 Grove Lane, London SE5 8RD.

Contrary to the specific requirement not to do so, Example 15.8 Mary Rose Trust reproduced, in its 1992 annual report, the auditors' report 'for information purposes only'.

Example 15.8 Mary Rose Trust
Annual report 1992 (extract) (31 December 1992):

> The following Financial Summary has been extracted from the Trust's statutory accounts for the year ending 31 December 1992 prepared in accordance with the Accounting Standard Committee's Statement of Recommended Practice number 2. Copies of the full accounts are available from the address shown on the back cover. The Auditor's report in respect of the statutory accounts is reproduced below for information purposes only.
>
> *Auditor's Report to the members of the Mary Rose Trust*
>
> (Company limited by Guarantee)
> We have audited the financial statements on pages 5 to 15 in accordance with Auditing Standards.
>
> In our opinion the financial statements give a true and fair view of the state of the Trust's affairs at 31 December 1992 and of its deficit for the year then ended and have been properly prepared in accordance with the Companies Act 1985.
>
> In our opinion the Trust is entitled under Section 248 of the Companies Act 1985 not to prepare group financial statements for the year ended 31 December 1992.
>
> Grant Thornton
> Registered Auditor,
> Chartered Accountants
> 26 April 1993

For charities which are not incorporated under the Companies Acts, sub-paras 7(a) and (b) of SORP 2 recommended that a full annual report should always be produced, together with details of how this may be obtained, and that simplified accounts should carry a statement explaining that they are not the full accounts and that they are not audited. Example 15.9 the Royal Society for the Protection of Birds provides this information.

Example 15.9 Royal Society for the Protection of Birds
Summary of the accounts (extract) (31 March 1994):

> The accounts on these pages are a summary of the RSPB's accounts. A copy of the audited accounts which contain the detailed information required by law or under best practice guidelines can be obtained from the Director of Finance at The Lodge for £4.
>
> The RSPB accounts were adopted by the RSPB Council on 5 July 1994. The RSPB's auditors, Price Waterhouse, have given an unqualified audit report on these accounts.

Some charities surveyed append auditors' reports to the non- statutory accounts. Example 15.10 Artists' General Benevolent Fund and Example 15.11 Mary Rose Trust, in its 1993 annual report, include reports which are not dissimilar to that used by auditors reporting on summary financial statements for listed public companies.

Example 15.10 Artists' General Benevolent Fund
Annual report (extract) (5 April 1993):

> In our opinion this summary financial statement is consistent with the annual audited financial statement.
>
> TUDOR JOHN *Chartered Accountants*
> Dated this 22nd day of June 1993

Example 15.11 Mary Rose Trust
Annual report 1993 (extract) (31st December 1993):

> In our opinion these summarised accounts are consistent with the full annual accounts of the Mary Rose Trust for the year ended 31 December 1993.
>
> Grant Thornton
> Chartered Accountants
> Portsmouth 3 May 1994

Attached to Example 15.4 Soldiers' Sailors' & Airmen's Families Association's summary accounts is an auditors' *statement* which, like Examples 15.10 and 15.11, refers to the consistency aspect but, also, includes the comment 'the extracts from the full Accounts do not contain sufficient information to allow for a complete understanding of the result for the year and state of affairs of the Charity', a form of 'health warning'.

Example 15.12 Youth Hostels Association (England and Wales) 1993/94 annual report includes accounts which are a 'simplified consolidated version covering the activities of the Association and the Company . . . they do not purport to be in statutory form' but have been reviewed by the auditors who 'are satisfied that they give a fair picture of the YHA's finances for the period'.

Example 15.12 YHA (England and Wales) Limited
1993/94 Annual report (extract) (28 February 1994):

> The accounts which follow are a simplified, consolidated, version covering the activities of the Association and the Company for the full twelve months. They do not purport to be in statutory form, but have been prepared in conjunction with the statutory accounts, and have been reviewed by the Auditors, who are satisfied that they give a fair picture of the YHA's finances for the period.

(D) The revised charity SORP

Summarised accounts should:

(a) be accompanied by a statement, signed on behalf of the trustees, that they are an extract from the full accounts (para 216);
(b) contain information relating to both the SOFA and the balance sheet (para 216);
(c) contain a 'health warning', a suitable form of which might be:
   'These summarised accounts may not contain sufficient information to allow for a full understanding of the financial affairs of the charity. For further information the full annual accounts, the auditor's or independent examiner's report on those accounts and the trustees' annual report should be consulted; copies of these can be obtained from (address)' (para 217);
(d) give the date the accounts were approved and whether they have been submitted to the Commissioners (para 218);
(e) state whether the full annual accounts have been audited, or independently examined. If so, the summary accounts should include a statement from the auditor, or independent examiner, giving his opinion as to whether those summarised accounts are *consistent* with the full annual accounts (para 219);
(f) state whether the auditor's, or independent examiner's, opinion was qualified (para 220). If so, the statement should give enough details to enable a reader to appreciate the significance of the qualification (para 221).

In respect of (f), para 221 states that 'it may not be necessary or even suitable to quote the report in full'. Charitable companies cannot, of course, quote this.

Paragraph 222 acknowledges that the trustees of charitable companies must, also, state whether the statutory accounts have been delivered to the Registrar.

Chapter 16 – Auditing

16.1 Introduction

The regulatory framework governing the audit of charities is more fully discussed in chapters **3** (see page 40) and, for smaller charities, **17** (see page 429).

In conducting an audit, auditors should have regard both to the SASs, issued by the APB, in general and to AG 301 *Charities*, issued in October 1981 by the then APC, in particular. In the light of the Regulations and the need for guidance thereunder, the APB is also taking the opportunity of reviewing and revising, the now somewhat outdated, AG 301. A Practice Note is to be issued in due course.

16.2 Objective and general principles

SAS 100 *Objective and general principles governing an audit of financial statements* sets out an overall summary of the objectives of an audit, discusses the concept of reasonable assurance and provides a link to the ethical guidance. SAS 100.1, which is a useful overall Auditing Standard for the entire series of SASs, states that:

> 'In undertaking an audit of financial statements the auditors should:
> (a) carry out procedures designed to obtain sufficient appropriate audit evidence, in accordance with Auditing Standards contained in SASs, to determine with reasonable confidence whether the financial statements are free of material mis-statement;
> (b) evaluate the overall presentation of the financial statements, in order to ascertain whether they have been prepared in accordance with relevant legislation and accounting standards;
> (c) issue a report containing a clear expression of their opinion on the financial statements.'

The application of SASs is neither more, nor less, onerous for charities than for other entities.

The auditors should:

(a) consider the terms of the engagement;
(b) plan, control and record the audit;

(c) obtain relevant and reliable audit evidence, including carrying out an overall review of the accounts; and
(d) make a report, addressed to the appropriate person(s), or body.

16.2.1 Considering the terms of the engagement

The scope of the audit will be conditioned both by the status of the charity and by the form of report to be given. Where the charity is, for example, a company, friendly or industrial and provident society, the minimum requirements will be laid down in statute. Where this is not so, the trust deed, or other constitutional document, should establish the terms of reference. A lack of clarity of the provisions of the trust deed, or other constitutional document, may highlight practical problems (see chapter **3**, page 52).

The trustees should be consulted, as they may wish to expand the scope of the audit beyond the minimum requirements. It should be borne in mind that any additional tests not ordinarily performed for the purposes of giving an opinion, may be more akin to 'tests for management' and, perhaps, subject to a separate fee. Whatever is agreed, SAS 140.1 of SAS 140 *Engagement letters* requires that:

> 'The auditors and the client should agree on the terms of the engagement, which should be recorded in writing'.

The purpose of a letter of engagement is to define clearly the extent of the responsibilities so as to minimise the possibility of any misunderstanding between the charity and auditor. The letter provides written confirmation of the acceptance of appointment, the scope of the audit and the form of report. If an engagement letter were not sent, there is scope for argument about the precise extent of the respective obligations of the charity, its trustees and the auditors.

Specifically but not exclusively, the letter should:

(a) explain the respective responsibilities, having particular regard to those under the Charities Acts, of the trustees and auditors;
(b) indicate that the trustees are responsible for the prevention and detection of fraud and other irregularities, but that the auditors will plan their audit so as to have a reasonable expectation of detecting material mis-statements in the accounting records resulting from fraud or other irregularities which may exist. This will be particularly important in the case of voluntary income – an area of difficulty for the auditors of many, especially smaller, charities;
(c) where the charity has branches (or similar), clarify their status and

whether or not their transactions, assets and liabilities should be 'consolidated' with the 'parent' charity's own accounts.

Before submitting the letter, the auditors should discuss its contents with the trustees, or other appropriate body, to ensure that its objectives and content are fully understood.

Existing letters should be reviewed annually both at the planning stage and at the conclusion of the audit to ensure their continuing applicability to the work to be performed.

16.2.2 Planning, controlling and recording

SAS 200.1 of SAS 200 *Planning* states:

> 'The auditors should plan the audit work so as to perform the audit in an effective manner'.

The planning should be documented in sufficient detail to explain the audit approach. SAS 200.2 requires the auditor to prepare a planning memorandum. While its form and content may vary depending on the size and complexity of the charity, the auditors should:

(a) obtain a knowledge of the business;
(b) assess risk and materiality;
(c) assess the adequacy of the accounting systems and, where appropriate, internal controls;
(d) determine the nature, timing and extent of the procedures;
(e) co-ordinate, direct, supervise and review the audit; and
(f) consider any other relevant matters (e.g., inappropriateness of the going concern presumption).

SAS 200.3 requires the auditors to prepare an audit programme setting out the nature, timing and extent of the planned procedures required to implement the planning memorandum. For charities, the use of a tailored audit programme may result in a more efficient and effective audit, rather than slavish completion of 'standardised' programmes.

Although the concept of planning may not alter as a result of the size and complexity of the charity, the timing and extent may vary on smaller engagements. For example, where accountancy work is carried out, in addition to carrying out the audit, this work should be taken into account when planning the nature, timing and extent of audit tests. As para 4 of chapter 8 of *Towards better auditing*, published by the ICAEW's Auditing Committee in 1993, states:

> 'At the planning stage the auditor needs to identify those audit objectives which preparing the accounts will help satisfy and design cost-effective audit work to meet the appropriate standards. Timing is therefore important – planning the audit should take place before any accountancy work so that staff are aware of the use to which their work will be put and can then document it accordingly. . . .'.

Therefore, where monthly (or other regular) management accounts are prepared on behalf of a charity, planning should take place before the first month's accounts of a new accounting period are prepared.

Proper planning assists in ensuring that appropriate attention is devoted to important areas of the audit, that potential problems are identified at an early stage and that the work is carried out efficiently and effectively.

16.2.3 Audit evidence

SAS 400.1 of SAS 400 *Audit evidence* states that:

> 'Auditors should obtain sufficient appropriate audit evidence to be able to draw reasonable conclusions on which to base the audit opinion'.

When designing their tests, para 44 of AG 301 suggests that the auditors should give special attention to the possibility of:

(a) understatement or incompleteness of the recording of all income including gifts in kind, cash donations and legacies;
(b) overstatement of cash grants or expenses;
(c) mis-analysis or misuse in the application of funds;
(d) mis-statement or omission of assets including donated properties and investments;
(e) the existence of restricted or uncontrollable funds in foreign or independent branches.

16.2.4 Accounting and internal control systems

SAS 300.3 of SAS 300 *Audit risk assessment* states:

> 'In planning the audit, auditors should obtain and document an understanding of the accounting system and control environment sufficient to determine their audit approach'.

After obtaining such an understanding, SAS 300.4 requires the auditors to make a preliminary assessment of control risk for material financial statement assertions. However, where the auditors conclude that, for example, it is likely to be inefficient to adopt an audit approach which relies on tests of control, they may plan the audit approach as if they had made an adverse preliminary assessment of control risk. In these circumstances, the auditors evidence will be obtained entirely from substantive tests.

However, para 49 of AG 301 states that, in considering internal controls, the auditors should take into consideration any related reporting requirements . . . : 'For example, the Friendly Societies Act 1974 requires the auditor to state in his report if a satisfactory system of control over transactions has not been maintained'. (This duty has since been repealed, replaced and widened by the Friendly Societies Act 1992.) Some of the internal controls which might be expected to be present in most charities are given in paras 52 to 62 of AG 301.

(Note: In some cases monitored or investigated during 1993 the Commissioners noted, *inter alia*, a lack of adequate internal control, which had the effect of 'impairing trustee control'. The Commissioners were keen to point out that effective management structures and controls and reporting procedures will minimise the risk to charity property.) (See chapter **2**, page 15, for a discussion of trustees' responsibilities.)

16.2.5 Risk areas

Donations

Donations may be received either through collecting boxes (or similar) or through the post.

AG 301 recognises that it may be difficult to ensure the completeness and accuracy of the recording of income from donations. Nonetheless, para 52 suggests that, in respect of the former method of collection, the following controls which might be expected to be present in most charities would be:

'(a) numerical control over collecting boxes and tins;
(b) satisfactory sealing of boxes and tins so that any opening prior to recording is apparent;
(c) regular collection and recording of proceeds from collecting boxes;
(d) dual control over counting and recording of proceeds.'

It would, also, be useful if the name of the charity were printed prominently on collecting boxes and tins. Some charities use collectors to put envelopes through letter boxes in the hope that the occupiers will make a contribution. Others put plastic bags through, asking for these to be filled with jumble or other bric-a-brac. AG 301 is silent as to the controls which may be present over these forms of donation. Invariably, formal controls (e.g., in the former case, pre-numbering of envelopes) are absent. Indeed, even if there were, for example, pre-numbering, this may not be a particularly effective control, as there may be no guarantee that they could all be accounted for. While all forms of fundraising involve some degree of risk, these forms involve greater risk and, perhaps, should be avoided, whenever possible.

The 1992 Annual Report of the Commissioners referred to a new, and rather disturbing, development in the method of raising funds. Paragraph 97 stated:

> 'One recent development in fundraising which is causing concern is the method being adopted by some charities of recruiting collectors by unsolicited telephone calls, made at random and without any checks to see if the individual is a fit and proper person to conduct a collection. Once an individual has agreed to act as a collector, he is supplied by the charity with a certificate of authority and a "flat pack" collection box which he is asked to assemble. The collector is instructed that on completion of the collection he should open the box in the presence of a third party, count the contents and send a cheque to the charity for the amount collected. The charities concerned appear to take little or no action if funds are not forwarded by individuals who have received collection boxes . . . we deprecate this kind of fundraising.'

This demonstrates that charities should have controls not only over collection monies but, also, *over the recruitment of collectors*, to ensure they employ only fit and proper persons. Furthermore, it is important for trustees to ensure that fundraising activities, as well as being in accordance with the aims and objectives of the charity, are carried out in the most effective and efficient way.

In respect of postal donations, para 53 of AG 301 states that the following controls which might be expected to be present are:

> '(a) dual control over the opening of mail;
> (b) immediate recording of donations on opening mail or receipt of cash.'

Post room operations should, also, be properly supervised by a responsible official.

Bank records

While applicable to all charities, para 62 of AG 301 suggests that for smaller charities the following controls will have particular significance:

> '(a) prompt banking of receipts;
> (b) independent agreement of banking records to receipt records;
> (c) regular bank reconciliations;
> (d) scrutiny of returned cheques for unusual or frequent endorsements;
> (e) adequate arrangements for bank signatories.'

Controls should be implemented to ensure that cheques cannot be signed singly. There should be two signatories (although, perhaps, subject to a *de minimis* limit, below which one signature may suffice), each of whom scrutinises the documents which support the payments; when paid, the supporting documents should be annotated as such to prevent their being used subsequently to support invalid payments; and cheques should be posted by someone other than the signatories. Checks of bank reconciliations and, subject to below, the scrutiny of paid cheques should be carried out by independent persons.

Although the scrutiny of paid cheques might still be regarded as an important audit procedure, in December 1993 the ICAEW's Auditing Committee published new guidance (FRAG 27/93) on the use of paid cheques by auditors. The guidance note was agreed with the British Bankers' Association and replaced that issued in 1982, in the light both of recent changes in auditing and banking practice and the additional security afforded by the Cheques Act 1992. The principal objectives of the guidance are:

(a) to encourage auditors to consider using alternative, more cost-effective ways of obtaining audit evidence (where possible) rather than examining paid cheques;
(b) to encourage auditors to advise clients to adopt rigorous controls over cheque payments; and
(c) where it is considered necessary to examine paid cheques, to encourage auditors to do so in a cost-effective manner that accords, as far as possible, with the banks' preferred methods for providing paid cheques.

Such controls, together with those relating to postal donations, might have prevented Miss Rosemary Aberdour, a former employee of the National Hospital for Neurology and Neurosurgery Development Foundation, from misappropriating some £2.7 million of the charity's funds.

Paragraphs 94 and 95 of the 1992 Annual Report of the Commissioners stated:

> '. . . She had the complete trust of the trustees and virtually ran the charity's finances on her own without any effective controls or checks . . . . Although not a signatory to any of the charity's building society accounts she managed to remove funds by forging the signatures of those who were. In addition, she directed further sums to the account of a separate fundraising committee outside the control of the charity. She opened the mail herself and, it appears, paid cheques into this account. She was a signatory to this account and by forging the second signature gained access to these funds also.

'. . . the person was allowed to handle the day-to-day receipt of donations unchecked and the trustees received no financial information about the charity . . . although the trustees were aware of the separate fundraising committee, they neither received nor asked for any detail of its position. They now recognise the need to have control over activities conducted in the name of the charity . . . .'.

This, also, highlights the risk which may exist in circumstances where there is a dominant personality, who effectively takes control and acts without regard and referral to the legally appointed trustees. The addition of a new trustee can often provide fresh insight into the way the charity is being administered and help to avoid this situation.

Expenditure and the apportionment of administration and fundraising expenses

In general, the audit of expenditure should be straightforward. The auditors should ensure that all expenditure is properly authorised and supported by valid invoices and receipts.

Problems may arise, however, in verifying that all expenditure is used for the purposes for which the money is given. This may be particularly so in relation to expenditure e.g., food, purchase of equipment etc., of international aid agencies running overseas projects, the responsibility for the proper application of which still rests with the trustees. Where the amounts are material, AG 301 suggests that it may be appropriate for the auditors to give consideration to a local audit.

Establishing that expenditure and year-end liabilities are not materially understated may be difficult. Year-end cut-off testing is, therefore, a vital part of the audit. The auditors should, also, assess the consistency of treatment of items from one year to the next. Both these tests may be difficult to perform but, as a minimum, the following year's records should be examined, together with the minutes of any relevant committee meetings.

A particularly sensitive area is the apportionment between administration and fundraising. In reviewing this apportionment, the auditors should consider its:

(a) basis and consistency with previous years;
(b) fairness; and
(c) consistency with the description in the accounting policies.

This aspect of a charity's activities is more fully discussed in chapter **7**, see page 197.

Apportionment will, also, be an important feature where the charity works closely with an associated non-charitable company. In order to ensure that the charity is not subsidising the activities of the non-charitable company, expenses, e.g., administration and accommodation costs incurred jointly, should be fairly apportioned.

Paragraph 94 of the 1991 Annual Report of the Commissioners stated:

> 'In the case of two inquiries, we found that charity funds had been inter-mingled with those of an associated non-charitable organisation because the accounting systems had not sufficiently differentiated between the two organisations. As a result charity funds were misapplied to non-charitable purposes . . . .'.

The Commissioners reported that, during 1991, they protected £0.5 million of charity funds which were at risk through lack of proper controls to distinguish between the assets and finances of charities and their associated organisations. Despite this, the 1993 Annual Report revealed continuing concern. Paragraph 87 stated (*inter alia*):

> ' . . . Where a charity has established a separate non-charitable trading company, it should not be seen merely as a paper exercise. The trading company is a separate entity and it is essential that its funds and those of the charity are kept separate and are separately accounted for; that loans by the charity to the trading company are generally on a secured basis, and that the charity does not subsidise the trading company in any way. To strengthen the distinction between a charity and its non-charitable trading company, it is advisable also to distinguish the names of the two organisations from each other to prevent confusion, both as to which of the organisations a potential donor is giving support . . . .'.

Grants receivable

In respect of grants receivable, para 57 of AG 301 suggests that the controls which might be appropriate are:

> '(a) regular checks that all sources of income or funds are fully exploited and appropriate claims made;
> (b) ensuring income or funds are correctly applied in accordance with the terms of the grant or loan;
> (c) comprehensive records of applications made and follow-up procedures for those not discharged.'

Complications may arise if there are claw-back conditions. A claw-back of grant may be required if, for example, the amount of expenditure falls below the budget level on which the amount of grant was determined. The auditors may need to assess whether a provision should be made for part-repayment of the grants received or whether a contingent liability note may suffice.

Hidden assets

Trustees should know what assets belong to the charity and who holds them. Paragraph 59 of AG 301 suggests that controls which might be present are:

> '(a) a register of fixed assets maintained including donated assets;
> (b) assets vested in the Official Custodian, where appropriate;
> (c) donated assets recorded at approximate market value, where appropriate;
> (d) depreciation calculated and recorded as for commercial enterprises, where the accounting policy requires.'

(Note: In respect of (b), the 1992 Act provided for the investment-holding function of the Official Custodian to be phased out.)

As part of their stewardship responsibilities, the trustees should, also, know the value of the assets which belong to the charity. Current values are, also, important for charities as the trustees must ensure that the assets are fully insured.

A paper by a group of researchers ('Charity accounting standards:Issues from charity researchers', compiled by the NCVO) states:

> 'We know very little about the value . . . of the assets held by the charity sector, and yet the proper application of assets is probably the longest-standing area of public concern about charities . . . . In some cases, valuable assets are held for years and carried in the accounts at nominal value, or even no value. A more accurate accounting of their true worth would paint a wholly different picture of the charitable sector, and the standards of its asset management. It is of critical importance that charity accounting standards make a contribution to the process of making the value . . . of charity assets transparent. Moreover, if charity trustees were themselves more aware of the worth of the assets, which it is their responsibility to manage, they might be more conscientious.'

Paragraph 1(2) of Sch 7 to the 1985 Act requires the difference between the book amount and the market value of land and buildings to be stated, if it is of such significance that, in the opinion of the trustees, the attention of members ought to to be drawn to it. Charities which are not bound by that Act are not required to comply and frequently do not. Neither, for that matter, do some charitable companies (see chapter **5**, page 128). This is chiefly because the cost of regular revaluations is prohibitive and not the best use of charitable funds. Where there are donor-imposed restrictions, such that the assets must be held in perpetuity, little need is seen for current values. Nonetheless, it might be considered necessary, were the accounts to give a true and fair view, that some indication of current values be given.

16.2.6 Letters of representation

SAS 440.1 of SAS 440 *Management representations* states that:

> 'Auditors should obtain written confirmation of appropriate representations from management before their report is issued'.

And, SAS 440.3 states:

> 'Auditors should obtain written confirmation of representations from management on matters material to the financial statements when those representations are critical to obtaining sufficient appropriate audit evidence'.

Paragraphs 5 and 6 of SAS 440 state that 'management' includes 'directors', which, in turn, means ' . . . or trustees of other forms of entity'. Accordingly, management representations are to be obtained for all audits.

Examples of specific issues which may be included in a management representation letter are:

(a) the extent of receipt of donated assets and services and their measurement and disclosure;
(b) confirmation of grants payable and that they are *intra vires*;
(c) confirmation that income or funds are correctly applied in accordance with the terms of the grants or loan;
(d) the basis, consistency and fairness of the apportionment of administration and fundraising expenses;
(e) the rationale for accounting for the charity as a going concern in circumstances where future donations finance current commitments; and
(f) confirmation that there have been no arrangements, transactions or agreements with trustees and their 'connected persons', or that, if there are any, they are fully disclosed in the accounts.

16.2.7 Review of the final accounts

SAS 470.1 of SAS 470 *Overall review of financial statements* states:

> 'Auditors should carry out such a review of the financial statements as is sufficient, in conjunction with the conclusions drawn from the other audit evidence obtained, to give them a reasonable basis for their opinion on the financial statements'.

Paragraph 46 of AG 301 points out that normal analytical review procedures, as applied to a commercial organisation, may need to be adapted in the case of a charity. It suggests that particular consideration be given to the relationship between appeals income and related expenses, and investments and income therefrom. Where applicable, a comparison of the funds raised by branches from one period to the next should be carried out and explanations received for significant variances. The auditors should consider whether the accounting policies are:

(a) appropriate to the activities, constitution and objectives of the charity;
(b) consistently applied; and
(c) adequately disclosed and fairly present the state of affairs and result for the year.

Consideration should, also, be given to the basis of:

(a) recognition of, and accounting for, income and expenses;
(b) presentation of income from fundraising activities (i.e., net or gross?);
(c) the apportionment of administration and fundraising expenses; and
(d) the capitalisation and depreciation of fixed assets.

In reviewing the accounts to ensure compliance with statutory and other requirements, the auditor may employ a checklist, or other *aide-mémoire.* A checklist for charities based on the revised SORP and the Regulations is provided in Appendix 1.

16.3 Reporting

As regards the form and content of auditors' reports, AG 301 needs to be read in conjunction with SAS 600 *Auditors' reports on financial statements.* The persons, or body, to whom, or to which, the report should be addressed and the statutory, or other, provisions under which the audit will have been conducted, will depend on the charity's constitution.

Paragraph 18 of SAS 600 states that the auditors' report on the accounts of a charitable company should be addressed to 'the members' (normally the shareholders) because the audit is undertaken on their behalf. The trustees should be clear who their members (i.e., as such companies will be limited by guarantee – the guarantors) are as, apart from other statutory rights, they must be given the full accounts. This might be particularly important where charities use the label 'members' more generally, for example to describe volunteers and supporters of the charity's work.

Auditors' reports on the accounts of other types of charity should be addressed to the appropriate person(s), as defined by statute, or by the terms of the engagement.

Paragraph 38 states that the auditors' report should be expressed in the context of the particular accounting requirements applicable to the accounts concerned and will normally include, in addition to that on the view given by the accounts, an opinion on whether or not those requirements have been satisfied. Thus, where appropriate, the auditors will state that the accounts have been properly prepared in accordance with the 1985 Act, relevant Acts relating to friendly societies and industrial and provident societies or to the specific Act of Parliament. Where the charity is not incorporated under an Act of Parliament, reference would normally be made to the trust deed, or other constitutional document, under which the accounts have been prepared, and audited.

For a charity incorporated under the Companies Acts, the report provided by Example 16.1 British Diabetic Association is typical.

Example 16.1 British Diabetic Association
Report of the auditors to the members (31 December 1993):

We have audited the financial statements on page 3 to 17 which have been prepared under the accounting policies set out on page 10.

Respective Responsibilities of Executive Council and Auditors

As described on page 17 the Executive Council are responsible for the preparation of financial statements. It is our responsibility to form an independent opinion, based on our audit, on those statements and report our opinion to you.

Basis of opinion

We conducted our audit in accordance with Auditing Standards issued by the Auditing Practices Board. An audit includes examination, on a test basis, of evidence relevant to the amounts and disclosures in the financial statements. It also includes an assessment of the significant estimates and judgements made by the Executive Council in the preparation of the financial statements, and of whether the accounting policies are appropriate to the Association's circumstances, consistently applied and adequately disclosed.

We planned and performed our audit so as to obtain all the information and explanations which we consider necessary in order to provide us with sufficient evidence to give reasonable assurance that the financial statements are free from material misstatement, whether caused by fraud or other irregularity or error. In confirming our opinion we also evaluated the overall adequacy of the presentation of information in the financial statements.

Opinion

In our opinion the financial statements give true and fair view of the state of affairs of the Association and the group as at 31 December 1993 and of the group surplus and cash flows for the year then ended and have been properly prepared in accordance with the Companies Act 1985.

Kidsons Impey
Registered Auditors
Chartered Accountants

London
7 May 1994

Where such a charity is, also, a housing association, reference will need to be made both to the 1985 Act and to the statutory requirements under which such associations also report – see Example 16.2 BEN-Motor & Allied Trades Benevolent Fund.

Example 16.2 BEN-Motor & Allied Trades Benevolent Fund
Auditors' report to the members (31 March 1994):

We have audited the financial statements on pages 5 to 19 which have been prepared on the basis of the accounting policies set out on page 9.

Respective responsibilities of directors and auditors

As described on page 1 the trustees are responsible for the preparation of financial statements. It is our responsibility to form an independent opinion, based on our audit, on those statements and to report our opinion to you.

Basis of opinion

We conducted our audit in accordance with Auditing Standards issued by the Auditing Practices Board. An audit includes examination, on a test basis, of evidence relevant to the amounts and disclosures in the financial statements. It also includes an assessment of the significant estimates and judgements made by the trustees in the preparation of the financial statements, and of whether the accounting policies are appropriate to the Fund's circumstances, consistently applied and adequately disclosed.

We planned and performed our audit so as to obtain all the information and explanations which we considered necessary in order to provide us with sufficient evidence to give reasonable assurance that the financial statements are free from material misstatement, whether caused by fraud or other irregularity or error. In forming our opinion we also evaluated the overall adequacy of the presentation of information in the financial statements.

Opinion

In our opinion the financial statements give a true and fair view of the state of the Fund's affairs as at 31 March 1994 and of its surplus for the year then ended and have been properly prepared in accordance with the Companies Act 1985 and the Registered Housing Associations (Accounting Requirements) Order 1992.

BDO Binder Hamlyn
Chartered Accountants
Registered Auditors

20 Old Bailey
London EC4M 7BH
25 August 1994

Both reports are addressed to *the members*, yet that of Example 16.3 Childline (a charitable company) is addressed to *the trustees*.

Example 16.3 Childline
Auditors' report to the trustees (31 March 1994):

We have audited the accounts in accordance with Auditing Standards.

Respective responsibilities of trustees and auditors

As described in the trustees' report, the trustees are responsible for the preparation of the accounts. It is our responsibility as auditors to form an independent opinion, based on our audit, on those accounts and to report our opinion to you.

Basis of opinion

We conducted our audit in accordance with Auditing Standards issued by the Auditing Practices Board. An audit includes examination, on a test basis, of evidence relevant to the amounts and disclosures in the accounts. It also includes an assessment of the significant estimates and judgements made by the trustees in the preparation of the accounts and of whether the accounting policies are appropriate to the charity's circumstances, consistently applied and adequately disclosed.

We planned and performed our audit so as to obtain all the information and explanations that we considered necessary in order to provide us with sufficient evidence to give reasonable assurance that the accounts are free from material misstatement, whether caused by fraud or other irregularity or error. In forming our opinion we also evaluated the overall adequacy of the presentation of the information in the accounts.

Opinion

In our opinion the accounts give a true and fair view of the state of the charity's affairs as at 31 March 1994 and of its surplus and cash flow for the year ended at that date.

In our opinion the charity is entitled to the exemption from preparing group accounts conferred by section 248 of the Companies Act 1985.

MOORES ROWLAND
Chartered Accounts, Registered Auditors, London

Note 2: Status of the company:

The company is limited by guarantee and has no share capital. The liability of each member in the event of winding up is limited to £1.

The company has obtained the consent of the Registrar of Companies to be exempt from the requirement to use the word 'Limited' in its name.

Example 16.4 The National Trust provides an example of an auditors' report, which is addressed to *the Council*, for a charity incorporated by special Act of Parliament.

Example 16.4 The National Trust
Auditors' report to the Council (28 February 1994):

We have audited the accounts on pages 34 to 47 which have been prepared under the accounting policies permitted by the National Trust Act 1971, and which are set out on pages 38 and 39.

RESPECTIVE RESPONSIBILITIES OF THE COUNCIL AND AUDITORS

As described above, the Council is responsible for the preparation of accounts. It is our responsibility to form an independent opinion, based on our audit, on those accounts and to report our opinion to you.

BASIS OF OPINION

We conducted an audit in accordance with Auditing Standards issued by the Auditing Practices Board. An audit includes examination, on a test basis, of evidence relevant to the amounts and disclosures in the accounts. It also includes an assessment of the significant estimates and judgements made by the Council in the preparation of the accounts, and of whether the accounting policies are appropriate to The National Trust's circumstances, consistently applied and adequately disclosed.

We planned and performed our audit so as to obtain all the information and explanations which we considered necessary in order to provide us with sufficient evidence to give reasonable assurance that the accounts are free from material misstatement, whether caused by fraud or other irregularity or error. In forming our opinion we also evaluated the overall adequacy of the presentation of information in the accounts.

OPINION

In our opinion the accounts give a true and fair view of the state of The National Trust's affairs at 28 February 1994 and of its income and expenditure and cash flows for the fourteen months then ended and have been properly prepared in accordance with the provisions of The National Trust Act 1971 and the Charities Act 1960.

Price Waterhouse,
Chartered Accountants
and Registered Auditors
30 June 1994

31 Great George Street, Bristol, BS1 5QD

Example 16.5 British Red Cross Society and Example 16.6 Soldiers' Sailors' & Airmen's Families Association provide examples of reports for charities incorporated by Royal Charter. Both reports are addressed to *the Council* and, in the latter example, reference is made to the 'engagement letter of 9th May 1989'.

Example 16.5 British Red Cross Society
Report of the auditors to the Council (31 December 1993):

We have audited the financial statements on pages 10 to 20 which have been prepared on the basis of the accounting policies set out on page 13.

Respective Responsibilities of the Trustees & Auditors

As described on pages 3 and 4, the Trustees require the Director General to prepare the financial statements for submission to the Finance Committee. It is our responsibility to form an independent opinion, based on our audit, on those statements and to report our opinion to you.

Basis of Opinion

We conducted our audit in accordance with Auditing Standards issued by the Auditing Practices Board. An audit includes examination, on a test basis, of evidence relevant to the amounts and disclosures in the financial statements. It also includes an assessment of the significant estimates and judgements made by the Trustees in the preparation of the financial statements, and of whether the accounting policies are appropriate to the charity's circumstances, consistently applied and adequately disclosed.

We planned and performed our audit so as to obtain all the information and explanations which we considered necessary in order to provide us with sufficient evidence to give reasonable assurance that the financial statements are free from material misstatement, whether caused by fraud or other irregularity or error. In forming our opinion we also evaluated the overall adequacy of the presentation of information in the financial statements.

Opinion

In our opinion the financial statements give a true and fair view of the state of the affairs of the Society's Central Funds as at 31 December 1993 and of its results for the year then ended and have been properly prepared in accordance with the requirements of the Royal Charter of Incorporation dated 3 September 1908 and supplementary Charters.

[signed]

20 Old Bailey
London EC4M 7BH
26th April 1994

BDO Binder Hamlyn
Chartered Accountants
Registered Auditors

Example 16.6 Soldiers' Sailors' & Airmen's Families Association Report of the auditors to the Council (31 December 1993):

We have audited the financial statements on pages 3 to 10 which have been prepared following the accounting policies set out on page 6.

Respective responsibilities of the Council and auditors

As described on page 11 the Council are responsible for the preparation of the financial statements. It is our responsibility to form an independent opinion based on our audit of those statements and to report our opinion. The accounts of branches included in the financial statements have been dealt with by the auditors to the individual branches.

Basis of Opinion

We conducted our audit in accordance with auditing standards issued by the Auditing Practices Board. All audit includes examination, on a test basis, of evidence relevant to the amounts and disclosures in the financial statements. It also includes an assessment of the significant estimates and judgements made by the Council in the preparation of the financial statements and of whether the accounting policies are appropriate to the charity's circumstances, consistently applied and adequately disclosed.

We planned and performed our audit so as to obtain all the information and explanations which we considered necessary in order to provide us with sufficient evidence to give reasonable assurance the financial statements are free from material misstatement, whether caused by fraud or other irregularity or error. In forming our opinion, we also evaluated the overall adequacy of the presentation of information in the financial statements.

Opinion

In our opinion, the financial statements give a true and fair view of the state of the charity's affairs as at 31 December 1993 and of its financial activities for the year then ended and have been properly prepared in accordance with the rules set forth in the schedule to the Royal Charter of Incorporation dated 25 January 1926, as amended by the supplemental Royal Charters, the regulations as currently adopted by the Association and our engagement letter of 9 May 1989.

71 Mark Lane
London
EC3R 7RD

Drury Thurgood & Co
Chartered Accountants
Registered Auditors

9 June 1993

Where a charity is not incorporated under an Act of Parliament, para 70 of AG 301 recommends that reference should normally be made to the trust deed, or other constitutional document, under which the accounts have been prepared. A review of auditors' reports of charities' accounts reveals that reference to the trust deed is seldom made. Some auditors, however, refer to the 1960 Act – see, for example, Example 16.4 The National Trust and Example 16.7 BLESMA.

Example 16.7 BLESMA
Report of the registered auditor (31 December 1993):

We have audited the financial statements on pages 11 to 20 which have been prepared under the accounting policies on pages 15 and 16.

Respective Responsibilities of Trustees and Auditors.

As described on page 9 the trustees are responsible for the preparation of the Association's financial statements. It is our responsibility to form an independent opinion, based on our audit, on those financial statements and to report our opinion to you.

Basis of Opinion

We conducted our audit in accordance with Auditing Standards issued by the Auditing Practices Board. An audit includes examination, on a test basis, of evidence relevant to the amounts and disclosures in the financial statements. It also includes an assessment of the significant estimates and judgements made in the preparation of the financial statements, and of whether the accounting policies are appropriate to the Association's circumstances, consistently applied and adequately disclosed.

We planned and performed our audit so as to obtain all the information and explanations which we considered necessary in order to provide us with sufficient evidence to give reasonable assurance that the financial statements are free from material misstatement, whether caused by fraud or other irregularity or error. In forming our opinion we also evaluated the overall adequacy of the presentation of the information in the financial statements.

Unqualified Opinion

In our opinion the financial statements give a true and fair view of the state of the Association's affairs as at 31 December 1993 and of the financial activities and cash flows for the year then ended and have been properly prepared in accordance with the Charities Act 1960.

Clark Whitehill
Chartered Accountants
and Registered Auditors

24 March 1994

For charities which are not incorporated under the 1985 Act, the different form of words employed by auditors suggests that more up-to-date guidance from the APB is needed.

Note 1 to para 71 of AG 301 states that:

> 'Whether the auditor should report on the net surplus/deficit or income and expenditure will depend on the statutory or constitutional provisions under which he is reporting. For example, if reporting under the Companies Acts, then Section 56(2)(b) of the 1967 Act applies and the income and expenditure account should disclose a net surplus or deficit, on which the auditor should express an opinion. However, under the Friendly and Industrial and Provident Societies Act 1974, the auditors' opinion would be on the income and expenditure.'

(While the statutory references require updating, the broad principles should remain the same.)

As regards charitable companies, Example 16.8 NCVO uses 'income and expenditure', but the narrative in that account is 'net surplus/(deficit)'. The report does not refer to the investment gains, the statement for which is positioned immediately after that account. Conversely, Example 16.9 Guide Dogs for the Blind Association uses the description 'surplus' (being the relevant narrative), but does refer to gains on the realisation of investments, the statement for which is similarly positioned.

Example 16.8 NCVO
Auditors' report to the members (part) (31 March 1993):

Opinion

In our opinion the financial statements give a true and fair view of the state of the company's affairs as at 31 March 1993 and of its income and expenditure for the year then ended and have been properly prepared in accordance with the Companies Act 1985.

Touche Ross & Co
Chartered Accountants and Registered Auditors
12 October 1993

Example 16.9 Guide Dogs for the Blind Association
Report of the auditors to the members (part) (31 December 1993):

Unqualified opinion

In our opinion the financial statements give a true and fair view of the state of the Association's affairs as at 31 December 1993 and of the surplus and gains on realisation of investments for the year ended on that date and have been properly prepared in accordance with the Companies Act 1985.

Clark Whitehill

London
29 March 1994

Chartered Accountants and
Registered Auditor

The auditors' report of Example 16.10 Action Research refers to the 'excess of income over expenditure', yet the narrative in that account is 'surplus/deficit'.

Example 16.10 Action Research
Report of the auditors to the members (31 October 1993):

We have audited the financial statements on pages 23 to 31.

RESPECTIVE RESPONSIBILITIES OF DIRECTORS & AUDITORS

As described on page 22, the Company's directors are responsible for the preparation of financial statements. It is our responsibility to form an independent opinion, based on our audit, on those financial statements and to report our opinion to you.

BASIS OF OPINION

We conducted our audit in accordance with Auditing Standards issued by the Auditing Practices Board, except that the scope of our work was limited as explained below.

An audit includes examination, on a test basis, of evidence relevant to the amounts and disclosures in the financial statements. It also includes an assessment of the significant estimates and judgements made by the directors in the preparation of the financial statements, and of whether the accounting policies are appropriate to the Company's circumstances, consistently applied and adequately disclosed.

We planned our audit so as to obtain all the information and explanations which we considered necessary in order to provide us with sufficient evidence to give reasonable assurance that the financial statements are free from material misstatement, whether caused by fraud or other irregularity or error. However, in common with other charities of similar size and organisation, the evidence available to us was limited because £1,563,378 of the Company's recorded income comprises of income from regional organisations which cannot be fully controlled until they are entered in the accounting records and there was no system of control over which we could rely for the purposes of our audit. There were no other satisfactory audit procedures that we could adopt to confirm that voluntary income was properly recorded.

In forming our opinion we also evaluated the overall adequacy of the presentation of information in the financial statements.

Except for any adjustments that might have been found to be necessary had we been able to obtain sufficient evidence concerning voluntary donations, in our opinion the financial statements give a true and fair view of the state of the Company's affairs as at 31 October 1993 and of its excess of income over expenditure for the year then ended and have been properly prepared in accordance with the Companies Act 1985.

KPMG Peat Marwick
Chartered accountants
Registered auditors
6 June 1994

Of the charities preparing a SOFA (see chapter **4**, page 95), Example 16.7 BLESMA uses the term 'financial activities', whereas Example 16.11 Save The Children Fund uses 'results', as does OXFAM.

Example 16.11 Save The Children Fund
Auditors' report to the members (part) (31 March 1994):

Opinion

In our opinion the financial statements give a true and fair view of the state of affairs of the Fund and of the group as at 31 March 1994 and of its results for the year then ended and have been properly prepared in accordance with the Companies Act 1985.

BDO BINDER HAMLYN
Chartered Accountants
Registered Auditors
20 Old Bailey
London
EC4M 7BH — 28 July 1994

Example 16.6 Soldiers' Sailors' & Airmen's Families Association uses the term 'financial activities', yet continues to prepare an income and expenditure account.

A survey of auditors' reports found some interesting features.

Although applicable, the form of report required by SAS 600 has not been employed by the auditors of Example 16.12 Cinema & Television Benevolent Fund. And, although a charitable company, that of Example 16.3 Childline does not refer to the 1985 Act.

16.12 Cinema & Television Benevolent Fund
Auditors' report to the members (31 March 1994):

We have audited the accounts on Pages 24 to 30 in accordance with Auditing Standards.

In our opinion the Accounts give a true and fair view of the state of affairs of the Cinema and Television Benevolent Fund at 31 March 1994 and of the results and cash flows for the year then ended.

KPMG Peat Marwick
Chartered Accountants
Registered Auditors

London
8 June 1994

Although there is no requirement to do so, most auditors refer to the accounting convention and policies which have been followed in preparing the accounts. The auditors' report of Example 16.10 Action Research, however, does not.

And, where the accounts, or accompanying information, do not include an adequate description of the directors' relevant responsibilities, Auditing Standard 600.3 requires the auditors' report to include such a

Example 16.13 Royal National Lifeboat Institution
Auditors' report to the committee of management (part) (31 December 1993):

> We have audited the accounts on pages 32 to 36 which have been prepared under the accounting policies set out on page 34.
>
> **Responsibilities of Executive Committee**
> The Charter, the Charities Act 1960 and the Charities (Statement of Account) Regulations 1960 require the Executive Committee to prepare accounts for each financial year. In preparing these accounts, the Executive Committee are encouraged to follow the recommendations outlined in Statement of Recommended Practice No. 2, 'Accounting by Charities' (issued by the Accounting Standards Committee in 1988).
>
> The Executive Committee consider that in preparing these accounts, they have used appropriate accounting policies, consistently applied and supported by reasonable and prudent judgements and estimates.
>
> The Executive Committee are responsible for keeping proper accounting records to enable them to ensure that the accounts comply with the Charities Act 1960 and the Charities (Statement of Account) Regulations 1960. They are also responsible for safeguarding the assets of the Institution and hence for taking reasonable steps for the prevention and detection of fraud and other irregularities.
>
> **Responsibilities of auditors**
> It is our responsibility to form an independent opinion, based on our audit, on those accounts and to report our opinion to you.
>
> **Opinion**
> In our opinion the accounts give a true and fair view of the state of the Institution's affairs at 31 December 1993 and of its income and expenditure and cash flows for the year then ended and have been properly prepared in accordance with the provisions of the Charities Act 1960.
>
> **Price Waterhouse** 24 March 1994
> Chartered Accountants
> and Registered Auditors
> Southampton

description of them. Example 16.13 Royal National Lifeboat Institution's auditors' report is such an example.

The opinion paragraph of the auditors' report of Example 16.14 Nuffield Nursing Homes Trust refers to the accounts having been properly prepared in accordance with '*the provisions of* the Companies Act 1985'.

Example 16.14 Nuffield Nursing Homes Trust
Report of the auditors (part) (31 December 1993):

> Opinion
>
> In our opinion the financial statements give a true and fair view of the state of affairs of the Trust and the group at 31 December 1993 and of the surplus and income on accumulated fund of the group for the year then ended and have been properly prepared in accordance with the provisions of the Companies Act 1985.
>
> GRANT THORNTON
> REGISTERED AUDITORS
> CHARTERED ACCOUNTANTS
> LONDON
> 30th March 1994

And, that of Example 16.7 BLESMA uses 'the report of the *registered auditor*' as part of its title.

16.3.1 Qualifications in auditors' reports

Completeness of income

The most common problem facing auditors, particularly those of smaller charities, will be the verification of the completeness of income from voluntary donations. An analogy may be drawn with many small commercial organisations regarding the verification of the completeness of income from cash sales. More often than not, formal control over cash receipts will be absent, with the consequential result that the auditors may be unable to determine whether or not all income to which the charity is entitled has been properly recorded in the accounting records. In these circumstances, and where they are unable to carry out reasonable alternative procedures to obtain sufficient audit evidence to support an unqualified opinion, the auditors should qualify their report. Example 8 of Appendix 2 to SAS 600 illustrates the form of wording which will satisfy the relevant Auditing Standard. An example is provided by Example 16.10 Action Research. Although withdrawn by SAS 600, the

Example 16.15 Friends of the Lake District
Report of the auditors to the members (31 December 1993):

We have audited the financial statements on pages 3 & 4 which have been prepared under the historical cost convention and the accounting policies set out on page 4.

RESPECTIVE RESPONSIBILITIES OF THE COMMITTEE AND AUDITORS

As described above the committee are responsible for the preparation of financial statements. It is our responsibility to form an independent opinion, based on our audit, on those statements and to report our opinion to you.

BASIS OF OPINION

We conducted our audit in accordance with Auditing Standards issued by the Auditing Practices Board. An audit includes examination, on a test basis, of evidence relevant to the amounts and disclosures in the financial statements. It also includes an assessment of the significant estimates and judgements made by the committee in the preparation of the financial statements, and whether the accounting policies are appropriate to the association's circumstances, consistently applied and adequately disclosed.

We planned and performed our audit so as to obtain all the information and explanations which we considered necessary in order to provide us with sufficient evidence to give reasonable assurance that the financial statements are free from material mis-statement, whether caused by fraud or other irregularity or error. In forming our opinion we also evaluated the overall adequacy of the presentation of information in the financial statements.

OPINION

This charity in common with many other similar organisations derives a substantial proportion of its income from voluntary donations which cannot be fully controlled until they are entered in the accounting records and therefore are not susceptible to independent audit verification.

Subject to the above, in our opinion the financial statements give a true and fair view of the state of the association's affairs at 31 December 1993 and of its surplus for the year then ended.

R.F. MILLER & CO
CHARTERED ACCOUNTANTS
REGISTERED AUDITORS
8 JUNE 1994 102 DUKE STREE, BARROW-IN-FURNESS

auditors of Example 16.15 Friends of the Lake District continue to use the 'subject to' form of qualification.

Reliance on other auditors

Some charities have branches (or similar) the results, assets and liabilities of which may be included in the charity's accounts. Sometimes these branches are audited by local auditors. Example 16.6 Soldiers' Sailors' & Airmen's Families Association is one such charity. The auditors make reference, within the 'respective responsibilities' section of their report, to the fact that 'the accounts of branches . . . have been dealt with by the auditors to the individual branches'.

Example 16.16 Leonard Cheshire Foundation (part)
Report of the auditors (30 September 1993):

> We have audited the financial statements from pages 6 to 15 which have been prepared under the historical cost convention and the accounting policies set out in Note 1. The financial statements have been compiled from the records of the Central Administration and two Foundation Homes which have been audited by us, and from adequate returns received from 107 Local Committees in the United Kingdom, representing Foundation Homes and Care At Home Services, not visited by us but subject to local audit.
>
> **Opinion**
>
> In our opinion the financial statements give a true and fair view of the state of affairs of The Foundation as at 30 September 1993 and of the excess of income over expenditure for the year then ended and have been properly prepared in accordance with the Companies Act 1985.
>
> Moore Stephens
> St Paul's House
> Warwick Lane
> London EC4P 4BN
>
> Chartered Accountants
> Registered Auditors
> 18 April 1994

This example is not unique. The auditors of Example 16.16 Leonard Cheshire Foundation take a somewhat similar view. In this case, however, the reference is made, not within but, before the section dealing with the respective responsibilities.

But should there be any reference at all? Are these circumstances not analogous to the group situation where some subsidiaries may be audited by auditors other than the primary auditor? It is the primary auditor who is ultimately responsible for the group accounts. As paras 22 and 23 of SAS 510 *The relationship of principal auditors to others* state:

> 'When the principal auditors are satisfied that the work of the other auditors is adequate for the purposes of their audit, no reference to the other auditors is made in the principal auditors' report'.

And:

> 'The principal auditors have sole responsibility for their audit opinion and a reference to the other auditors in the principal auditors' report may be misunderstood and interpreted as a qualification of their opinion or a division of responsibility, neither of which is appropriate'.

The SAS extends the scope of guidance previously set out in AG 415 to circumstances other than those involving group accounts.

Depreciation and the writing off of fixed assets

As reported in chapter **8** (see page 224), some charities no longer depreciate their freehold buildings. As also reported, this is a practice which has attracted a mixed reception from auditors. Neither Example 8.12 Church Missionary Society, nor Example 8.13 SENSE, depreciate their freehold buildings with the latter, but not the former, providing the reason. Neither charity's accounts attracted a qualification. Conversely, Church Lads' and Church Girls' Brigade used not to depreciate its buildings (it changed its policy in its 1993 accounts), yet did attract a qualification. Example 8.2 Cystic Fibrosis Research Trust (see chapter **8**, page 212) does not provide depreciation on its freehold property, presumably on the basis of the wording given in note 9 to its 1994 accounts, being that 'in the opinion of the Trustees the market value of the property is considerably in excess of its book value'. (Its auditors' report was unqualified.) Paragraph 9 of SSAP 12 (Revised), however, states that:

> 'It is not appropriate to omit charging for the depreciation of an asset on the grounds that its current market value is greater than its net book amount . . . '.

Non-consolidation of non-charitable trading subsidiaries

This issue is discussed in depth in chapter **13** (see page 340).

Going concern

In circumstances where charities without significant endowments or accumulated funds are dependent on future income to finance future (or, indeed, current) commitments arising from the continuation of their activities, AG 301 prompts auditors to question whether the going concern basis of accounting is appropriate.

SAS 130 *The going concern basis in financial statements*, which applies to the audit of accounts for accounting periods ending on or after 30 June 1995 (although earlier adoption is encouraged), requires auditors to take an active, rather than a passive, approach. Auditing Standard 130.2 requires them to assess the adequacy of the means by which the directors have satisfied themselves that it is appropriate for them to adopt the going concern basis in preparing the accounts. To achieve this, the auditors should 'make enquiries of the directors and examine appropriate available financial information and . . . plan and perform procedures specifically designed to identify any material matters which could indicate concern about the entity's ability to continue as a going concern'.

Paragraph 67 of AG 301 suggests that the auditors should take account of the amount of, and trends in, income and expenditure since the year end, any forecasts and management representations as to future income and expenditure and, where relevant, the market value of the charity's tangible assets. Experience of past appeals may, also, be a persuasive factor.

Paragraph 24 of SAS 130 suggests, however, that the entity's (and auditors') procedures may not always need to be elaborate in order to provide sufficient appropriate audit evidence, and that this is particularly likely to be the case in respect of entities with uncomplicated circumstances, e.g., smaller entities. Thus, apart from the accounting records required by law, the directors might not, as a matter of course, prepare periodic cash flow and other budgets, forecasts or other management accounts information.

However, a lack of more elaborate procedures may not apply to smaller charities. In their 1993 Annual Report, the Commissioners reported that few charities looked at in that year had prepared spending plans and budgets at the beginning of their accounting year. 'Trustees can often be optimistic about finance, but optimism is no substitute for realistic planning, including contingency planning, and regular monitoring of the actual financial situation against there plans. *Basic financial planning is essential for even the smallest of charities.*' More charities were being identified as potentially insolvent with risks both to charitable funds and to the trustees themselves . . . : 'sound budgeting and cash flow management can both prevent such situations arising and help to protect trustees from the consequences of insolvency'.

One fund-seeking charity is Example 16.17 British Heart Foundation. The position regarding future commitments is explained, not in the audited accounts, but in the report of the Council. Being conscious of the need to make adequate provision for future obligations, the Council has set up a specific fund the objective of which is to meet, in full, the Foundation's commitment to chairholders. This fund is not yet at a level such that these future commitments may be satisfied. The Council

16.17 British Heart Foundation
Report of the Council (part) (31 March 1994):

Chairs Maintenance Fund

The Foundation regards the support for its Chairs of Cardiovascular Medicine as the keystone of its research funding. These centres of medical excellence at universities and hospitals provide a secure base on which to build additional research initiatives and almost all chairholders are, in fact, assisted by means of other BHF grants. They must therefore be supported consistently and enthusiastically by the Foundation, without producing any concerns about the Foundation's ability to continue funding. In order to demonstrate this commitment and ensure that funds will be available whatever the future economic climate for fundraising, the Council set up a Chairs Maintenance Fund in the Foundation's Balance Sheet. The fund is represented by an investment portfolio the ultimate objective of which is to meet in full the Foundation's commitment to the 25 chairholders. At 31 March 1994 an actuarial valuation of the obligations to existing chairholders came to £72.4m so that the Foundation's investments at that date, at actuaries current valuation, would only have met 58 per cent of the liability. Actuaries report further that a transfer of £2.5m in each of the next 15 years will see the fund fully financed to the extent of its current commitments.

Note 9: Chairs Maintenance Fund:

The Foundation finances a number of chairs of cardiovascular medicine at universities and teaching hospitals, which are awarded for a varying number of years. Independent actuaries have assessed the Foundation's commitments at 31 March 1994 to be £72,363,000 (1993 £69,882,000).

	1994	*1993*
	£000	*£000*
At 1 April 1993	45,693	*35,729*
Transfer from Income and Expenditure Account	3,250	*3,250*
	48,943	*38,979*
Change in market value during the year	5,207	*6,714*
At 31 March 1994	54,150	*45,693*

It is the intention, as and when resources allow, to build up the fund of investments so as eventually to provide funding to meet, in full, the Foundation's commitments.

The Chairs Maintenance Fund is represented by investments at market value (note 12).

reports that 'At 31 March 1994 an actuarial valuation of the obligations to existing chairholders came to £72.4m so that the Foundation's investments at that date, at actuaries current valuation, would only have met 58% of the liability'.

While there is some narrative in note 9, a case may be made for including, in that note, some of the detail which appears in the report of the Council. This could be supported by further details (e.g., principal assumptions used) of the actuarial valuation. After all, the liability is not contingent, it is actual.

Although a preference may be made for it to be given in a separate note, rather than within the accounting policies, the trustees of Example 16.18 War on Want provide a clear statement of the position regarding future funding.

Example 16.18 War on Want
Note 1: Accounting policies (part) (31 March 1994):

> Future funding
>
> The majority of the company's income is from grants which are subject to annual review and are not guaranteed for future periods. Furthermore, certain granting bodies reserve the right to clawback grants which have been underspent and to withdraw any grant by giving an agreed period of notice. No allowance is made in these financial statements for any costs attributable to terminating contractual arrangements in the event of a significant withdrawal of funds.

Other uncertainties

Example 16.19 National Federation of Community Organisations includes, within debtors, an amount due from its trading subsidiary. According to the note, the recoverability of the debt is currently being negotiated with that company's directors and, until those negotiations are concluded, 'the recoverability of the debt in the foreseeable future is uncertain'.

Example 16.19 National Federation of Community Organisations Note 5: Debtors (31 March 1994):

	1994	*1993*
	£	*£*
Trade Debtors	2,757	*3,137*
Amounts owed by subsidiary	34,115	*23,490*
Other Debtors	4,508	*4,630*
Prepayments	2,582	*9,852*
	43,962	*41,109*

The recovery of the amount owed by the subsidiary is at present being negotiated with the subsidiary's Directors. Until such time as these negotiations are concluded, the recoverability of the debt in the foreseeable future is uncertain.

The financial statements of the subsidiary at 31 March 1994 show the aggregate amount of its Capital and Reserves as being £42,085 deficit and its loss for that year was £3,492.

Auditors' report to the members (part):

Basis of Opinion

We conducted our audit in accordance with Auditing Standards issued by the Auditing Practices Board. An audit includes examination, on a test basis, of evidence relevant to the amounts and disclosures in the Financial Statements. It also includes an assessment of the significant estimates and judgements made by the Directors in the preparation of the Financial Statements, and of whether the accounting policies are appropriate to the charity's circumstances, consistently applied and adequately disclosed.

We planned and performed our audit so as to obtain all the information and explanations which we considered necessary in order to provide us with sufficient evidence to give reasonable assurance that the Financial Statements are free from material misstatement, whether caused by fraud or other irregularity or error. In forming our opinion we also evaluated the overall adequacy of the presentation of information in the Financial Statements.

Opinion

In our opinion the Financial Statements give a true and fair view of the state of the charity's affairs at 31 March 1994 and of its results for the year then ended and have been properly prepared in accordance with the provisions of Companies Act 1985, applicable to small companies.

Feltons
Registered Auditors
Chartered Accountants
12 Sheet Street
Windsor

17 June 1994

It is neither easy to see why a provision against the debt has not been made, nor why the auditors have not referred to this in their report, given that the amount of the debt, of £34,115, represents 36 per cent and 10 per cent of reported net assets and turnover respectively. SAS 600.6(b) states that:

> 'When an inherent uncertainty exists which
>
> (i) in the auditors' opinion is fundamental, and
> (ii) is adequately accounted for and disclosed in the financial statements, the auditors should include an explanatory paragraph referring to the fundamental uncertainty in the section of their report setting out the basis of their opinion.')

Chapter 17 – Smaller charities

17.1 Introduction

Many smaller charities are managed, and services provided, entirely by lay volunteers. More often than not, there are no professional resources, nor, if there were, would there be any, or enough, resources to pay for them.

Some of those who work with these charities took the view that the proposals of the ED were onerous and likened them to the use of a sledgehammer to crack a nut. One of the major concerns was the threshold, then of £25,000, for the preparation of accounts to a true and fair view standard and the burden which compliance with that would have imposed on those charities. It is understood that both the ASB and the eighth Deregulation Task Force raised the same concern.

It is clearly very important to strike a proper balance between the requirements for supervision and the need to minimise burdens. Accordingly, in August 1993, as part of the consultation process, an eighth Deregulation Task Force (additional to the seven business task forces) was established with the mission of examining the regulation of charities and voluntary organisations. (This Task Force considered a broad range of regulations and legislation, including the Charities Acts.) The Task Force published its report in July 1994. Some of the recommendations have been implemented by the Deregulation and Contracting Out Act 1994. Others have been implemented by statutory instrument (The Charities Act 1993 (Substitution of Sums) Order 1995 (SI 1995 No . . .*)).

Paragraph 13 of the revised charity SORP states that a charity is treated for accounting purposes in the 1993 Act as a small charity if it is:

(a) not a charitable company; and
(b) its gross income in a financial year does not exceed £100,000.

The Commissioners are preparing, as a companion to the revised SORP, a guide for the small charity, *Accounting for the smaller charity*, for those

* *This SI will be issued at the same time as that relating to the Regulations.*

circumstances where accounts are prepared on the receipts and payments basis. Charity trustees are afforded a certain degree of flexibility regarding preparation of the receipts and payments account. They may prepare the receipts and payments account and statement of assets and liabilities using this guide. Alternatively, they may use the pre-printed standard forms of accounts, which will be available from the Commissioners. It is understood that these will offer a ready-made form which complies with recommended practice for small charities.

17.2 The 1993 Act

17.2.1 Charities whose gross income does not exceed £1,000

Charities with gross income (see chapter **3**, page 50 for a definition) which does not exceed £1,000 and which have neither a permanent endowment nor the use or occupation of any land and are not required to register, must maintain proper accounting records, prepare (a simpler form of – see below) accounts and make those accounts available to the public on request.

Unless any requirement of law or trust deed has any provision to the contrary, there is no requirement for an audit or independent examination. There is, also, no duty to prepare a trustees' annual report or to submit the accounts to the Commissioners.

If the charity trustees do decide to register, they will be subject to the same requirements as in **17.2.2** below.

17.2.2 Charities whose gross income and total expenditure do not exceed £10,000

The Task Force introduced a new regulatory band – a *light touch* band – which had not been in existence before. It is for those charities which have gross income and total expenditure which do not exceed £10,000 in a financial year.

(A) Preparation of accounts

Charity trustees must keep proper accounting records and prepare accounts. The charity trustees may elect to prepare a simpler form of accounts ('an account and statement'), comprising:

(a) a receipts and payments account; and
(b) a statement of assets and liabilities,

rather than accounts (a statement of accounts) to a true and fair view standard.

The Commissioners are preparing, as a companion to the revised SORP, a guide for the smaller charity, for those circumstances where accounts are prepared on the receipts and payments basis (see above).

(B) Audit or independent examination?
Subject to any requirement of either law or of the Commissioners, or to any provision in the trust deed, charity trustees of these charities do not have to have their account and statement (or statement of accounts) audited or independently examined. This will allow many smaller charities, e.g., local lay-volunteer charities, which use treasurers who may have had little, or no, training and experience in accounting, but have diligently trained themselves in book-keeping, to continue to act for them.

(C) Trustees' annual report
The trustees' must prepare an annual report.

Regulations 10(1)(a),(c), (2) and (3) prescribe the information required by such charities.

Regulation 10(1)(a) requires, in addition to specifying the financial year, a brief summary of the charity's main activities and achievements during the year in relation to its objects.

And, reg 10(2) requires the following to be given:

(a) the name of the charity, as it appears in the register and any other name by which it makes itself known;
(b) the charity registration number and, if it is a charitable company, the company registration number;
(c) its principal address and, in the case of a charitable company, its registered office;
(d) a description of the trusts of the charity;
(e) the names of the charity trustees and any other person who, at any time during the financial year, was a trustee for, or of, the charity and of any person, or body, entitled to appoint a charity trustee of the charity;
(f) a description of the charity's organisational structure; and
(g) a description of any assets held by the charity, or by any charity trustee or other trustee for, or of, the charity on behalf of another charity, and particulars of any special arrangements made with

respect to such assets and of the objects of the charity on whose behalf the assets are held.

In the case of a particular charity or class of charities, or of a particular financial year of a charity or class of charities, reg 10(3) permits the Commissioners to dispense with the requirement, in para 2(e), to give the name of a trustee, where they are satisfied that its disclosure could lead to that person being placed in any personal danger.

Because there is no requirement for the charity trustees to submit their annual report to the Commissioners, such charities do not routinely engage in the surveillance regime. If the Commissioners request that report, however, the charity trustees must submit it within the prescribed time limit. Where that request is made before the end of seven months after a financial year to which that report relates, within ten months of the end of that financial year; in any other case, within three months of the date of the request. In either case, the Commissioners may, for any special reason, allow a longer period.

The charity trustees are required to keep, for at least six years from the end of the financial year to which a report relates, any annual report which they have not routinely submitted to the Commissioners.

(D) Annual return
These charities will have to prepare a simplified annual return.

17.2.3 Charities whose gross income does not exceed £100,000 (but whose gross income or total expenditure exceeds £10,000)

(A) Preparation of accounts
Such charities must keep proper accounting records. Where a charity's gross income in a financial year does not exceed £100,000, the charity trustees may, for that year, elect to prepare:

(a) a receipts and payments account; and
(b) a statement of assets and liabilities,

instead of a statement of accounts.

In circumstances where the charity is trading, committed to substantial expenditure or holding significant investments, preparation of true and fair view accounts is advised, even though a charity may need only to prepare accounts on a receipts and payments basis.

(B) Audit or independent examination?
To whatever standard the accounts are prepared, they must be independently examined, or audited. The accounts must be submitted to the Commissioners, together with the annual return.

(C) Trustees' annual report
For charities whose gross income or total expenditure exceeds £10,000 in a financial year, the annual report must, in addition to stating the financial year to which it relates, be a review of:

(a) all activities, including material transactions, significant developments and achievements, of the charity during that year in relation to its objects;
(b) any significant changes in those activities during the year;
(c) any important post balance sheet events; and
(d) any likely future developments in those activities.

The further information relating to the charity and its trustees and officers, as required by reg 10(2) and (3), is, also, required.

Unless they are excepted from registration with the Commissioners and have chosen not to register voluntarily, charitable companies must file an annual report and their own statutory accounts (prepared under the 1985 Act), if their gross income or total expenditure exceeds £10,000 or if they are requested to provide that information by the Commissioners.

(D) Annual return
These charities, if registered, will have to submit an annual return.

17.3 The revised charity SORP

Paragraphs 13 to 21 deal with small charities.

The charity trustees should prepare an annual report and, unless the governing instrument stipulates otherwise, an account of the charity's receipts and payments for the year, together with a statement of assets and liabilities.

A receipts and payments account does not purport to show a true and fair view of the charity's financial activities and state of affairs. SSAPs, FRSs etc. will, therefore, not generally be applicable. In summarising the financial information, para 17 states that the only fundamental accounting concept which should be 'assumed' is that of consistency.

Nonetheless, many of the explanations and recommendations in the SORP, while primarily applicable to the accounts of larger charities, will, also, apply to some degree where the receipts and payments basis is adopted. In particular, para 19 recommends that the charity's unrestricted funds are distinguished from any permanent endowment and other restricted funds. And, unless immaterial, restricted funds should be distinguished from each other.

Where a charity changes from preparing accounts on the receipts and payments basis to full accounts, or vice versa, the comparatives must be restated.

Chapter 18 – Income tax, corporation tax and capital taxes

18.1 Exemptions for charities

18.1.1 Introduction

Most categories of income enjoyed by a charity are exempt from tax; either because its sources of finance are outside the scope of tax completely, for example the receipt of legacies, or they are given specific exemption by s505 ICTA 1988. Specific exemption does not apply automatically and certain conditions must be met. The principal restrictions on exemption occur when a charity does not apply its income for charitable purposes and the circumstances in which this may apply are discussed below. The text of s505 ICTA 1988 is set out in Appendix 6. The exemptions from tax to which it refers apply equally to income tax and corporation tax. A charity may pay either of these, the determining factor between the two being the constitution of the charity.

18.1.2 Non-taxable sources of income

In general, legacies and donations are outside the scope of tax. The exceptions to this are:

(a) donations made under a deed of covenant which, because of their annual nature, come within the scope of Schedule D Case III;
(b) donations received under 'Gift Aid', also within the scope of Schedule D Case III; and
(c) income accrued since the date of death on a legacy.

These are granted specific exemption subject to the conditions applying in s505 ICTA 1988.

It should be noted that a donation which is received by a charity from another charity is actually, in principle, taxable under Schedule D Case III by virtue of s505(2) ICTA 1988. However again such payments may be exempted by that section provided the relevant conditions contained in s505 ICTA 1988 are satisfied.

18.1.3 Specific exemptions

Section 505 ICTA 1988 specifically exempts from tax the following sources of income:

(a) income in respect of rents and profits arising from land otherwise taxable under Schedules A and D, so far as it is employed for charitable purposes;
(b) income arising under Schedules C, D and F in respect of yearly interest, annuities, annual payments and dividends where the income forms part of the income of a charity or is applicable to charitable purposes only, and only so far as it is actually applied to charitable purposes;
(c) profits of a trade carried on by a charity if the profits are applied solely to the purposes of the charity and either:
   (i) the trade is exercised in the course of the actual carrying out of a primary purpose of the charity;
   or
   (ii) the work in connection with the trade is mainly carried by beneficiaries of the charity.

The statutory provisions only exempt yearly interest from tax. The Revenue therefore have produced an Extra-statutory Concession B9 which extends that exemption to other bank interest, to interest and dividends payable gross by a building society, and to profits from discounting transactions. There is no exemption from interest which is not yearly interest and which is not received from a bank. So, for example, it would be inadvisable for a charity to establish a funding arrangement with a trading subsidiary which provided for payment of short interest as this would be taxable in the hands of the charity.

In order for the exemptions under s505 ICTA 1988 to apply, a claim must be made within six years of the end of the tax year to which the claim relates. In practice a claim is required only for income which is received gross as the claim for repayment on dividends and other income received under deduction of tax is sufficient in itself to constitute a s505 claim. The claims should be made on form R68(1990) and submitted to Inland Revenue Claims Branch, Charity Division, St John's House, Merton Road, Bootle, Merseyside L69 9BB. Tax reclaims on dividends and taxed income can be made at any stage during a tax year provided the trustees submit the relevant vouchers to Claims Branch.

Charities can also arrange for certain types of income to be received gross in which case no reclaim is necessary. If a charity provides a bank or building society with proof of its charitable status, then interest will not be deducted from deposit accounts. Similarly, in the case of government securities, the Bank of England will pay interest to charities gross on submission by the charity of a registration slip issued by the Charity Commission.

Following FA 1993, in which the rate of tax credits on dividends was reduced from 25 per cent to 20 per cent, charities are entitled until 1996/97 to an additional reclaim of a proportion of the dividend. This additional reclaim must be claimed on form R68(TR) and the time limit for the claim is two years from the end of the charity's chargeable period in which the dividend is received.

Example 18.1

The fractions of a net dividend which charities will receive as an additional tax credit in the transitional period are:

1993/94	1/15
1994/95	1/20
1995/96	1/30
1996/97	1/60

For a net dividend received each year of £8,000 with an associated reclaimable tax credit of £2,000, a charity will be able to claim an additional tax credit as follows:

1993/94	1/15 × 8,000 = £533.33
1994/95	1/20 × 8,000 = £400.00
1995/96	1/30 × 8,000 = £266.67
1996/97	1/60 × 8,000 = £133.33

Finally it should be noted that no specific exemption applies for income received under Schedule D Case VI which will therefore be taxable on receipt by a charity. This would include, for example, a premium paid by a charity for underwriting a share issue.

Charitable purposes

Generally, if an application of funds is in pursuit of the charitable objects of a charity's constitution, then it is 'applied for charitable purposes'.

For exemption under s505 to apply the income or profits arising must be employed for charitable purposes. Using a charity's income for non-charitable purposes not only has serious consequences for taxation purposes, but may also be challenged by the Charity Commission. The Commissioners and the Inland Revenue have appropriate powers to inform each other when they learn of charitable funds being misapplied.

The question of whether or not income is applied for charitable purposes was considered in the case of *CIR* v *Helen Slater Charitable Trust Ltd* (1981 STC 471). This case concerned the grant of funds from one charity to another. The funds received by the second charity were not however spent 'in the field' but were largely accumulated in the second charity. The Court held that the trustees of the first charity had nevertheless applied their funds for charitable purposes. The making of grants was in accordance with the charity's objects and, unless the first charity actually knew that the funds would be misapplied by the second charity, the making of such a grant was actually an application for charitable purposes.

The receipt of the grant by the second charity did not constitute income or a capital gain of the charity and therefore did not fall within the statutory provisions.

Legislation was introduced in s30(1) FA 1986 to reverse this decision so that a receipt in similar circumstances now constitutes Schedule D Case III income in the hands of the recipient charity and is therefore subject to similar considerations on the application for charitable purposes. This now forms s505(2) ICTA 1988. A payment made in such circumstances by a charity is nevertheless still considered to be a payment for charitable purposes only.

The case however also considered the accumulation of income and whether or not this constituted an application for charitable purposes. The point had been considered inconclusively in earlier cases, and in the *Helen Slater* case Lord Justice Oliver commented (at 477d):

> 'Charitable trustees who simply leave surplus income uninvested cannot, I think, be said to have "applied" it at all and, indeed, would be in breach of trust. But if the income is reinvested by them and held, as invested, as part of the funds of the charity, I would be disposed to say that it is no less being applied for charitable purposes than it is if it is paid out in wages to the secretary.'

As the case was decided on other grounds, this statement constitutes obiter dicta but nevertheless has strong persuasive force. It suggests that were charitable trustees to make conscious investment decisions on funds to be accumulated, then this constitutes an application for charitable purposes.

It is important to emphasise that, for tax purposes, as illustrated in the Helen Slater case, the provisions relating to application for charitable purposes apply only to income and gains which rely on exemption from tax under s505 ICTA 1988 and on s256 TCGA 1992. Therefore donations or legacies which are not within the charge to tax escape this requirement. No such distinction of course applies to the

Commissioners when considering whether capital or income has been applied for charitable purposes.

18.1.4 Trading income

Introduction

The restrictions which apply to trading income received by charities are more restrictive than for all other types of income except that received under Schedule D VI. In a similar way, trading profits must be applied for charitable purposes but the wording of the provision is slightly different. Section 505(1)(e) ICTA 1988 exempts trading profits 'if the profits are applied solely to the purposes of the charity' along with other conditions discussed below. In strictness this is capable of a narrower interpretation than 'for charitable purposes only' as it implies that funds must be applied to further the objects of a particular charity. So, for example, if a charitable educational trust were to make a donation to, say, the RSPCA then although this would be applying funds for charitable purposes, it may not necessarily be viewed as being applied solely to the purposes of the charity in question. This is however a subtle distinction, and in practice exemption for trading income is normally not applicable because of the further conditions that must be satisfied.

Further conditions for exemption of trading income

Exemption from tax under Schedule D in respect of trading profits only applies

> 'if the profits are applied solely to the purposes of the charity and either –
> (i) the trade is exercised in the course of the actual carrying out of a primary purpose of the charity; or
> (ii) the work in connection with the trade is mainly carried out by beneficiaries of the charity.' (s505(1)(e) ICTA 1988).

Both these criteria may be demonstrated to some extent in the production of magazines by charities for the homeless. A primary purpose of such a charity is to inform the public at large of the problems of homelessness so that increased awareness can lead to a drive for resolution of the problem. As the magazine is also sold by homeless people who are beneficiaries of the charity, the second criterion is also fulfilled.

However, these exemptions are narrow in their application and many trading activities commonly carried out by charities will not be covered. There is some logic in the legislation in that the result of the tax system should not be to give a competitive advantage to charities relative to non-charitable businesses. However, the support given to the use of subsidiary companies which covenant their profits to charity (see below) does seem somewhat to belie this principle. Similar logic also gave rise to regulations governing trading issues for VAT purposes.

The Revenue have however published an Extra-statutory Concession to cover certain areas in which they do not consider that charities are likely to be competing in a major way with other taxable businesses. The concession is reproduced in Appendix 7 and exempts from tax profits from bazaars, jumble sales, and similar activities subject to certain conditions being satisfied. The conditions effectively limit the application of the concession to events which take place on an occasional basis only and are clearly in support of charitable activities. They are largely to ensure that the charity is not actively competing with other tax paying businesses.

Trading companies

The usual way for a charity to structure its affairs so that its trading income does not effectively suffer tax is through the use of a subsidiary company. Taxable trading can be routed through the company and the profits passed back to the charity in tax efficient form. There are three ways in which a trading company can pass profits back to the charity in a tax efficient manner: deed of covenant; Gift Aid or dividend.

Deed of covenant

The trading subsidiary enters into a deed of covenant with the charity agreeing to pay the equivalent of its taxable profits to the charity on an annual basis. This then is paid after deduction of income tax and the charity receives an annual payment on which the income tax can be reclaimed.

The main problem that arises is that the covenant, in order to qualify as a charge on income in the trading company's corporation tax computation for that year, must be paid before the end of the accounting period. This of course will be before the final profit figure is known. In practice, provided the profits that are paid up to the charity are equal to or exceed the final profit figure this does not give rise to a problem as the Revenue will repay any income tax paid which is subsequently shown to be excessive.

The procedure for making such repayments is informal. It is of course a requirement that the recipient charity repay the excess to the captive company. The Revenue have, in some instances however, adopted the approach that an overpayment in one year can be set off against the following year's payment where the repayments would otherwise be small and the level of administration required disproportionately high.

Example 18.2

Charity Co corporation tax computation year ended 31 December 1994

	£
Trading income	600
Less: allowable expenses	(400)
Schedule D Case I	200
Schedule D Case III	100
Less: charge on income	(300)
Profits chargeable to corporation tax	nil
Amount paid to charity	225
Amount paid to Inland Revenue	75
	300
Amount received by charity	225
Charity reclaims from Inland Revenue	75
	300

Care should be taken in the wording of profit shedding covenants as excessive payments can cause cash flow problems for the company and may also lead to other consequences discussed under 'non-qualifying expenditure' below. Further problems will arise in particular where the company has a high level of disallowable expenditure so that profits for accounting and tax purposes are appreciably different. If the level of profit to be paid over to the charity is higher than the accounts profit (assuming in this instance that cash flow is directly referable to accounting profit) then the company will require additional funding. If this is likely to be the case, then the wording of the deed of covenant may need to be altered to ensure that the level of profit paid over takes account of the deficit. This may result in the company paying a small amount of corporation tax.

Prior to 1986 it was possible for a company to pay income gross to the charity under a group income election. This was stopped in what is now s339(3) ICTA 1988 and it is now possible that a charity may suffer a tax flow disadvantage while the Revenue validate their claim for repayment of income tax. The Revenue therefore published Statement of Practice 3/87 stating that they were prepared to make provisional repayment under these circumstances provided certain conditions are met. The Statement of Practice is reproduced in Appendix 8.

Gift Aid

The mechanism of giving to a charity using Gift Aid is outlined in chapter **20**. It is possible for a company to make a payment using Gift

Aid in the same way as an individual. However, a trading company using this method of paying out profits suffers from a number of disadvantages. If a Gift Aid donation based on an estimated profit figure proves to be excessive, then the facility for repayment is not available as it is with the deed of covenant. The tax may therefore prove to be irrecoverable by the donor company. There is also a VAT problem in that companies using Gift Aid as a mechanism rather than paying using a profit shedding covenant are not entitled to zero rate the sale of donated goods.

Dividends

This is no longer as tax efficient as it once was as a method of shedding profits to a charity because of the reduction of the rate of ACT in FA 1993. As the small companies rate of tax is no longer equal to the ACT rate, trading subsidiaries are not able to recover their tax in full even if their corporation tax rate is within the small companies band. Charities are entitled to a transitional relief which increases the amount of tax they can reclaim on dividends received but this relief lasts only until 1996/97.

Example 18.3

Charity Subco Corporation Tax Computation Year ended 31 March 1995

	£
Schedule D Case I	25,000
Schedule D Case II	5,000
Profits chargeable to corporation tax	30,000
Corporation tax payable @ 25%	7,500
Less: ACT paid	(6,000)
Mainstream corporation tax liability	1,500
Dividend payable to charity	24,000
ACT payable to Inland Revenue	6,000
MCT liability payable to Inland Revenue	1,500
	31,500
Dividend received by charity	24,000
Tax credit reclaimed from Inland Revenue	6,000
Additional tax credit under FA 1993 transitional rules 1/20 × 24,000	1,200
	31,200

As with the deed of covenant route the situation may arise (as above) that the company has a net cash outflow which will need to be addressed.

Despite the additional liability to corporation tax, the dividend route should not be overlooked entirely, as it may be useful in certain circumstances. If a payment made under a deed of covenant or Gift Aid in a particular year is insufficient then a dividend paid in a later period can result in ACT being carried back to cover the tax paid (if any) in the preceding year. Alternatively it can be carried forward to future accounting periods.

Loans

The financing of a trading subsidiary by means of a loan from the charity has already been considered. It should be noted however that a loan from a trading subsidiary to a charity is inadvisable. This is because a trading subsidiary is likely to be a close company within the definition of s414 ICTA 1988. The trustees of the charity will then be treated as participators in a close company. This means that any loans made by the subsidiary to a participator in a close company comes within the scope of s419 ICTA 1988 and an amount of deemed ACT is payable on the making of the loan. This will not be recoverable by the charity.

18.1.5 Non-qualifying expenditure

Restriction of relief

The earlier enactment of s505 ICTA 1988 did not fully address the misapplication of funds by a charity. The requirement that income be applied for charitable purposes only applies to income which would otherwise be taxable. Although tax exemption could be lost if a particular source of taxable income was misapplied and was not therefore used for charitable purposes, it was still possible for charities to misapply other sources of income which were not within the scope of s505. These would include for example legacies and some donations. Legislation was therefore enacted in FA 1986 to restrict exemption on taxable sources of income where a charity had incurred non-qualifying expenditure.

Section 505(3) ICTA 1988 provides:

> 'If in any chargeable period of a charity –
> (a) its relevant income and gains are not less than £10,000; and
> (b) its relevant income and gains exceed the amount of its qualifying expenditure; and
> (c) the charity incurs, or is treated as incurring, non-qualifying expenditure;
> relief shall not be available (for income tax, corporation tax or capital gains tax) for so much of the excess as does not exceed the nonqualifying expenditure incurred in that period.

The following definitions are relevant:

1 Relevant income and gains are any taxable income of the charity and income for which s505 ICTA 1988 gives exemption, and capital gains which would be chargeable if the conditions in s256 TCGA 1992 relating to charitable exemption were not fulfilled.
2 Qualifying expenditure is expenditure incurred for charitable purposes only but also includes commitments which the charity has entered into either before or during the period in question, even though the expenditure may not yet have been incurred. However, it should be noted that a payment made to a body outside the United Kingdom is not qualifying expenditure unless the charity has taken reasonable steps to ensure that the payment will be applied for charitable purposes (s506(3) ICTA 1988).
3 Non-qualifying expenditure is defined in s506 ICTA 1988 as 'expenditure which is not qualifying expenditure' however it is extended to include investments and loans which are not qualifying.

If a charity incurs both qualifying and non-qualifying expenditure in any period, then the above provisions will not bite unless the relevant income and gains exceeds the amount of qualifying expenditure. If the relevant income is less than the qualifying expenditure then no restriction on exemption will apply in that period. However the non-qualifying expenditure can then be carried back to earlier periods ending not more than six years before the end of the period in which the expenditure was incurred.

If however, the non-qualifying expenditure to be carried back can be shown by the charity to be expenditure of non-taxable sums then the carry back provisions do not apply. Non-taxable sums are donations, legacies and other sums of a similar nature which are not within the charge to tax. If under the above provisions only part of a charity's relevant income and gains still qualify for exemption then the charity can specify which of its income it would prefer to restrict. In these circumstances a charity will normally ensure that exemption is lost from covenanted donations last as a restriction on this income in the charity's hands means that higher rate relief for the covenantor will also be restricted.

The mechanism of the provisions is illustrated in the example below. The procedure should be followed in a number of stages.

(a) Has the charity actually incurred non-qualifying expenditure?
If not, there is no restriction of relief.
(b) Do relevant income and gains exceed £10,000?
If not, there is no restriction of relief in that year.

(c) Do relevant income and gains exceed qualifying expenditure? If not there is no restriction of relief in that year.
(d) Calculate the excess of relevant income and gains over qualifying expenditure. Tax relief on income is restricted to the lower of that excess and the actual amount of non-qualifying expenditure. Having dealt with the restriction of relief in that year, then the previous six years should be considered, taking later periods first.
(e) Look at the year in which the non-qualifying expenditure was incurred. Does the aggregate of qualifying and non-qualifying expenditure in that year exceed relevant income and gains? If not, no further restriction is required.
(f) Calculate the extent to which the excess represents non-qualifying expenditure. This is then called 'unapplied non-qualifying expenditure'.
(g) Does unapplied non-qualifying expenditure exceed non-taxable sums received during the year? If not, no further restriction is required. If so, the excess only is carried back to earlier years.
(h) Taking each earlier year in turn, later years first, go back to stage (d) in the process and restrict tax relief accordingly.

Example 18.4

A charity has the following income and expenditure for three years:

		£
Year 1	Covenant income	30,000
	Deposit interest	5,000
	Qualifying expenditure	20,000
	Non-qualifying expenditure	5,000
Year 2	Covenant income	30,000
	Deposit interest	5,000
	Qualifying expenditure	25,000
Year 3	Covenant income	30,000
	Deposit interest	5,000
	Legacy	10,000
	Non-qualifying loan	25,000

Following the stages above:

Year 1	Relevant income and gains	35,000
	Qualifying expenditure	(20,000)
	Excess	15,000
	Non-qualifying expenditure	5,000

Tax relief on income restricted by £5,000.

The charity would elect for the restriction to apply to deposit interest, thus preserving higher rate relief for convenantors.

		£
Year 2	No non-qualifying expenditure.	
Year 3	Relevant income and gains	35,000
	Qualifying expenditure	(25,000)
	Excess	10,000
	Non-qualifying expenditure	25,000

Tax relief on income restricted by £10,000.

Looking at earlier years:

Relevant income and gains in Year 3	35,000
Total qualifying and non-qualifying expenditure	(50,000)
Excess	15,000

Unapplied non-qualifying expenditure £15,000.

	Non taxable sums	10,000
	Unapplied non-qualifying expenditure	(15,000)
	Excess to carry back	5,000
Year 2	Relevant income and gains	35,000
	Qualifying expenditure	(25,000)
	Excess	10,000
	Unapplied non-qualifying expenditure	5,000

Relief on income restricted by £5,000.

Sch 20 ICTA 1988

The definition of non-qualifying expenditure is extended by s506 ICTA 1988 to include investments and loans which are not 'qualifying' under Sch 20 ICTA 1988.

Investments qualifying under Sch 20 include:

(a) Those authorised by Sch 1 Trustee Investment Act 1961 (excluding mortgages).
(b) Common investment funds.
(c) Land (but excluding an interest in land which is held as a security on a debt).
(d) Quoted shares, including USM shares.
(e) Unit trusts.

(f) Bank deposits paying interest at a commercial rate (not as part of a back to back loan arrangement).
(g) Certificates of deposit.

If an investment is not covered by the above, a charity may make a claim to the Revenue that the loan or other investment is made for the benefit of the charity and not for the avoidance of tax. The Schedule does not cover unquoted shares, and therefore the funding of a trading subsidiary comes within the scope of non-qualifying expenditure. A claim should always be made under Sch 20 para 9 when such arrangements are being considered. There is no formal clearance procedure for the claim, but the Revenue will normally confirm that a proposed investment would be regarded as qualifying for the purposes of s506 ICTA 1988.

The address to which claims should be sent is Inland Revenue, Claims Branch, Trusts & Charities, St John's House, Merton Road, Bootle L69 9BB.

When considering whether or not an investment or loan comes within the scope of Sch 20, the Revenue consider particularly if it is actually made 'for the benefit of the charity' (Sch 20 para 9(1) ICTA 1988). The fact that a subsidiary company is wholly owned by a charity and all its profits are paid up using a deed of covenant is not considered relevant. The matters which they have indicated they would take into account are:

(a) whether the loan is covered by adequate security;
(b) whether a commercial rate of interest is charged; and
(c) whether a formal loan agreement exists which provides repayment terms for the loan.

When a trading company is first set up, adequate security may be difficult to establish. Assuming however that the company is likely to make profits, and indeed if this is not the case the investment would not be advisable for the charity, then the payment of a commercial rate of interest is actually of benefit to the charity. This is one way in which amounts can be paid by the company to the charity other than by deed of covenant.

The interest payable must be annual interest as the receipt of short interest from a captive company is not exempt from tax on receipt by the charity. The company must therefore deduct income tax from the payment and it will be deductible as a charge on income.

18.2 Capital gains tax

Similar exemptions for capital gains accruing to charities are given by s256 TCGA 1992. Under this section a gain shall not be a chargeable gain if it is applicable and applied for charitable purposes. There is a claw back of capital gains tax if property held on charitable trust ceases to be subject to those trusts. The text of s256 TCGA 1992 is reproduced in Appendix 10.

Where an asset is given away or otherwise disposed of in a non-arm's length transaction, basic CGT legislation provides that a capital gain will arise based on the market value of the asset in question. Where the gift is to a charity however, s257 TCGA 1992 provides that the transaction is deemed to have taken place at such a consideration as would create neither a gain nor a loss for the donor.

18.3 Inheritance tax

Gifts to charities both on death and during a lifetime are exempt from IHT. Section 23(6) IHTA 1984 expands this by providing that a property is given to charity 'if it becomes the property of charities or is held on trust for charitable purposes only'. There is a possibility of utilising this relief in conjunction with Gift Aid to maximise tax reliefs available and this is considered in more detail in chapter **20**.

18.4 Stamp duty

Charities are exempt from stamp duty under the following headings in Sch 1 Stamp Act 1891:

(a) Conveyance or Transfer on Sale;
(b) Conveyance or Transfer of any kind not hereinbefore described;
(c) Lease or Tack (s129 FA 1982).

The most common forms of stamp duty therefore, i.e., those relating to land, shares and leases, are not payable by a charity. The exemption is however subject to compulsory adjudication. Adjudication matters are dealt with at The Stamp Office, Adjudication Section, Ridgworth House, Liverpool Gardens, Worthing, West Sussex BN11 1XP.

Chapter 19 – VAT and charities

19.1 General

19.1.1 Introduction

The exemptions which apply to income tax and corporation tax for charities unfortunately do not apply to VAT. Charities may be liable to register for VAT and therefore charge VAT on the goods and services they provide (their supplies) and must also pay VAT on many goods and services they acquire (their inputs). The liability to register for VAT depends on a number of factors. The principal factor to consider is whether or not an organisation is carrying on a business. If this is found to be the case, then the status of the supplies that the organisation is making has to be ascertained. Under the VAT legislation, goods and services supplied can either be fully taxable at the standard rate, zero rated, exempt or outside the scope of VAT. A person carrying on a business will be liable to register if his taxable supplies exceed the VAT threshold (from 30 November 1994 £46,000 per annum). Voluntary registration is also possible below this limit, and may be particularly useful where supplies are zero rated as this then enables input tax to be reclaimed.

It is not the intention of this chapter to set out in detail the general rules on the operation of VAT. The topics covered are those which are particularly relevant to charities. Customs themselves produce a booklet on VAT and charities, 701/1/95 which gives helpful guidance on many of the points discussed below.

19.1.2 Carrying on a business

No liability to VAT will arise if a charity can establish that it is not actually carrying on a business. However in many cases this may be very difficult. The definition of business for VAT purposes is substantially wider than that used for income and corporation tax. The fact that an association is non-profit making does not in itself mean that a business is not being carried on. The matter has been considered by the Courts principally in the case of *Customs & Excise Commissioners* v *Morrison's Academy Boarding Houses Association* (1978 STC 1), and were well summarised in *Customs & Excise* v *Lord Fisher* (1981 STC 238) paraphrased as follows:

(1) Statute provides in s94(1) VAT Act 1994 that '"business" includes any trade, profession or vocation' and it is thus clear that a wide meaning of 'business' is intended.
(2) 'In determining whether any particular activity constitutes a business it is necessary to consider the whole of that activity as it is carried on in all its aspects:'
(3) There are certain criteria which may indicate whether or not a business is being carried on:
    (a) 'whether the activity is a "serious undertaking earnestly pursued" or "a serious occupation, not necessarily confined to commercial or profitmaking undertakings"'
    (b) 'whether the activity is an occupation or function activity pursued with reasonable or recognisable continuity;'
    (c) 'whether the activity has a certain measure of substance as measured by the quarterly or annual value of taxable supplies made'
    (d) 'whether the activity was conducted in a regular manner and on sound and recognised business principles'
    (e) 'whether the activity is predominantly concerned with the making of taxable supplies to consumers for a consideration'
    (f) 'whether the taxable supplies are of a kind which, subject to differences of detail, are commonly made by those who seek to profit from them.'

The Morrison's Academy case is frequently cited by Customs and, as can be seen from the above, the criteria which may be used are widely drawn.

Certain activities are excluded from the definition of business, these include the services of employees and activities which are no more than an activity for pleasure and social enjoyment. Nevertheless the term is sufficiently broad as to include membership subscriptions to clubs and admission charges to premises. However s94(3) VAT Act 1994 specifically excludes from that definition the subscription to a body whose objects are 'in the public domain and are of a political, religious, philanthropic, philosophical or patriotic nature, . . .' but only if the 'subscriber' obtains no facility or advantage . . . other than the right to participate in its management or receive reports on its activities.

In other words, members of an organisation which qualifies under the above conditions, who receive nothing but a report of the organisation's activities etc., do not pay VAT on the subscriptions. This exemption is strictly applied and is unlikely to apply to the activities of many charities. In the tribunal case *The English speaking Union of the Commonwealth* (1980 VATTR 184) the members concerned received a journal which contained items other than mere reports of the activities of the society. This was held to be a benefit to the members and thus the exemption in s94(3) did not apply. The association was therefore carrying on a business and its subscriptions were taxable.

As has already been stated, it is possible under VAT legislation to be carrying on a business without making a profit. Nevertheless Charities Notice 701/1/95 referred to above states that welfare services and related goods supplied by charities are non-business when made consistently below cost to distressed people for the relief of their distress. Their definition of below cost is that the cost of providing the welfare is subsidised as to at least 15 per cent from the charity's own funds; in other words in most cases from non-business income such as donations.

It should however be noted that in order for a business to exist there must be some consideration. Supplies made for which no consideration in any form passes are not supplies in the course of a business. However where an organisation receives grants and donations but also makes supplies where consideration has passed, then the organisation may still be considered to be carrying on a business. The relevance then of the donation income and the other income will be for apportionment purposes only.

19.1.3 The status of charitable supplies

Once it is established that a charity is liable to VAT on its business activities then it is necessary to establish the status of the various supplies it makes. It is particularly important to distinguish between those supplies which are outside the scope of VAT and therefore the business, and those supplies which are made in the course of the business but are exempt. The latter will give rise to a disallowance of input tax under partial exemption calculations, whereas input tax which is related to non-business supplies is excluded from partial exemption calculations.

Donations and grants are outside the scope of VAT provided that nothing is given in return. They are therefore classed as a non-business activity of the charity. The sale of donated goods is a business activity but is zero rated by Sch 8 Group 15 VAT Act 1994. A typical charity shop will therefore need to distinguish between goods which are donated for sale and goods which are bought in. The supply of bought in goods is standard rated if the goods themselves would normally be standard rated. The zero rating of donated goods may also be applied to companies selling donated goods, which pay all their profits to charity using a profit shedding covenant. However the legislation states that the company must covenant all its profits to a charity. In principle therefore, where a company sheds its profits by means of a Gift Aid payment, zero rating does not apply.

19.1.4 VAT registration for branches

If an organisation's taxable supplies exceed the annual turnover limit, then registration is compulsory except where all supplies are zero rated. A national charity may however be organised into a series of branches which individually may not exceed the turnover limit. Customs will normally require the charity to register as one national business unless the branches are 'constitutionally and financially independent'. The factors taken into consideration include whether or not membership of a branch automatically gives national membership, and whether or not the local branch keeps a separate bank account and has control over its own financial resources. Customs would also look at the constitution of the charity and if necessary can direct that it register nationally as one business.

The principle can be extended to independent fundraising committees whose members may not be members of the national charity. Provided the committee is responsible for its own expenditure and is legally independent of the main body then, if the value of the supplies is below the annual threshold, tickets and other sales relating to a fundraising event will not be taxable.

19.1.5 Fundraising

The organisation of events for fundraising purposes is in general a business activity. The income thus generated is not therefore outside the scope of VAT. However Sch 9 Group 12 VAT Act 1994 states that 'the supply of goods and services by a charity in connection with a fundraising event organised for charitable purposes by a charity or jointly by more than one charity' is exempt. It also exempts the 'supply of goods and services by a qualifying body in connection with a fundraising event organised exclusively for its own benefit.' Qualifying bodies for these purposes are trade unions and other professional bodies as defined in Sch 9 Group 9 Item 1. It should be stressed however that this exemption does not apply to all fundraising events.

The definition in the Act says that a fundraising event means 'a fete, ball, bazaar, gala show, performance or similar event, which is separate from and not forming any part of a series or regular run of like or similar events.' The emphasis is therefore on the irregular nature of an event, the purpose of the legislation being to ensure that a charity does not gain a competitive advantage over non-charitable persons organising similar events. So a theatrical performance on a single night would qualify as exempt under this heading, but if the performance were to be repeated over three nights the provisions would not apply. Similarly a car boot sale held as a one-off event one Sunday would be exempt, but if such sales were held every Sunday in the same location then again the provisions would not apply.

Customs & Excise Notice 701/1/95 provides detailed advice on frequency of events which would constitute taxable supplies. A national charity can hold the same event in a number of different locations without affecting the exemption, but a programme of events, although reasonably spaced, which are sold on a season ticket would not be exempt.

The notes to Group 12 now also state that the same treatment is extended to a company wholly owned by a charity and whose profits are paid to the charity either by 'a deed of covenant or trust or otherwise'. The profit shedding mechanisms which are therefore acceptable for these purposes are more widely defined than those for the sale of donated goods.

If the event is classified as exempt then there are obviously no further implications for the charging of VAT. If not, other considerations must then be taken into account. If the price of a ticket is chargeable to VAT, it may be possible to split the price between the cost of admission and a voluntary donation. Customs will only accept this if the cost of admission on the ticket is comparable with other commercial events. This will then mean that VAT is only chargeable on the proportion of the total cost which represents the cost of the entrance to the event. The disadvantage of this method is that the donation element must be voluntary and the charity will therefore lose money if some ticket holders decide not to contribute to the donation element. It is not possible for the charity to give any return for the donation, so that for example prior allocation of seats to those having paid the donation would render the whole amount taxable.

Where companies have paid amounts to charities to secure sponsorship for an event, then Customs' position has been that if the benefits provided to the company are minimal then the supply is exempt. If however the benefits were substantial then all the amounts paid are liable to VAT, even though the amount paid by the company will often be significantly in excess of the value of the benefits received. This view was recently challenged in a VAT tribunal where a theatre had provided the following nominal benefits in return for a minimum subscription of £150:

(a) Personalised brass plaque displayed on each seat.
(b) Acknowledgement on board featured in the main foyer.
(c) Limited edition print of the theatre.
(d) Priority booking for two gala evenings.

The value of the benefits was estimated to be around £5 and the theatre contended that VAT should be payable on that amount only. Although this view was upheld in the tribunal it was reversed in the Court of Session and VAT was held to be due on the full amount (*Customs & Excise Commissioners* v *Tron Theatre Ltd* 1994 STC 177). It must therefore be likely that Customs will now harden their stance when any benefits which may qualify as goods and services are given in return for sponsorship payments.

Finally, coffee mornings and jumble sales can be held as frequently as desired without incurring any liability to VAT. It is considered unlikely by Customs that these are areas in which significant competitive advantage can be obtained.

19.2 Special reliefs for charities

19.2.1 Summary

In addition to the general principles discussed above there are a number of special reliefs which apply to charities. These provide that certain goods or services provided to charity or in some cases to disabled persons are zero rated or exempt. The following items may be zero rated:

1 The construction of a new building for non-business charitable purposes.
2 Talking books and wireless sets for the blind. Schedule 8 Group 4 VAT Act 1994.
3 Life boats and associated equipment. Schedule 8 Group 8 VAT Act 1994.
4 Drugs, medicines and aids for the handicapped. Schedule 8 Group 12 VAT Act 1994.
5 Donated goods sold by a charity. Schedule 8 Group 16 VAT Act 1994.
6 Medical equipment. Schedule 8 Group 16 VAT Act 1994.
7 Advertising. Schedule 8 Group 15 VAT Act 1994.
8 The supply of medical goods to a charity. Schedule 8 Group 15 VAT Act 1994.

These services are exempt:

1 Educational services where the charity is an 'eligible body' and youth clubs. Schedule 9 Group 6 VAT Act 1994.
2 Welfare services. Schedule 9 Group 7 VAT Act 1994.
3 Charges by religious communities to resident members. Schedule 9 Group 7 VAT Act 1994.
4 Fundraising events. Schedule 9 Group 12 VAT Act 1994.

Many of the above are subject to certain conditions and these are considered in more detail below.

19.2.2 Zero-rated supplies

The construction of a new building for non-business charitable purposes

A contractor can zero rate his construction services and goods in connection with the construction of a building for non-business charitable use. It is not, however, possible to zero rate architects' fees, surveyors' fees or the fees of other persons acting in a consultancy or supervisory role.

Zero rating also applies to the first grant of a major interest in a non-business charity building. A major interest is either a freehold or a lease exceeding 21 years.

From 1 July 1994 it has also been possible to treat the conversion of a non-residential building into a non-business charity use building as being zero rated.

Talking books for blind and handicapped and wireless sets for the blind

The above are zero rated when supplied to the Royal National Institute for the Blind, the National Listening Library or other similar charities. Radios and cassette recorders are zero rated when supplied to any charity if used by that charity for loan to the blind.

The zero rating does not cover the supplies of these items by the charity concerned. This is governed by the rules on business activities outlined above. It may therefore be covered by the charitable activities for the relief of distress. If the items are consistently supplied at below cost then the supply will not constitute a business activity and VAT will not be chargeable. However if this is not the case, then the supply will be taxable.

Drugs, medicines, aids for the handicapped etc.

Group 12 zero rates many items supplied to an individual handicapped person or to a charity which makes them available by sale or otherwise to handicapped persons. Zero rating only applies however if the goods are for the domestic or personal use of the handicapped person. Handicapped in this context means chronically sick or disabled. The items covered by this group are wide ranging and are changed frequently.

19.2.3 Zero-rated items under Group 16

Group 16 provides a number of reliefs specifically for charities.

The sale by a charity of donated goods is zero rated as stated earlier. The donation of the goods by the donor is also zero rated if their sale by the charity would be zero rated. This means that a business can recover its input tax on such goods. Similarly zero rating applies if such goods are exported by a charity.

Fuel and power for charity use

The provision for zero-rating fuel and power for charity use covered supplies of coal, gas, fuel oil, electricity, heat or air conditioning when it was supplied to a charity for use otherwise than in the course of furtherance of a business. Zero rating ended on 31 March 1994 and from 1 April 1994 the rate is 8 per cent. Where the goods are used partly for business and partly not, the whole amount may be subject to the lower rate provided the business use does not exceed 40 per cent. In other cases apportionment will be necessary.

Group 16 also covers medical equipment which is bought for donation to 'an eligible body' if the goods are purchased with funds provided by a charity or from voluntary contributions. An eligible body is defined in the legislation and is principally a health authority or non-profit making hospital. If an eligible body purchases goods itself with funds provided by a charity or from voluntary contributions, then these goods may also be zero rated. The goods concerned are generally medical and scientific equipment etc., for use in medical research, training, diagnosis or treatment.

The supply of advertising to a charity may be zero rated if the advertisement is for the raising of money or for making known the objects or reason for the objects of the charity. The wording to fulfil these conditions may be minimal and may form part of the charity's logo but must nevertheless be present. Customs now also accept that a recruitment advertisement by a charity can qualify for zero rating, provided again that it contains a qualifying advertisement.

This provision should not be confused with the sale of advertising by a charity for example in one of its publications. All advertising sold by a charity in a journal etc., may be zero rated provided that at least 50 per cent of the advertisements are from private individuals and do not advertise a business connection.

The supply of a medicinal product to a charity which provides care or medical or surgical treatment for human beings or animals, or is engaged in medical research, is also zero rated where the goods supplied are solely for the use of the charity providing such care.

In all such cases where the zero rating depends on the circumstances of the purchaser such as the example above, a certificate must be provided to the supplier.

19.2.4 Exempt supplies

The provision of educational research by a school, university or similarly defined institution is exempt. In addition educational research of a kind provided by a school or university or training for any trade, profession or employment is also exempt but only if the provision is otherwise than for profit. In Charities Notice 701/1/95 it is stated that 'otherwise than for profit' means that any profit made is applied solely to the furtherance of the activity that generated it. So if any profit is used for a different charitable activity the supply is standard rated.

Schedule 9 Group 6 VAT Act 1994 also exempts the provision by a youth club or association of youth clubs of the facilities available to its members. This exemption covers facilities in return for member subscriptions, but does not include the provision of food and drink and entertainment etc.

Schedule 9 Group 6 VAT Act 1994 exempts supplies otherwise than for profit by a charity of welfare services and goods supplied in connection therewith. See above for the meaning of 'otherwise than for profit.' Examples of welfare services include residential care for elderly and handicapped people, the provision of accommodation in hostels for the homeless and in children's homes, children taken into care etc. The phrase 'otherwise than for profit' in this context should not be confused with the provision which states that welfare services provided for the relief of distress consistently below cost are outside the scope of VAT as being non-business supplies. The distinction is a fine one.

Finally, Sch 9 Group 6 also exempts the supply 'otherwise than for profit' of goods and services incidental to the provision of spiritual welfare by a religious community to a resident member of the community in return for a subscription or other consideration paid as a condition of membership.

As stated at the beginning of this chapter, Customs Notice 701/1/95 is a useful source of guidance on the VAT treatment of charities and the reliefs available. Other Customs notices cover some of these reliefs in more detail.

Chapter 20 – Giving to charity

There are currently four ways in which an individual can give to a charity in a tax efficient manner: deeds of covenant; Gift Aid; give as you earn scheme and legacies. The first two are the most widely used and are more effective from the charity's point of view than the give as you earn scheme, principally because the give as you earn scheme benefits the donor only and not the charity. This section deals with the characteristics of each together with some associated pitfalls.

20.1 Deeds of covenant

Deeds of covenant have been a popular form of giving to charity for some time. To satisfy the requirements of the Inland Revenue, there are a number of criteria which must be fulfilled. The way in which the covenant is worded is of paramount importance.

(a) A covenant form must state that it is a deed.
(b) It must be signed and delivered by the covenantor in the presence of a witness.
(c) The covenant must provide for annual payments to be made year by year and must cover a minimum period.
(d) A covenant cannot be backdated. Previous Revenue practice was to allow a payment earlier in a tax year to be validated retrospectively by a deed of covenant. However Revenue Statement of Practice 4/90 stated that this would no longer apply to covenants issued after 31 July 1990.

The Revenue also publish a model deed for a form of covenant by an individual to a charity. This is reproduced in Appendix 9.

20.1.1 Minimum period

A covenant must be capable of lasting more than three years and in practice covenants are usually drawn up for a four year period. It is now also possible to draw up a covenant which will expire at the later of four years from the date of the covenant and, for example, the termination of membership of the charity after that date. Before the FA 1992 the Revenue took the view that such covenants were invalid after the original four years had expired. This is no longer the case, and a suggested wording has been issued by the Revenue as follows:

> 'I promise to pay (the charity) during my lifetime, such a sum as after deduction of income tax at the basic rates amounts to £ . . . . per annum, provided that I may revoke in writing this deed of covenant at any time after the expiry of 4 years from . . . . (enter here the date on which the first payment is due to be made under the deed).'

20.1.2 Benefits to donor

A covenanted payment to a charity must represent pure income profit for the charity. Therefore the charity cannot give any benefit to the donor in return for the covenanted payment. In practice the Revenue are prepared to accept small benefits (up to 25 per cent of a subscription payment) without invalidating the covenant.

Legislation was introduced in FA 1989 to enable certain charities to grant free admission to their sites in return for a covenanted membership subscription. This allows charities such as The National Trust to grant free admission to members even though this benefit is perhaps not small relative to the cost of the membership subscription. The legislation however only applies to a charity if its sole or main purpose is:

(a) the preservation of property for the public benefit; or
(b) the conservation of wildlife for the public benefit.

Corporate giving via deeds of covenant

The majority of individual covenants are now worded as net deeds so that the amount of tax recovered by the charity is currently $\frac{25}{75}$ of the amount of the gift. It is however still possible to enter into 'gross' deeds of covenant, which specify a gross amount to be paid less the basic rate of income tax then in force. Such deeds are generally preferred by companies who do not pay income tax but deduct an amount equivalent to the basic rate from their covenanted donation and pay this on completion of the relevant CT61.

20.2 Gift Aid

Gift Aid as a mechanism for giving money to charity has two major advantages over a deed of covenant. The first is that it is significantly simpler to administer. The donor simply completes a form stating that tax has been deducted from the payment and passes this to the charity with the donation. Indeed it is not strictly necessary to complete the form at the time the donation is made. It can be completed, often at the charity's request, after the donation has been received. Secondly, Gift Aid applies to one-off payments and thus there is no necessity to commit the donor to regular giving over four years. Now that the minimum amount which can be paid over under Gift Aid has been reduced to £250, the popularity of this method is increasing.

Gift Aid payments and also payments under deed of covenant may be made by companies, and as with individuals the payment is treated as a charge on income. The company deducts income tax from the payment and pays over the tax to the Revenue under the provisions of Sch 16 ICTA 1988 in the normal way. The minimum limit for payment to charities by close companies is £250. There is no minimum limit on payments made by non-close companies and the maximum limit which applied when the legislation was first introduced has now been repealed.

20.2.1 Benefits to donor

There is provision in the legislation to ensure that charities do not give benefits to donors in return for a payment under Gift Aid. Section 25 FA 1990 states that any benefit received by the person making the payment, or any person connected with him, must not exceed two and a half per cent of the amount of the gift or £250. The gift must also not be conditional on or associated with the acquisition of property by the charity unless this acquisition is by way of gift from the donor.

Because the Gift Aid route is simpler to administer than a deed of covenant, donors may wish to terminate their covenants early and replace them with Gift Aid donations. The Revenue however appear to take the view that the donor has received a benefit in the revocation of the covenant and thus the Gift Aid payment is not valid. Early termination of covenants to be replaced by Gift Aid may not therefore be advisable.

20.2.2 Mechanism of tax relief

For both Gift Aid payments and payments under deeds of covenant it is now usual for the net amount to be included on the face of the deed or Gift Aid certificate. For Gift Aid payments, the prescribed form specifies this and the donor has no choice.

Thus a donor makes a payment under Gift Aid of £300 from which basic rate tax has been deducted. The gross equivalent of this payment is therefore £400, and the charity is entitled to reclaim £100 from the Inland Revenue.

If the donor is a higher rate taxpayer, then he will be entitled to further relief of 15 per cent of £400, i.e., £60. The gross amount of the payment to charity will be included on the donor's tax return at the end of the fiscal year and the higher rate relief claimed. If the donor wishes to pass the benefit of this higher rate relief on to the charity, then he will need to increase the amount of the net payment made under Gift Aid. In the example above, if the net payment were increased to £375, the gross equivalent being £500, the charity would receive a £125 tax repayment. The donor would then receive £75 higher rate relief after the end of the tax year and his net outlay would therefore be £300. Deeds of covenant can of course be worded in a similar way. A proviso to this is that if the charity applies its funds for non-charitable purposes (see below) then higher rate relief for a donor may be restricted.

It is of course necessary for the taxpayer to have sufficient taxable income to cover the covenanted or Gift Aid payment. If this is not the case then tax will be assessed on the donor under s348 ICTA 1988 and paid to the Revenue.

20.3 Payroll deduction scheme

More commonly known as the give as you earn scheme this is a method of giving to charities which in fact benefits the donor rather than the charity and so will not be discussed in any detail. The mechanism of the scheme is that the employer deducts an amount specified by the employee from gross pay and this amount is not taxable on the employee. Payments under this scheme cannot exceed £900 in any year of assessment. In most cases the employee will receive a book of vouchers, similar to a cheque book, from the Charities Aid Foundation which he can then use to make gifts to charities of his choice. The charity is not entitled to reclaim any further tax on these payments.

The Charities Aid Foundation (CAF) acts as a type of clearing house and pays funds on to the charity concerned at the request of the employee. It performs a similar service for individuals who can set up an account there using covenanted donations. The donor issues instructions to the CAF to pay amounts to specific charities from the account.

20.4 Legacies

Transfers to charities are exempt from inheritance tax and thus reduce the tax burden on an estate. There are a number of ways in which wills can be drafted to maximise the effect of this relief, particularly where the estate is substantial and the testator wishes to split the disposition between a charity or charities and individuals. A certain amount of planning can also ensure that even a small pecuniary legacy to a charity can be structured so as to take advantage of maximum tax reliefs available.

If a testator wishes to leave say £5,000 to charity and specifies this in his will, then the only tax relief obtained is exemption from inheritance tax. However if, rather than passing the amount directly to the charity, it is passed to an individual with the expressed wish that the individual should then pass this amount on to charity, the amount will still qualify for inheritance relief under s143 IHTA 1984, provided the recipient makes the gift within two years of the date of death. The recipient making the gift to the charity can also claim relief under Gift Aid provided his taxable income is sufficient.

On a net gift of £5,000 the charity may reclaim £1,667 from the Inland Revenue. If the donor is also a higher rate taxpayer he will then receive further higher rate relief of £1,000. In all therefore tax relief of 93 per cent of the original legacy has been enjoyed in aggregate by all sources.

A similar result can be obtained even though the testator does not express a wish that the gift be passed to charity by the beneficiary entering into a deed of variation under s142 IHTA 1984. However it should be noted that the Revenue have recently mounted an attack, particularly on the above form of precatory legacy, and care should therefore be taken in implementing such arrangements.

20.5 Other gifts to charities

If a person including a company carrying on a trade or profession provides the services of an employee to a charity free of charge then the costs of that employee will still be deductible as a trading expense under s86 ICTA 1988 even though they may otherwise fail under the 'wholly and exclusively' rule. Gift Aid payments and payments under deed of covenant must be paid in cash. Where assets are transferred to a charity, no income tax relief is due.

However, no capital gains tax is chargeable on assets transferred to charities. In such circumstances nevertheless some planning may be necessary. If the asset which is to be given has a high base cost and the capital gains tax payable would not therefore be large, then it may be preferable to sell the asset to a third party before making the gift to charity and making a payment of the proceeds to charity as a Gift Aid donation. The tax relief obtained in this way may well exceed the capital gains tax payable provided the donor has sufficient taxable income. Consider the following example.

In January 1990 Julius inherited a painting on the death of his father with a probate value of £35,000. Its value is now £50,000 and he decides to gift the asset to a local theatre to fund a major appeal. Julius' taxable income is £85,000 a year from various sources, but he does not intend to realise any other capital gains in the current tax year.

Were he to gift the asset directly to the theatre, there would be no tax implications for Julius, and the charity would no doubt sell the picture and realise £50,000. However, were Julius to sell the picture himself and donate the proceeds to the theatre using Gift Aid, the following consequences would ensue:

1 Julius would pay capital gains tax of £562.

Proceeds		50,000	
Costs	35,000		
Indexation	7,595		
		42,595	
		7,405	
Annual exemption		(6,000)	
Gain		1,405	at 40%
		=£562	

2 The charity would receive £50,000 plus tax credit of £16,667, giving total income for the charity of £66,667.

3 Julius would receive higher rate tax relief of 66,667 × 15%, i.e., £10,000.

It would therefore be advisable both for him and the charity to follow the latter route.

Appendix 1 – Disclosure checklist

*(**Caution**: this disclosure checklist has been compiled from the draft Regulations and the revised charity SORP issued on 1 February 1995. The consultation period on the former was completed on 17 May. As a result of that consultation, changes may be made to the Regulations and there may be consequential changes to the revised SORP.)*

*(**Note**: this checklist has been compiled for those charities preparing accounts to a true and fair view standard i.e., those with gross income which exceeds £100,000.)*

The following abbreviations have been used:

App	Appendix (to the SORP)
para	paragraph
Pt	Part
Reg	Regulation
s	section
Sch	Schedule

General requirements

	Ref
Is the charity required to comply with the Regulations?	s42 Reg 4
Is the charity required to comply with the SORP?	SORP para 6
Is the charity subject to the requirements of another parallel statutory regime? If so, have the recommendations of the SORP been adapted, as appropriate, to comply with those requirements?	SORP para 8
Have the recommendations of the SORP been adapted to comply with any requirements imposed by the charity's governing instrument?	SORP para 8
Do the annual report and accounts contain:	s45 Reg 3

	Ref
(a) a separate trustees' annual report?;	SORP para 26(a)
(b) a SOFA?;	Reg 3(2)(a) SORP para 22(a)
(c) where applicable, a summary income and expenditure account?;	SORP para 22(b)
(d) a balance sheet?;	Reg 3(2)(b) SORP para 22(c)
(e) where applicable, a cash flow statement?;	SORP para 22(d)
(f) notes to the accounts?	Reg 4 SORP para 22(e)
Do the accounts show a true and fair view of the financial activities during the year and of the state of affairs at the balance sheet date?	Sch Pt III para 1(1) SORP para 5
Where additional information to that which the Regulations and SORP require is needed for the accounts to give a true and fair view, has that information been given?	Sch Pt III para 1(2) SORP para 5
Where compliance with the Regulations or SORP is inconsistent with that view, has the provision been departed from and have particulars of that departure, the reasons for it and its effect been disclosed in the notes?	Sch Pt III para 1(3) SORP para 5
Have the accounts been prepared in accordance with:	SORP para 32
(a) the going concern concept?;	
(b) the accruals concept?;	

	Ref
(c) the consistency concept?;	
(d) the prudence concept?; and	
(e) with due regard to substance over form?	
Has there been consistency of accounting treatment within each financial year and from one year to the next?	SORP App 2(c)
Have the assets and liabilities been measured in accordance with the methods and principles in the SORP?	Sch Pt III para 4
Are corresponding amounts for the immediately preceding year given for all items shown in the accounts?	Sch Pt III para 2(1) & Pt IV para 1(p) SORP para 23
If not comparable, have the comparatives been adjusted and particulars of the adjustment and reasons for it been disclosed in the notes?	Sch Pt III para 2(2)
Has the duration of the current and previous periods been stated?	SORP para 23
Is there a statement as to whether or not the accounts have been prepared in accordance with applicable FRSs, SSAPs and SORPs? Have particulars of any material departure therefrom and the reasons been given?	Sch Pt IV 1(q) SORP paras 34 & 35

Accounting principles and rules

Have the principal accounting policies adopted been disclosed?	Sch Pt IV para 1(a) SORP paras 31 & 35

	Ref
Specific mention of the following is recommended:	
(a) donations, legacies and other forms of voluntary income or benefit;	SORP para 35(a)
(b) grants receivable and payable;	SORP para 35(b)
(c) basis of allocation of fundraising, publicity, support and administration costs;	SORP paras 35(c) & 151
(d) specific activities, e.g. research;	SORP para 35(d)
(e) investment assets and income;	SORP para 35(e)
(f) realised and unrealised gains and losses;	SORP para 35(f)
(g) valuation, capitalisation and depreciation of fixed assets for the charity's use;	SORP para 35(g)
(h) netting off of income and expenditure;	SORP para 35(h)
(i) subscriptions for life membership;	SORP para 35(i)
(j) stocks;	SORP para 35(j)
(k) commitments and the use of designated funds.	SORP para 35(k)
Are the descriptions clear, fair and brief?	SORP para 31
Are the assets and liabilities included at the following amounts:	Sch Pt III para 4
(a) fixed assets for the charity's use, at cost less depreciation?;	SORP para 174(a)

	Ref
(b) investments held as fixed assets at market value?;	SORP paras 174(b) & 194
(c) current assets at the lower of cost and net realisable value?;	SORP para 174(c)
(d) liabilities at settlement value?	SORP para 174(d)
Is all expenditure on the acquisition, enhancement, production or installation of fixed assets for the charity's use capitalised?	SORP para 185
(***Note:*** *receipts of such fixed assets by way of gift should be similarly capitalised.)*	
Are fixed assets with finite lives suitably depreciated and charged against charitable expenditure, as appropriate?	SORP para 189
Is the basis for measuring gifts in kind disclosed?	SORP paras 107 & 108
Have branches been properly accounted for?	SORP paras 45–49
If there has been a change in accounting policy:	
(a) is it justifiable on the grounds that it will give a fairer presentation of the transactions and of the disposition of the charity's net assets?	SORP App 2(c)
(b) if material, has the change, the reasons and its effect been disclosed?	Sch Pt IV para 1(q)
(c) if material, has it been treated as a prior year adjustment?	SORP App 2(c)

Trustees' annual report

	Ref
(The trustees' annual report should be a comprehensive review and explanation of the accounts. It is important that those seeking to interpret the accounts should be able to refer to the review and explanation in the annual report.)	SORP para 24
Has the trustees' annual report been prepared as a separate document?	s45 SORP para 26(a)
Does the report include all additional information which the trustees are required by law to report?	SORP para 26
Have the trustees confirmed that the accounts comply with current statutory requirements and with those of the governing instrument?	SORP para 26
Are the following legal and administrative details included (either as part of the report or appended to it):	SORP paras 26(a) & 27
(a) the full name of the charity and any other name by which it makes itself known?	Reg 10(2)(a) SORP para 27(a)
(b) an indication of the nature of its governing instrument and how it is constituted?	SORP para 27(b)
(c) the charity and, if applicable, company registration number?;	Reg 10(2)(b) SORP para 27(b)
(d) the name of the trustees, their nominating bodies (or other method of appointment), the names of any management committee, and the names of the principal officers?	Reg 10(2)(e) SORP para 27(c)
(e) the principal, or registered, address of the charity?	Reg 10(2)(c) SORP para 27(d)
(f) the names and addresses of bankers, solicitors, auditors, investment or other advisers etc.?	SORP para 27(e)
(g) details of any restrictions on the charity's operations?	SORP para 27(f)

	Ref
(h) a summary of the charity's specific investment powers?	SORP para 27(g)
Is the financial year specified?	Reg 10(1)
Does the trustees' annual report contain an explanation of what the charity is trying to achieve and how it is going about it? Is there:	
(a) an explanation of the charity's objects?;	Reg 10(2)(d) SORP para 28(a)(i)
(b) a summary of the policies adopted to further those objects?	SORP para 28(a)(ii)
(c) any material changes in the policies since the last report, together with the reasons, or a statement that there have been none?;	SORP para 28(a)(iii)
(d) a description of the way the charity is organised?	Reg 10(2)(f) SORP para 28(a)(iv)
Does the report contain a review of the charity's development, activities and achievements during the year, enabling the user to judge its effectiveness and to appreciate:	Reg 10(1)(b) SORP para 28(b)
(a) the general progress of the charity and its achievements during the year?;	SORP para 28(b)(i)
(***Note:*** *ideally, this overview should be supported by statistical information showing e.g., number of beneficiaries reached; number of times the charity's services were called upon, the unit costs for services provided etc.)*	
(b) important events during the year affecting the charity or the areas in which it works, and how the charity has responded to them?;	SORP para 28(b)(ii)

	Ref
(c) the extent to which the charity is dependent on the services of unpaid volunteers, donations-in-kind and other intangible income not evaluated or explained in the accounts?	SORP para 28(b)(iii)
Does the report contain a review of the transactions, and financial position of the charity and an explanation of the salient features of the accounts?	Reg 10(1)(b) SORP para 28(c)
*(**Note:** this review should put the accounts into an accurate perspective so that they may be readily understood and should show how the charity aims to achieve its objectives.)*	
Is the review sufficiently informative to enable the user to appreciate:	
(a) how the funds have been applied and the significance of material movements in the SOFA?;	Reg 10(1)(b) SORP para 28(c)(i)
(b) the purposes for which the assets are being held and their estimated value, if materially different from that shown in the accounts?;	SORP para 28(c)(ii)
(c) the financial position at the balance sheet date in the context of future plans and commitments, particularly in respect of on-going items of expenditure, projects not yet completed and obligations not yet met?;	Reg 10(1)(b) SORP para 28(c)(iii)
(d) the reasons for any changes to the accounting policies and the effect?;	SORP para 28(c)(iv)
(e) the performance of any subsidiary and associated undertakings whose results are included in the consolidated accounts or in the notes?;	SORP para 28(c)(v)
(f) the effects on present and future accounts of any revaluations of fixed assets (other than investments) made in the period?;	SORP para 28(c)(vi)
(g) the extent to which the charity may be financially dependent upon the support of any individuals, corporations, or classes of donors known to play a key role in its affairs?;	SORP para 28(c)(vii)

	Ref
(h) the nature of any post balance sheet events?;	Reg 10(1)(b) SORP para 28(c)(viii)
(i) the progress on any projects the charity was specifically set up to undertake?;	SORP para 28(c)(ix)
(***Note***: *the review should give cumulative figures of funding and expenditure on the project to date, with estimates of the additional costs and period of time required to complete it.)*	
(j) that any investments held have been acquired in accordance with the powers in the governing instrument?	SORP para 28(c)(x)
Does the report confirm (or otherwise) that, on a fund-by-fund basis, the assets are available and adequate to fulfil the obligations of the charity, with specific reference to:	SORP para 28(d)
(a) any likely delays or shortfalls in realising those assets into cash?;	SORP para 28(d)(i)
(b) any commitments or guarantees which are disclosed in the accounts?	SORP para 28(d)(ii)
Does the report contain a review of the relationships between the charity and its connected charities and with any other charities and organisations with which it co-operates in the pursuit of its charitable objectives?	SORP para 28(e)
(***Notes:***	
1 the purpose of this part of the report is to ensure that the user is aware of the wider organisational context(s) in which the charity is operating;	
2 the 'annual report' should include:	SORP para 51
(a) the names of the connected charities, principal contact addresses and the nature of the relationship between the charities; and	
(b) particulars of any material transactions between the charities.)	

	Ref
Does the charity act as custodian trustee? If so, does the report:	Reg 10(1)(g) SORP para 29
(a) describe the assets held in this capacity?;	
(b) show how this activity falls within the objects?;	
(c) give details of the arrangements for safe custody and segregation of such assets from the charity's own?	
Is the trustees' annual report approved by the trustees, as a body, and signed by one on their behalf?	Reg 10(1)(c)
Is the date of approval given?	SORP para 30

Statement of financial activities

*(**Note**: the SOFA must show the total incoming resources and their application, together with any other increase/decrease during the financial year.)*	Sch Pt I para 1
Does the SOFA and reconciliation of funds statement show the following main headings:	Sch Pt I para 1 SORP para 73
(a) incoming resources before transfers and revaluations?;	
(b) direct charitable expenditure?;	
(c) other expenditure?;	
(d) total expenditure?;	
(e) gross transfers between funds?;	Sch Pt I para 3(c)
(f) net incoming resources before revaluations and investment asset disposals?;	Sch Pt I para 3(d)

	Ref
(g) gains and losses on revaluation and investment asset disposals; (i) gains or losses on disposal of investment assets?; (ii) unrealised gains or losses on revaluation of investment assets?; (iii) unrealised gains or losses on revaluation of fixed assets for the charity's use?;	Sch Pt I para 3(e)
(h) net movement of funds?;	Sch Pt I para 3(f)
(i) resources used for net acquisitions?;	SORP para 86
(j) total funds brought forward?;	Sch Pt I para 3(g)
(k) total funds carried forward?	Sch Pt I para 3(h)
*(**Note**: where there has been a material change in the year in total resources applied for fixed assets for the charity's use, this fact should be stated in the notes. Where the change is 'very large' in the context of total income or expenditure, this note should immediately follow the reconciliation of funds.)*	SORP para 86
Are the total figures analysed, in columnar form, distinguishing between unrestricted, restricted and endowment funds?	Sch Pt I para 4 SORP para 74
Are incoming resources analysed under the following headings, where material:	Sch Pt I para 3 SORP para 90
(a) donations, legacies and similar?	
(b) grants receivable?;	
(c) investment income?;	

	Ref
(d) income from trading activities: (i) which are in furtherance of the charity's objects?; (ii) which are for commercial or fundraising purposes?;	Sch Pt I para 3(a) (iii)(A) & (B)
(e) other (e.g., net gains on disposal of fixed assets for use by the charity)?	
***(Notes**:* *1 gross incoming resources should be summarised in the SOFA in a manner appropriate to the charity. It should allow a user to gain an accurate appreciation of the principal elements, but should not be excessively detailed. Supporting analyses should be provided in the notes;*	SORP paras 87 & 88
2 within this section the indivdiual sub-headings may be changed in order to present a true and fair view of the charity's activities.)	SORP para 96
Is investment income analysed between:	SORP para 128
(a) investment properties?;	
(b) investments listed on a recognised stock exchange, including ones valued by reference to such investments?;	
(c) investments in subsidiary and associated undertakings or in companies which are connected persons?;	
(d) other unlisted securities?;	
(e) cash held as part of the investment portfolio?; and	
(f) other?,	
and is there a further analysis for each of the above categories between that arising on investment assets in and outside the UK?	SORP para 128
Are all incoming resources, as far as is practicable, shown gross?	SORP paras 99, 122 & 133

	Ref
*(**Note**: in certain cases, e.g., small fundraising events, it may be more informative for the net amount to be shown in the SOFA. In such a case, the reason for netting and, where material, an estimate of the gross funds and the deducted expenditure should be given in the notes.)*	
Is taxed income grossed up, with the tax recoverable shown as a debtor?	SORP para 134
Is income collected for the charity but not yet handed over, or in collecting boxes , etc., appropriately estimated and shown as 'collections in progress'?	SORP paras 113 & 114
Are grants receivable credited to the SOFA as soon as the conditions for receipt have been satisfied?	SORP para 117
Is direct charitable expenditure analysed under the following headings:	Sch Pt I para 3(b) SORP para 92
(a) grants payable?;	
(b) other direct expenditure on charitable objectives, appropriately analysed?;	
(c) depreciation/losses on disposal of fixed assets used for charitable purposes?; and	
(d) support costs?	
*(**Note**: within this section the individual sub-headings may be changed in order to present a true and fair view of the charity's activities.)*	
Is other expenditure analysed under the following headings:	Sch Pt I para 3(b) SORP para 93
(a) fundraising and publicity costs?;	
(b) administration costs?; and	

	Ref
(c) other expenditure?	
*(**Note**: within this section the individual sub-headings may be changed in order to present a true and fair view of the charity's activities.)*	SORP para 96
*(**Note**: the natural classification of expenditure may be given in the notes.)*	SORP para 136
For material grants to institutions, state:	Sch Pt IV para 1(k) SORP para 137
(a) the name of the recipient?; and	
(b) the aggregate amount of grants made to that recipient in the financial year?	
*(**Notes**:*	
1 this may be given in the SOFA or the notes. Alternatively, this information may be given in a separate publication, provided the notes refer to this and the amounts are reconciled to the charge in the accounts;	
2 in the case of any one recipient, all grants in aggregate in any year equal to or greater than £1,000 should be regarded as material and disclosed;	SORP para 138
3 unless contained in a separate publication, disclosure should be limited to the largest 50 grants, or such larger number as is considered necessary to convey a proper understanding of the charity's grant-making activities;	
4 if the trustees consider that disclosure may prejudice the recipient institution, or the charity's activities, they should give their reasons in the notes instead;	SORP para 138(a)
5 where a charitable foundation finds it necessary to make anonymous grants, the details need not be disclosed, but the notes should give the total amount;	SORP para 138(b)
6 in the cases of 4 and 5, details of the grants must be disclosed separately, in writing, to the Commissioners, or other regulatory body, explaining in full the reasons for non-disclosure, or why the charity is seeking anonymity.)	

	Ref
For grants to individuals, is the number and aggregate amount disclosed?	SORP para 139
Are interest-free loans shown as debtors and only written off as direct charitable expenditure if irrecoverable?	SORP para 140

Balance sheet

(***Note***: *the balance sheet must show the state of affairs of the charity at the end of the financial year)*	Sch Pt II para 1
Are the assets of the charity sub-divided between fixed assets (including investments and investment properties) and current assets (including investments for trading)?	SORP para 171
Have fixed assets been divided into:	Sch Pt II para 2(a)
(a) intangible assets?;	
(b) tangible assets for the charity's use?; and	
(c) investments?	
Have current assets been divided into:	Sch Pt II para 2(b)
(a) stocks and work in progress?;	
(b) debtors?;	
(c) investments?;	
(d) cash at bank and in hand?	
Are the liabilities divided between current and long-term liabilities?	Sch Pt II para 2(c) & (f) SORP para 172
Is there a heading for net current assets, or liabilities?	Sch Pt II para 2(d)

	Ref
Is there a heading for total assets less current liabilities?	Sch Pt II para 2(e)
Is there a heading for provisions for liabilities and charges?	Sch Pt II para 2(g)
Has the figure for net assets been given?	Sch Pt II para 2(h)
Where the use of any income is so severely restricted, has it been disclosed as 'deferred income' on the balance sheet, with suitable explanation in the notes?	SORP para 103
Have the charity's funds been divided into:	Sch Pt II para 2(i)
(a) unrestricted income funds?;	
(b) income funds which are restricted as to their use?;	
(c) capital funds?	
Has the balance sheet been approved by the trustees, as a body, and signed by one on their behalf? Is the date of approval given?	Reg 3(6) SORP para 30

Notes to the accounts

Have tangible fixed assets been analysed into:	Sch Pt IV para 1(1)(i)
(a) freehold interests in land and buildings?;	
(b) any other interest in land and buildings?;	
(c) plant and machinery?;	
(d) fixtures, fittings and equipment?;	
(e) payment on account and assets in the course of construction?	

	Ref
Are all assets of material value held for continuing use in the charity's activities:	SORP para 183
(a) classified as fixed assets for charity use;	
(b) segregated in the notes between those used for direct charitable purposes and those used for other purposes?	
Have material movements of tangible fixed assets and fixed asset investments been disclosed?	Sch Pt IV para 1(1) (iii)
Are any of the charity's fixed assets excepted from capitalisation? If so, have:	SORP para 187
(a) details of the assets' insured value; and	
(b) what use is made of them, been given?	
*(**Notes**:* *1 the information about uncapitalised fixed assets should be such that a user can appreciate their age and scale;* *2 the above information need not be disclosed if publication would prejudice the efficient working of the charity.)*	
Have fixed asset investments been analysed according to the major categories of investment? Are investment assets analysed between:	Sch Pt IV para 1(1) (ii) SORP para 195
(a) investment properties?;	
(b) investments listed on a recognised stock exchange, including ones valued by reference to such investments?;	
(c) investments in subsidiary and associated undertakings or in companies which are connected persons?;	
(d) other unlisted securities?;	

	Ref
(e) cash held as part of the investment portfolio?; and	
(f) other?	SORP para 195
and is there a further analysis for each of the above categories between that arising on investment assets in and outside the UK?	
Are there further details showing how the portfolio is structured?	SORP para 196
*(**Note**: this should indicate direct and indirect investment in listed securities, details of any material investments (any over 5 per cent by value of the portfolio) and any material restrictions applying on realisation.)*	
Is the value of investments allotted to the narrower and wider ranges disclosed?	SORP para 198
Where an investment is held within more than one of the charity's funds, are the funds to which it belongs made clear?	SORP para 197
If the charity has revalued any of its fixed assets, is this fact stated and the dates and basis of valuation been given? Where values are determined otherwise than by reference to readily available market prices, is the name and qualification of the valuer given? If that person is an employee or trustee of the charity, is that disclosed?	SORP para 175
Has the historical cost of investment assets been stated?	SORP para 194
Where the market is thought by the trustees not to be capable of absorbing a shareholding due to its size, or nature, without a material effect on the price, has the position been summarised? Are the trustees able to give an opinion on how much that price should be adjusted?	SORP para 178
Have debtors been further analysed into:	Sch Pt IV para 1(m)

	Ref
(a) trade debtors?;	
(b) amounts owed by any institution or body corporate which is a connected person of the charity?;	
(c) other debtors?; and	
(d) prepayments and accrued income?	
Are both current and long-term creditors analysed into:	Sch Pt IV para 1(n)
(a) loans and overdrafts?;	
(b) trade creditors?;	
(c) amounts owed to any institution or body corporate which is a connected person of the charity?;	
(d) other creditors?; and	
(e) accruals and deferred income?	
For all material charitable commitments accrued, have:	SORP para 200
(a) the amount charged in the SOFA;	
(b) when each payment is likely to be made; and	
(c) the movement on previously reported accrued commitment,	
been given?	
For all material commitments in respect of specific charitable projects not charged in the accounts, have:	SORP para 199
(a) the amounts involved;	
(b) when the commitments are likely to be met; and	

	Ref
(c) the movements on previously reported commitments,	
been given?	
*(**Note**: similar particulars should be given for all other material binding commitments.)*	
Where there are contingent liabilities, have:	Sch Pt IV part 1(o) SORP para 207
(a) the amount, or estimated amount;	
(b) its legal nature;	
(c) whether any valuable security has been provided and, if so, what; and	
(d) the uncertainties expected to affect its outcome,	
been given?	
*(**Note**: full details should be given where a contingent liability is offset by a related counter-claim.)*	SORP para 206
Are all material guarantees, and the conditions under which liabilities might arise thereunder, disclosed?	SORP para 202
If any of the charity's assets are subject to a charge, have:	Sch Pt IV para 1(i) SORP para 208
(a) particulars of those assets;	
(b) the amount of the loan/liability and its proportion to the present value of those assets,	
been given?	

	Ref
Have the amounts, interest and repayment terms of all inter-fund loans been given?	SORP para 209
Where there are loans to trading subsidiaries, has the security provided, the interest payable and the repayment terms been given?	SORP para 209
Is there a description of the nature and purposes of all of the charity's significant funds?	Sch Pt IV para 1(b) SORP para 43
*(**Notes**:*	
1 the precise purpose of all designated funds should be given;	SORP App 3(1)
2 there should be an explanation of the nature of transfers out of, and allocations to, designated funds and the reasons for them.)	SORP para 44
Is there a description of incoming resources which represent capital, according to whether or not that capital is permanent?	Sch Pt IV para 1(f)
Are the assets and liabilities analysed between the funds?	SORP para 36(a)
Is there an indication whether or not sufficient resources are held in an appropriate form to enable each fund to be applied in accordance with restrictions imposed?	SORP para 36(a)
Are all funds in deficit separately disclosed and is the matter referred to and explained in the trustees' annual report?	SORP para 37
Where the trustees have changed the accounting reference date, is there a statement of their reasons?	Sch Pt IV para 1(r)
Have the total emoluments of employees, their average number, and the number whose emoluments fell within each band of £5,000 from £30,000 been given?	SORP paras 160 & 161

	Ref
Has auditors' or independent examiner's remuneration been analysed between:	Sch Pt IV para 1(j) SORP para 162
(a) audit, or independent examination, services?;	
(b) other services?	
*(**Notes**:* *1 in respect of (b) above, the SORP recommends that the figure for other services be further analysed e.g., between taxation, financial advice, consultancy etc.;*	
2 where consolidated accounts are prepared, the amounts to be disclosed are those for the group.)	SORP para 163
Where ex-gratia payments are made otherwise than as an application of funds for charitable purposes, has the total amount or value of any:	SORP para 164
(a) payment;	
(b) non-monetary benefit; or	
(c) other expenditure of any kind; or	
(d) waiver of rights to property to which the charity is entitled,	
been given?	
*(**Note**: where the trustees require the authority of the Court, the Attorney General or the Commissioners, the nature and date of that authority for each such payment should be disclosed.)*	SORP para 165
Where indemnity insurance has been purchased, is that fact and the costs involved given?	Sch Pt IV para 1(d) SORP para 159
For material transactions, contracts, arrangements etc., with trustees or connected persons have:	Sch Pt IV para 1(e) SORP para 154

	Ref
(a) the amounts involved;	
(b) the terms and conditions,	
been given?	
(***Notes***:	
1 contracts of employment will not usually be material;	SORP para 155
2 transactions involving trustees, whether directly or indirectly, will always be material.)	SORP para 156
Where a trustee has received remuneration, directly or indirectly, from either:	Sch Pt IV para 1(c) SORP para 157
(a) the charity; or	
(b) a company which the trustees control, has that fact, the source and amount been given?	
(***Notes***:	
1 para 1(c) of Pt IV requires the remuneration of any person connected with the charity and the name of the person to be given. The remuneration may be paid directly or indirectly from the charity's funds or from any institution or body corporate which is a connected person;	
2 where the trustees have received no such remuneration, that fact should be stated.)	SORP para 157
Where trustees have been reimbursed for any expenses incurred, have the following been stated:	SORP para 158
(a) aggregate amount?;	
(b) nature of the expenses?; and	
(c) number of trustees reimbursed?	
(***Note***: *where the trustees have received no such reimbursement, that fact should be stated.)*	SORP para 158

	Ref
For each connected person which is an institution or body corporate, have the following been stated:	Sch Pt IV para 1(h)
(a) name?;	
(b) description of the nature of the relationship with the charity?;	
(c) its activities, including, where material, its turnover, net result for the corresponding financial year?; and	
(d) any qualification expressed in an auditor's report?	
Is there a description of the sources, by category, of any material grants?	SORP para 120
Where material legacies to which the charity has entitlement are not accounted for, has that fact and an estimate of the amounts receivable been stated?	SORP para 106
Are there analyses of administration and support costs?	SORP paras 152 & 153
Has any other information which may reasonably assist a user to understand the accounts been disclosed?	Sch Pt IV para 1(f)

Cash flow statement

Has a cash flow statement been prepared, in accordance with FRS 1, if the charity has two or more of the following size qualifications?	SORP para 210
(a) gross resources in excess of £2.8 million;	SORP App 2
(b) a balance sheet total greater than £1.4 million;	
(c) more than 50 employees.	

Consolidated accounts

Have consolidated accounts been prepared, regardless of the size of the charity group?	SORP paras 54 & 55

	Ref
Have 'entity' accounts for the parent also been prepared?	SORP para 56
Have the activities of subsidiaries been consolidated on a line-by-line basis in the SOFA, unless inappropriate?	SORP paras 63 & 64
Where the trading activity of a subsidiary is shown as a single line entry in the SOFA (or summary income and expenditure account), has the full profit and loss account been given in the notes?	SORP para 65
Have the assets and liabilities been consolidated on a line-by-line basis?	SORP para 66
Has the name of each subsidiary and particulars of the charity's shareholding, or other controlling interest, been given?	SORP para 58
Are funds, other than funds used in carrying out the charitable objectives, retained by subsidiaries shown under an appropriate separate heading in the consolidated accounts?	SORP para 42
If consolidated accounts are not prepared, has the reason been stated? Is the aggregate amount of the total investment of the charity in its subsidiary undertakings stated? For each subsidiary, is the following stated:	SORP para 59

(a) its name?;

(b) particulars of the charity's shareholding or other controlling interest?

(c) how its activities relate to the charity's?;

(d) if material, the aggregate amount of its capital and reserves at the year end?;

(e) if material, a summary of its turnover and expenditure, and of its profit or loss for the year?;

Ref

(f) particulars of any qualifications contained in the auditors' report on its accounts, and any note or reservation in those accounts which call attention to a matter which, that note or reservation apart, would have been referred to in such a qualification?

(***Note***: *it is particularly important that the presentation is sufficiently detailed to distinguish the assets and liabilities and transactions of the charity from those of its subsidiary(ies) and that the turnover and results of the latter are clearly stated. Expenditure for charitable purposes (including support costs), fundraising and publicity costs, and administration costs should be separately disclosed.)*

SORP para 60

Has the charity any associated undertakings? If so and consolidated accounts are prepared, has the following been stated:

SORP para 67

(a) the name of those undertakings?;

(b) particulars of the charity's shareholding or other interest?

Has the interest been equity-accounted for?

SORP para 67

If consolidated accounts are not prepared, has the following been stated:

SORP para 67

(a) the name of the undertaking?;

(b) particulars of the charity's shareholding or other interest?;

(c) if material, the aggregate amount of its capital and reserves at the year end?; and

(d) if material, its turnover and result for the year?

Summary income and expenditure account

Is this account derived from, and cross-referenced to, the corresponding figures in the SOFA?

SORP para 167

	Ref
Have the following been shown:	SORP para 168
(a) gross income from all sources, excluding non-charitable trading activities, inter-fund transfers and revaluations of fixed assets?;	
(b) income from non-charitable trading activities (if shown net, are the turnover and expenses shown as an inset?)?;	
(c) net gains/losses from disposals of all fixed assets belonging to the charity's income funds?;	
(d) transfers from endowment funds?;	
(e) total income?;	
(f) total expenditure from income funds?;	
(g) net income or expenditure for the year?	
*(**Notes**: 1 a summary income and expenditure account should be prepared where either statutory requirements or accounting and reporting standards or the requirements of the charity's governing instrument dictate; 2 where the charity has no endowment fund movements, both for the current and previous year, the summary income and expenditure account may be omitted. In such cases, the SOFA should show the amount of the net revaluation gains/losses for the year in a separate section, after prominent sub-totals entitled 'net income/expenditure for the year'. The SOFA would, thus, comprise two parts: the account of income and expenditure for the year; and, the statement of total recognised gains and losses.)*	SORP para 70

Summarised accounts

(Regardless of the intended circulation of any summarised accounts, the full annual report and accounts should always be prepared.)	SORP para 215
If summarised accounts are prepared:	

	Ref
(a) are they a fair and accurate summary of the full accounts?	SORP para 25
(b) do they contain information relating both to the balance sheet and the SOFA?	SORP para 216
(c) do they contain an appropriate 'health warning'?;	SORP para 217
(d) are they accompanied by a statement, signed on behalf of the trustees, which contains the following:	
(i) that they are a summary of the information extracted from the full accounts?;	SORP para 216
(ii) the date on which the annual report and accounts were approved, whether they have been submitted to the Commissioners and, for charitable companies, whether they have been delivered to the Registrar?;	SORP paras 218 & 222
(iii) whether or not the full annual accounts have been audited/independently examined? If so, there should be a report by the auditor/independent examiner stating: • whether, in his opinion, the summarised accounts are consistent with the full annual accounts; • whether his opinion on the full accounts was qualified or not; and • if qualified, the report given in the summarised accounts should be sufficient to enable a user to appreciate the significance of the auditor's/independent examiner's reservations.	SORP paras 219 & 220

Appendix 2 – The Charities (Accounts and Reports) Regulations 1995 (SI 1995 No . . . (Draft Statutory Instrument)

Made	*1995*
Laid before Parliament	*1995*
Coming into force	*1995*

The Secretary of State in exercise of the powers conferred upon him by sections 42, 44, 45 and 86(3) of the Charities Act 1993(**a**), and after such consultation as is mentioned in section 86(4) of that Act, hereby makes the following Regulations:

Citation and commencement

1. These Regulations may be cited as the Charities (Accounts and Reports) Regulations 1995 and shall come into force on 1995.

Interpretation

2. In these Regulations, the expression –

'connected person', in relation to a charity, shall be construed in accordance with Schedule 5 to the 1993 Act;

'financial year' shall be construed in accordance with regulation 5 below; and

'the 1993 Act' means the Charities Act 1993.

(**a**) 1993 c.10; section 42 was amended by the Charities Act 1993 (Substitution of Sums) Order 1995 (S.I. 1995/) and section 45 was amended by section 29 of the Deregulation and Contracting Out Act 1994 (c.40) and by Part II of Schedule I to the Companies Act 1985 (Audit Exemption) Regulations 1994 (S.I. 1994/1935).

Form and content of statements of accounts

3. – (1) Subject to regulation 4 below, the requirements as to form and contents of a statement of accounts prepared in accordance with section 42(1) of the 1993 Act are those set out in the following provisions of this regulation.

(2) The statement shall consist of the following, that is to say –
(a) a statement of financial activities which satisfies the requirements set out in Part I of the Schedule to these Regulations; and
(b) a balance sheet which satisfies the requirements set out in Part II of that Schedule.

(3) The statement shall be prepared in accordance with the methods and principles specified and referred to in Part III of the Schedule to these Regulations.

(4) There shall be provided by way of notes to the accounts the information specified in Part IV of the Schedule to these Regulations.

(5) Part V of the Schedule to these Regulations shall have effect for the purposes of defining expressions used in that Schedule.

(6) The balance sheet shall be signed by one or more of the charity trustees of the charity, each of whom has been authorised to do so, and shall specify the date on which the accounts to which the statement relates were approved by the charity trustees in accordance with those trusts.

Form and contents: special cases

4. – (1) Regulation 3 above does not apply in the case of a charity which is –
(a) a common investment fund established by a scheme under section 24 of the 1993 Act, other than a fund the trusts of which provide for property to be transferred to the fund only by or on behalf of a participating charity of which the charity trustees are the trustees appointed to manage the fund; or
(b) a common deposit fund established by a scheme under section 25 of the 1993 Act.

[(2) In the case of a charity (other than an exempt charity) which is a registered housing association within the meaning of the Housing Associations Act 1985(**a**) and whose registration has been recorded under section 5(3) of that Act, the requirements as to form and contents of a statement of accounts prepared in pursuance of section 42(1) of the 1993 Act are those for the time being laid down by order of the Secretary of State under section 24 of that Act of 1985(**b**) as the accounting requirements for registered housing associations.]

Financial year

5. – (1) The financial year of a charity shall, for the purposes of the 1993 Act and regulations made thereunder, be determined in accordance with the following provisions of this regulation.

(2) The first financial year of a charity shall be –

(a) in the case of a charity which is established before the date on which these Regulations come into force, the period beginning with the day immediately following the end of the period in respect of which a statement of accounts was required to be prepared under any statutory provision contained in or having effect under an Act of Parliament applicable to that charity before the coming into force of section 42 of the 1993 Act and ending with the accounting reference date of the charity or such other date, not more than seven days before or after the accounting reference date, as the charity trustees may determine;

(b) in the case of a charity which is established on or after the date on which these Regulations come into force, the period beginning with the day on which the charity is established and ending with the accounting reference date of the charity or such other date, not more than seven days before or after the accounting reference date, as the charity trustees may determine.

(3) Subsequent financial years of a charity begin with the day immediately following the end of the charity's previous financial year and end with its accounting reference date or such other date, not more than seven days before or after the accounting reference date, as the charity trustees may determine.

(**a**) 1985 c.69; the expressions 'housing association' and 'registered' are defined in accordance with section 102.

(**b**) Section 24 was amended by section 59 of, and Part I of Schedule 6 to, the Housing Act 1988 (c.50).

(4) The accounting reference date of a charity shall, for the purposes of this regulation, be –

(a) in the first financial year of a charity which is established before the date on which these Regulations come into force, such date, not less than 6 months nor more than 18 months after the date on which that financial year began, as the charity trustees may determine;

(b) in the first financial year of a charity which is established on or after the date on which these Regulations come into force, such date, not less than 6 months nor more than 18 months after the date on which the charity was established, as the charity trustees may determine;

(c) in any subsequent financial year of a charity, the date 12 months after the previous accounting reference date of the charity or such other date, not less than 6 months nor more than 18 months after the previous accounting reference date of the charity as the trustees may determine:

Provided that –

(i) the charity trustees shall not exercise their powers under sub-paragraph (c) of this paragraph so as to determine an accounting reference date in respect of any financial year which is consecutive, or follows immediately after a financial year which is consecutive, to a previous financial year in respect of which that power was exercised; and

(ii) the charity trustees shall exercise their powers under sub-paragraph (a) or (c) of this paragraph so as to determine a date earlier or later than 12 months from the beginning of the financial year only where satisfied that there are exceptional reasons to do so (which reasons shall be specified in the notes to the accounts in accordance with regulation 3(4) above and Part IV of the Schedule to these Regulations).

Annual audit of charity accounts

6. – (1) The duties of an auditor carrying out an audit of the accounts of a charity under section 43 of the 1993 Act(**a**) shall be those specified in the following provisions of this regulation.

(2) Where a statement of accounts has been prepared under section 42(1) of the 1993 Act for the financial year in question the auditor shall

(**a**) Section 43 was amended by section 28 of the Deregulation and Contracting Out Act 1994.

make a report on that statement to the person or persons who appointed him which –

(a) states the name and address of the auditor and the name of the charity concerned and the person or persons who appointed him;

(b) is signed by him or, where the office of auditor is held by a body corporate or partnership, in its name by a person authorised to sign on its behalf and states that the auditor is a person falling within paragraph (a) or, as the case may be, (b) of section 43(2) of the 1993 Act;

(c) is dated and specifies the financial year in respect of which the accounts to which it relates have been prepared;

(d) specifies that it is a report in respect of an audit carried out under section 43 of the 1993 Act and in accordance with regulations made under section 44 of that Act;

(e) states whether in the auditor's opinion the statement of accounts complies with the requirements of regulation 3 or, as the case may be, 4, above and, in particular, gives a true and fair view of the state of affairs of the charity at the end of, and of the financial activities or, as the case may require, income and expenditure of the charity in, the financial year in question;

(f) where the auditor has formed the opinion –

(i) that accounting records have not been kept in respect of the charity in accordance with section 41 of the 1993 Act; or

(ii) that the statement of accounts does not accord with those records; or

(iii) that any information contained in the statement of accounts is inconsistent in any material respect with the report of the charity trustees prepared under section 45 of the 1993 Act in respect of the financial year in question; or

(iv) that any information or explanation to which he is entitled under regulation 8 below has not been afforded to him,

contains a statement of that opinion and of his grounds for forming it.

(3) Where a receipts and payments account and statement of assets and liabilities have been prepared under section 42(3) of the 1993 Act for the financial year in question the auditor shall make a report on that account and statement to the person or persons who appointed him which –

(a) states the name and address of the auditor and the name of the charity concerned and the person or persons who appointed him;

(b) is signed by him or, where the office of auditor is held by a body corporate or partnership, in its name by a person authorised to sign on its behalf and states that the auditor is a person falling within paragraph (a) or, as the case may be, (b) of section 43(2) of the 1993 Act;

(c) is dated and specifies the financial year in respect of which the accounts to which it relates have been prepared;

(d) specifies that it is a report in respect of an audit carried out under section 43 of the 1993 Act and in accordance with regulations made under section 44 of that Act;

(e) states whether in the auditor's opinion –

  (i) the receipts and payments account and statement of assets and liabilities are [properly prepared] [in all material respects complete and accurate]; and

  (ii) the account and statement adequately distinguish any material special trust or other restricted fund of the charity;

(f) where the auditor has formed the opinion –

  (i) that accounting records have not been kept in respect of the charity in accordance with section 41 of the 1993 Act; or

  (ii) that the account and statement do not accord with those records; or

  (iii) that any information or explanation to which he is entitled under regulation 8 below has not been afforded to him,

contains a statement of that opinion and of his grounds for forming it.

(4) The auditor shall, in preparing his report for the purposes of paragraph (2) or, as the case may be, (3) above, carry out such investigations as will enable him to form an opinion as to the matters specified in sub-paragraph (e) and (f) of that paragraph.

(5) The auditor shall communicate to the Commissioners, in writing, any matter of which the auditor becomes aware in his capacity as such which relates to the activities or affairs of the charity or of any institution or body corporate which is a connected person in relation to the charity and which the auditor has reasonable cause to believe is, or is likely to be, of material significance for the exercise, in relation to the charity of the Commissioners' functions under section 8 (general power to institute inquiries) or 18 (power to act for protection of charities) of the 1993 Act.

(6) Where an auditor appointed by charity trustees ceases for any reason to hold office he shall send to the charity trustees a statement of any circumstances connected with his ceasing to hold office which he considers should be brought to their attention or, if he considers that there are no such circumstances, a statement that there are none; and a copy of any statement sent to the charity trustees under this paragraph (except a statement that there are no such circumstances) shall be sent to the Commissioners.

Independent examination of charity accounts

7. An independent examiner who has carried out an examination of the accounts of a charity under section 43 of the 1993 Act shall make a report to the charity trustees which –

- (a) states his name and address and the name of the charity concerned and the names of the charity trustees;
- (b) is signed by him and specifies any relevant professional qualifications or professional body of which he is a member;
- (c) is dated and specifies the financial year in respect of which the accounts to which it relates have been prepared;
- (d) specifies that it is a report in respect of an examination carried out under section 43 of the 1993 Act and in accordance with any directions given by the Commissioners under subsection (7)(b) of that section which are applicable;
- (e) states whether or not any matter has come to the examiner's attention in connection with the examination which gives him reasonable cause to believe that in any material respect –
  - (i) accounting records have not been kept in respect of the charity in accordance with section 41 of the 1993 Act; or
  - (ii) the accounts do not accord with those records; or
  - (iii) in the case of an examination of accounts a statement of which has been prepared under section 42(1) of the 1993 Act, the statement of accounts does not comply with any of the requirements of regulation 3 above except the requirements specified in paragraph 1 of Part III of the Schedule to these Regulations;
- (f) states whether or not any matter has come to the examiner's attention in connection with the examination to which, in his opinion, attention should be drawn in the report in order to enable a proper understanding of the accounts to be reached;
- (g) where any of the following matters has become apparent to

the examiner during the course of the examination, namely, that –

(i) there has been any material expenditure or action which appears not to be in accordance with the trusts of the charity; or

(ii) any information or explanation to which he is entitled under regulation 8 below has not been afforded to him; or

(iii) in the case of an examination of accounts a statement of which has been prepared under section 42(1) of the 1993 Act, any information contained in the statement of accounts is inconsistent in any material respect with the report of the charity trustees prepared under section 45 of the 1993 Act in respect of the financial year in question,

contains a statement to that effect.

Audit and independent examination: supplementary provisions

8. – (1) An auditor or independent examiner carrying out an audit or examination of the accounts of a charity under section 43 of the 1993 Act shall have a right of access to any books, documents and other records (however kept) which relate to the charity concerned and which the auditor or examiner in question considers it necessary to inspect for the purposes of carrying out the audit or, as the case may be, examination.

(2) Such an auditor or independent examiner shall be entitled to require, in the case of the charity concerned, such information and explanations from past or present charity trustees or trustees for the charity, or from past or present officers or employees of the charity, as he considers it necessary to obtain for the purposes of carrying out the audit or, as the case may be, examination.

Dispensations from audit or examination requirements

9. – (1) The Commissioners may, in the circumstances specified in paragraph (2) below, dispense with the requirements of section 43(2) or (3) of the 1993 Act in the case of a particular charity or of a particular financial year of a charity.

(2) The circumstances referred to in paragraph (1) above are where the Commissioners:

(a) are satisfied that the accounts of the charity concerned are required to be audited in accordance with any statutory provision contained in or having effect under an Act of Parliament which, in the opinion of the Commissioners, imposes requirements which are sufficiently similar to the requirements of section 43(2) for those requirements to be dispensed with;

(b) are satisfied that the accounts of the charity concerned for the financial year in question have been audited or, as the case may be, examined in accordance with requirements or arrangements which, in the opinion of the Commissioners, are sufficiently similar to the relevant requirements of section 43 of the 1993 Act applicable to that financial year of that charity for those requirements to be dispensed with;

(c) are satisfied that there has in the financial year in question been no transaction on the part of the charity concerned which would be required to be shown and explained in the accounting records kept in pursuance of section 41 of the 1993 Act;

(d) consider that, although the financial year in question of the charity concerned is one to which subsection (2) of section 43 of the 1993 Act applies, there are exceptional circumstances which justify the examination of the accounts by an independent examiner instead of their audit in accordance with that subsection, and the accounts have been so examined,

and where the charity trustees of the charity concerned have supplied to the Commissioners any report made to them with respect to the accounts of that charity for the financial year in question which the Commissioners have requested.

Annual reports

10. – (1) The report on the activities of a charity during the year which is required to be contained in the annual report in respect of each financial year of the charity prepared under section 45 of the 1993 Act shall specify the financial year to which it relates and shall –

(a) in the case of any financial year of a charity in which neither its gross income nor its total expenditure exceeds £10,000, be a brief summary of the main activities and achievements of the charity during the year in relation to its objects;

(b) in the case of any financial year of a charity in which its gross income or total expenditure exceeds £10,000, be a review of all activities, including material transactions, significant developments, and achievements of the charity during the year in relation to its objects, any significant changes in those activities during the year, any important events affecting those activities which have occurred since the end of the year and any likely future developments in those activities; and

(c) in either case, be dated and be signed by one or more of the charity trustees, each of whom has been authorised in accordance with the trusts of the charity to do so.

(2) The information relating to a charity and to its trustees and officers which is required to be contained in that annual report shall be –

(a) the name of the charity as it appears in the register and any other name by which it makes itself known;

(b) the number assigned to it in the register and, in the case of a charitable company, the number with which it is registered as a company;

(c) the principal address of the charity and, in the case of a charitable company, the address of its registered office;

(d) a description of the trusts of the charity;

(e) the names of the charity trustees and any other person who has at any time during the financial year in question been a trustee for or of the charity and of any person or body entitled to appoint a charity trustee of the charity;

(f) a description of the organisational structure of the charity;

(g) a description of any assets held by the charity, or by any charity trustee or other trustee for or of the charity on behalf of another charity, and particulars of any special arrangements made with respect to such assets and of the objects of the charity on whose behalf the assets are held.

(3) The Commissioners may, where they are satisfied that, in the case of a particular charity or class of charities, or of a particular financial year of a charity or class of charities, the disclosure of the name of any person required by paragraph (2)(e) above to be contained in the annual report of a charity could lead to that person being placed in any personal danger, dispense with the requirement in that paragraph so far as it applies to the name of any such person.

[One of Her Majesty's Principal Secretaries of State]

Home Office
1995

SCHEDULE **Regulation 3**

FORM AND CONTENTS OF STATEMENTS OF ACCOUNTS

PART 1
STATEMENT OF FINANCIAL ACTIVITIES

1. The statement of financial activities shall show the total incoming resources and application of resources, together with any other increase or decrease in the resources, of the charity during the financial year in respect of which the statement of accounts is prepared.

2. The information required by paragraph 1 above shall be analysed by reference to –

(a) the nature of the incoming resources or application of resources, or other increase or decrease in resources, concerned in accordance with paragraph 3 below; and
(b) the type of fund to which it relates, in accordance with paragraph 4 below.

3. The analysis required by paragraph 2(a) above is as follows:

(a) all incoming resources other than those required to be entered by sub-paragraph (e) below, divided into –
  (i) incoming resources from donors;
  (ii) income from investment;
  (iii) income from trading activities –
    (A) which are in furtherance of the objects of the charity; and
    (B) which are for commercial or fund-raising purposes; and
  (iv) any other material incoming resources;
(b) all resources expended, divided into –
  (i) expenditure directly relating to the objects of the charity;
  (ii) expenditure in support of charitable activity;
  (iii) expenditure on fund-raising and publicity;
  (iv) expenditure on the administration of the charity; and
  (v) any other expenditure;
(c) gross transfers between the funds of the charity;
(d) net incoming resources for the financial year before calculation of gains or losses on disposal or revaluation of fixed assets (that is to say, the aggregate of all amounts entered in pursuance of sub-paragraphs (a), (b) and (c) above);

(e) any gains or losses on disposal or revaluation of fixed assets, divided into –
  (i) gains or losses on disposal of investment assets;
  (ii) unrealised gains or losses on revaluation of investment assets; and
  (iii) unrealised gains or losses on revaluation of fixed assets for use by the charity;
(f) net movement in funds in the financial year (that is to say, the total of all entries made in pursuance of sub-paragraphs (d) and (e) above);
(g) the total of funds brought forward from the previous financial year; and
(h) the total of funds carried forward to the next financial year (that is to say, the amount entered in pursuance of sub-paragraph (f) above plus the amount entered in pursuance of sub-paragraph (g) above).

4. The analysis required by paragraph 2(b) above is as follows:
(a) unrestricted income funds;
(b) income funds which are restricted as to their use;
(c) capital funds; and
(d) the total for all funds of the charity (that is to say, the total of the amounts entered in pursuance of sub-paragraphs (a), (b) and (c) above).

Part II
Balance Sheet

1. The balance sheet shall show, by reference to the information specified in paragraph 2 below, the state of affairs of the charity as at the end of the financial year in respect of which the statement of accounts is prepared.

2. The information referred to in paragraph 1 above is as follows:
(a) fixed assets, divided into –
  (i) intangible assets;
  (ii) tangible assets for use by the charity; and
  (iii) investments;
(b) current assets, divided into –
  (i) stock and work in progress;
  (ii) debtors;
  (iii) investments;
  (iv) cash at bank and in hand;
(c) short-term creditors;
(d) net current assets or liabilities (that is to say, the difference

between the total amount entered in pursuance of sub-paragraph (b) above and the total amount entered in pursuance of sub-paragraph (c) above);

(e) total assets after deduction of current liabilities (that is to say, the total amount entered in pursuance of sub-paragraph (a) above plus the amount entered in pursuance of sub-paragraph (d) above);

(f) long term creditors;

(g) provisions for liabilities or charges;

(h) net assets (that is to say, the amount entered in pursuance of sub-paragraph (e) above less the total amounts entered in pursuance of sub-paragraphs (f) and (g) above); and

(i) funds of the charity, divided into –

(i) unrestricted income funds;

(ii) income funds which are restricted as to their use; and

(iii) capital funds.

PART III
METHODS AND PRINCIPLES

1. – (1) The statement of financial activities shall give a true and fair view of the financial activities of the charity in, and the balance sheet shall give a true and fair view of the state of affairs of the charity at the end of, the financial year in respect of which the statement of accounts is prepared.

(2) Where compliance with Part I, or, as the case may be, Part II and Part IV of this Schedule would not be sufficient to give a true and fair view, the necessary additional information shall be given in the accounts or a note to them.

(3) If in special circumstances compliance with any of those provisions is inconsistent with the requirement to give a true and fair view, the charity trustees shall depart from that provision to the extent necessary to give a true and fair view; particulars of any such departure, the reasons for it and its effect shall be given in a note to the accounts.

2. – (1) In respect of every amount required by paragraph 3 or 4(d) of Part I of this Schedule to be shown in the statement of financial activities or by Part II of this Schedule to be shown in the balance sheet, the corresponding amount for the financial year immediately preceding that to which the statement or balance sheet relates shall also be shown.

(2) Where that corresponding amount is not comparable with the amount to be shown for the item in question in respect of the financial

year to which the statement of financial activities or balance sheet relates, the former amount shall be adjusted; particulars of any material adjustment under this sub-paragraph shall be disclosed in a note to the accounts.

(3) This paragraph applies in relation to an item which would be required to be shown were there no such amount for the financial year in respect of which the statement of accounts is prepared in any case in which a corresponding amount is required to be shown for the immediately preceding financial year.

4. The values of assets and liabilities of the charity shall, for the purposes of entry in the accounts, be determined in accordance with the methods and principles for inclusion of assets and liabilities in the balance sheet set out in the Statement of Recommended Practice for Accounting by Charities issued on 1995.

PART IV
NOTES TO THE ACCOUNTS

1. The information to be provided by way of notes to the accounts is as follows:

(a) a description of the accounting policies of, and accounting assumptions made by, the charity trustees, including any material change in these, the reason for such change and its effect (if material) on the accounts;

(b) a description of the nature and purpose of all significant funds of the charity;

(c) a statement as to whether any remuneration or other benefits (together with the monetary value of such benefits) has been paid or is payable to any person connected with the charity directly or indirectly from the funds of the charity or from the property of any institution or body corporate which is a connected person in relation to the charity and the name of that person;

(d) particulars of the cost to the charity of –

(i) any policies of insurance against loss arising from the neglect or default of any of the charity trustees or trustees for the charity; or

(ii) indemnifying the charity trustees, or any of the trustees, for the charity in respect of the consequences of any such loss;

(e) particulars of any transaction undertaken in tne name of or on behalf of the charity in which any person connected with the charity has a material interest;

(f) a description of any incoming resources which represent capital, according to whether or not that capital is permanent endowment;

(g) an itemised analysis of any material movement between any of the restricted funds of the charity, or between a restricted and an unrestricted fund of the charity, together with an explanation of the nature and purpose of each of those funds;

(h) the name of any institution or body corporate which is a connected person in relation to the charity, together with a description of the nature of the charity's relationship with that institution or body corporate and of its activities, including, where material, its turnover and net profit or loss for the corresponding financial year of the institution or body corporate and any qualification expressed in an auditor's report on its accounts;

(i) particulars of any loan or guarantee secured against any of the assets of the charity;

(j) particulars of any remuneration paid to an auditor or independent examiner in respect of auditing or examining the accounts of the charity and particulars of any remuneration paid to him in respect of any other services rendered to the charity;

(k) particulars of any grant made by the charity to another institution of which any relevant recommended accounting practice requires disclosure;

(l) an analysis of any entry in the balance sheet relating to fixed assets –

    (i) in the case of tangible assets for use by the charity, according to the following categories –

        (A) freehold interests in land and buildings;

        (B) any other interest in land or buildings;

        (C) plant and machinery;

        (D) fixtures, fittings and equipment;

        (E) payment on account and assets in course of construction;

    (ii) in the case of investments, according to the major categories of investment;

    [(iii) in either case, which records any material movement in assets during the financial year to which the balance sheet relates];

(m) an analysis of any entry in the balance sheet relating to debtors, according to the following categories –

    (i) trade debtors;

(ii) amounts owed by an institution or body corporate which is a connected person in relation to the charity;
(iii) other debtors; and
(iv) prepayments and accrued income;

(n) an analysis of any entry in the balance sheet relating to creditors (whether short-term or long-term creditors), according to the following categories –
(i) loans and overdrafts;
(ii) trade creditors;
(iii) amounts owed to any institution or body corporate which is a connected person in relation to the charity;
(iv) other creditors; and
(v) accruals and deferred income;

(o) the following particulars of any contingent liability, that is to say, its amount or estimated amount, its legal nature and whether any valuable security has been provided by the charity in connection with that liability and, if so, what;

(p) in the case of any amount required by any of the preceding sub-paragraphs to be disclosed, the corresponding amount for the financial year immediately preceding that to which the accounts relate;

(q) a statement as to whether or not the accounts have been prepared in accordance with any applicable accounting standards and statements of recommended practice and particulars of any material departure from those standards and practices and the reasons for such departure;

(r) where the charity trustees have exercised their powers under regulation 5(4)(b) above, a statement of their reasons for doing so, and

(s) any other information which is required by these Regulations to be disclosed in a note to the accounts or which may reasonably assist the user to understand the statement of accounts.

PART V
INTERPRETATION

In this Schedule the following expressions have the meanings hereafter assigned to them –

'long-term creditor' means an amount falling due after more than one year from the end of the financial year;

'provisions for liabilities or charges' means any amount retained as reasonably necessary for the purpose of providing for any liability or loss which is either likely to be incurred, or certain to be incurred but uncertain as to amount or as to the date on which it will arise; and

'short-term creditor' means an amount falling due within one year.

EXPLANATORY NOTE

(This Note is not Part of the Regulations)

These Regulations, which extend only to England and Wales, make provision with respect to the accounts of charities, the financial years of a charity, the requirements relating to audit or examination of charity accounts and the annual reports of charity trustees.

Regulation 3 and the Schedule to the Regulations prescribe the form and contents of statements of accounts prepared by charity trustees under section 42 of the Charities Act 1993 ('the 1993 Act'), including the information to be provided by way of notes to the accounts and the methods and principles applicable.

Regulation 4 deals with the form and contents of the accounts of common investment funds and common deposit funds (which are governed by the Charities (Common Investment and Deposit Funds) (Accounts) Regulations 1995: S.I. 1995/) and registered housing associations (which must comply with the Housing Associations Act 1985).

Regulation 5 defines the financial year of a charity for the purposes of the 1993 Act and Regulations.

Regulation 6 deals with the duties of auditors and the report which they are required to make. Regulation 7 deals with the reports of independent examiners. Regulation 8 makes supplementary provision with respect to audit and independent examination and regulation 9 prescribes the circumstances in which dispensation from the requirement to have accounts audited or examined may be given by the Charity Commissioners.

Regulation 10 deals with the annual reports which charity trustees are required to make to the Charity Commissioners.

The Recommended Practice for Accounting by Charities referred to in Part III of the Schedule to the Regulations may be obtained from [the Charity Commission].

By virtue of the Charities Act 1993 (Commencement and Transitional Provisions) Order 1995 (S.I. 1995/) these Regulations apply only to financial years of a charity commencing after they come into force.

Appendix 3 – Extract from the Charities Act 1993: Part VI Charity accounts, reports and returns

PART VI

CHARITY ACCOUNTS, REPORTS AND RETURNS

Duty to keep accounting records

41. – (1) The charity trustees of a charity shall ensure that accounting records are kept in respect of the charity which are sufficient to show and explain all the charity's transactions, and which are such as to –

(a) disclose at any time, with reasonable accuracy, the financial position of the charity at that time, and

(b) enable the trustees to ensure that, where any statements of accounts are prepared by them under section 42(1) below, those statements of accounts comply with the requirements of regulations under that provision.

(2) The accounting records shall in particular contain –

(a) entries showing from day to day all sums of money received and expended by the charity, and the matters in respect of which the receipt and expenditure takes place; and

(b) a record of the assets and liabilities of the charity.

(3) The charity trustees of a charity shall preserve any accounting records made for the purposes of this section in respect of the charity for at least six years from the end of the financial year of the charity in which they are made.

(4) Where a charity ceases to exist within the period of six years mentioned in subsection (3) above as it applies to any accounting records, the obligation to preserve those records in accordance with that subsection shall continue to be discharged by the last charity trustees of the charity, unless the Commissioners consent in writing to the records being destroyed or otherwise disposed of.

(5) Nothing in this section applies to a charity which is a company.

Annual statements of accounts

42. – (1) The charity trustees of a charity shall (subject to subsection (3) below) prepare in respect of each financial year of the charity a statement of accounts complying with such requirements as to its form and contents as may be prescribed by regulations made by the Secretary of State.

(2) Without prejudice to the generality of subsection (1) above, regulations under that subsection may make provision –

- (a) for any such statement to be prepared in accordance with such methods and principles as are specified or referred to in the regulations;
- (b) as to any information to be provided by way of notes to the accounts;

and regulations under that subsection may also make provision for determining the financial years of a charity for the purposes of this Act and any regulations made under it.

(3) Where a charity's gross income in any financial year does not exceed £25,000, the charity trustees may, in respect of that year, elect to prepare the following, namely –

- (a) a receipts and payments account, and
- (b) a statement of assets and liabilities,

instead of a statement of accounts under subsection (1) above.

(4) The charity trustees of a charity shall preserve –

- (a) any statement of accounts prepared by them under subsection (1) above, or
- (b) any account and statement prepared by them under subsection (3) above,

for at least six years from the end of the financial year to which any such statement relates or (as the case may be) to which any such account and statement relate.

(5) Subsection (4) of section 41 above shall apply in relation to the preservation of any such statement or account and statement as it applies in relation to the preservation of any accounting records (the references to subsection (3) of that section being read as references to subsection (4) above).

(6) The Secretary of State may by order amend subsection (3) above by substituting a different sum for the sum for the time being specified there.

(7) Nothing in this section applies to a charity which is a company.

Annual audit or examination of charity accounts

43. – (1) Subsection (2) below applies to a financial year of a charity ('the relevant year') if the charity's gross income or total expenditure in any of the following, namely –

(a) the relevant year,

(b) the financial year of the charity immediately preceding the relevant year (if any), and

(c) the financial year of the charity immediately preceding the year specified in paragraph (b) above (if any),

exceeds £100,000.

(2) If this subsection applies to a financial year of a charity, the accounts of the charity for that year shall be audited by a person who –

(a) is, in accordance with section 25 of the Companies Act 1989 [1989 c.40.]. (eligibility for appointment), eligible for appointment as a company auditor, or

(b) is a member of a body for the time being specified in regulations under section 44 below and is under the rules of that body eligible for appointment as auditor of the charity.

(3) If subsection (2) above does not apply to a financial year of a charity, then (subject to subsection (4) below) the accounts of the charity for that year shall, at the election of the charity trustees, either –

(a) be examined by an independent examiner, that is to say an independent person who is reasonably believed by the trustees to have the requisite ability and practical experience to carry out a competent examination of the accounts, or

(b) be audited by such a person as is mentioned in subsection (2) above.

(4) Where it appears to the Commissioners –

(a) that subsection (2), or (as the case may be) subsection (3) above, has not been complied with in relation to a financial year of a charity within ten months from the end of that year, or

(b) that, although subsection (2) above does not apply to a financial year of a charity, it would nevertheless be desirable for the accounts of the charity for that year to be audited by such a person as is mentioned in that subsection,

the Commissioners may by order require the accounts of the charity for that year to be audited by such a person as is mentioned in that subsection.

(5) If the Commissioners make an order under subsection (4) above with respect to a charity, then unless –

(a) the order is made by virtue of paragraph (b) of that subsection, and

(b) the charity trustees themselves appoint an auditor in accordance with the order,

the auditor shall be a person appointed by the Commissioners.

(6) The expenses of any audit carried out by an auditor appointed by the Commissioners under subsection (5) above, including the auditor's remuneration, shall be recoverable by the Commissioners –

(a) from the charity trustees of the charity concerned, who shall be personally liable, jointly and severally, for those expenses; or

(b) to the extent that it appears to the Commissioners not to be practical to seek recovery of those expenses in accordance with paragraph (a) above, from the funds of the charity.

(7) The Commissioners may –

(a) give guidance to charity trustees in connection with the selection of a person for appointment as an independent examiner;

(b) give such directions as they think appropriate with respect to the carrying out of an examination in pursuance of subsection (3)(a) above;

and apply any such guidance or directions may either be of general application or apply to a particular charity only.

(8) The Secretary of State may by order amend subsection (1) above by substituting a different sum for the sum for the time being specified there.

(9) Nothing in this section applies to a charity which is a company.

Supplementary provisions relating to audits etc.

44. – (1) The Secretary of State may by regulations make provision –

(a) specifying one or more bodies for the purposes of section 43(2)(b) above;

(b) with respect to the duties of an auditor carrying out an audit

under section 43 above, including provision with respect to the making by him of a report on –
(i) the statement of accounts prepared for the financial year in question under section 42(1) above, or
(ii) the account and statement so prepared under section 42(3) above,
as the case may be;

(c) with respect to the making by an independent examiner of a report in respect of an examination carried out by him under section 43 above;

(d) conferring on such an auditor or on an independent examiner a right of access with respect to books, documents and other records (however kept) which relate to the charity concerned);

(e) entitling such an auditor or an independent examiner to require, in the case of a charity, information and explanations from past or present charity trustees or trustees for the charity, or from past or present officers or employees of the charity);

(f) enabling the Commissioners, in circumstances specified in the regulations, to dispense with the requirements of section 43(2) or (3) above in the case of a particular charity or in the case of any particular financial year of a charity.

(2) If any person fails to afford an auditor or an independent examiner any facility to which he is entitled by virtue of subsection (1)(d) or (e) above, the Commissioners may by order give –
(a) to that person, or
(b) to the charity trustees for the time being of the charity concerned, such directions as the Commissioners think appropriate for securing that the default is made good.

(3) Section 727 of the Companies Act 1985 [1985 c.6.] (power of court to grant relief in certain cases) shall have effect in relation to an auditor or independent examiner appointed by a charity in pursuance of section 43 above as it has effect in relation to a person employed as auditor by a company within the meaning of that Act.

Annual reports

45. – (1) The charity trustees of a charity shall prepare in respect of each financial year of the charity an annual report containing –
(a) such a report by the trustees on the activities of the charity during that year, and

(b) such other information relating to the charity or to its trustees or officers,

as may be prescribed by regulations made by the Secretary of State.

(2) Without prejudice to the generality of subsection (1) above, regulations under that subsection may make provision –

(a) for any such report as is mentioned in paragraph (a) of that subsection to be prepared in accordance with such principles as are specified or referred to in the regulations;

(b) enabling the Commissioners to dispense with any requirement prescribed by virtue of subsection (1)(b) above in the case of a particular charity or a particular class of charities, or in the case of a particular financial year of a charity or of any class of charities.

(3) The annual report required to be prepared under this section in respect of any financial year of a charity shall be transmitted to the Commissioners by the charity trustees –

(a) within ten months from the end of that year, or

(b) within such longer period as the Commissioners may for any special reason allow in the case of that report.

(4) Subject to subsection (5) below, any such annual report shall have attached to it the statement of accounts prepared for the financial year in question under section 42(1) above or (as the case may be) the account and statement so prepared under section 42(3) above, together with –

(a) where the accounts of the charity for that year have been audited under section 43 above, a copy of the report made by the auditor on that statement of accounts or (as the case may be) on that account and statement;

(b) where the accounts of the charity for that year have been examined under section 43 above, a copy of the report made by the independent examiner in respect of the examination carried out by him under that section.

(5) Subsection (4) above does not apply to a charity which is a company, and any annual report transmitted by the charity trustees of such a charity under subsection (3) above shall instead have attached to it a copy of the charity's annual accounts prepared for the financial year in question under Part VII of the Companies Act 1985, [1985 c. 6.] together with a copy of the auditors' report on those accounts.

(6) Any annual report transmitted to the Commissioners under subsection (3) above, together with the documents attached to it, shall be kept by the Commissioners for such period as they think fit.

Special provision as respects accounts and annual reports of exempt and other excepted charities

46. – (1) Nothing in sections 41 to 45 above applies to any exempt charity; but the charity trustees of an exempt charity shall keep proper books of account with respect to the affairs of the charity, and if not required by or under the authority of any other Act to prepare periodical statements of account shall prepare consecutive statements of account consisting on each occasion of an income and expenditure account relating to a period of not more than fifteen months and a balance sheet relating to the end of that period.

(2) The books of accounts and statements of account relating to an exempt charity shall be preserved for a period of six years at least until the charity ceases to exist and the Commissioners consent in writing to their being destroyed or otherwise disposed of.

(3) Nothing in sections 43 to 45 above applies to any charity which –
- (a) falls within section 3(5)(c) above, and
- (b) is not registered.

(4) Except in accordance with subsection (7) below, nothing in section 45 above applies to any charity (other than an exempt charity or a charity which falls within section 3(5)(c) above) which –
- (a) is excepted by section 3(5) above, and
- (b) is not registered.

(5) If requested to do so by the Commissioners, the charity trustees of any such charity as is mentioned in subsection (4) above shall prepare an annual report in respect of such financial year of the charity as is specified in the Commissioners' request.

(6) Any report prepared under subsection (5) above shall contain –
- (a) such a report by the charity trustees on the activities of the charity during the year in question, and
- (b) such other information relating to the charity or to its trustees or officers,

as may be prescribed by regulations made under section 45(1) above in relation to annual reports prepared under that provision.

(7) Subsections (3) to (6) of section 45 above shall apply to any report required to be prepared under subsection (5) above as if it were an

annual report required to be prepared under subsection (1) of that section.

(8) Any reference in this section to a charity which falls within section 3(5)(c) above includes a reference to a charity which falls within that provision but is also excepted from registration by section 3(5)(b) above.

Public inspection of annual reports etc.

47. – (1) Any annual report or other document kept by the Commissioners in pursuance of section 45(6) above shall be open to public inspection at all reasonable times –

- (a) during the period for which it is so kept; or
- (b) if the Commissioners so determine, during such lesser period as they may specify.

(2) Where any person –

- (a) requests the charity trustees of a charity in writing to provide him with a copy of the charity's most recent accounts, and
- (b) pays them such reasonable fee (if any) as they may require in respect of the costs of complying with the request,

those trustees shall comply with the request within the period of two months beginning with the date on which it is made.

(3) In subsection (2) above the reference to a charity's most recent accounts is –

- (a) in the case of a charity other than one falling within any of paragraphs (b) to (d) below, a reference to the statement of accounts or account and statement prepared in pursuance of section 42(1) or (3) above in respect of the last financial year of the charity the accounts for which have been audited or examined under section 43 above;
- (b) in the case of such a charity as is mentioned in section 46(3) above, a reference to the statement of accounts or account and statement prepared in pursuance of section 42(1) or (3) above in respect of the last financial year of the charity in respect of which a statement of accounts or account and statement has or have been so prepared;
- (c) in the case of a charity which is a company, a reference to the annual accounts of the company most recently audited under Part VII of the Companies Act 1985 [1985 c. 6.]; and
- (d) in the case of an exempt charity, a reference to the accounts of the charity most recently audited in pursuance of any

statutory or other requirement or, if its accounts are not required to be audited, the accounts most recently prepared in respect of the charity.

Annual returns by registered charities

48. – (1) Every registered charity shall prepare in respect of each of its financial years an annual return in such form, and containing such information, as may be prescribed by regulations made by the Commissioners.

(2) Any such return shall be transmitted to the Commissioners by the date by which the charity trustees are, by virtue of section 45(3) above, required to transmit to them the annual report required to be prepared in respect of the financial year in question.

(3) The Commissioners may dispense with the requirements of subsection (1) above in the case of a particular charity or a particular class of charities, or in the case of a particular financial year of a charity or of any class of charities.

Offences

49. Any person who, without reasonable excuse, is persistently in default in relation to any requirement imposed –

(a) by section 45(3) above (taken with section 45(4) or (5), as the case may require), or

(b) by section 47(2) or 48(2) above,

shall be guilty of an offence and liable on summary conviction to a fine not exceeding level 4 on the standard scale.

Appendix 4 – Extract from SI 1994 No 1935 'The Companies Act (Audit Exemption) Regulations 1994

PART II
AMENDMENTS OF CHARITIES ACT 1993

6. In section 45 of the Charities Act 1993(**e**) (annual reports), in subsection (5), for the words 'the auditors' report' there shall be substituted the words 'any auditors' report or report made for the purposes of section 249A(2) of that Act'.

7. In section 47 of that Act (public inspection of annual reports etc.), in subsection (3) for paragraph (c) there shall be substituted the following paragraph –

'(c) in the case of a charity which is a company, a reference to the most recent annual accounts of the company prepared under Part VII of the Companies Act 1985 in relation to which any of the following conditions is satisfied –
- (i) they have been audited;
- (ii) a report required for the purposes of section 249A(2) of that Act has been made in respect of them; or
- (iii) they relate to a year in respect of which the company is exempt from audit by virtue of section 249A(1) of that Act; and'.

(**e**) 1993 c. 10.

Appendix 5 – Extracts from The Deregulation and Contracting Out Act 1994: sections 28 to 30 and from Schedules 11 and 17

Annual audit or examination of charity accounts

28. – (1) Section 43 of the Charities Act 1993 [1993 c. 10.] (annual audit or examination of charity accounts) shall be amended as follows.

(2) In subsection (3) (which requires a charity's accounts for a financial year to be audited or independently examined if its gross income and total expenditure in that year, and each of the two previous financial years, is £100,000 or less) after 'a charity' there shall be inserted 'and its gross income or total expenditure in that year exceeds £10,000'.

(3) In subsection (8) (power of Secretary of State to amend sum specified in subsection (1)) after '(1)' there shall be inserted 'or (3)'.

Annual reports of charities

29. – (1) In section 45 of the Charities Act 1993 (annual reports) in subsection (3) (automatic duty to transmit annual report to the Commissioners) for the words from the beginning to 'a charity' there shall be substituted 'Where in any financial year of a charity its gross income or total expenditure exceeds £10,000, the annual report required to be prepared under this section in respect of that year'.

(2) After that subsection there shall be inserted –

'(3A) Where in any financial year of a charity neither its gross income nor its total expenditure exceeds £10,000, the annual report required to be prepared under this section in respect of that year shall, if the Commissioners so request, be transmitted to them by the charity trustees –

(a) in the case of a request made before the end of seven months from the end of the financial year to which the report relates, within ten months from the end of that year, and

(b) in the case of a request not so made, within three months from the date of the request,

or, in either case, within such longer period as the Commissioners may for any special reason allow in the case of that report.'

(3) In subsection (4) of that section, for 'any such annual report' there shall be substituted 'any annual report transmitted to the Commissioners under this section'.

(4) In subsection (5) of that section, for 'subsection (3) above' there shall be substituted 'this section'.

(5) In subsection (6) of that section, for 'subsection (3) above' there shall be substituted 'this section'.

(6) At the end of that section there shall be inserted –

'(7) The charity trustees of a charity shall preserve, for at least six years from the end of the financial year to which it relates, any annual report prepared by them under subsection (1) above which they have not been required to transmit to the Commissioners.

(8) Subsection (4) of section 41 above shall apply in relation to the preservation of any such annual report as it applies in relation to the preservation of any accounting records (the references in subsection (3) of that section being read as references to subsection (7) above).

(9) The Secretary of State may by order amend subsection (3) or (3A) above by substituting a different sum for the sum for the time being specified there'.

(7) In section 46(7) of that Act (application of section 45(3) to (6) to annual reports under section 46(5)) after 'section 45' there shall be inserted '(as originally enacted)'.

(8) In section 49 of that Act (penalty for persistent default in relation to certain requirements) in paragraphs (a), after '45(3)' there shall be inserted 'or (3A)'.

Annual returns by charities

30. – (1) Section 48 of the Charities Act 1993 [1993 c. 10.] (annual returns by registered charities) shall be amended as follows.

(2) In subsection (1) (duty to prepare annual return) at the beginning there shall be inserted 'Subject to subsection (1A) below,'.

(3) After subsection (1) there shall be inserted –

'(1A) Subsection (1) above shall not apply in relation to any financial year of a charity in which neither the gross income nor the total expenditure of the charity exceeds £10,000.'

(4) At the end there shall be inserted –

'(4) The Secretary of State may by order amend subsection (1A) above by substituting a different sum for the time being specified there.'

SCHEDULE 11

Charities Act 1993 (c. 10)

12. In section 47(3) of the Charities Act 1993 –
   (a) paragraph (a) shall be omitted, and
   (b) in paragraph (b), for the words from 'such' to '46(3) above' there shall be substituted 'a charity other than one falling within paragraph (c) or (d) below'.

SCHEDULE 17

Chapter or Number	Title	Extent of repeal
1992 c. 41.	The Charities Act 1992.	Section 67(3)(b) and the word 'but' immediately preceding it.

Appendix 6 – s505 ICTA 1988

505. Charities: general

(1) Subject to subsection (2) and (3) below, the following exemptions shall be granted on a claim in that behalf to the Board –

(a) exemption from tax under Schedules A and D in respect of the rents and profits of any lands, tenements, hereditaments or heritages belonging to a hospital, public school or almshouse, or vested in trustees for charitable purposes, so far as the same are applied to charitable purposes only;

(b) . . .

(c) exemption –

(i) from tax under Schedule C in respect of any interest, annuities, dividends or shares of annuities,

(ii) from tax under Schedule D in respect of any yearly interest or other annual payment, and

(iii) from tax under Schedule F in respect of any distribution,

where the income in question forms part of the income of a charity, or is, according to rules or regulations established by Act of Parliament, charter, decree, deed of trust or will, applicable to charitable purposes only, and so far as it is applied to charitable purposes only;

(d) exemption from tax under Schedule C in respect of any interest, annuities, dividends or shares of annuities which are in the names of trustees and are applicable solely towards the repairs of any cathedral, college, church or chapel, or of any building used solely for the purposes of divine worship, so far as the same are applied to those purposes;

(e) exemption from tax under Schedule D in respect of the profits of any trade carried on by a charity, if the profits are applied solely to the purposes of the charity and either –

(i) the trade is exercised in the course of the actual carrying out of a primary purpose of the charity; or

(ii) the work in connection with the trade is mainly carried out by beneficiaries of the charity.

(2) Any payment which –

(a) is received by a charity from another charity; and
(b) is not made for full consideration in money or money's worth; and
(c) is not chargeable to tax apart from this subsection; and
(d) is not, apart from this subsecton, of a description which (on a claim) would be eligible for relief from tax by virtue of any provision of subsection (1) above;

shall be chargeable to tax under Case III of Schedule D but shall be eligible for relief from tax under subsection (1)(c) above as if it were an annual payment.

(3) If in any chargeable period of a charity –
(a) its relevant income and gains are not less than £10,000; and
(b) its relevant income and gains exceed the amount of its qualifying expenditure; and
(c) the charity incurs, or is treated as incurring, non-qualifying expenditure;

relief shall not be available under either subsection (1) above or section [256 of the 1992 Act] for so much of the excess as does not exceed the non-qualifying expenditure incurred in that period.

(4) In relation to a chargeable period of less than 12 months, subsection (3) above shall have effect as if the amount specified in paragraph (a) of that subsection were proportionately reduced.

(5) In subsection (3) above 'relevant income and gains' means –
(a) income which apart from subsection (1) above would not be exempt from tax together with any income which is taxable notwithstanding that subsection; and
(b) gains which apart from section 256 of the 1992 Act would be chargeable gains together with any gains which are chargeable gains notwithstanding that section.

(6) Where by virtue of subsection (3) above there is an amount of a charity's relevant income and gains for which relief under subsection (1) above and section 256 of the 1992 Act is not available, the charity may, by notice to the Board, specify which items of its relevant income and gains are, in whole or in part, to be attributed to that amount, and, for this purpose, all covenanted payments to charity (within the meaning of section 647A(7) shall be treated as a single item; and if within 30 days of being required to do so by the Board, a charity does not give notice under this subsection, the items of its relevant income and gains which are to be attributed to the amount in question shall be such as the Board may determine.

(7) Where it appears to the Board that two or more charities acting in concert are engaged in transactions of which the main purpose or one of the main purposes is the avoidance of tax (whether by the charities or by any other person), the Board may by notice given to the charities provide that, for such chargeable periods as may be specified in the notice, subsection (3) above shall have effect in relation to them with the omission of paragraph (a).

(8) An appeal may be brought against a notice under subsection (7) above as if it were notice of the decision of the Board on a claim made by the charities concerned.

Appendix 7 – Extra-statutory Concessions

C4 Trading activities for charitable purposes

Bazaars, jumble sales, gymkhanas, carnivals, firework displays and similar activities arranged by voluntary organisations or charities for the purpose of raising funds for charity may fall within the definition of 'trade' in TA 1988, s832, with the result that any profits will be liable to corporation tax. Tax is not, however, charged on such profits provided all the following conditions are satisfied –

- the organisation or charity is not regularly carrying on these trading activities;
- the trading is not in competition with other traders;
- the activities are supported substantially because the public are aware that any profits will be devoted to charity; and
- the profits are transferred to charities or otherwise applied for charitable purposes.

Appendix 8 – Statements of practice

SP 3/87 (26 March 1987) Repayment of tax to charities on covenanted and other income

1. FA 1986 contains provisions designed to deal with certain abuses of the tax reliefs for charities. These include a requirement that tax should in all cases be deducted at source from covenant payments by companies to charities FA 1986, s30(2) inserting ICTA 1970, s248(8a), now ICTA 1988, s339(7). Charities are entitled to claim repayment of the tax, provided that they meet the conditions for tax exemption on their income.

2. This statement describes the procedure which the Revenue are adopting in order to minimise any delay in making repayments of tax to charities. Pargraphs 3–8 deal with the particular case of 'profit-shedding' covenants. Pargraph 9 makes it clear that the same principles will be applied to other repayment claims by charities.

Profit-shedding covenants

3. Many charities set up subsidiary companies to carry on fund-raising activities. The profits of such a subsidiary are usually covenanted to the charity, relieving the subsidary of its corporation tax liabilities. Prior to FA 1986, many of those companies were, under the group relief rules, able to make such covenant payments gross, so that it was unnecessary for the charity to claim repayment.

4. Under ICTA 1988, s505(2), however, such payments are now required to be made under deduction of tax at source. The charity will thus have received income under deduction of tax and will qualify for repayment of the tax if it is otherwise eligible for tax exemption under the normal rules.

5. In examining claims for repayment it is the Revenue's practice in appropriate cases to verify, by reference to the tax records of the person making the payment, that the amount claimed is correct and that the tax deducted from the payment has, where necessary, been accounted for. This can take some time.

6. In order to minimise any cash flow disadvantage for charities while awaiting repayment, the Revenue are prepared to repay provisionally the tax apparently suffered without awaiting the results of the verification process described above, provided that –

(a) the identity of the charity and the subsidiary, and their relationship to each other, are all well known in advance of the claim; and

(b) the Revenue are satisfied that the affairs of the charity are otherwise in order, and

(c) the repayment claim is not otherwise likely materially to exceed the amount ultimately due.

7. In order to obtain corporation tax relief, the subsidary company must make its payment during the accounting period in which the profits arise, even though the true profit for corporation tax purposes may not be known for some months after the end of that period. Most companies therefore make a payment which to some extent exceeds the likely profit, accounting for tax on the full amount and adjusting the payments later.

8. It follows that, when the verification referred to above is complete, the tax paid over by the subsidiary, and the tax repayment made to the charity, may prove to be excessive. The Revenue will in such cases have power, under the provisions of TMA 1970, s30 (as amended by FA 1982, s149) to recover the over-repayment from the charity by assessment. In practice, however, unless the amount over-repaid is significant in relation to the sum claimed, it will normally be collected from subsequent repayment claims. Similarly the excess paid over by the subsidiary will be repaid to it by the inspector or set against any other tax liabilities.

Other income

9. Similar procedures for provisional repayment of tax and verification of claims will be adopted, so far as appropriate, where charities receive other income under deduction of tax, for example from other covenanted donations or from investments.

Appendix 9 – Deeds of covenant – model versions approved by the Inland Revenue

Version 'A'

[Form of covenant by an *individual* to a *charity* for use in *England and Wales* from 31 July 1990]

DEED OF COVENANT

Notes

To ....

[Name of Charity]

I promise to pay you for . . . . . . years, or until I die if earlier, such a sum as after deduction of income tax at the basic rate amounts to 1

£ 2

each [week] [month] [quarter] [year] 3

from [the date shown below] [. . . . .]. 4

Signed and delivered 5

Date ....

Full Name ....

Address ....

Witnessed by:

Signed ....

Full Name ....

Address ....

Notes

1 Enter the period of the covenant, which must be longer than *three years.*
2 Enter the amount you will be paying to the charity.
3 Delete as appropriate to show how often you will make the payment.
4 Delete as appropriate. If you choose to enter an actual date *it must not be earlier than the date you sign the deed.*
5 You must sign the form and enter the date you actually sign it in the presence of the witness, who should also sign where shown.

Appendix 10 – s256 TCGA 1992

CHARITIES AND GIFTS OF NON-BUSINESS ASSETS ETC.

256. Charities

(1) Subject to section 505(3) of the Taxes Act and subsection (2) below, a gain shall not be a chargeable gain if it accrues to a charity and is applicable and applied for charitable purposes.

(2) If property held on charitable trusts ceases to be subject to charitable trusts –

- (a) the trustees shall be treated as if they had disposed of, and immediately reacquired, the property for a consideration equal to its market value, any gain on the disposal being treated as not accruing to a charity, and
- (b) if and so far as any of that property represents, directly or indirectly, the consideration for the disposal of assets by the trustees, any gain accruing on that disposal shall be treated as not having accrued to a charity,

and an assessment to capital gains tax chargeable by virtue of paragraph (b) above may be made at any time not more than 3 years after the end of the year of assessment in which the property ceases to be subject to charitable trusts.

Index